Anglo-Saxon Studies   1

THE DRAMATIC LITURGY OF ANGLO-SAXON ENGLAND

This volume presents an examination of the liturgical rituals of the high festivals from Christmas to Ascension in late Anglo-Saxon England, particularly in the secular church. It expands the current knowledge of liturgical practice in a period where there is little direct evidence, using vernacular homilies and sermons – important but neglected sources of information – to explore the extent to which monastic practices were extended to the secular church. The performative nature of liturgy and its spiritual, emotional and educative value receive particular attention; the author argues that preachers were often unconsciously influenced by the liturgical experience of an episode rather than by the biblical narrative which they were ostensibly retelling.

Dr M. BRADFORD BEDINGFIELD gained his D.Phil. at Oxford University.

Anglo-Saxon Studies

ISSN 1475–2468

General editors
John Hines
Catherine Cubitt

'Anglo-Saxon Studies' aims to provide a forum for the best scholarship on the Anglo-Saxon peoples, from the end of Roman Britain to the Norman Conquest, and including comparative studies involving adjacent populations and periods. Both new research and major reassessments of central topics are welcomed.

Originally founded by Professor David Dumville as 'Studies in Anglo-Saxon History', the series has now broadened in scope under new editorship to take in all of the principal disciplines of archaeology, art history, history, language and literature. Inter- or multi-disciplinary studies are encouraged.

Proposals or enquiries may be sent directly to the editors or the publisher at the addresses given below; all submissions will receive prompt and informed consideration.

Professor John Hines, School of History and Archaeology, Cardiff University, Cardiff, Wales, UK CF10 3XU

Dr Catherine Cubitt, Centre for Medieval Studies, University of York, The King's Manor, York, England, UK YO1 2EP

Boydell & Brewer, PO Box 9, Woodbridge, Suffolk, England, UK IP12 3DF

THE DRAMATIC LITURGY OF ANGLO-SAXON ENGLAND

M. Bradford Bedingfield

THE BOYDELL PRESS

First published 2002
The Boydell Press, Woodbridge

ISBN 0 85115 873 0

BX
1977
. G7
B43
2002

The Boydell Press is an imprint of Boydell & Brewer Ltd
PO Box 9, Woodbridge, Suffolk IP12 3DF, UK
and of Boydell & Brewer Inc.
PO Box 41026, Rochester, NY 14604–4126, USA
website: www.boydell.co.uk

A catalogue record for this book is available
from the British Library

Library of Congress Cataloging-in-Publication Data
applied for

This publication is printed on acid-free paper

Typeset by Joshua Associates Ltd, Oxford
Printed in Great Britain by
Antony Rowe Ltd, Chippenham, Wiltshire

Contents

Plates

Acknowledgements

This book is a development of my Oxford D.Phil. thesis, "Dramatic Ritual and Preaching in Late Anglo-Saxon England" (1999). I owe a tremendous debt of gratitude to my doctoral supervisor, Professor Malcolm Godden, whose guidance and patience made this possible. Among the many people who have kindly offered valuable suggestions, I would like to thank John Blair, Gale Owen-Crocker, Jonathan Evans, Joyce Hill, John Hines, Christopher A. Jones, Sarah Larratt Keefer, Jerome Mitchell, Heather O'Donoghue, William Provost, and Barbara Raw. I extend special thanks to Helen Gittos for her continuous advice while I was adapting the thesis for publication. I am grateful to the Bibliothèque nationale in Paris, the Bibliothèque municipale in Rouen, the Bodleian Library, the British Library, the Parker Library (Corpus Christi College, Cambridge), and the University Library at Cambridge University for kindly allowing me access to their materials. A generous grant from the Lynne Grundy Memorial Trust was instrumental in the completion of the original thesis, and I am indebted to my parents, Rebecca and Tom Campen, for years of emotional and financial support. Finally I would like to thank my fiancée, Agnieszka Wróblewska, for everything.

Abbreviations

ASE	*Anglo-Saxon England*
ASPR	Anglo-Saxon Poetic Records
BC	*Eleven Old English Rogationtide Homilies* (Bazire and Cross 1982)
BL	British Library
CCSL	Corpus Christianorum Series Latina
CH I	*Ælfric's Catholic Homilies: The First Series* (Clemoes 1997)
CH II	*Ælfric's Catholic Homilies: The Second Series* (Godden 1979)
CSASE	Cambridge Studies in Anglo-Saxon England
DBL	*Documents of the Baptismal Liturgy* (Whitaker 1970)
EETS	Early English Text Society
EHR	*English Historical Review*
HBS	Henry Bradshaw Society
JTS	*Journal of Theological Studies*
LME	*Ælfric's Letter to the Monks of Eynsham* (Jones 1998)
LSE	*Leeds Studies in English*
NRSV	New Revised Standard Version
n.s.	new series
o.s.	original series
OEC	Old English Corpus
OR	*Ordo romanus/Ordines romani* (Andrieu 1931)
PMLA	*Publications of the Modern Language Association of America*
PL	Patrologia Latina
s.s.	supplementary series
SPCK	Society for Promoting Christian Knowledge
TBL	*The Baptismal Liturgy* (Whitaker 1981)

Liturgical witnesses

Additional 28188	London, BL MS Additional 28188
Æthelwold	The Benedictional of Æthelwold (Prescott 1988)
Anderson	The Anderson (or Brodie) Pontifical (Conn 1993)
Bobbio	The Bobbio Missal (Lowe 1917)
CB	The Canterbury Benedictional (Woolley 1917)
Claudius (I and II)	The Claudius Pontificals (Turner 1971)
Concordia	*Regularis Concordia* (Symons 1953; Kornexl 1993)

Corpus 41	Cambridge, Corpus Christi College MS 41 (Grant 1978)
Corpus 44	Cambridge, Corpus Christi College MS 44 (Corpus-Canterbury Benedictional)
Corpus 163	Cambridge, Corpus Christi College MS 163 (Roman-German Pontifical)
Corpus 422	Cambridge, Corpus Christi College MS 422 (The Red Book of Darley)
Darley	Corpus 422
Dunstan	The Dunstan (or Sherborne) Pontifical (Conn 1993)
Durham	The Durham Collectar (Corrêa 1992)
'Egbert'	The 'Egbert' Pontifical (Banting 1989)
Gelasian	The Gelasian Sacramentary (Wilson 1894)
Gothicum	*Missale Gothicum* (Bannister 1917)
Gregorian	The Gregorian Sacramentary (Deshusses 1971)
Lanalet	The Lanalet Pontifical (Doble 1937)
Leofric Collectar	The Leofric Collectar (Dewick and Frere 1914)
Leofric Missal	The Leofric Missal (Warren 1883)
Magdalen Pontifical	The Pontifical of Magdalen College (Wilson 1910)
New Minster	The Missal of the New Minster (Turner 1962)
RGP	The Romano-German Pontifical (Vogel and Elze 1963)
Robert Benedictional	The Benedictional of Archbishop Robert (Wilson 1903)
Robert Missal	The Missal of Robert of Jumièges (Wilson 1896)
Samson	Cambridge, Corpus Christ College MS 146 (The Samson Pontifical)
Stowe	The Stowe Missal (Warner 1906)
Vitellius A.vii	London, BL MS Cotton Vitellius A.vii
Winchcombe	The Winchcombe Sacramentary (Davril 1995)
Winchester Troper	The Winchester Troper (Frere 1894)
Wulstan	The Portiforium of Saint Wulstan (Hughes 1958)

1

Introduction

THE STUDY of the Anglo-Saxon liturgy is just coming into its own. The last few decades have seen increasing activity in cataloguing, editing, and analysing the relevant manuscripts. The liturgy of the Anglo-Saxon church certainly warrants the attention. Although not much can be said about the liturgy before the tenth century,[1] enough (mostly second-hand) evidence exists to paint the picture of a liturgy that reflects the influence of at least the Irish, Gallican, and Roman churches, and probably more. When Augustine arrived in Canterbury in 597, in an attempt to revive a Christian church in the British Isles that had been largely smothered by Anglo-Saxon migrations, he was given a mandate by Pope Gregory to marry the best of local traditions with the practice of Rome, and this approach remained a dynamic in subsequent reforms. This sort of philosophy surely encouraged a diverse liturgy, but the paucity of surviving liturgical manuscripts from before the tenth century stunts our appreciation of it. The loss of evidence for Christian observance before the mid to late tenth century is generally attributed to the Viking ravages of the preceding century.[2] To what extent the continuity of Christian worship was crippled or changed during this period we will probably never know. We can develop a much clearer picture, however, of the liturgical activities of the later Anglo-Saxon church as the Benedictine Reform spurred the production of a plethora of liturgical books and other documentary witnesses to what has recently been referred to as a "period of national liturgical experiment and innovation."[3] Through the activities of (most notably) Dunstan (Archbishop of Canterbury, 960–88), Oswald (Bishop of Worcester from 961, and Archbishop of York, 972–92), and Æthelwold (Bishop of Winchester, 963–84), working with the protection and support of King Edgar (959–975), the English church saw a burst of activity during this period. Quite a few

---

[1] For a description of the pre-tenth-century Anglo-Saxon liturgical environment, see Catherine Cubitt, *Anglo-Saxon Church Councils c. 650–c. 850* (London, 1995), pp. 125–47; Sarah Foot, " 'By water in the spirit': the administration of baptism in early Anglo-Saxon England," in *Pastoral Care Before the Parish*, ed. Blair and Sharpe (Leicester, 1992), pp. 171–92; and the entries in R. Pfaff, ed. *The Liturgical Books of Anglo-Saxon England* (Kalamazoo, 1995).

[2] On the effects of the Vikings on Anglo-Saxon production of liturgical books, and in particular the evidence for continuity, see David Dumville, *Liturgy and the Ecclesiastical History of Late Anglo-Saxon England* (Woodbridge, 1992), pp. 96ff.

[3] Christopher Jones, "The Book of the Liturgy," *Speculum* 73.3 (1998), p. 685.

monasteries were founded or refounded, the excesses of secular members of religious communities were punished, and an attempt was made to standardize religious experience in the key monastic centres in England.[4] This attempt is evident most notably in the *Regularis Concordia*, drawn up by Æthelwold in the early 970s and widely distributed. The *Concordia* echoes Gregory's instruction to Augustine as part of its own mandate, to join the best of the liturgy of the Frankish churches with local English traditions.[5] From about the same time, troping and polyphonic singing were adapted and developed in England, a style of manuscript illumination referred to as the 'Winchester School' flourished, and many of the English liturgical books that have survived from before the Conquest were compiled.[6] Although this apparent renewed activity may not have been as original or as ubiquitous as some critics have assumed, from the surviving documentary evidence the *Concordia* represents (at least symbolically) something of a turning point in the stability and vigour of liturgical and devotional experience in Anglo-Saxon England.

The tenth century is also the starting point for those attempting to map the development of dramatic exercise in the Western church. It would be some time before Western Europe would develop liturgical ritual that most critics today would be comfortable calling 'drama,' but the beginnings of this development, in the form of rituals that seem to exhibit some characteristics of drama, are generally traced to this period. The *Concordia* contains an early example of one of the earliest and most famous of these liturgical elaborations, the *Visitatio Sepulchri*, the visit to the sepulchre during which the three Marys hear the pronouncement of the angel that Christ has risen and witness the proof of the Resurrection. The *Concordia*'s oft-quoted instructions for the *Visitatio*, performed at Matins on Easter

---

[4] For a recent summary of the external history of the church at this time, see H. R. Loyn, *The English Church, 940–1154* (New York, 2000). See also F. Barlow, *The English Church, 1000–1066* (Hamden, 1963).

[5] Lucia Kornexl, *Die Regularis concordia und ihre altenglische Interlinearversion* (Munich, 1993); see also T. Symons, ed. and trans. *Regularis concordia Anglicae nationis monachorum sanctimonia-liumque: the Monastic Agreement of the Monks and Nuns of the English Nation* (London, 1953). It has been noted by Joyce Hill ("The 'Regularis Concordia' and its Latin and Old English Reflexes," *Revue Bénédictine* 101 (1991), pp. 299–315), Lucia Kornexl (*Die Regularis concordia*, pp. lvii–lxxxiii, xcvi–clv), and Christopher Jones (*Ælfric's Letter to the Monks of Eynsham* (Cambridge, 1998), pp. 21–7) that the *Concordia* has a rather "obscure textual history" (*LME*, p. 21). While I have used Kornexl's edition throughout, I also give references to Symons' edition.

[6] See Richard Gem, "Tenth-Century Architecture in England," *Settimane di Studio del Centro Italiano* 38 (1991), pp. 803–36; J. J. C. Alexander, "The Benedictional of St. Æthelwold and Anglo-Saxon Illumination of the Reform Period," in *Tenth-Century Studies*, ed. David Parsons (London, 1975), pp. 169–83; Francis Wormald, "The 'Winchester School' before St. Æthelwold," in *England Before the Conquest*, ed. Clemoes and Hughes (Cambridge, 1971), pp. 305–13; D. Talbot Rice, *English Art 871–1100* (Oxford, 1952), esp. pp. 173ff. Critics of various artistic forms recognize a period of prosperity stemming from the Reform. Rice's comments about the 'Winchester style' are representative: "... after [the year 960] the new style burst into full flower with surprising vigour and richness" (183). See also the essays in *St. Dunstan: His Life, Times and Cult*, ed. Nigel Ramsay, Margaret Sparks, and Tim Tatton-Brown (Woodbridge, 1992).

morning, present a ritual that, with its apparent consciousness of costuming, dialogue, and role-playing, "marks the beginnings of liturgical drama in England," according to the *Blackwell Encyclopaedia of Anglo-Saxon England.*[7] Where did this 'drama' come from, in a tenth-century text from Anglo-Saxon England? Is this really something new, the birth of a new form of worship involving a mimetic presentation of Christian history? What is happening in the tenth-century English church that makes critics want to see in it the birth of liturgical drama?

One does not often find the words 'Anglo-Saxon' and 'drama' spoken together, and for good reason. George Anderson, in his *The Literature of the Anglo-Saxons*, devotes only six pages to "Old English Literature and the Drama." Pointing out the lack of any extant evidence of secular drama, he looks at poetic passages that "imply drama" or "illustrate a dramatic atmosphere."[8] His most prominent example is the dialogue between Mary and Joseph in the Old English poem *Christ I.*[9] Old English literature is also rich in monologues and dialogues that, albeit with a very loose definition of the word, one is tempted to interpret as dramatically-inspired. Julia Bolton Holloway has discussed the dramatic Adoration of the Cross ceremony as reflected in *The Dream of the Rood.*[10] Dramatic voice is often explored in relation to poems like *The Seafarer* and *The Wanderer*. Old English sermons and homilies are full of narratives, many of which contain dramatically used direct discourse. Nicholson and Clough discuss dramatic dialogues in the Vercelli homilies, as does Ruth Waterhouse in Ælfric's saints' lives.[11]

Still, interpretation of monologues or dialogue from poetry or prose as 'drama' depends upon a performance in which a role is undertaken. While it is compelling to imagine a particularly histrionic preacher presenting such passages mimetically, the fact that they are almost universally subjugated to very down-to-earth instruction and didactic exhortation does not seem to suggest this; at least, it prevents us from discussing them in terms of 'drama,' without corollary evidence indicating how they might have been presented. As for poetic monologues, while I cannot agree with Anderson that "drama . . . demands the interplay of two or more characters,"[12] speculations about the relationship between Old English poetry and 'drama' are simply that. For Anderson, because of its compelling use of dialogue between Mary and Joseph in *Christ I* and in the Last Judgement

[7] Michael Lapidge, et al., eds. *The Blackwell Encyclopaedia of Anglo-Saxon England* (Oxford, 1999), p. 389. The *Visitatio* is discussed at length, below, pp. 156–70.

[8] George Anderson, *The Literature of the Anglo-Saxons* (Princeton, 1949; repr. 1997), p. 207.

[9] Discussed below, pp. 218–22.

[10] Julia Bolton Holloway, "'The Dream of the Rood' and Liturgical Drama," in *Drama in the Middle Ages*, ed. Davidson and Stroupe (New York, 1990), pp. 24–42.

[11] Francis Clough, "Introduction," in *The Vercelli Book Homilies*, ed. Nicholson (Maryland, 1991), pp. 1–15; Ruth Waterhouse, "Ælfric's Use of Discourse in Some Saints' Lives," *ASE* 5 (1976), pp. 83–103.

[12] Anderson, *The Literature of the Anglo-Saxons*, p. 207.

scene in *Christ III*, "the one poem in Old English literature which [in certain parts] comes nearest in form to a play is . . . *Christ*."[13] While, in his opinion, these passages are "more advanced than liturgical drama" of the same period, their singularity forces him to conclude that, "to judge from the literature which [the Anglo-Saxon] has left behind him . . . it is difficult to see him as the possessor of any strong dramatic sense or the mimetic artist of vivacity and imagination."[14] While Anderson's summary analysis is now somewhat dated in many respects, this predisposition that the Anglo-Saxons had no developed sense of the possibilities of dramatic activity remains.

RITUAL AND REPRESENTATION

Regardless, it is to Anglo-Saxon England that critics look for what is probably the most celebrated example of pre-twelfth-century dramatic ritual, the *Visitatio Sepulchri*. There are almost as many theories as to the origin of its central *Quem quaeritis* dialogue as there are critics[15] but, regardless of origin, its use in the *Regularis Concordia* seems to indicate some kind of dramatic sensibility, at least among English monks. Indeed, most of the dramatic rituals of the Easter season to which critics point as the origins of liturgical drama are featured in the *Concordia*. The apparent strength of dramatic ritual in Anglo-Saxon England, compared to the lack of secular drama, prompts Anderson to attribute the dramatic structure of *Christ*'s Mary and Joseph dialogue to the liturgy (specifically the antiphons for Advent).

Some critics have drawn connections between Old English literature and the liturgy,[16] enough so to suggest that the power of liturgical ritual was perhaps more pervasive than the traditional focus on a handful of rituals (and the *Visitatio* in particular) implies, and that the experience of dramatic liturgy may not have been confined to the monastery. Generally, however, when these rituals have been discussed it has been in the context of the development of drama, looking forward to the representational drama of the later Middle Ages. There is a tremendous difference between dramatic ritual and the kind of 'dramatic tradition' or established 'theater' that Anderson is looking for, or the 'representational mode' that critics of drama

---

[13] Anderson, *The Literature of the Anglo-Saxons*, p. 207.

[14] Ibid. p. 209.

[15] For a summary of many key arguments see David A. Bjork, "On the Dissemination of *Quem quaeritis* and the *Visitatio sepulchri* and the Chronology of their Early Sources," *Comparative Drama* 14.1 (1980), pp. 46–69.

[16] See, for example, Barbara Raw's chapter on "Biblical literature: the New Testament," in *The Cambridge Companion to Old English Literature*, ed. Godden and Lapidge (Cambridge, 1991), pp. 227–42, in which she discusses reflections of the Holy Week liturgy (including the *Regularis Visitatio*) in Old English poetry.

are exploring. In failing to make adequate distinctions between ritual and drama in this period (a notoriously difficult distinction to make), critics have been unable to decide consistently whether to discuss dramatic ritual like the *Visitatio* as a highly symbolic (and therefore, implicitly, unrealistic) form or as an emerging representational mode. Anderson's assertion that the Mary and Joseph dialogue is "more advanced" than the ritual demonstrates the tendency of many critics to judge early dramatic cere-monies in terms of the characteristics of later dramas, thereby understating their dramatic power. The *Visitatio* ritual, in particular, tends to be seen as a primitive forerunner of the relatively complex Resurrection plays of the later Middle Ages, particularly in its lack of verisimilitude. The three Marys are monks, wearing copes. They carry thuribles of incense rather than spices. The 'angel' at the sepulchre wears an alb and holds a palm-twig in his hand. The empty linen is held up and presented to the clergy. The actions are ritualistic, not realistic. Such ritualistic expressions, however, might have, for the late Anglo-Saxons, served to draw the participants into a reenactment of Christian history much more effectively than more 'realistic' ones could have. The predisposition that ritual expression is distant or removed from what it is commemorating stands in the way of interpreta-tions of the Anglo-Saxon liturgy. The power of symbolism widely recog-nized in other artistic forms in Anglo-Saxon England should likewise be recognized in dramatic ritual, helping us appreciate how a tenth-century English Christian might relate to something like the *Visitatio*.

Clifford Davidson, in his discussion of "Space and Time in Medieval Drama," discusses the fallacy of expecting what we consider verisimilitude in medieval drama, looking at, in particular, iconographic expression. He points to illustrations of the Abraham and Isaac story, in which the wood that Isaac carries to his own sacrifice is in the shape of a cross. As Davidson argues, the sacrifice finds its meaning in its foreshadowing of Christ's sacrifice. The Christian community was trained to see history as "stamped or marked through certain events or individuals,"[17] each of which had a very real connection with Christ. A viewer is more meaningfully drawn into the Isaac story via symbolic expression than realistic, for symbolically Isaac can prefigure Christ, making the representation more applicable to con-temporary viewers.

It is easy to underestimate the power of symbols in Anglo-Saxon Christianity. The relationship between the symbol and what it symbolizes is real enough to belie the modern predisposition that ritualistic expression, relying as it does on symbols, is somehow unrealistic. Barbara Raw describes how art can imbue a church with divine power, providing "a way of entering the next world."[18] Church art, by surrounding the faithful

---

[17] Clifford Davidson, "Space and Time in Medieval Drama," in *Word, Picture, and Spectacle*, ed. Davidson (Kalamazoo, 1984), p. 51.

[18] Barbara Raw, *Anglo-Saxon Crucifixion Iconography* (Cambridge, 1990), p. 16.

with the presence of Christ and his saints, transforms the church into a branch of the heavenly church, making it "a place where man could enter into communion with the citizens of heaven."[19] Portrayals of events in Christian history are important not as historical instruction, but rather as means to "make men aware of their role as citizens of heaven."[20] As such, historical accuracy is not particularly important. Raw notes that a drawing of the Maundy in the mid-eleventh-century Tiberius Psalter "represents the event according to contemporary monastic practice,"[21] a ritualistic practice that bore little resemblance to the original Maundy. Rather than muting the effectiveness of the portrayal, the drawing translates the original event into the artist's present. If eleventh-century Maundy participants were trained to understand that their ceremony was a reactualization of the original, then there is no reason to think that they saw the ceremony as unrealistic. They wash each others' feet, just as Christ demonstrated that they should do.

One of the functions of pastoral instruction is to explain the significance of ceremonies like the Maundy. If the original event is interpreted in terms of the ritual, and is clearly explained that way to the participants from the beginning, it is natural for the congregation to conflate the two, giving them a ritualistically distorted view of history. Circularly, it might not even occur to them (or at least it might not matter to them) that the reenacted event is historically inaccurate. A modern example of this usurpation of history by ritual expression is found in portrayals of Christ's triumphal entry. Often dominant in movie, stage, or Sunday School reenactment of the event is the palm-waving crowd. There is no scriptural evidence, however, indicating that palms were held aloft. The first three gospel accounts mention, if anything, only branches laid in the road alongside cloaks, and John's account does not specify what was done with the palms. Still, those who have been trained ritualistically to wave palms in the air will see no discrepancy; indeed, they might come to relate to the Palm Sunday ceremony by means of the waving palms. More powerfully for the Anglo-Saxon Christian, who garnered his understanding of biblical history primarily through the liturgy, ritualistic, symbolic interpretation can seem more real than what to us is 'realistic.'

Demonstrating the degree of this conflation, many Old English 'historical' stories tend to take on a very ritualistic feel. The Blickling Assumption of the Virgin Mary illustrates the blurred distinction between the perception of 'actual' events and the habitual, ritualistic mode of interpreting such events.[22] The characters seem to process rather than walk. Mary is presented a palm-twig upon hearing the news of her approaching Assumption. A Jewish leader tries to take the palm-twig and desecrate it (an action that,

---

[19] Raw, *Anglo-Saxon Crucifixion Iconography*, p. 16.
[20] Ibid. p. 8.
[21] Ibid. pp. 14–15, n. 60.
[22] Richard Morris, ed. and trans. *The Blickling Homilies* (London, 1874–89; reprint 1967), pp. 136–59.

except typologically, would have no meaning) and, after being stuck to Mary's bier by angels and being converted (in a rather strong-armed fashion), processes around the city holding aloft the palm-twig, curing the blindness of the other formerly belligerent Jews, ritualistically reminiscent of Moses' serpent in the wilderness. The addresses of the characters are often ritual prayers, written in Latin. Many of them are explained at the end, with the idea that those speaking them now are in the direct presence of the characters in the story. As a narrative like the Blickling Assumption demonstrates, appreciation of these early Christian stories in ritualistic terms contextualizes them as something more than just history, something that may have a direct impact on contemporary Christians, and which can be made personally accessible through ritual expression, when those raised on this symbolic, liturgical language have been educated about the significance of the individual elements. Narratives with this sort of flavour reflect on paper what is expressed actively in the liturgy, the ability of liturgical symbolism to personalize commemoration, to juxtapose the participants of dramatic liturgical ritual with Christian history. It is ritual's ability to make the participants an active part of the events reactualized that makes it 'dramatic.'

O. B. Hardison in *Christian Rite and Christian Drama* explores this dynamic of liturgical reactualization, driven by what he calls the "principle of coincidence," in great detail, drawing on Amalarius' dramatic interpretation of the Mass.[23] Coincidence, for Hardison, stems from the desire for literal identification, spatially and temporally, with commemorated figures and events. Clifford Flanigan described the principle of coincidence when he asserted that "the words and gestures of a ritual are thought to be charged with a power of reactualization so that the event imitated is believed rendered present."[24] The theory of transubstantiation in the Eucharist, along with explicitly-made recollections of Passover and the Last Supper, is perhaps the most obvious example of this reactualization. Throughout the Holy Season, ceremonies were often timed to correspond temporally with commemorated events, and liturgical action was intended to recall the commemorated biblical action.

Gregory Dix in *The Shape of the Liturgy* discusses in detail the power of Eucharistic ceremonies, illustrating, in short, their ability to bring the participant into the presence of the Passover, the Last Supper, and the entire community of Christians.[25] Ælfric makes this simultaneous impact

---

[23] O. B. Hardison, *Christian Rite and Christian Drama* (Baltimore, 1965). Hardison's exploration of the dramatic nature of the Mass and of the church year is fundamental to any subsequent study of dramatic ritual, including this one. On versions of Amalarius' works in Anglo-Saxon manuscripts, see Dumville, *Liturgy*, pp. 135–6.

[24] C. Clifford Flanigan, "The Fleury Playbook, the Traditions of Medieval Latin Drama, and Modern Scholarship," in *The Fleury Playbook: Essays and Studies*, ed. Campbell and Davidson (Kalamazoo, 1985), p. 3.

[25] Gregory Dix, *The Shape of the Liturgy* (Westminster, 1945).

explicit in his *Sermo de Sacrificio in Die Pascae*.[26] He connects the Passover and the Last Supper by specifying that the doorposts of the Israelites' houses were marked with 'Tau,' the 'cross-sign,' and by reiterating God's command, in both instances, to 'Do this in remembrance.' He points out that the manifold sacrifices of the Israelites symbolized Christ's body. The entire community of Christians, past and present, are invoked in the sanctified loaf and wine by the mixing of water, which signifies the folk, with the sacraments, and by the words of Paul, "Be that which you see on the altar, and receive that which you yourself are . . . We many are one loaf and one body." While the bulk of the text is dedicated to explaining that "Micel is betwux þære ungesewenlican mihte þæs halgan husles and þam gesewenlican hiwe,"[27] reflecting the tendency to take signification literally, Ælfric emphasizes that the sacraments are spiritually "soþlice æfter halgunge Cristes lichama and his blod."[28] He reinforces his point with two stories of Eucharistic manifestations. The first involves an angel carving up an infant in Mass, after which it is converted to the sacraments and communicated. The second relates a mass of Gregory in which a doubting woman is convinced upon seeing a bloody fingertip in place of the sacraments. Concluding his discussion with reminders of the Last Judgement and Christ's sacrifice, Ælfric trains his audience to see the Eucharist as a juxtaposition, not literal but still quite real, of a series of events throughout Christian history. His purpose is simply to make sure that Christians have a clear understanding of the meaning of the Eucharist, that they approach the ceremony with the correct mindset. While this purpose necessitates mitigating a too-literal view of the sacraments (a view that perhaps misled some into worshipping the sacraments themselves rather than the Christ dwelling spiritually within them), it also compels Ælfric to invoke the very real, direct presence of the former participants of Passover and of the Mass, as well as Christ himself. As with the figures and events represented in painting and sculpture, Ælfric makes it clear that the invoked presence of Christ is to be understood as, if not literal, just as real as if Christ were literally present. Those being enlightened by Ælfric's sermon, then, will interact with the Eucharist, and with the rest of the liturgy, in such a way that the actions involved carry out this juxtaposition of present with past, making them players in a sort of timeless Christian history, aware of the significance of their actions and the degree of their personal participation.

This sort of reenactment is not hindered by ritualistic expression; rather, it depends upon it. Discussions of the *Visitatio* as an 'emerging representational mode,' making baby-steps towards drama in its early recognition of

---

[26] Malcolm Godden, ed. *Ælfric's Catholic Homilies: The Second Series* (London, 1979), pp. 150–60.
[27] "There is a great difference between the unseen might of the holy Eucharist and its visible form."
[28] Ibid. p. 153. "Truly after the blessing Christ's body and his blood."

the fundamentals of mimesis, miss the point. It is exactly those elements of the *Visitatio* that critics looking for representational drama consider weakest, elements of ritual adherence that stunt the emerging mode (most notably the ritual presentation of the gravecloth to the audience), that make the dramatic ritual work, for the Anglo-Saxons. Descriptions of the *Visitatio* as embryonic drama emphasize the actions, clothing, and characterization of the 'actors,' the three monks representing the women and the one standing in for the angel at the tomb. What is most important here, however, is the role taken over by all present, by the celebrants, by what some might call the 'audience,' and anything happening 'onstage' is there not for its own sake but primarily to enhance the participatory role undertaken by the congregation. It is communal reenactment, rather than presentation, and the end result is to enhance the sympathetic identification between the larger congregation and the women at the tomb.

The concern here, a concern evident in liturgical ritual throughout the festivals commemorating the events of Christ's life, is to establish a connection between all the faithful and their biblical models. The gospel accounts for the major events in Christ's life set forth as models certain figures, the shepherds at Christmas, the three magi at Epiphany, Simeon at Candlemas, the people of Jerusalem at the triumphal entry, and the three Marys at Easter. Liturgical commemoration picks up on this biblical dynamic. The liturgy of the late Anglo-Saxon church might be called 'dramatic' because it recognizes and develops these associations to the degree that the liturgical participants are trained to feel that, for the time of the commemoration, they have some sort of connection with these biblical figures, speaking with their voices and relating to Christ as had they, experiencing what those invoked experienced, and learning what they learned. What we do not see, at any stage in the Anglo-Saxon liturgy, is the sort of mimetic playing evident in both ecclesiastical and secular society in later Medieval England, nothing like the mystery cycles of the fourteenth and fifteenth centuries, or even the imaginative complex of liturgical and secular dramatic forms represented in the twelfth-century Anglo-Norman *Jeu D'Adam*. This is why it is more appropriate to refer to ceremonies like the *Visitatio* not as 'drama' but as 'dramatic ritual,' and those who attempt to describe this sort of thing as drama must resort to a language heavily qualified by quotation marks (a 'quasi-play,' the 'actors,' the 'audience,' the 'playing area,' etc.). Although, as modern critics often exhort, drama is in some ways essentially ritualistic, drama and ritual are nevertheless distinct forms of communal participation. One of the primary distinctions has to do with the inclusive nature of ritual. To oversimply a complex web of relationships for the sake of argument, while drama certainly involves the 'drawing-in' of the audience so that they will empathize with the protagonists onstage, in dramatic ritual like the *Visitatio*, the congregation themselves become the protagonists in the story. The kind of characteristics familiar in modern drama seen in the *Visitatio* (costuming, dialogue, mimetic impersonation), and often asserted as necessary determinants for drama, are not what drive these liturgical ceremonies, but are inventive trappings added to a pre-existing core of dramatic ritual, a core established by symbolic invocation and communal identification. The liturgy of the late Anglo-Saxon church was certainly innovative. Perhaps its most exciting innovation was in recognizing this dynamic of establishing sympathetic associations with biblical models, a dynamic intrinsic to the liturgy, and in developing the ritual to take greater advantage of this strategy.

The potential for some sort of dramatic relationship with the liturgy is inherent in the liturgical forms of the church from a very early stage, and when Amalarius of Metz (c. 775–852/3) describes the ninth-century Frankish liturgy as dramatic, he is not creating new ceremonies, but is rather interpreting the various relationships between liturgical celebrants and biblical figures and events embedded in the liturgical forms.[29] The Anglo-Saxons inherited the core of their liturgy from the continent, which already included the potential for sympathetic identification. However, as their liturgy developed, new liturgical forms often emphasized and enhanced this connective potential. The *Visitatio* is of this nature. As I will demonstrate, the surrounding liturgy for Easter involves some relationship between the celebrant and the three women at the tomb. The *Concordia* expands upon this, drawing out this connection and emphasizing it in the ritual presentation of the grave-cloth to the congregation, making the congregation one with the women, hearing the angel and seeing the proof of the Resurrection. This is the central mechanism of dramatic ritual, and appears here not as a quasi-dramatic, partly successful experiment, but as a naturalized part of the Anglo-Saxon liturgy. When we appreciate it in its own context, by examining the symbolic significance of its elements to its contemporaries, rather than comparing the actions to those of people separated by hundreds of years, there is no particular reason to see this sort of dramatic ritual as any less a reenactment of the revelation at the tomb than what we see in later centuries. It is this context on which I would like to focus, in order to examine the degree to which the forces behind the *Visitatio* are at work elsewhere in the late Anglo-Saxon liturgy.

In summary, what I hope to demonstrate in regard to the dramatic nature of the liturgy of this period is threefold. Firstly, the liturgy inherited by the tenth-century Anglo-Saxons was inherently set up to encourage identification with biblical figures, lending it the dramatic potential recognized by Amalarius in the ninth century. Of course, dramatic potential does not necessarily make for dramatic ritual, but this is one of the problems that the

---

[29] See Jean Michel Hanssens, ed. *Amalarii episcopi opera liturgical omnia*, vol. 2 (Vatican City, 1948).

Anglo-Saxon church, at least from the tenth century if not before, seems to be addressing. Secondly, Anglo-Saxon adaptations of the liturgy indicate various attempts to draw out sympathetic, participatory aspects of the liturgy and highlight them. We can see this addressed explicitly in the *Concordia*, and more subtly in many liturgical manuscripts of the period (see for instance the emphasis given identification with the original crowd in the Palm Sunday liturgy and developments of the song of Simeon in the Candlemas procession). The liturgical innovations of the Anglo-Saxons were in many respects targeted at clarifying and elaborating the relationship between the participant and the biblical model. Thirdly, Anglo-Saxon vernacular preaching texts demonstrate an interest in highlighting central aspects of this involvement, especially for the laity, so that the congregation can participate with a conscious appreciation that what they are engaging in is a reenactment, a usurpation of voice and action for contemporary edification. Both in forms inherited from continental models and in those developed creatively by the Anglo-Saxon church (insofar as we can identify these), it is this strategy of sympathetic connection, a sort of ritualistic role-playing, that allows us to describe liturgical ritual in dramatic terms.

SOURCES

Because my primary interest is in the various contexts of the *Visitatio*, I will focus on the time period between the compilation of the *Regularis Concordia* and the end of the Anglo-Saxon period (around 1100). I will examine primarily three bodies of evidence. The first is the *Concordia* itself, along with texts directly derived from it. The second is the liturgical manuscripts of the period. Most of these were compiled after the *Concordia*, and a few of them quote the *Concordia* in their rubrical apparatus. I have included brief descriptions of the more important liturgical manuscripts cited in this study (those which are cited in more than one context). For manuscripts mentioned in only one context, I will give information about date and provenance as they occur.[30]

---

[30] The following descriptions are summaries for the sake of reference. They are based on the following works: Pfaff, *The Liturgical Books of Anglo-Saxon England* (cited by individual chapter); Dumville, *Liturgy*, pp. 66ff; Andrew Prescott, "The Structure of English Pre-Conquest Benedictionals," *British Library Journal* 13 (1987), pp. 118–58; Helmut Gneuss, "Liturgical Books in Anglo-Saxon England and their Old English Terminology," in *Learning and Literature*, ed. Lapidge and Gneuss (Cambridge, 1985), pp. 91–141; J. Brückmann, "Latin Manuscript Pontificals and Benedictionals in England and Wales," *Traditio* 29 (1973), pp. 391–9; N. R. Ker, *Catalogue of Manuscripts Containing Anglo-Saxon* (Oxford, 1957). See, in particular, Pfaff and Gneuss for more comprehensive surveys of the relevant manuscripts and some of the problems involved in classifying and interpreting them.

Gelasian Sacramentary   The term 'Gelasian' refers to a type of liturgical book rather than a single manuscript. Liturgists distinguish two types of 'Gelasian' Sacramentaries, the Old Gelasian (represented by the single copy in Vatican MS Regenensis 316; ed. Wilson) and the eighth-century Gelasian, of which there are many examples.[31] I will refer only to the Old Gelasian, as edited by Wilson. This represents a Roman liturgy which was Gallicanized after reaching Gaul in the eighth century. It may be that the Gelasian type was predominant in England before the tenth century. In any event, it was one of the models used for English liturgical books.

Gregorian Sacramentary   The primary model for at least the late Anglo-Saxon liturgy, however, was the Gregorian Sacramentary.[32] It similarly represents a type of book rather than a single manuscript. Sometime between 784 and 791, Charlemagne, in an attempt to align the Carolingian liturgy with Roman practice, asked Pope Hadrian to send a copy of the sacramentary used in Rome. This "Hadrianum" type of sacramentary was intended for festal use by the pope himself, and was consequently found insufficient for daily use. The book was supplemented with Gelasian and Gallican forms, creating the type of sacramentary known as the Supplemented Hadrianum.[33] This type of massbook found its way into England at some point in the ninth or tenth century, and its influence is clearly evident in the extant Anglo-Saxon manuscripts. However, Anglo-Saxon books differ in many regards, due to the convoluted mix of Gelasian and Gregorian elements (as well as possible influence from sacramentaries derived from other countries and original composition). Unless otherwise specified, references to this type will assume the Supplemented Hadrianum.

Æthelwold Benedictional   The Benedictional of St. Æthelwold (London, BL MS Additional 49598; ed. A. Prescott, "The Text of the Benedictional of St. Æthelwold," in *Bishop Æthelwold*, ed. Barbara Yorke (Woodbridge, 1988), pp. 119–47; Prescott p. 120; Gneuss no. 301; Brückmann p. 431) does seem to be connected to the saint. Its scribe, Godeman, claims that the book was commissioned by Æthelwold, giving us a date for its composition of 963–84 (Æthelwold's tenure as bishop of Winchester). It is important to this

---

[31] See Cyrille Vogel, translated by William G. Storey and Niels Krogh Rasmussen, *Medieval Liturgy* (Washington, 1988), pp. 61ff, for a discussion of the definitions of 'Gregorian,' 'Gallican,' and 'Gelasian,' and of the difficulties in ascertaining a 'pure' form of each. See also Eric Palazzo, translated by Madeleine Beaumont, *A History of Liturgical Books* (Minnesota, 1998), pp. 35ff. In short, any liturgy existing in any extant text is in varying degrees a mix of these types.

[32] See R. Pfaff, "Missals," pp. 7–11, for a discussion of the introduction of the Gregorian sacramentary into England, perhaps in the late ninth or early tenth century.

[33] For the history and types of Gregorian sacramentaries, see Palazzo, *A History of Liturgical Books*, pp. 48ff.

study for a number of reasons, including its links to the *Concordia*, its influence on subsequent benedictionals, and its rich illustrations of key biblical scenes.[34]

Anderson Pontifical   The Anderson (or Brodie) Pontifical (London, BL MS Additional 57337; ed. Marie A. Conn, *The Dunstan and Brodie (Anderson) Pontificals: An Edition and Study* (University of Notre Dame, 1993); Dumville p. 77; Prescott p. 121; Gneuss no. 302; Brückmann pp. 431–2) is a Christ Church, Canterbury, book of c. 1000, containing both pontifical and benedictional material. It has affinities with other Anglo-Saxon books of the period, including the Benedictional of Æthelwold and the tenth-century Dunstan Pontifical, and has a particularly rich set of prayers for the blessing of the palms on Palm Sunday.[35]

Canterbury Benedictional   This Christ Church, Canterbury, book (London, BL MS Harley 2892; ed. Woolley, *The Canterbury Benedictional* (London, 1917); Prescott pp. 132–3; Gneuss no. 429; Brückmann p. 440) is perhaps the most important witness to the Anglo-Saxon liturgy, in that it demonstrates in many respects original composition or purposeful revision of liturigical *ordines*. It can be dated to c. 1023–30, and includes not only episcopal prayers but also a good deal of pontifical material.[36] Prescott, who dates the book to just after 1023 and who gives a table demonstrating the mixing of Gallican, Gregorian, and native English elements in these prayers, considers this book to be "the climax of the tradition of benedictionals begun under St. Æthelwold." Apart from being one of the most interesting, and most original, *ordines* for the Maundy Thursday Chrism Mass extant in Anglo-Saxon books,[37] it contains extensive *ordines* for the Ash Wednesday Dismissal of public penitents, the Maundy Thursday Reconciliation, and the Candlemas and Palm Sunday blessings and processions. That some kind of importance was attached to these festivals is perhaps indicated by their expansive treatment here. In places, the rubrical directions quote the *Concordia* (see, for example, the instructions for Palm Sunday, pp. 22–8).

Darley/Corpus 422   This book, also known as the Red Book of Darley, has not yet been edited (Cambridge, Corpus Christi College MS 422; Dumville

---

[34] Nelson and Pfaff, "Pontificals and Benedictionals," in *The Liturgical Books*, p. 90; Deshman, *The Benedictional of Æthelwold* (Princeton, 1995). Prescott ("The Structure") charts the relationship between the Æthelwold Benedictional and other Anglo-Saxon books.

[35] Ibid. pp. 91–2.

[36] See Nelson and Pfaff, "Pontificals and Benedictionals," p. 92.

[37] On the various strains of the chrism mass in England, and the originality of the Canterbury *ordo*, see Christopher A. Jones, "The Chrism Mass in Later Anglo-Saxon England," in *Ritual and Belief*, ed. Bedingfield and Gittos (forthcoming).

pp. 74–5; Gneuss no. 111; Ker no. 70). In addition to a tenth-century copy of the Old English poem *Solomon and Saturn*, it contains a wide variety of liturgical and devotional texts, including some office material. It seems to have been compiled around the year 1060, apparently for a parochial context in Derbyshire.[38] Particularly interesting are the Old English computistical material and the Old English translations of baptismal rubrics.[39]

Lanalet Pontifical   Several different locations have been postulated for the provenance of this early eleventh-century book (Rouen, Bib. mun. MS 368 (A. 27); ed. G. H. Doble, *Pontificale lanaletense* (London, 1937); Dumville pp. 86–7; Prescott p. 128; Gneuss no. 922; Ker no. 374), including Crediton, St. Germans, and Wells.[40] In any event, it seems to be a West Country text, and features distinctive forms for a number of festivals, including Palm Sunday, the Maundy Thursday Chrism Mass, and the rites for public penance. It may have belonged to Lyfing, a monk from Winchester and Bishop of Crediton (1027–46). Prescott describes it as consisting of "recently composed English blessings . . . added to a basic Winchester text."

Leofric Missal   The Leofric Missal (Oxford, Bodleian Library, MS Bodley 579; ed. Warren, *The Leofric Missal* (Oxford, 1883); Dumville p. 82; Prescott p. 121; Gneuss no. 585; Brückmann pp. 446–8) is an extremely complicated book, and one that belies summary description.[41] The core of the book, consisting of year-round Mass readings for both Temporale and Sanctorale festivals, is generally described as having derived from northeastern France in the ninth century. Over the next two centuries, however, after making its way to England in the early tenth century, additions were made by a number of hands, at times simply alterations or marginal additions of single feasts and at times larger blocks of liturgical material. As such, it is difficult to judge the date and provenance of a particular form in the book. Three layers of material were discerned by Warren. The original, ninth-century material is referred to as Leofric A. Leofric B (a calendar and computistical material) was appended in the mid-tenth century in England. Leofric C consists of several substrata of liturgical material (including some pontifical material) added to the book (appended or written in blank spaces) over the course of the tenth and eleventh centuries,

---

[38] See Pfaff, "Massbooks," in *The Liturgical Books*, pp. 21–4; Alicia Corrêa, "Daily Office Books," in *The Liturgical Books*, pp. 54, 56–7.

[39] See Sarah Larratt Keefer, "Manuals," in *The Liturgical Books*, p. 102; R. I. Page, "Old English Liturgical Rubrics in Corpus Christi College, Cambridge, MS 422," *Anglia* 96 (1978), pp. 149–58.

[40] See Nelson and Pfaff, "Pontificals and Benedictionals," p. 93.

[41] For a survey of arguments regarding date, provenance, and layers of addition, see Pfaff, "Massbooks," pp. 11–14. A new edition of the Leofric Missal, which will challenge many previous assumptions about the history and structure of the book, is being prepared for the Henry Bradshaw Society by Nicholas Orchard.

possibly at Exeter, where the book was given to the cathedral church by its bishop, Leofric (1050–72). Most of my quotations from Leofric will refer to Leofric A. Material drawn from Leofric C will be designated as such.

Leofric Collectar   The Leofric Collectar (London, BL MS Harley 2961; ed. Dewick and Frere, *The Leofric Collectar* (London, 1914–21); Gneuss no. 431) is an Exeter book, compiled while Leofric was bishop there (1050–72). This is a particularly useful witness for this study, as it was intended for the use of the secular clergy. Because it includes not just texts for the monastic office (as adapted for secular devotion) but also psalm incipits and other choral material, it "represents a dramatic improvement in structure and content over the earlier collectars."[42]

New Minster Missal   On summarizing the evidence for the date and nature of the remarkably full Missal of the New Minster (Le Havre, Bibl. mun. MS 330; ed. D. H. Turner, *The Missal of the New Minster, Winchester* (London, 1962); Gneuss no. 837), written for the New Minster probably in the 1070s, Pfaff conjectures that "it may reflect a genuinely new blend of English and Continental elements."[43] Although the book is missing a lot of material (it has only Temporale forms beginning from Easter Friday, a Sanctorale, and some votive prayers), it shows a good deal of creativity, and it reflects a liturgy different in many respects from earlier New Minster books. It is one of the few witnesses to the Candlemas liturgy, and includes musical material that many other missals omit.

Robert Benedictional   The Benedictional of Archbishop Robert (Rouen, Bib. mun. MS 369 (Y.7); ed. H. A. Wilson, *The Benedictional of Archbishop Robert* (London, 1903); Dumville p. 87; Prescott pp. 124–5; Gneuss no. 923) dates it from the 980s, and while it seems to reflect New Minster practice, it was apparently compiled for a bishop.[44] It contains a benedictional followed by pontifical material. Prescott charts these blessings and their sources (pp. 141–7).

Robert Missal   The sacramentary known as the Missal of Robert of Jumièges (Rouen, Bibl. mun. MS 274 (Y.6); ed. H. A. Wilson, *The Missal of Robert of Jumièges* (London, 1896); Dumville p. 87; Gneuss no. 921) is monastic in origin, and may reflect the observance of Ely or Peterborough, with possible connections to Christ Church, Canterbury. It was composed most likely before the year 1013.[45] It includes mass forms, and at times other

---

[42] Corrêa, "Daily Office Books," p. 51.
[43] See Pfaff, "Massbooks," pp. 28–30.
[44] For more detail and alternate dating, see Nelson and Pfaff, "Pontificals and Benedictionals," p. 94.
[45] See ibid. 15–19 for further bibliography.

liturgical material, but does not contain episcopal blessings. However, as a number of books survive that consist primarily of these blessings, the Robert Missal may or may not reflect an episcopal model. In any event, it is one of the most important witnesses to Anglo-Saxon observance, and it includes the liturgy for the Candlemas procession (as do the New Minster Missal and the Canterbury Benedictional).

Winchcombe Sacramentary This massbook (Orléans, Bib. mun. MS 127 (105); ed. Davril, *The Winchcombe Sacramentary* (London, 1995); Dumville pp. 80–81; Gneuss no. 867) was compiled in the late tenth century, either at Winchcombe abbey or, possibly, at Ramsey. Although it includes references to the English saint Kenelm, it seems to have been written for use not in England but in France (perhaps Fleury), and therefore must be used with caution, in that some forms may indicate knowledge rather than practice of a particular liturgical element in England.[46]

Winchester Troper The label 'Winchester Troper' actually refers to two related manuscripts (Cambridge, Corpus Christ College MS 473, the Corpus Troper (Gneuss no. 116); Oxford, Bodleian Library, MS Bodley 775, the Bodleian or Æthelred Troper (Gneuss no. 597)) which were amalgamated and edited as *The Winchester Troper* by Frere (London, 1894).[47] As troping seems to have been a relatively new development at the time of the Benedictine Reform, this is one of the more fertile areas for examination of Anglo-Saxon liturgical elaborations. While many of the tropes found in these manuscripts are clearly of Frankish origin, there are quite a few original English elements as well. Both manuscripts represent tenth-century Winchester usage (Old Minster). The manuscript copy of the Corpus Troper dates from the late tenth or early eleventh century, and that of the Bodleian Troper from the mid-eleventh century. In addition to tropes both manuscripts also contain some gradual material.[48]

Wulstan Portiforium This late-eleventh-century book (Cambridge, Corpus Christ College MS 391; ed. Anselm Hughes, *The Portiforium of Saint Wulstan* (London, 1956–7); Gneuss no. 104; Ker no. 67) "is by far the most comprehensive representative of the breviary to survive in Anglo-Saxon England." It was written for monastic use at Worcester under Bishop Wulfstan (II, 1062–95).[49] In addition to its remarkably full office material, a psalter, a hymnal, and several other texts, it includes a series of prayers in Old English and in Latin, including some devotional prayers related to the Adoration of the Cross liturgy on Good Friday. It is also

[46] See Pfaff, "Massbooks," pp. 14–15, for further bibliography.
[47] See E. C. Teviotdale, "Tropers," in *The Liturgical Books*, pp. 39–44, for further bibliography.
[48] K. D. Hartzell, "Graduals," in *The Liturgical Books*, pp. 35–7.
[49] See Teviotdale, "Tropers," pp. 57–8.

one of the few Anglo-Saxon books to provide forms for the Rogationtide processions.

As one might expect given the importance of Winchester and Canterbury in the tenth-century reforms, many of these books either represent the liturgies of these two ecclesiastical centres or were in varying degrees influenced by them. Exeter and Worcester are also important, and are represented in the extant texts. While the concentration of texts in these major centres makes it difficult to postulate about more parochial permutations of the liturgy, it does allow for comparison with the ceremonies represented in the *Concordia*, developed itself primarily with Winchester and Canterbury in mind. Especially interesting is the fact that the witnesses from these two major centres demonstrate sequential development. It would seem that both Winchester and Canterbury were frequently interested in revision and updating of liturgical *ordines*.[50]

Bridging the gap between the *Concordia* and the later liturgical witnesses, and most important to my analysis of Anglo-Saxon liturgical innovation, are the vernacular preaching texts of the period, especially those of Ælfric (c. 955–c. 1010; a monk of Winchester and Cerne Abbas, and Abbot of Eynsham from 1005). Between the years 990 and 994, Ælfric composed two series of sermons, known as the Catholic Homilies.[51] He provides sermons for all of the major festivals of the church calendar. Although it is not his primary purpose, Ælfric frequently comments in these two series on the liturgy, in a way that gives us some insight into the nature of Anglo-Saxon participation in these liturgical events. There are a number of links between Ælfric and the liturgical schema presented in the *Concordia*. In his preface to his First Series, in an address to Archbishop Sigeric of Canterbury, he calls himself a pupil of St. Æthelwold, who played a central role in drawing up the document.[52] Ælfric was trained by him at Winchester before being sent to Cerne Abbas around the year 987. Sometime later, around the year 1005, Ælfric adapted the *Concordia*, synthesizing it with a version of the commentaries of Amalarius, in his *Letter to the Monks of Eynsham*.[53] He comments from time to time on the liturgy in his other sermons as well, and gives a rough outline of the more important festivals in his pastoral letters for Wulfstan.[54] Whatever the particular liturgy followed by Ælfric at Winchester, or at

[50] See Turner, *The Missal of the New Minster*, and also Prescott, "The Structure," on innovation at Winchester. See Jones, "The Chrism Mass in Later Anglo-Saxon England," on the interest, evident in CB, in collecting various forms of the Chrism rite for creation of a new one. See also Bedingfield, "Public Penance in Anglo-Saxon England," *ASE* (forthcoming), on CB's innovative rites for the Dismissal and Reconciliation of penitents.

[51] Apart from the editions of Peter Clemoes, ed. *Ælfric's Catholic Homilies: The First Series* (Oxford, 1997) and Godden (CH II), see also Godden, *Ælfric's Catholic Homilies: Introduction, Commentary, and Glossary* (London, 2000).

[52] See Godden, *Ælfric's Catholic Homilies: Introduction*, p. xxix.

[53] See Jones, *LME*.

[54] Bernhard Fehr, ed. *Die Hirtenbriefe Ælfrics* (Hamburg, 1914), pp. 68ff.

Cerne Abbas, or at Eynsham, Ælfric was clearly in many respects a product of this Benedictine Reform, and would have been intimately familiar with innovative rituals like the *Visitatio*, possibly even participating in some way in their development and performance. The evidence available in Ælfric's sermons is particularly important given his general interest in instruction. Although he writes his sermons with both lay and monastic audiences in mind,[55] he shows a particular concern for making sure the lay congregations of England understand just what they are doing in the course of Christian worship, as is evident in his explanation of the Eucharist. This interest takes the form not only of explicit instruction regarding the liturgy, but also of more subtle hints as to the relationship between biblical history and ritual expression.[56] When he does deal with ritual, his mechanism for interpreting and packaging the liturgy is remarkably consistent, and is consonant with the dramatic mechanism described above in regards to the *Visitatio*, in that he uses the preaching as an opportunity to span the gap between what is happening in the liturgy and the understanding of his audience. In particular, as I will attempt to show, Ælfric emphasizes these biblical models, and at times explicitly instructs his audience to emulate them in the liturgy. At other times, especially in his gospel translations, he deals with these models more subtly in ways that increase the sense of identification between them and the contemporary faithful. Anglo-Saxon vernacular preaching texts (featuring but not exclusive to the sermons of Ælfric) reflect the liturgy, even to the point of allowing liturgical form to invade and usurp biblical accounts, and it is through the preaching texts that the folk are trained to appreciate and relate to the symbolic elements of the liturgy.

CONTINENTAL INFLUENCE AND NATIVE PRACTICE

Apart from these three central bodies of evidence, I will from time to time draw upon the homilies of Wulfstan (Bishop of Worcester and Archbishop of York, 1003–1023), anonymous homilies including the vernacular sermons of the Blickling and Vercelli manuscripts (most of which were probably composed in the first half of the tenth century),[57] earlier devo-

---

[55] See Godden, *Ælfric's Catholic Homilies: Introduction*, pp. xxiii–xxvii.

[56] Particularly interesting are his revisions of the gospel text, made to reflect the ritual more than the historical event. On this see Bedingfield, "Reinventing the Gospel: Ælfric and the Liturgy," *Medium Ævum* 68, no. 1 (1999), pp. 13–31.

[57] However, many of these sermons were transmitted into eleventh-century texts, at times with the apparent purpose of using them in a preaching context, and so they do yet have relevance to post-*Concordia* liturgical appreciation. See the introduction to D. G. Scragg, ed. *The Vercelli Homilies and Related Texts* (Oxford, 1992), as well as Scragg, "Cambridge, Corpus Christi College 162," in *Anglo-Saxon Manuscripts and Their Heritage*, ed. Pulsiano and Treharne (Aldershot, 1998), pp. 71–84, for examples of eleventh-century manuscripts which integrate these earlier homilies. See also the descriptions of Ælfrician manuscripts in the introductions to CH I and CH II, many of which include sermons from the Blickling or Vercelli collections.

tional books (such as the ninth-century Book of Cerne), and the poems of Anglo-Saxon England (most of which probably predate the Reform by some time), many of which reflect, in one way or another, liturgical dynamics. Most of this evidence must be used with caution, as we have very little idea what the liturgy of these periods would have consisted of, and therefore how they relate to the dramatic liturgy of the later period. Much of the innovation reflected in the *Concordia* was imported by the Reformers, some of whom were trained on the Continent, from Frankish centres (named in the *Concordia* are Fleury and Ghent[58]). It is generally believed that the *Quem quaeritis* (the heart of the *Visitatio*) was developed on the continent and integrated into the English liturgy at some point in the tenth century. To what extent the rest of the *Concordia* represents importation rather than native practice we will probably never know, without clear evidence for the pre-existing English liturgy.[59] However, that the earlier Anglo-Saxons had some sort of liturgy is certain, and that that liturgy encouraged, in some respects, a participatory relationship with the events commemorated is not unlikely, given the intensity of that relationship reflected in poems like *The Dream of the Rood*, in devotional practices like those in the Book of Cerne, and in these earlier homilies. I will use this earlier evidence, then, to demonstrate that the dynamics behind the participatory liturgy evident in the *Concordia*, in Ælfric's interpretations, and in the later liturgical books, were already present to some extent in the Anglo-Saxon relationship with the liturgy, such that what we see in the later tenth century represents an integration of good and useful continental practices into a preexisting liturgical paradigm, along the lines of Gregory's instruction to Augustine to marry together the best of differing practices, an instruction with which the *Concordia* begins.[60]

That Anglo-Saxon reception of continental practices generally represents something more than mere transmission is by now a commonplace.[61] Christopher A. Jones describes how Ælfric's creative use of Amalarius "demonstrates the now-familiar point that reception of Carolingian sources was productive rather than merely passive."[62] In describing tenth-century

---

[58] Kornexl, *Die Regularis concordia*, p. 6; Symons, *Regularis concordia*, p. 3.
[59] See Symons, "Regularis Concordia: History and Derivation," *Tenth-Century Studies*, ed. Parsons (London, 1975). While certain practices seem clearly to have English precedent, such as the special prayers for the royal family, the frequent communion, and the ringing of bells at certain occasions, most of the more dramatic elements are of uncertain origin. The problem is compounded by the fact that many aspects of the liturgy would have existed both in England and on the continent, such that the influence of Fleury and Ghent on the compilation of the *Concordia* might in many respects amount to amalgamation rather than importation.
[60] Kornexl, *Die Regularis concordia*, pp. 5–6; Symons, *Regularis concordia*, p. 3.
[61] See in particular Veronica Ortenberg, *The English Church and the Continent in the Tenth and Eleventh Centuries: Cultural, Spiritual, and Artistic Exchanges* (Oxford, 1992), who argues that "the borrowing of Continental elements, when it took place, was never indiscriminate, but prompted by a deliberate choice" (264).
[62] Jones, "The Book of the Liturgy," p. 681.

changes in ecclesiastical territorial organization regarding church revenue, John Blair argues that, while these changes demonstrate Carolingian influence, they are "also founded on old insular practice . . . This context warns against any simple model of a Carolingian parochial system imported ready-made to England."[63] D. Talbot Rice, discussing continental influence on tenth-century art forms, asserts that "Whatever the external influences may have been, and however important, it must, on the other hand, be stressed that the essential character of later Anglo-Saxon art was above anything else its Englishness."[64] Similarly, while indebtedness to continental liturgical practices is heavy, the *Concordia*, the liturgical reflections of Ælfric, and the later liturgical manuscripts all demonstrate reinventions of a variety of sources in line with English aesthetics. Indeed, some new research into the Anglo-Saxon liturgy seems to be indicating that the influence may have been reciprocal, with continental books reflecting some Anglo-Saxon practices.[65] Description of liturgical practice in terms of 'native' or 'imported' is tricky, and generally oversimplistic, and, due to the paucity of the evidence, it is perhaps more revealing to ask what the late Anglo-Saxons did with the liturgical material available to them, either native or new, than to ask where the individual elements might have come from. As such, while I will attempt to discuss native and imported practices where the evidence is suggestive, I will focus instead on evidence that indicates active interpretation or revision of these rituals, demonstrating Anglo-Saxon interest in developing the liturgy to take greater advantage of its dramatic potential.

MONASTIC v LAY

In particular, and especially relevant in light of the evidence afforded by vernacular preaching texts, I will emphasize the way in which this experience has been extended to the laity. Even where liturgical ceremonies seem to cater exclusively to a monastic milieu, the general extension of monastic observance to the secular clergy in late Anglo-Saxon England would surely have placed these ceremonies in a broader context. Secular clergy were encouraged to observe the monastic Offices, and many bishops were trained in monasteries.[66] As such, although the extant liturgical witnesses are

---

[63] Blair, *The Church in Anglo-Saxon Society* (forthcoming). I am grateful to Dr Blair for advance access to this study.

[64] Rice, *English Art*, p. 251.

[65] As Prescott explains, "The benedictionals and pontificals in England quickly became known and admired abroad" ("The Structure," p. 129). On Anglo-Saxon influence on continental liturgy see also Yitzhak Hen, "The liturgy of St Willibrord," *ASE* 26 (1997), pp. 41–62; Hen, "Rome, Anglo-Saxon England and the formation of the Frankish Liturgy," *Revue bénédictine* 112 (forthcoming 2002); Christopher A. Jones, "The Chrism Mass in Later Anglo-Saxon England."

[66] See Lapidge, *The Blackwell Encyclopaedia*, pp. 84–7, for a discussion of the relationship between Anglo-Saxon cathedral clergy and the monasteries.

fundamentally on a monastic model, they were intended for much wider use and would have influenced observance of the liturgy throughout England. The exhortation to observe monastic hours, as with Ælfric's attempts to include a broader demographic in the monastic liturgical and devotional imperatives, provided a mechanism for making monastic innovation accessible to the community.[67] In line with this effort to extend monastic practice to the general Christian community is a care for including the laity in the liturgical establishment of dramatic identification. Ælfric makes this effort clear in his descriptions of liturgical practices, designed to make his audience appreciate the models set up for them in the liturgy. It is difficult, however, to determine the exact role of the laity in a liturgy that is in many ways fundamentally monastic. I examine the evidence for the respective dramatic roles of the laity and the monastic participants in respect to Candlemas, Palm Sunday, *Tenebrae*, the *Adoratio* and *Depositio*, and Rogationtide. Although the evidence is best examined case by case, some general observations can be made. Not unexpectedly, the dramatic experience of monks would surely have been much richer, and in some ceremonies where the participation of both laity and monks can be demonstrated, the monks are given greater responsibilities for creating the juxtaposition of present and biblical worlds by enhancing visual representation (see for example *Tenebrae* and the *Depositio*). Nevertheless, the dramatic identifications set up for each festival are clearly meant to apply equally to all participants. The temptation to describe in a few cases the monk/layman dichotomy as an actor/audience dynamic falls apart because of the fluid nature of the monastic 'role-playing.' The function of this enhanced monastic role is not to present a character in any extended or developed way, but rather to enhance the atmosphere of the liturgical reenactment so that the 'role' undertaken by all present is intensified. The unified nature of the dramatic experience is most clear at Candlemas, Palm Sunday, and Rogationtide, but is fundamental to the liturgical reenactment throughout the year.

*

---

[67] See M. McC. Gatch, "The Office in Late Anglo-Saxon Monasticism," in *Learning and Literature*, pp. 341–62, on Ælfric's use of the monastic Night Office in his sermons. Malcolm Godden summarizes Ælfric's position: "Much of this mixture [of monastic and lay interests] no doubt reflects Ælfric's own situation as a monk of Winchester and a learned scholar setting out to mediate the world of Christian learning to the ordinary laity and clergy of his time. . . . the surviving manuscripts of the Catholic Homilies are particularly associated with monastic cathedrals such as Canterbury, Winchester, and Worcester, where monks would be heavily engaged in pastoral work for the laity." (*Ælfric's Catholic Homilies: Introduction*, pp. xxv, xxvii). See also J. Hill, "Monastic Reform and the Secular Church: Ælfric's Pastoral Letters in Context," in *England in the Eleventh-Century*, ed. Carole Hicks (Stamford, 1992), pp. 103–18.

See John Blair, *The Church in Anglo-Saxon Society* (forthcoming), on the possible use of processions by minster churches to encourage affiliation among the laity in response to the proliferation of parish churches, and in other respects on the pastoral responsibilities that many minsters had in Anglo-Saxon society for the surrounding layfolk.

Naturally enough, the cycle of liturgical ritual, following the church year, begins at Christ's birth and ends with Advent. Homiliaries, customaries, and summaries of the church year like the Old English verse Menologium are all based on this structure, and all draw a good deal of significance from it. It is fitting that Christ was born and grew up in a cold dark world[68] and that he was reborn at spring. All of the important saints and all of the important events of Christ's life are commemorated each year, giving them a sense of timelessness. Advent, coming as it does at the end of the year, often takes on a dual meaning, looking forward both to Christ's birth and to the Last Judgement, as relationships between poetic accounts of the Last Judgement and the lyrics for Advent indicate. The church year symbolically encompasses the entirety of Christian history, pointing to the Last Judgement. This ideal is evident in the monastic desire to read the whole of scripture over the course of the year during the Night Office. As Gatch demonstrates, Ælfric assumes this ideal (with alterations) and applies it, at least in spirit, to his cycles of homilies.[69] He provides complete cycles of exegetical and catechetical material for the church year so that Christians will understand the nature and significance of its highlighted days and be able to relate personally to the people and events remembered on those days. Vernacular preaching, explaining and bolstering the rituals, helps participants encompass the Christian universe over the course of the year and understand their places in it, as well as what they must do to have a place in the rapidly approaching heavenly kingdom to which the events of the year are leading them.

My approach is to explore the establishment of dramatic association in the liturgical forms for each major festival (focusing on the Temporale), along with the recursive influence between vernacular preaching and the liturgy. That this period in the history of the liturgy was an innovative one means that liturgical witnesses can be quite disparate. Especially regarding relatively newer parts of the liturgy, like the blessings of the candles, the ashes and the palm-twigs, apparently original prayers interact with more established forms in different ways in different texts. Many of the manuscripts seem to be interrelated, but because liturgical books represent collections of different ceremonies, some of these may be connected to a particular witness and not others, or only some may be intended for actual use. To complicate the problem, there was no clear idea in Anglo-Saxon England of just what each type of liturgical book should contain. Missals, sacramentaries, benedictionals, and pontificals are extremely fluid cate-

---

[68] The period from Christmas Eve through the Purification of Mary on 2 February symbolically encapsulates Christ's childhood, including his birth, the Slaughter of the Innocents two days later (historically two years later), his Circumcision, and the Purification, at which time Christ was presented to Simeon.

[69] Gatch, "The Office in Late Anglo-Saxon Monasticism," pp. 341–62.

gories when used in regards to Anglo-Saxon liturgical books. It was assumed that a priest or bishop would use several different books in combination in the performance of the liturgy, perhaps relying for some elements on memory and local traditions. Even when we do have fairly well-provided texts, there are always questions concerning the date and provenance of each book. Even when we have a fairly good idea that a certain text was written at a certain place and a certain time (a rare case being the Canterbury Benedictional), the nature of liturgical books is such that we can not always assume that the presence of a particular form in the book indicates its use in the local liturgy. These are just some of the problems facing those who would attempt to explicate the pre-Sarum liturgy in England.[70] As such, my approach, which is to look for the most interesting and pertinent liturgical forms from a range of texts, lays itself open to the criticism that I end up explicating a liturgy that did not actually exist at any particular place and time. However, while I will attempt, where possible, to place witnesses in their appropriate contexts, my concern is not to try to delineate exactly how the liturgy was performed in certain places in England (a task that, if possible, requires a good deal more research than has been done to date, and than is possible here). Instead, I hope to explore the state of the late Anglo-Saxon liturgy in relation to the establishment of dramatic association and the way new and deviant liturgical forms and practices reveal a general 'dramatic conscious-ness.' This consciousness is evident throughout the developing liturgy (though, given the scattered nature of the liturgical witnesses, can only be presented as flashes here and there). Vernacular preaching texts reveal a care for spreading the effects of this 'dramatic' strategy beyond the key monastic centres in England.

In summarizing the state of the liturgy in post-Reform England, Richard Pfaff urges caution in our appreciation of turn-of-the-millennium ritual:

> Inferences drawn from the few major liturgical books that survive whole, like the Benedictional of Æthelwold or the Missal of Robert of Jumièges, might lead us to the supposition that the liturgical life of England was as rich and complex c. 1000 as it was in, say, 1400. This is almost certainly a false impression. The sophistic-ated and elaborate liturgy practised at Æthelwold's Winchester or Dunstan's Canterbury or (to take a secular example) Leofric's Exeter cannot safely be extrapolated beyond a couple of dozen major establishments. Surprisingly little is known about the liturgical performance even in minster churches, and very little indeed about that in the emerging parish churches.[71]

As the energy behind the late Anglo-Saxon liturgical innovations came from these major, especially monastic, centres, the most full liturgical witnesses tend to assume a fairly large community, often a mixed one,

---

[70] See Gatch, "Old English Literature and the Liturgy: Problems and Potential," *ASE* 6 (1977), pp. 237–47, for an overview of some of these difficulties.
[71] Lapidge, *The Blackwell Encyclopaedia*, p. 293.

pursuing a liturgy driven by monks but also (to an uncertain degree) including the secular clergy and the laity. Envisioning the effects of these liturgical models on more parochial churches, especially those not in the proximity of a monastic community, is difficult at best, although at least one witness[72] seems to involve a parochial interpretation of a larger model. Again, this process of parochial translation is a far more difficult problem than can be tackled here. What I do hope to demonstrate is that the effort to enliven and extend the appreciation of the liturgy by making the participants liturgically juxtaposed with biblical figures, a process explored by the Carolingians but creatively expanded by the Anglo-Saxons, was evident wherever liturgical innovations took place. This care for the dramatic quality of the liturgy extended from the cathedrals, in strictly episcopal rituals such as the blessing of the oils and the Reconciliation of Penitents on Maundy Thursday, to the monasteries, in rituals like the *Visitatio*, to the broader community, for inclusive rituals like the Adoration of the Cross and the Easter Vigil, to the countryside, for public processions like Rogationtide. I will explore the various ways in which the establishment of sympathetic identification was used throughout the church year, focusing on Christmas, Epiphany, Candlemas, Ash Wednesday and Lent, Palm Sunday, Holy Week, Easter, Rogationtide and the Ascension, Pentecost, and Advent. Exploring the contexts of this liturgical innovation will demonstrate the degree to which Anglo-Saxon appreciation of the dramatic potential of the liturgy was realized both in creative expansion of the liturgy and in the vernacular preaching texts that identified and enhanced this dramatic dynamic.

---

[72] Corpus 422, the Red Book of Darley. As a loose collection of liturgical materials and devotional prayers, this is an uncertain, if compelling, witness to this process of translation.

2

Christmas and Epiphany

THE JUXTAPOSITION of biblical history with contemporary participants dominates the Anglo-Saxons' relationship with the liturgy from
the very beginning of the liturgical year, at Christmas. The liturgy for
Christmas and for Epiphany, explicated and explored in various ways by
vernacular writers, demonstrates the mechanisms for the establishment of
identification that drive dramatic liturgical ritual. Today, we tend to think
of Christmas as the highlight of the Christian year and a time that more
than any would appeal to dramatic sensibilities; it was, however, relatively
undervalued in the early Middle Ages. Augustine, for whom the festival was
fairly new, considered Christmas a *memoria* and Easter a *sacramentum*.
Although the importance of Christmas grew, it was still by the tenth century
greatly overshadowed by Easter. While the *Concordia* outlines specific
directions for Christmas worship, it is treated no more fully than is the
festival for the Purification of St. Mary on February 2, and its directions
seem a footnote compared to the extensive instructions for Easter. Still, the
manipulation of certain liturgical images and themes in the extant sermons
(there are six, four of which are by Ælfric), coupled with the liturgical
innovations added to the Christmas celebration in France and England at
this time, attest to a strong appeal for the commemoration of the
incarnation and birth of Christ in Anglo-Saxon England.

The third-century *De Pascha Computus* claims that Christ was born on
28 March, reflecting an early desire to correlate his birth with the creation of
the world.[1] The earliest references to a 25 December birth in the West are
found in the mid-fourth century. In the Orient, Epiphany was the original time
for this celebration. The *Peregrinatio Aetheriae* describes a midnight Mass at
the Grotto of the Nativity in Bethlehem, followed by a dawn procession back
to Jerusalem. This ritual was added to the Roman Christmas by the fifth
century, and a 'crib chapel' in a basilica dedicated to Mary was constructed
for the purpose (hence the name of the first Christmas Mass, *Ad Sanctam
Mariam Maiorem ad Praesepe*). In the morning is the *Mane Prima Ad
Sanctam Anastasiam*, originally an independent celebration from Byzantium

---

[1] See L. Duchesne, *Christian Worship* (London, 1949), pp. 257ff; Jungmann and Brenner, trans.
The Mass of the Roman Rite (New York, 1950), pp. 266–77; John Gunstone, *Christmas and
Epiphany* (London, 1967); and Thomas Talley, *The Origins of the Liturgical Year* (New York,
1986), pp. 235ff.

that was modified into a second Christmas Mass while retaining an understated commemoration of Anastasia. The third Mass is the principal one, the original Roman Christmas Mass, *In Natali Domini Ad Sanctum Petrum*. The gospel for this Mass is the beginning of John and the Mass texts correspondingly focus on the wonder of the incarnation and divine birth. Adding to these three Christmas Masses a Christmas Eve vigil, we can perceive a progression in themes over the course of the Christmas celebration. The Vigil Mass, *Vigilia Natalis Domini*, looking forward to the birth, picks up the prophetic themes of Advent and focuses them on the upcoming fulfilment of God's promise. The midnight Mass, because of its temporal coincidence with the incidents leading up to the birth (as well as, originally, its spatial coincidence, in Jerusalem and Rome), focuses on the story of the birth itself, and on the imagery of Christ as the 'rising Sun.' Light imagery dominates the ritual through sunrise, in the *Mane Prima*. Finally, the principal Mass celebrates the union of the divine and the human in the newborn Christ and its consequences for the celebrants.

Vernacular homilies openly adopted the main themes of Christmas – the fulfilment of prophecy, the light overcoming darkness, Christ as the rising Sun, and the union of heaven and earth in Christ – demonstrating the close relationship between the preaching and the liturgy. The celebrants are the hearers of the prophets, promised a Saviour. They are those who, having walked in darkness, have seen a great light. They are the shepherds, sung to by the host of angels, told of the glorious birth, and led to worship and ponder God made man. The Christmas liturgy establishes this kind of identification, while the preaching explains and solidifies it. This invocational juxtaposition of the voices of the Israelites and of the shepherds with the celebrants makes the commemoration a dramatic liturgical reenactment of the experience of those awaiting and hearing the news of Christ's birth.

From Chapter on Christmas Eve, when the festival of the Lord's Nativity is announced, there is a conscious increase in solemnity, building expectation in the celebrants. The Vigil Mass brings the feeling of expectation nurtured in Advent into focus. The Mass forms in the Leofric Missal are nicely representative.[2] In these prayers, the feelings of expectation are personalized in the participants as they ask God to make them watchful of the coming birth, to make them worthy to see it, and to be a part of it. Specifically, the celebrants are to see themselves, loosely, as the people of Israel, expecting a fulfilment of prophecy. For Vespers, the *Concordia* prescribes "antiphonae congrue de ipsa completione temporis,"[3] and these antiphons, derived from Old Testament prophecy, strengthen this identification, as do the antiphons for Vespers in the Leofric Collectar:

---

[2] See Warren, *The Leofric Missal*, pp. 62–3.
[3] Kornexl, *Die Regularis concordia*, p. 59; see also Symons, *Regularis concordia*, p. 28, "Antiphons befitting the fulfillment of the time."

Super psalmos [Ant]. Iudea et Heirusalem, nolite timere, cras egrediemini et dominus erit vobiscum.

Ant. Orietur sicut sol salvator mundi et descendet in uterum virginis sicut ymber super gramen, alleluia.

Ant. Dum ortus fuerit sol de celo, videbitis regem regum procedentem tamquam sponsum de thalamo suo.

Ant. Gaude et letare, Hierusalem, quia rex tuus venit tibi, de quo prophete praedixerunt, quem angeli semper adorant, cui cherubin et seraphin sanctus sanctus sanctus proclamant.[4]

The promises of God to the people of Israel to provide a Saviour become promises to the celebrants, as the general sense of 'tomorrow' as used in Old Testament prophecy is made literal. This direct use of tense is intensified in the *Capitula* and response for Vespers:

Capitula. Paratus esto, Israhel, in occursum domini. Ecce, enim veniet tibi, salus a domino celeriter . . . cuius gloria mane videbitur super terram.

R̊. Iudea et Hierusalem, nolite timere, cras egrediemini et dominus erit vobiscum.

V̊. . . . videbitis auxilium domini super vos, cras egrediemini. Gloria patri et filio et spiritui sancto, cras.

V̊. Hodie scietis quia veniet dominus.[5]

The dramatic nature of this use of prophecy does not involve the 'playing of a part.' There is no clear 'designation of roles' in this exchange, no Isaiah or Jeremiah crying out, clearly delineated from the responding populace. None is necessary, however, as each speaker can be simultaneously a prophet of God, inspired by the Spirit, and one of the people of Israel, crying out to each other to prepare themselves for the Lord's coming. What is important here is not so much the delineations of role-playing as the effort to make present biblical dynamics for contemporary edification. The expectations of Israel before Christ's advent and those of the participants are super-imposed, such that the celebrants become part of the general mass of the darkness-enwrapped people of God, told to expect the imminent coming of a Saviour and to prepare themselves.

Most notably, they are told to expect to see Christ rising 'like the sun.' Light is the dominant image from this point until after sunrise. The *Capitula* for *Completorium*, echoing the correlation between light and Christ's coming, proclaims, "Propter Sion non tacebo et propter Hierusalem non

[4] Dewick and Frere, *The Leofric Collectar*, p. 19. "Judea and Jerusalem, do not be afraid, tomorrow you will go forth and the Lord will be with you./ The Saviour of the world will rise like the sun and descend in the womb of the virgin like rain over the grass, alleluia./ When the sun is rising in the sky, you will see the king of kings proceeding like a bridegroom from his marriage-bed./ Rejoice and be glad, Jerusalem, because your king comes to you, about whom the prophets prophesied, whom the angels perpetually adore, to whom cherubim and seraphim proclaim, 'Holy, Holy, Holy.'"

[5] Ibid. "Be prepared, Israel, for meeting with the Lord. Lo, indeed he will come to you, salvation from the Lord quickly . . . whose glory will be seen in the morning over the earth./ Judea and Jerusalem, do not be afraid, tomorrow you will go forth and the Lord will be with you./ You will see the help of the Lord over you, tomorrow you will go forth. Glory to the father and the son and the Holy Spirit, tomorrow./ You will know today because the Lord will come."

quiescam, donec egrediatur . . . ut lampas accendatur."[6] This image is developed in the first Christmas Mass, *In Nocte*. The focus of this Mass is the Christmas story itself, which resonates with light imagery. Most important for the liturgy is the announcement to the shepherds. It is here that the people of God are first told that Christ has been born, and this announcement is concurrent with light, as the 'Glory of the Lord shone about them.' The importance of this scene to the liturgy is further attested by the return of the *Gloria*, the announcement of the angels to the shepherds, which had been absent during Advent. It is this announcement that the Christmas celebrants come to expect during the *In Nocte* Mass, as the gospel reading ends with it. The *Capitula* begs, "Deus, qui hanc sacratissimam noctem veri luminis fecisti illustratione clarescere, da, quaesumus, ut cuius lucis mysteria in terra cognovimus . . ."[7] The emphasis here is on the union of heaven and earth, such that, as the *Capitula* for Christmas Matins (from Isaiah 9:2) proclaims, "Populus gentium qui ambulabat in tenebris vidit lucem magnam; habitantibus in regione umbre mortis, lux orta est eis,"[8] allowing them to see heavenly things, and be a part of them.

It is at sunrise that these promises come to fruition. The *Concordia* specifies that the second Christmas Mass, the Morrow Mass (or *In Aurora*) must be said in the early dawn,[9] and it suggests ways to rearrange the offices to make sure. Ælfric's Letter to the Monks of Eynsham, partially derived from the *Concordia*, delineates the pre-dawn order:

> At Vespers of Christmas, antiphons appropriate to the fulness of time shall be sung at the psalms. At Vigils on this night, two shall sing the fourth responsory together, in order that it may be done with greater reverence. And after the gospel they shall wash, then the mass *in nocte* shall take place, followed by Lauds of the day. And if the day has not yet dawned, they shall sing Lauds of All Saints; but if it has dawned, they shall celebrate the matutinal mass (which is to be celebrated at daybreak) and then sing [Lauds] of All Saints.[10]

The importance of ritual coincidence with sunrise mimics a similar use of light and darkness at Easter. This relationship between Christmas and

---

[6] Dewick and Frere, *The Leofric Collectar*, p. 19. "Near Zion I will not be silent and near Jerusalem I will not rest, until he comes forth . . . so that the light is kindled."

[7] Warren, *The Leofric Missal*, p. 63. "God, you who made this most holy night bright with the illumination of the true light, grant us, we pray, that we may perceive the mystery of this light on earth."

[8] Dewick and Frere, *The Leofric Collectar*, p. 20. "The people of the nation who walked in darkness have seen a great light; for those who lived in the country of the shadow of death, a light has risen."

[9] Kornexl, *Die Regularis concordia*, pp. 59–60; Symons, *Regularis concordia*, p. 29.

[10] *LME*, p. 117. "Vespere Nativitatis Domini canantur antiphone congrue de ipsa completione temporis ad psalmos. In cuius noctis vigilia in quarto responsorio, ut honorificentius agatur, duo simul cantent. Et post evangelium lavent se et fiat missa de nocte, deinde matutinales laudes de die. Et, si nondum diei aurora eluxerit, cantent laudes de omnibus sanctis; si autem eluxerit, celebrent missam matutinalem quae in lucis crepusculo celebranda est, et dehinc canant de omnibus sanctis." All translations from *LME* are those provided by Jones.

Easter is hinted at in the *Concordia*'s directions for Chapter on Christmas Vigils, which states (as does Ælfric's Letter) that for the announcement of the feast, "Sabbato quoque sancto pascae, dum a puero *Resurrectio Domini nostri Ihesu Christi* legitur.' "[11] The Christmas festival was always concerned with light; the time of the Roman Christmas is a natural one for celebrating the triumph of light over darkness, for its inception is to some degree a response to the pagan *Natalis Solis Invicti*, celebrated on 25 December in fourth-century Rome, the winter solstice according to the Julian calendar.[12] However, the explicit connection between Christmas and Easter heightens the importance of light at Christmas, marking Christmas sunrise as both the new light given to those who had dwelt in darkness and a precursor of the light of the Risen Christ.

This Mass is the one that was originally composed for the Byzantine Anastasia. After it was translated to the Roman Christmas, however, it was altered to apply more specifically to Christmas. As such, the version in the Leofric Missal has two *Capitulae*, two *Praefationes*, and two *Ad Complenda*, a first specific to Anastasia and a second for Christmas. The second *Capitula* and *Praefatio* state:

> C: Da nobis quaesumus, omnipotens deus, ut qui nova incarnati verbi tui luce perfundimur, hoc in nostro resplendeat opere, quod per fidem fulget in mente.
> P: . . . nostri salvatoris hodie lux vera processit, quae clara nobis omnia et intellectu manifestavit et visu.[13]

The position of the participant is as one over whom the light of the new birth has shone, and to whom the proclamation 'Glory be to God in the highest, and on earth peace to men who are of good will' has been given. This is the critical moment in the Christmas celebration; as such, it is not surprising that the most evocative liturgical innovations for Christmas were composed for the period up to dawn. A set of tropes probably written in the tenth century for the *Prima Mane* (or the *Inlucescente Mane*) celebrates the new light:

> Iam fulget oriens, iam praecurrunt signa;
> Iam venit dominus illuminare nobis, alleluia:/ *Lux fulgebit hodie super nos*
> Quia pax hominibus nata est et aeterna laetitia,/ *Quia natus est nobis dominus*

---

[11] Kornexl, *Die Regularis concordia*, p. 58; see also Symons, *Regularis concordia*, p. 28. "It shall be done in the same way as on Holy Saturday, when *Resurrectio Domini nostri Ihesu Christi* is read out by one of the children."

[12] Noële Denis-Boulet (*The Christian Calendar* (London, 1960), p. 51) speculates that the founding of St. Peter's in the fourth century near a pagan worship site for the solstice may have been part of the introduction of Christmas.

[13] Warren, *The Leofric Missal*, p. 64. "Grant us we pray, Almighty God, that for us, who are covered by the new light of your incarnate word, this may shine brightly in our works, what by faith shines in the mind. . . . today the true light of our Saviour has come forth, which has made all clear to us in sight and in understanding."

Ex virgine matre et homo factus in mundum,/ *Et vocabitur admirabilis deus,*
    princeps pacis, pater futuri seculi
Terribilis et potens venturus ad iudicandum saeculum,/ *Cuius regni non erit finis.*
. . . Hodie inluxit nobis dominus, eia/ *Lux fulgebit* . . .[14]

As the end of Advent represents both the beginning and the end of the Christian year, and thus of the Christian time-line, it is not surprising to see images of the new birth juxtaposed with those of the Second Coming. Most notable here, however, is the repeated *Iam*, playing on the coincidence with sunrise, and emphasizing the direct participation of the celebrants, such that, seeing the sun rise, they are also seeing Christ coming 'to illuminate us.' This participation is, here again, described in terms of receiving light and hearing that 'peace is born for men.' The implied relationship with the shepherds is developed throughout the liturgy for this period.[15] The gospel for the dawn Mass is Luke 2:15–20, in which the shepherds, having just received the *Gloria*, go to see the child. It is at this time that the 'light rises' for the shepherds as they see the promise expressed in the *Gloria* fulfilled; so too for the celebrants.

Also notable here is the shift in tense from future on Christmas Eve ('The Lord will shine . . .') to present, at sunrise, to past, for the rest of Christmas, emphasizing that, symbolically, the events of Christmas are unfolding as the celebrants keep vigil. This shift is evident in the following exchange, also extant in the Winchester Troper, titled *Versus Ante Officium [Canendi] in Die Natalis Domini.* It was written by Tuotilo of St. Gall (d. c. 913), who may have composed an early version of the *Quem quaeritis.*[16] It exists in late Anglo-Saxon England as part of a family of recent compositions, probably imported from the continent, which includes the *Quem quaeritis in sepulchro* for Easter and the *Quem quaeritis in praesepe* for Christmas. The latter trope is a direct reworking of the Easter trope for Christmas, including a dramatic *Adest hic* to mimic the Easter trope's *Non est hic.* While the Christmas *Quem quaeritis* does not exist in any Anglo-Saxon text, it can be found in a closely related French troper for the monastery of St. Magliorii. Directly following the Christmas *Quem quaeritis* in Magliorii is the following piece, which is also extant in (and here printed from) the Winchester Troper. Its question and answer format is compelling:

Primo Dicant Cantores
Hodie cantandus est nobis puer, quem gignebat ineffabiliter ante tempora pater, et
eundem sub tempore generavit inclita mater.

---

[14] Frere, *The Winchester Troper,* p. 4. "Now shines the rising sun, now precede the signs;/ Now the Lord comes to illuminate us, alleluia (The light will shine today over us)./ Because peace is born for men and eternal joy (Because the Lord is born to us)/ From a virgin mother and shaped as a man in the world (And he will be called wonderful God, Prince of Peace, father of the future world)/ Coming terrible and powerful to the judgement of the world (Whose reign will not end)./ Today the Lord has begun to dawn for us, lo! (The light will shine)."

[15] See, for example, Dewick and Frere, *The Leofric Collectar,* p. 21.

[16] Frere, *The Winchester Troper,* p. xvi.

Item Dicant Alteri
Quis est iste puer tam magnis praeconiis dignum vociferatis? Dicite nobis ut conlau-
datores esse possimus.
Item Praetitulati Cantores.
Hic enim est quem praesagus et electus symmista dei ad terras venturum.[17]

As with the Christmas *Quem quaeritis*, and the Vigil prophecies, this
dialogue is somewhat removed from any kind of direct, representational
identification. The associations are more general, if no less evocative. The
speakers are abstracts of those at the time of the birth, hearing the news of
the Son and seeking him. Their exchange focuses the imperatives of the
people of Israel at the Saviour's advent onto the contemporary celebrants,
to come to terms with what they have seen, and been told, to participate in
Christ's coming by recognizing and praising him as did the shepherds. The
dialogue is dramatic in that it heightens the participants' association with
those trying to see the promised Saviour, making them active seekers and
proclaimers. By seeking out and praising Christ, they can attain the peace
and unity with God that was promised them in prophecy the previous night.

The union of God and man has, by Christmas Day, transported the
faithful from the cold, dark world to a new fellowship with heaven,
symbolized by the new light. As such, the faithful must come to terms
with their position in the new light by putting away their relationship with
the old world. This is the primary aim of the rest of the Christmas liturgy,
and its implementation directly reflects similar liturgical imperatives right
after Easter. The *Concordia* prescribes for Chapter on Christmas Day a
special form of confession here and at Easter:

> Finita prima, venientes ad capitulum, post cetera spiritualis aedificationis colloquia
> petant humili devotione omnes fratres veniam ab abbate, qui vices Christi agit,
> postulantes multiplicium indulgentiam excessuum, dicentes *Confiteor*; et abbas
> respondeat *Misereatur*. Demum ipse abbas, solotenus se prosternens, eadem a
> fratribus petat. Idem modus confessionis prima paschalis solempnitatis die ita
> agatur.[18]

The ceremony is at its heart an expression of the liturgical imperatives of
Christmas Day. This confession reflects the participants' sense of living in a
new state of being and their subsequent need to sever ties with the old world
in the wake of the previous night's experience. This is also the dominant

---

[17] Ibid. pp. 4–5. "Today we are to sing of the Son, whom the father begat ineffably before time, and
the same one whom the glorious mother bore under time./ Who is this Son whom such great
heralds declare worthy? Tell us that we may praise him highly./ This indeed is the one who was
foretold and the chosen right hand of God, coming to the earth."

[18] Kornexl, *Die Regularis concordia*, p. 60; see also Symons, *Regularis concordia*, p. 29. "When
Prime has ended, all of the brothers, assembling for Chapter, after other words of spiritual
edification, shall with humble devotion together beg pardon of the abbot, who takes the place of
Christ, asking forgiveness for their many failings and saying the *Confiteor*; then the abbot shall
respond *Misereatur*. Next the abbot, prostrate to the earth, himself shall ask pardon of the
brethren. The same manner of confession shall be observed in the same way on the first day of the
Paschal feast."

tone of the principal Mass of the day, *In Natali Domini ad Sanctum Petrum*. The forms for the day pray for God's clemency for sins, invoking the newborn son as the agent of the cleansing of flesh, and proclaiming that those who glory in the birth of the son are removed from contagions and the adverse of the world.[19] These prayers stem from an attempt to certify the celebrants' newfound unity with God, much as is done at the *Concordia* confession and the parallel confession at Easter Chapter. While they may not literally return to their flocks rejoicing, as did the shepherds, the liturgy for Christmas Day represents an attempt to do the same thing in spiritual terms, to recognize the change in the world that has given them a newfound reconciliation with heaven, the birth of God as man, by putting away the old world and exercising their new ability to perceive heavenly things. These dynamics are inherent in the early liturgical forms (such as those in the Leofric Missal), and are developed further in later creative additions to the liturgy.

These themes are also picked up and reinforced in vernacular preaching texts, both pre- and post-Reform. The extant sermons for Christmas (four by Ælfric and two from the Vercelli Book, dating from the early tenth century) do not always specify for which Mass they are intended (or indeed if they were intended to be used in a service, as Ælfric's Lives of Saints homily surely was not), and as such we cannot follow the overnight time-line as clearly as we can with the liturgy. All six start with some mention of Christ born both human and divine, reflecting the reading and the main theme of the principal Mass, although Ælfric's First Series sermon (CH I.ii) and Vercelli V, discussing Luke's account of the birth, would be well suited to the midnight Mass. Vercelli V hints at such a use when the narration of the birth is broken to emphasize that Christ was "hire frumbearn, on þas niht þe nu toniht wæs."[20] Also, Vercelli VI makes clear that it is intended for Christmas Day itself, as it specifies that certain portentous events happened "gyrsandæg," "þæs ðe dryhten on niht geboren wæs."[21] Ælfric's Christmas sermon for his Second Series (CH II.i) is somewhat more esoteric, discussing the theological complexities of the incarnation and Mary's maidenhood, although the lengthy recitation of prophecies recalls a good bit of the liturgy for the festival. Ælfric's third piece, beginning the Lives of Saints, is even more theological, and has little dramatic resonance.[22] His fourth piece for the occasion, Pope's I, is an exegesis on the beginning of John, the reading for the principal Mass.[23] I will deal primarily with Vercelli V and Ælfric's CH I.ii. These two sermons, because they deal with the story

---

[19] Warren, *The Leofric Missal*, pp. 64–5.

[20] Scragg, *The Vercelli Homilies*, p. 112. "Her first-born, on the night which was now, tonight."

[21] Ibid. p. 129. "Yesterday . . . on the night during which the Lord was born."

[22] W. W. Skeat, ed. and trans. *Ælfric's Lives of Saints*, vol. I (London, 1890–1900; reprint 1966), pp. 10–23. A later version of this piece survives as Belfour's IX (A. O. Belfour, ed. *Twelfth-Century Homilies in MS Bodley 343* (London, 1909), pp. 78–96).

[23] J. C. Pope, ed. *Homilies of Ælfric*, vol. I (London, 1967), pp. 191–225.

of the birth itself rather than some of the theology around it, resonate with the themes and imperatives established in the liturgy. The insertion of "on þas niht þe nu toniht wæs"[24] into the gospel account of Vercelli V puts the reading and its explanation in the context of the temporal coincidence established in the liturgy. In CH I.ii, Ælfric reveals more subtly recognition of the concurrence of past events and present commemoration in comparing the current congregation with those participating in the census that brought Mary to Bethlehem. The strongest commemorative association, however, is with the shepherds, to whom the *Gloria* was announced. In both of these Christmas sermons, the congregation is made to sympathise with the shepherds, hearing the *Gloria*, seeing the infant Christ, and returning home to proclaim it to the people.

The introduction of the *Gloria in excelsis deo* to the liturgy is the climax of the Christmas celebration[25] and it figures prominently in Ælfric's sermon. Ælfric presents it in Latin, the only Latin passage in the narrative, and then, in the explanatory passage, repeats it twice, specifying between the two recitations that there "færlice wurdon æteowede fela þusend engla ði læs þe wære geþuht anes engles ealdordom to hwonlic to swa micelre bodunge."[26] The announcement is specifically one of peace announced to the shepherds, as it is announced to the liturgical participants at Christmas. In line with the juxtaposition of biblical shepherds and contemporary celebrants, Ælfric expands the use of the shepherds in his sermon, such that the entire narrative and all of the Christmas themes are set around them. In particular, the shepherds represent "þa halgan lareowas on Godes gelaðunge, þe sint gastlice hyrdas geleaffulra saula"[27] who are called upon to make known what has been revealed to them, to 'proclaim the heavenly vision' as did the shepherds. More generally, the shepherds come to signify all those to whom the *Gloria* has been announced and over whom the new light has shone (or all those who have heard the *Gloria* announced in the Christmas liturgy). The light that accompanied that announcement is described as representing the union of heaven and earth:

> . . . gelome wurdon englas mannum æteowode on ðære ealdan æ, ac hit nis awriten þæt hi mid leohte comon ac se wurðmynt wæs þises dæges mærðe gehealden, þæt hi mid heofenlicum leohte hi geswuteledon, þa ða þæt soðe leoht asprang on þeostrum.[28]

---

[24] Scragg, *The Vercelli Homilies*, p. 112.
[25] According to Duchesne, *Christian Worship*, p. 265, n. 1, "Before the sixth century it was not the custom of Rome to sing the *Gloria in excelsis* except at the Feast of Christmas, and then only at the nocturnal Mass. It is to Pope Symmachus (498–514) that we owe its use on Sundays and festivals."
[26] CH I.ii, p. 194. "Suddenly were revealed many thousands of angels, lest it be thought that the authority of one angel was too small for such a great announcement."
[27] Ibid. p. 193. "The holy teachers in God's church, who are the spiritual shepherds of the souls of the faithful."
[28] Ibid. p. 194. "Often were angels revealed to men in the Old Testament, but it is not written that

The 'true light' of the announcement is conflated with the light of Christ, "se soða dæg, se ðe todræfde mid his tocyme ealle nytennysse þære ealdan nihte, 7 ealne middaneard mid his gife onlihte."[29] This light is accompanied by a reconciliation with the angels. Ælfric, after explaining that, following the Lord's advent, mankind was no longer allowed to worship angels, concludes:

> Nu we sind getealde Godes ceastergewaran 7 englum gelice. Uton for ðy hogian þæt leahtras us ne totwæman fram ðysum miclum wurðmynte. Soðlice menn sindon godas gecigede; heald for ðy, þu mann, þinne godes wyrðscipe wið leahtrum, for ðan þe God is geworden man for ðe.[30]

This passage explains the liturgical themes of Christmas Day, under which celebrants cast off the old world and come to terms with living in a new light, with which heavenly things can be seen and related to.

Ælfric then focuses this idea on the shepherds themselves. Exercising their newfound vision, they go to see Christ. Ælfric puts the reading for the primary Mass, the beginning of the gospel of John, dealing with the incarnation, into the mouths of the shepherds, creating a link between the liturgical themes for morning (light and new vision) and afternoon (the incarnation). Following the shepherds' proclamation of the incarnation, Ælfric explains that "Ne mihte ure mennisce gecynd Crist on ðære god-cundlican acennydnesse geseon, ac þæt ilce word wæs geworden flæsc 7 wunode on us, þæt we hine geseon mihton."[31] More important here than the union of God and humanity is the ability of the shepherds to see it. After further explaining the incarnation, Ælfric again couches his discussion in the words of the shepherds:

> hi cwædon, uton geseon þæt word þe geworden is, for ðan ðe hi ne mihton hit geseon ær ðan þe hit geflæschamod wæs, 7 to menn geworden.[32]

He sums up his discussion of Christ's incarnation, Joseph's role, and Mary's maidenhood by asserting firmly that "Ða hyrdas gesawon 7 oncneowan be ðam cilde, swa swa him gesæd wæs."[33] As in the liturgy for the day, it is through sight, specifically the shepherds' sight, that these mysteries have significance for contemporary celebrants.

---

they came with light, but that distinction was held for the glory of this day, that they revealed themselves with heavenly light, at the time when the true light sprang up in the darkness."

[29] CH I.ii, p. 194. "The true day, he who drove out with his coming all of the ignorance of the old night, and illuminated all the earth with his gift."

[30] Ibid. p. 195. "Now we are reckoned God's city-dwellers and like angels. Let us therefore strive that sins not separate us from this great honour. Truly men are called gods; keep therefore, man, your godly dignity against sins, because God is made man for you."

[31] Ibid. p. 196. "Our human kind could not see Christ in that divine birth, but that same Word was made flesh and dwelt in us, that we might see him."

[32] Ibid. "They said, let us see that Word that was made, because they could not see it before it was incarnate, and became human."

[33] Ibid. "The shepherds saw and recognized that child, just as was said to them."

Having seen and recognized the child, it is left to the shepherds, and to the celebrants, to live in that new state. For the shepherds, that meant returning "wuldriende 7 herigende God on eallum ðan ðingum þe hi gehyrdon 7 gesawon,"[34] with which Ælfric concludes his exegesis. He mentions that the shepherds are commemorated a mile east of Bethlehem, "on Godes cyrcan geswutelod þam ðe ða stowe geneosiað,"[35] and exhorts that "we sceolon geefenlæcan þysum hyrdum, 7 wuldrian 7 herian urne drihten . . . us to alysednysse, 7 to ecere blisse."[36] It is this imperative that drives the celebrants to renew themselves in the Christmas confession and in the primary Mass, identifying with those who have seen Christ, recognized him, and attained redemptive unity with heaven.

The Vercelli Christmas homilies reveal the same awareness of liturgical dynamics, but more heavily emphasize the announcement of the *Gloria* as a harbinger of peace, accompanied by heavenly light. The homilist of Vercelli V begins with a recounting of the Christmas narrative according to Luke (following the reading for midnight Mass),[37] breaking in at the mention of Christ's birth with the assertion that this happened "on þas niht þe nu toniht wæs."[38] This addition to the gospel narrative connects the biblical story with the contemporary commemoration. The homilist then continues the gospel account as it discusses the shepherds watching over their sheep. As the angel appears and announces the *Gloria*, the narrative breaks off, and the homilist goes into a lengthy discussion of the state of the Roman empire under the emperor Augustus Octavianus, who ruled at the time of Christ's birth. The world under Augustus, claims the homilist, was at peace. Men did not carry weapons, and the emperor forgave all people in his kingdom of their crimes. The peaceful state of the world and the amnesty granted by Augustus signified the coming of Christ, who would do the same thing in spiritual terms. The peace of Christ is established in the *Gloria*, and the homilist subjugates his long discussion of Augustus' reign to the biblical/liturgical announcement of peace.

The importance of light imagery in the liturgy is likewise reflected here. The liturgy proclaims repeatedly, "solis orto," and the relationship between Christ and the sun is developed in the Vercelli sermons. One of the tokens of Christ's upcoming birth in Vercelli V is a wonder viewed by Augustus at the

---

[34] Ibid. p. 197. "Glorifying and praising God for all of the things that they heard and saw."

[35] Ibid. "In God's church, revealed to those who seek the place."

[36] Ibid. "We must imitate these shepherds, and glorify and praise our Lord . . . for our redemption and for eternal life."

[37] The modern appellation 'Midnight Mass' is a little misleading, here, referring more generally to 'some time in the night.' At an early stage, before the institution of the Mass for Anastasia (the current *In Aurora*), this mass took place closer to dawn, and was then pushed back to cock-crow, *in gallicantu*, a more fitting time for the birth and the annunciation to the shepherds than is midnight (Vercelli VI specifies that Christ was born "ær morgensteorra upeode" ("before the morning-star arose") (Scragg, *The Vercelli Homilies*, p. 130)).

[38] Scragg, *The Vercelli Homilies*, p. 112.

third hour on Christmas Eve, involving "gyldnes hringas onlicnes ymbutan þa sunnan . . . þæt is þonne ure hælend Crist, þæt he mid his fægernesse gewlitgode þa sunnan þe us nu dæghwamlice lyhteð."[39] Vercelli VI has a sun with "þryfealde gyldene hringe" ("a threefold golden ring") and mentions that "sio sunne beorhtor scan þonne hio æfre ær scine."[40] In addition, for seven nights before the birth, "sio sunne æt midre nihte ongan scinan swa swa on sumera þonne hio hattost 7 beorhtost scinð. þæt tacnode þæt he þas eorðlican sunnan nihtes scinende him to gisle beforan sende."[41] This prophetic use of light strengthens the climactic importance of Christmas sunrise for the faithful, for while the actual birth took place 'before the morning-star came up,' and while, for the original shepherds, it was still dark when the angels presented themselves,[42] the appearance of Christ in the world is conflated with the announcement to the shepherds. These events are tied together liturgically with the period between cock-crow and sunrise, as evident in the above hymn and antiphon for Prime from the Leofric Collectar.

The significance of this light, as explored in the liturgy and described in preaching, is that it allows believers newfound perception and unity with heaven. Its use in Vercelli V is couched within an association with the shepherds. As in Ælfric's sermon, the shepherds are defined as "lareowas" ("teachers") and the announcement of the angel is described as engendering a "leohtlicor" ability to perceive spiritual things:

> And we hyrdon ær on þam godspelle þæt hyrdas wæron on þam ilcan lande wæccende, 7 bi him stod dryhtnes engel 7 hie ymbscan heofonlices leohtes byrhto. þa hyrdas getacnodan þa godan lareowas 7 gedefe aldoras ða þe geornlice healdað þæt Cristes yrfe þæt wæron þa leaffullan menn. And gif hie arfæstlice healdað 7 wel læraþ þæt geleaffulle Godes folc, þonne bioð hie rumlice onlyhte mid godcundre gife, 7 þa gastlican gerynu him bioð leohtlicor ontyned þonne oðrum mannum, for þan ðe hie mid Godes lufan healdað ða getreowan gesomnunge Godes folces.[43]

[39] Scragg, *The Vercelli Homilies*, p. 114. "Rings around the sun in the likeness of gold . . . that is then our Lord Christ, that he with his fairness adorned the sun which now daily illuminates us." Such images of Christ bettering the sun are often described in the context of the Christian takeover of the *Natalis Solis Invicti*. Gunstone, *Christmas and Epiphany*, p. 20, notes a third-century burial chamber under St. Peter's in Rome, the ceiling of which has a mosaic of what seems to have been Helios, in his fiery chariot, turned into Christ.

[40] Ibid. p. 129. "The sun shone brighter than it had ever before shone." See J. E. Cross, "Portents and Events at Christ's Birth," *ASE* 2 (1973), pp. 209–20, for a discussion of the sources of these apocryphal signs.

[41] Scragg, *The Vercelli Homilies*, p. 129. "The sun in the middle of the night began to shine just as in the summer, when it is hottest and shines brightest. That symbolized that he sent before him the earthly sun shining at night as a hostage/assurance."

[42] Outside the reading of the gospel at the nocturnal Mass, the *Gloria* first appears in the Leofric Collectar as an antiphon for Matins (Dewick and Frere, *The Leofric Collectar*, p. 20).

[43] Ibid. p. 119. "And we heard before in the gospel that the shepherds were keeping watch in that same land, and God's angel stood by them and the brightness of heavenly light shone about them. The shepherds signified the good teachers and kind elders, those who eagerly keep that inheritance of Christ, who are the believing men. And if they piously keep and teach well the

The common definition of the shepherds as "lareowas" is widened by the Vercelli homilist to include more generally "þa leaffullan menn," allowing the wider audience to see themselves as having a responsibility to guard the flock and, ultimately, to pass on the announcement of the angels. It is important that all present at Christmas hear the *Gloria* and see this light, as that is the ultimate point of the liturgical commemoration. The light not only inspires new vision; it also allows a reconciliation with the angels, as the homilist explains:

> Ær þæt wære, þæt ure hælend wære on menniscum lichoman acenned, ær we hæfdon æfre wonisse 7 unsybbe wið englum, 7 we wæron aworpene 7 ascadene fram hiora beorhte 7 fram hiora clænnisse þurh earnunge þære ærestan scylde 7 þurh oðre synna dæghwamlice, 7 æfter ðam þe heofones cyning underhnah ures lichoman tyddernesse, ne forsawan þa englas usse untrumnesse ne usse tiedernesse, ac hie sona cyrdon to ure sibbe 7 ure lufan, for þan þe hie gesawon þæt ðurh Cristes acennednesse heofona rices eðel scolde gefylled bion. For þan hie mannum budon sybbe . . .[44]

The descending of Christ's divinity into the human form is the first step in reversing the debasement of humanity following the expulsion from Paradise. As the homilist goes on to explain, this reversal makes humanity equal with the angels, able to attain to the purity necessary for humanity to enter heaven. The homilist ends with a description of the joys of heaven made available by the new state of being. The heart of the Vercelli sermon, as with Ælfric's, is a treatment of the progression of the Christmas liturgy from darkness to light, from despair to hope, from blindness to new vision and the ability to move towards heaven. These two sermons make clear to their respective congregations just what is happening in the liturgy from Christmas Eve to the principal Mass on Christmas Day and how they should relate to it. What they make most clear is that the position of the congregation at Christmas is that of the shepherds.

The celebration of Christmas here is not so much a presentational re-creation as it is an invocation of the images and emotions surrounding the original, commemorated events, interpreted to apply to contemporary participants. Already represented in the liturgy of Christmas by the late Anglo-Saxon period are the people of Israel who dwelt in darkness and the shepherds. The celebrants of the liturgy assume their words and share their hopes and fears. Elaborations on the liturgy in the tenth century, like those

---

believing folk of God, then they will be abundantly alight with godly grace, and the spiritual mysteries will be to them shining brighter than to other men, because they with God's love keep the faithful assembly of God's folk."

[44] Ibid. 119–20. "Before our Lord was born in a human body, we had always wickedness and strife with the angels, and we were cast away and separated from their brightness and from their clearness through the reward of that first crime and through other daily sins, and after the king of heaven submitted to the frailty of our body, the angels did not despise our infirmity or our frailty, but they immediately turned to our peace and our love, because they saw that through Christ's birth should the homeland of the kingdom of heaven be filled. Therefore they offered peace to men . . ."

in the Winchester Troper, pick up on these identifications and enhance them. Ælfric's expansive treatment of, in particular, the shepherds, helps the congregation appreciate the sympathetic mindset with which they should approach the liturgical experience.

THE CHRISTMAS OCTAVE

The octave of Christmas, following that of Easter, stems out of a desire to maintain the sense of victory and heavenly unity attained on Christmas Day. Jungmann outlines the history of the Christmas octave.[45] Its development parallels that of Easter, as does the feast day itself, although its unity is much looser than Easter's octave. By the seventh century, Christmas' octave consisted only of an eighth day, which was really a commemoration of Mary (*Natale s. Mariae*), and the liturgy still reflects this history. The name *festum Circumcisionis*, also attributed to this day, is of Gallican origin, and entered the Roman liturgy with the tenth century RGP. Since in the Orient, and in the Gallican liturgy, Epiphany was as great a feast, with an older tradition, the day could be seen as much as a pre-festival of Epiphany as an Octave of Christmas. Still, the liturgy of the Octave, by this period, is tied wholly to that of Christmas. The relationships of the intervening days are, however, somewhat more dubious. Jungmann postulates that "the feast of St. Stephen had been already fixed in the Orient before Christmas was introduced, and that it was then also transferred to Rome."[46] Likewise, the festival for St. John the Apostle on 27 December is not particularly relevant. The feast of Holy Innocents is pertinent, of course, as it continues the story of Christ's flight into Egypt, although its liturgical and homiletic emphasis is on the relationship of the innocents to Christ's Passion, more than his birth.[47] Therefore, as the importance of Christmas grew and its octave solidified, these festivals, in particular that of St. Stephen, were consciously emended to fit the season more directly, much as was the case with the second Christmas Mass for Anastasia.

Generally, this period is characterized by a sense of maintaining or furthering the solemnity of Christmas, in particular its final tone of reconciliation with heaven. The *Concordia* (as well as Ælfric's Letter to

---

[45] Jungmann, *The Mass of the Roman Rite*, pp. 266–77.

[46] Ibid. p. 270.

[47] Gunstone, *Christmas and Epiphany*, p. 59, notes that the most primitive gospel for Christmas Day in Rome, before the introduction of Epiphany to the West, may have been Matthew 2, rather than Luke 2. This may explain the position of Holy Innocents' Day, as their story directly follows that of the adoration of the Magi and the escape to Egypt in Matthew 2.

The liturgy for Holy Innocents' Day in the Leofric Collectar (Dewick and Frere, *The Leofric Collectar*, pp. 31–4) is dominated by the form "Hi sunt qui . . ." or "Isti sunt qui . . ." which Ælfric seems to mimic in his conclusion to his homily for the day; "Hi sind ða ðe Criste folgiað on hwitum gyrlum . . ." ("They are those who follow Christ in white robes . . ." CH I.v, p. 223).

the Monks of Eynsham[48]) specifies that certain antiphons for Christmas are to be repeated until the Octave day, and two sets of antiphons in the Leofric Collectar are labelled *Antiphone de Natale Domini usque Oct. Domini* and *De Sancta Maria usque Oct. Domini*, demonstrating a sense of octave unity. The *Concordia* also prescribes for this time (specifically "between the feasts of the Innocents and the Octave of Christmas") two customs that stem not from the continent but from "the practice of the native people of this country," as follows:

> . . . quia *Gloria in excelsis Deo* ob tantae festivitatis honorificentiam ad missam celebratur, ad nocturnam et ad vesperam uti ad missam, sicut in usum huius patriae indigenae tenent, omnia signa pulsentur. Nam honestos huius patriae mores ad Deum pertinentes, quos veterum usu dedicimus, nullo modo abicere, sed undique, uti diximus, corroborare decrevimus. Ad matutinas vero ob rem praedictam, licet *Te Deum laudamus* non canatur et evangelium minime festivo more legatur, cerei tamen accendantur et signa pulsentur omnia et turribulum turificando deportetur.[49]

Ælfric's Eynsham Letter also stresses the use of bells and candles to signify the importance of the period. These customs attempt to extend the solemnity of Christmas through the week, turning ferial days into pseudo-feast days.

The earlier festival days were similarly adapted. While the liturgy for St. Stephen's feast is almost entirely absent of Christmas themes, the *Praefatio* attempts obliquely to link the two:

> Beati stephani levitae simul et martyris natalitia recolentes, qui fidei, qui et sacrae militae, qui dispensationis et castitatis egregiae, qui praedicationis mirabilisque constantiae, qui confessionis ac patientiae nobis exempla veneranda proposuit. Et ideo nativitatem filii tui merito prae ceteris passioni suae festivitate prosequitur, cuius gloriae sempiternae primus martyr occurrit.[50]

Ælfric's Second Series sermon for the Nativity of St. Stephen develops this liturgical assertion. Following a long list of 'wonders and cures' is a short passage attempting to explain the day's relevance to Christmas:

> Stephanus . . . is se forma cyðere þe ærest æfter Cristes upstige to heofenan rice wuldorful becom. He filigde Cristes fotswaðum swiðe nean, and his gebysnunge

---

[48] See *LME*, p. 117.

[49] Kornexl, *Die Regularis concordia*, pp. 61–2; see also Symons, *Regularis concordia*, p. 30. ". . . because the *Gloria in excelsis Deo* is sung at Mass, due to the solemnity of so great a feast, all of the bells shall ring at Nocturns and Vespers as at Mass, as is the practice of the native people of this country. Surely the respected practices of this land, belonging to God, the use of which we learned from our elders, we should in no way cast aside, but from all sides, as we said before, we should determine to strengthen [our practice]. Truly for this same reason, although the *Te Deum laudamus* is not sung nor the gospel read in the manner of a feast day, candles nevertheless shall be lit at Matins and all of the bells shall peal and the thurible shall be carried around, burning."

[50] Warren, *The Leofric Missal*, p. 132. "We remember the birth of the blessed Stephen, deacon and martyr, he who displayed a venerable example for us of faith, of the holy army, of stewardship and extraordinary chastity, of wonderful praise and of steadfastness, of confession and patience. And therefore his festival follows the nativity of your son, worthy before the other passions, with whose glory eternally the first martyr occurs."

arfæstlice geefenlæhte. . . . He is fyrmest on martyrdome and fyrmest on lareowdome for ðan þe he eallum cyðerum Cristes bysne æteowode.[51]

While the passage illustrates Stephen's importance, it in no way explains why his festival should be concurrent with Christmas rather than Easter or the Ascension. Ælfric makes the connection more explicit in his First Series homily for the day, concluding:

> Gyrstandæg gemedmode ure drihten hine sylfne þæt ðysne middaneard þurh soðre menniscnysse geneosode. Nu todæg se æþela cempa Stephanus fram lichamlicre wununge gewitende sigefæst to heofenum ferde. Crist nyðer astah mid flæsce bewæfed; Stephanus up astah þurh his blod gewuldorbeagod. Gyrstandæig sungon englas "Gode wuldor on heannyssum"; nu todæg hi underfengon Stephanum blissigende on heora geferrædene.[52]

Here, Ælfric subsumes the celebrants' appreciation of Stephen in an extension of the triumphs of Christmas. On Christmas, the door to heaven was opened. The next day, the protomartyr went through. The *Gloria* has not ended; rather, it continues on this day, with Stephen adding his voice. This is the kind of continuity that the liturgical addendum is intended to provide. Ælfric's First Series of Catholic Homilies pays tribute to the importance and unity of this period by devoting five homilies to it, CH I.ii–vi, representing each festival day, in a collection that otherwise has to be somewhat selective.

While the ties to Christmas of the two feast days following St. Stephen's are less specific, the Mass for the first Sunday after Christmas revives them, exulting in the fact that Christ has come to earth and taken human form for the restoration of mankind and repeating the *Ad Complendum* from the Christmas midnight Mass.[53] Finally, the liturgy for the Octave Mass sums up the week:

> Deus . . . cuius hodie circumcisionis diem et nativitatis octavum celebrantes, tua, domine, mirabilia veneramur. Quia quae peperit et mater et virgo est, qui natus est et infans et deus est. Merito caeli locuti sunt, angeli gratulati, pastores laetati, magi mutati, reges turbati, parvuli gloriosa passione coronati . . . da, quaesumus, plebi tuae ut gustae mortiferae profanitatis abiecto, puris mentibus ad epulas aeternae salutis accedat.[54]

---

[51] CH II.ii, p. 17. "Stephan . . . is the first martyr, who first after Christ's ascension became glorified in the heavenly kingdom. He followed Christ's footsteps very closely, and imitated his example piously . . . He is the first of the martyrs and the first of the teachers, because he demonstrated Christ's example to all martyrs."

[52] CH I.iii, p. 205. "Yesterday our Lord humbled himself, who sought this earth through true humanity. Now today the noble champion Stephen travelled to heaven, departing victorious from the bodily dwelling. Christ descended, enclosed in flesh; Stephen ascended, crowned through his blood. Yesterday, the angels sang 'Glory to God on high'; now today they received Stephen, rejoicing in their company."

[53] See Warren, *The Leofric Missal*, p. 65.

[54] Ibid. p. 52. "God . . . whose day of circumcision and octave of the nativity we celebrate today, Lord, we venerate your miracles. Because he whom mother and virgin bore is born infant and God. Rightly the heavens are speaking, angels giving thanks, shepherds rejoicing, magi

While Ælfric's sermon for the day is devoted to a discussion of circumcision and its relationship to baptism, looking more forwards to Epiphany than backwards to Christmas, the liturgy for the day demonstrates the celebrants' continuation of the victory of Christmas.

In the Gallican liturgy, as part of the build up to Epiphany, themes of the Circumcision dominate. The *Missale Gothicum*[55] contains pages of collects praising the circumcision as a precursor to the upcoming baptism and as an illustration of the 'spiritual circumcision' that Christians should undergo, excising the carnal. The Gregorian ignores the Circumcision, calling the day instead *In Octabas Domini* and focusing on Mary.[56] The commemoration in the Gelasian, representing a mix of the Gallican and the more austere Roman liturgies, calls the Mass *In Octavas Domini*, but has a long Preface, consisting of the passage above until "passione cornonati," reading instead of "hodie circumcisionis diem, et nativitatis octavum celebrantes" simply "hodie octavas nati celebrantes tua."[57] This bit is followed by a second passage, telling of the oxen and asses recognizing Christ in the manger and of him circumcised and then raised up by Simeon in the temple. The Gelasian version serves as a nodal point for the celebration of Christ's childhood, looking back to Christmas week and forward to the presentation to Simeon. The versions in the Robert and Leofric Missals owe much more in form to the Gelasian than to the Gregorian. The Gelasian summation passage above, while not in the pre-supplemented Gregorian, is in the Supplement, but much of the Supplement was itself taken from the Gelasian, and the remaining mass texts for the day are almost verbatim from the Gelasian (the Gregorian has completely different passages). Still, the Preface for the day in Robert and Leofric is that of the Supplement, the reworking of which tightens the Mass into a simple recapitulation of Christmas week. There is little sense of a developed commemoration of the circumcision in the Anglo-Saxon liturgical witnesses because of the Gregorian emphasis on New Year's Day as the Octave of Christmas, not as a circumcision day. As such, Ælfric's focus on the circumcision does not indicate its liturgical importance; rather, as the day is dominated by a simple recapitulation of Christmas, his concern is more in exegesis of the gospel and in warning against pagan New Year practices, following Augustine's treatment of the day. His explication of the significance of the circumcision also allows him to prepare his audience for a discussion of baptism at Epiphany.

---

converted, kings troubled, infants crowned with glorious passion . . . grant, we pray, your people that from the deadly taste of abject profanity with pure minds they may approach the eternal feasts of salvation."
[55] See Bannister, *Missale Gothicum*, pp. 16–20.
[56] See Deshusses, *Le sacramentaire grégorien*, p. 112.
[57] Wilson, *The Gelasian Sacramentary*, p. 9.

EPIPHANY

Christmas and Epiphany were originally feasts of the same event. In the fourth-century East, Epiphany was the celebration of the birth of Christ. Its origin is related to that of Christmas in the West. The Eastern calendar of Amenemhet I of Thebes (c. 1996 BC) placed the winter solstice on the sixth of January. As such, this day drew the same kind of religious fervour as did 25 December in the west. Gunstone relates a description of a fourth-century ritual in Alexandria on this day. The ritual involved hymns and a vigil in an underground sanctuary. At cock-crow, an icon was processed outside, then back again, "And if anyone asks them what manner of mysteries these might be, they reply, saying: 'Today at this hour Kore, that is the Virgin, has given birth to Aion.' "[58] Epiphany is primarily a festival of Christ's 'appearing'; as such, it is not surprising to find images of light and sunrise similar to those expressed in the Christmas liturgy.[59] The first hymn for Epiphany in the Leofric Collectar, at Nocturns, is *Ihesus refulsit*, and the hymn *Iam lucis orto*, so prominent at Christmas, is repeated several times here, most notably at Prime.[60] The use of light is as pronounced here as it was at Christmas, and it serves the same function, to allow the celebrants to see and recognize the newly revealed Christ.

In the late fourth and early fifth centuries, Christmas spread to the East and Epiphany to the West,[61] and Christian exegetes such as Augustine struggled to iron out the redundancies:

> Only a few days ago we celebrated the Lord's birthday. Today we are celebrating with equal solemnity, as is proper, his Epiphany, in which he began to manifest himself to the Gentiles. On the one day the Jewish shepherds saw him when he was born; on this day the magi coming from the east adored him. Now, he had been born that Cornerstone, the peace of the two walls coming from very different directions, from circumcision and uncircumcision. Thus they could be united in him who had been made our peace, and "who has made both one." This was foretokened in the Jewish shepherds and the Gentile magi. From this began what was to grow and to bear fruit throughout the world. Let us, therefore, with joy of the spirit hold dear these two days, the Nativity and the Manifestation of our Lord. The Jewish shepherds were led to him by an angel bringing the news; the Gentile magi by a star showing the way . . . [The magi] were the first-fruits of the Gentiles; we are the people of the Gentiles.[62]

---

[58] See Gunstone, *Christmas and Epiphany*, pp. 14–15.
[59] Early service books use the title *Apparitio Domini* to refer alternately to Christmas and Epiphany.
[60] Dewick and Frere, *The Leofric Collectar*, pp. 39ff.
[61] Epiphany was first observed in Rome in the early-mid fifth century, possibly under Leo the Great. Christmas was introduced to the East in the fourth century, but was not kept in Jerusalem until the second half of the sixth century.
[62] Quoted in Gunstone, *Christmas and Epiphany*, pp. 50–51. See also T. C. Lawler, trans. *St. Augustine: Sermons for Christmas and Epiphany* (Maryland, 1952), p. 164.

Here, Epiphany is described as a widening and clarification of the Christmas experience, in much the same way as Paul widened evangelism by extending it to the Gentiles. At Christmas, as the people of Israel in darkness, they heard and saw the birth of Christ. At Epiphany, as the Gentiles, they celebrate his manifestation to the rest of the world. This identification with the Magi, orchestrated in much the same way as were the Christmas identifications, permeates the liturgy for the day and encompasses Ælfric's discussion of it.

As with Christmas, the liturgy for Epiphany is dominated by light imagery, both in the specific use of the star, leading the Magi to the birthplace, and in the general sense of illumination. The Collect for the Vigil Mass in the Leofric Missal begs, "Corda nostra . . . venturae festivitatis splendor inlustret, quo mundi huius tenebris carere valeamus, et perveniamus ad patriam claritatis aeternae."[63] The Preface describes more specifically the star, an "index perpetua virginalis"[64] set up to announce to the magi by heavenly judgement the birth of Christ. The *Ad Complendum* sums up the anticipatory state of the participants:

Inlumina . . . populum tuum, et splendore gratiae tuae cor eius semper accende, ut salvatoris mundi, stella famulante, manifestata nativitatis mentibus eorum et reveletur.[65]

Speaking of 'your people' as the Magi, making their way to see the nativity, sets up the permutations on that identification in the liturgy of the day itself.

Epiphany commemorates three New Testament events:[66] the adoration of the Magi, the baptism of Christ, and the wedding at Cana. The third of these is more thematic than commemorative: the idea of the union of Christ and the church, in which terms the wedding at Cana is discussed here, is an extension of the imperatives of baptism. The Benedictional of St. Æthelwold has two illustrations introducing the day, depicting the approach of the three kings to the cradle and the baptism. In the Gallican liturgy, the baptism takes a prominent place, as Epiphany, celebrating the birth of Christ from Mary, was a primary day for baptism. For the Anglo-Saxons, it is presented primarily as a vehicle for asserting the Trinitarian doctrine. The Masses largely ignore it, except for a benediction from the Leofric Missal (also extant in Æthelwold) describing the dove as intended 'to demonstrate

---

[63] Warren, *The Leofric Missal*, pp. 66–7. "Let the splendor of this coming festival illuminate our hearts, by which we may be free from the darkness of this world, and come to the native land of eternal brightness."

[64] Ibid. "A perpetual virginal sign."

[65] Ibid. p. 66. "Illuminate . . . your people, and with the brilliance of your grace let their hearts always be kindled, so that by the attending star the manifestation of the birth of the Saviour of the world may be revealed to their minds."

[66] As an Old Testament parallel of these, the revelation of God to Moses through the burning bush is also invoked. An antiphon from the Leofric Collectar repeats, "Rubum quem viderat moyses incombustum . . ." (Dewick and Frere, *The Leofric Collectar*, p. 38).

the holy spirit.'[67] A verse from the Leofric Collectar, invoking the dove, focuses on the presence of all three members of the Trinity.[68] It is the Magi, however, who dominate the day; they are the focus of the gospel reading, Ælfric and the Benedictional of Æthelwold treat them first, and their voices, taken over by the participants, carry the liturgy.

In his Letter to the Monks of Eynsham, Ælfric (quoting Amalarius by name) makes clear that, in the Night Office, the participants are to think of themselves as the Magi coming to see Christ:

> At Nocturns we sing the psalm 'Our God is our refuge' out of sequence, because the Magi came to worship the Lord before he had been baptized; and we therefore sing the antiphon 'Come let us praise (the Lord with joy)' first, and afterwards 'The stream of the river maketh (the city of God) joyful.'[69]

The attention given the order of antiphons here shows some care for the temporal order of things and for the primacy of the Magi in Epiphanal commemoration. The Collect for the Epiphany Mass begins with them, making them analogous to the celebrants: "Deus, qui hodierna die unigenitum tuum gentibus, stella duce, revelasti; concede propitius ut qui iam te ex fide cognovimus, usque ad contemplandam speciem tuae celsitudinis perducemur."[70] They are called in another oration for the day "gentium primitiis" ("the first-fruits of the Gentiles") and the *Ad populum* at the end of the Mass extends their experience to the rest of the Gentiles.[71] Strengthening this connection, the celebrants repeatedly take over the voices of the Magi. An antiphon just preceding the Vigil Mass (from the Leofric Collectar) says, "Magi viderunt stellam et dixerunt adinuicem, 'hoc signum magni regis est; eamus et inquiramus eum et offeramus ei munera, aurum thus et mirram.'"[72] At the Offertory, the celebrants sing, "Rex ubi Iudea est natum quem novimus ecce/ *Vidimus stellam eius in oriente et venimus cum muneribus adorare dominum.*"[73] An earlier trope sums up the themes for the day, focusing them on the voices of the Magi:

> Aecclesiae sponsus, illuminator gentium, baptismatis sacrator, orbis redemptor
> *Ecce advenit*

[67] See Warren, *The Leofric Missal*, p. 67.
[68] Dewick and Frere, *The Leofric Collectar*, p. 39.
[69] *LME*, p. 119. "Ad nocturnas canius psalmum 'Deus noster refugium' preposteto ordine, quia magi venerunt adorare Dominum antequam baptizatus esset; et ideo cantamus antiphonam 'Venite adoremus eum' prius et postea 'Fluminis impetus laetificat.'"
[70] Warren, *The Leofric Missal*, p. 67. "God, who on this day revealed your only-begotten to the Gentiles, led by a star, grant help that we who recognized you today by faith may be led to observing the splendor of your highness."
[71] Ibid.
[72] Dewick and Frere, *The Leofric Collectar*, p. 39. "The Magi saw the star and said together, 'This is a sign of the great king; let us go and seek him and offer him gifts, gold and frankencense and myrrh.'"
[73] Frere, *The Winchester Troper*, p. 13. "Look where a king has been born in Judea, whom we recognize (We have seen his star in the east and have come with gifts to adore the Lord)."

Quem reges gentium cum muneribus mysticis Hierosolimam requirunt, dicentes,
    "ubi est qui natus est/ *dominator dominus*
Vidimus stellam eius in oriente et agnovimus regem regum natum esse,
Cui soli debetur honor, gloria, laus et iubilatio."[74]

In particular, the Magi are offering gifts. The liturgy for the day echoes over and over that the Magi offered him "aurum thus et mirram." The gifts have traditionally been understood as representing the triune nature of the infant Christ as King, God, and man, and this interpretation is explored in the liturgical forms.[75] At Christmas, the faithful were to imitate the shepherds by rejoicing in and proclaiming the new state of being. Here, they are to imitate the Magi by offering with the Magi that which the gifts signify. As with Christmas, the offering of the gifts by the Magi, and by identification that of the celebrants, represents a voluntary offering of oneself to God, and a subsequent union (with a focus on the recognition of his triune nature). The marriage at Cana is brought into the scope of the festival as a symbol of that marriage, a fulfilment of offering to Christ, and of baptism. An antiphon for Epiphany Matins unites these themes in an interesting way:

Hodie caelesti sponso iuncta est ecclesia, quoniam in Iordane lavit christus eius crimina; currunt cum muneribus magi ad regales nuptias et ex aqua facto vino laetantur convivae.[76]

The baptism and the wedding at Cana are here described as catalysts by which the church has been united with Christ; the Magi, and with them the celebrants, join the party by the offering of their gifts and by partaking of the wine at the banquet, as do the celebrants during the Mass. Having the Magi at Cana serves no narrative purpose except to subsume the commemorated events for the day in the priority of contemporary edification. All three events are invoked here, and the identification with the Magi is enhanced by putting their words into the mouths of the celebrants, but all this is done so that they will have a harmonious place in Christ's newlywed church.

Ælfric discusses these themes in his First Series sermon for Epiphany, focusing on the example of the Magi. He begins his explication of the gospel by explaining why the day is referred to as "Godes geswutelungdæg" ("God's revealing-day"). He mentions the manifestation to the three

---

[74] Ibid. p. 12. "Betrothed of the church, illuminator of the Gentiles, consecrator of baptism, redeemer of the world (Lo, he comes)/ He whom the kings of the gentiles seek with mystic gifts in Jerusalem, saying, 'Where is he who has been born (Ruler Lord)?/ We saw his star in the east and we recognized that the king of kings had been born/ To whom alone is fitting honor, glory, praise and jubilation.'"

[75] See for example Dewick and Frere, *The Leofric Collectar*, p. 42.

[76] Dewick and Frere, *The Leofric Collectar*, p. 40. "Today the church has been joined with the divine bridegroom, because Christ washed away its sins in the Jordan; the Magi hasten with gifts to the royal wedding and the banquet guests are made joyful by the wine made from water."

45

kings, "þe fram eastdæle middaneardes hine mid þrimfealdum lacum gesohton."[77] For the baptism (which he discusses more thoroughly in his Second Series sermon), he repeats the same passage that the liturgy used to represent it; "se halga gast on culfran hiwe uppon him gereste, 7 þæs fæder stemn of heofenum hlude swegde, þus cweðende, 'Ðes is min leofa sunu þe me wel licað; gehyrað him.' "[78] For the wedding at Cana, he mentions only that he turned water into wine ('manifesting that he is the true Creator'), for, as with the offering of the gifts, it is this part of the story that the contemporary celebrants mimic in the Mass itself. The rest of the sermon deals with the story of the Magi and their relationship with Ælfric's audience. Ælfric presents a reworked version of the Augustinian passage quoted above, explaining the difference between the revelations of Christmas and Epiphany:

> On þam forman dæge his gebyrdtide he wearð æteowod þrim hyrdum on Iudeiscum earde þurh ðæs engles bodunge. On þam ylcum dæge he wearð gecyd þam þrim tungelwitegum on eastdæle þurh ðone beorhtan steorran, ac on þysum dæge hi comon mid heora lacum. Hit wæs gedafenlic þæt se gesceadwisa engel hine cydde þam gesceadwisum Iudeiscum, þe Godes æ cuðon, 7 þam hæþenum, þe ðæs godcundan gesceades nyston, na þurh stemne ac þurh tacn wære geswutelod.[79]

Ælfric uses Augustine's cornerstone model to bring the two 'walls' together, explaining that "he geþeodde his gecorenan of Iudeiscum folce, 7 þa geleaffullan of hæþenum, swilce twegen wagas to anre gelaðunge. . . . he us gegaderode mid anum geleafan to þam healicum hyrnstane, þæt is to annysse his gelaðunge."[80] It is through the Magi's gifts and baptism that this unity is realized, and through the water turned to wine that it is celebrated.

In particular, the Magi recognize Christ's triune status. They do so first through their own statements, each of which is repeated in the liturgy. They ask "hwær is se ðe acenned is" ("where is he who was born") knowing him to be "soðne man" ("true man"), "Iudea cyning" knowing him to be "soþne cyning," and "We comon to þy þæt we us to him gebiddan" ("We came so that we might pray to him") because he is "soðne god." Explications such as this must have influenced how the liturgy was understood, for when these lines are repeated as antiphons and responses, those

---

[77] CH I.vii, p. 233. "Who from the East of the earth sought him with threefold gifts."

[78] Ibid. p. 233. "The Holy Ghost rested upon him in likeness of a dove, and the voice of the father resounded loudly from the heavens, thus saying, 'This is my dear son, who pleases me well; listen to him.' "

[79] Ibid. p. 233. "On that first day, his birthday, he was revealed to the three shepherds in the land of the Jews through the angel's announcement. On that same day he was revealed to the three wise men/star-prophets in the East through the bright star, and on this day they came with their gifts. It was fitting that the wise angel proclaimed him to the wise Jews, who knew God's law, and to the heathens, who did not know this godly understanding, not through a voice but through a sign was it revealed."

[80] Ibid. p. 234. "He joined together his chosen from the Jewish folk and the faithful of the heathens, just as two walls into one congregation. . . . he gathered us with one faith to the lofty cornerstone, that is to the unity of his church."

repeating them are reminded that, in taking on the voices of the Magi, they are recognizing and worshipping him along with them, in the same way.

In describing the star as an acknowledgment by creation of Christ, Ælfric kicks off a lengthy discussion of "gewyrd," intended to refute those who saw the star as something greater than Christ, such that "se steorra his gewyrd wære."[81] This is a dangerous heretical position, and one that Ælfric feels compelled to treat with here, as such a view would destroy the imperatives of the season. Those who believe in destiny also tend to believe, as Ælfric explains, that those who sin do so by destiny, while to offer with the Magi and partake of the changed wine, one must recognize choice and personal responsibility. Having established this, Ælfric goes on to explain the meaning of the gifts: gold for a king, frankincense for the True God, and myrrh for his humanity. He describes heretics as those who do not give all three gifts, such that those who believed that he was a king, but would not grant him divinity, offered him gold but not frankincense, and so on. He then extends this imperative to his audience, exhorting:

> Uton we geoffrian urum drihtne gold, þæt we andetton þæt he soð cyning sy 7 æighwær rixie. Uton him offrian stor, þæt we gelyfan þæt he æfre god wæs se þe on þære tide man æteowode. Uton him bringan mirran, þæt we gelyfan þæt he wæs deadlic on urum flæsce, se þe is unþrowiendlic on his godcundnysse.[82]

Finally, he makes clear how, practically, each who has undertaken to offer him these gifts can interpret the act in terms of their personal spiritual lives, or 'how they, in a moral sense, apply to us.' To offer gold, he explains, is to engender wisdom. Frankincense is prayer. Myrrh is the mortality of the flesh, such that we can offer him myrrh by denying our carnal nature.

This discussion is based on a recognition of the superimposition of the Magi and the celebrants in the act of the liturgy, and by asserting again and again the importance of this identification, the association made during the liturgy is strengthened. When the celebrants cry out "We saw his star in the east and came with gifts to adore the Lord," they are doing so, with the Magi, acknowledging his triune nature and presenting themselves for membership in God's church. This identification is more important than maintaining the narrative, for the strength of it brings the Magi out of their context and into the marriage at Cana, just as are the celebrants. The Magi and the celebrants together, the people of the Gentiles, offer themselves to the unity of the church.

The terms of this move towards union are the same here as at Christmas – darkness to light, ignorance to revelation, carnal nature to unity with heavenly things. The end result of the season, for those who have

---

[81] Ibid. p. 235. "The star was his fate."

[82] Ibid. p. 239. "Let us offer to our Lord gold, so that we acknowledge that he is true king and rules everywhere. Let us offer frankincense, so that we grant that he was always God, he who in that time became visible to humanity. Let us bring myrrh, so that we grant that he was mortal in our flesh, he who is unsuffering in his divinity."

participated in it, is membership in the earthly church. This status, the consummation of this season, is the launching point for the next, whereby the faithful must move from salvation to heaven, by way of some earthly pitfalls, in Lent and Easter. Recognition of what remains in the Christian pilgrimage to heaven is the point of Ælfric's final exhortation, based on the fact that the Magi had to return to their country by another way. The faithful have left Paradise, but they are now able to begin the move back:

> Ac us is micel neod þæt we þurh oðerne weg þone swicolan deofol forbugon, þæt we moton gesælilice to urum eðle becuman, þe we to gesceapene wæron. We sceolon, þurh gehyrsumnysse 7 forhæfednysse 7 eadmodnysse, anmodlice to urum eþele stæppan, 7 mid halgum mægnum þone eard ofgan, þe we þurh leahtrum forluron.[83]

The Vercelli homily for Epiphany (Vercelli XVI) ends in the same vein, using many of the same expressions. This is particularly interesting, since the Vercelli homily has been discussing baptism (in particular discussing how the water acknowledged Christ and enforcing a Trinitarian understanding of the baptism, based on the same declaration of the Father mentioned by Ælfric and used as an antiphon in the Leofric Collectar). Having accepted the Trinitarian truth illustrated in the baptismal story, the homilist asserts that "þæt fægere rice 7 þa eadignesse 7 ða myclan wyrðmendo we sculon nu heononforð ofer eorðan geearnian þurh micel gewinn 7 þurh micel ellen 7 þurh manigfealde sorge."[84] Pointing out the sins of our forefathers that drove them out of paradise, he continues; "nu se man se ðe þæt þenceð, þæt he of þysse gehrorenlican worulde þone heofonlican rice begite, he ðonne sceall eallinga oðerne weg gefaran 7 oðrum dædum don."[85] Describing what must be done (humility, obedience, forsaking the world, prayer, etc.), he concludes, "þurh þas lare . . . 7 þurh ðas dæda, þa þe ure mæssepreostas us tæcaþ 7 lærað, þonne sceolon we ðone weg eft gefaran to heofona rice."[86] While the Magi are themselves never mentioned, the reference to them is clear. Despite focusing on a different topic, he concludes his sermon with the same exhortation as would Ælfric, ensuring that his audience understand their newfound unity with the church and what they must do between now and Easter. It is through the identification with those in darkness and with the shepherds at Christmas,

---

[83] CH I.vii, p. 240. "But for us, there is great need that we flee the deceitful devil through another way, so that we may happily come to our homeland, in which we were created. We must, through obedience and continence and humility, single-mindedly proceed to our homeland, and with holy might attain our homeland, which we lost through sins."

[84] Scragg, *The Vercelli Homilies*, p. 273. "That fair kingdom and that blessedness and that great glory we must now henceforth earn on earth through great struggle and through great contention and through manifold sorrows."

[85] Ibid. "Now the man who desires that he might from this transitory world attain the heavenly kingdom must travel altogether another way and do other deeds."

[86] Ibid. p. 274. "Through this teaching . . . and through these deeds, those which our mass-priest teaches and instructs us [to do], then must we afterwards travel the road to the heavenly kingdom."

and with the Magi at Epiphany, dramatically assumed in the liturgical commemoration, that they have entered the church, and it is in this dramatic mode of appreciating Christian history that they will proceed towards the Resurrection.

3

Candlemas

CANDLEMAS is one of the most intriguing feast-days in late Anglo-Saxon England, and it attracts some of the liturgical year's most interesting innovations in establishing dramatic identification. As the commemoration of the purification of Mary required by the law of Moses forty days after the birth of a first-born male child, and highlighted by the presentation of the infant Christ to Simeon and his dramatic response, it constitutes a thematic denouement to the commemorated events of Christmas and Epiphany. However, the liturgical plan for Candlemas has been explicitly made to reflect that of Palm Sunday, as both the *Regularis Concordia* and Ælfric's Second Letter for Wulfstan indicate. As such, Candlemas, and, in particular, the candle, resonates with the images and imperatives of the entire Temporale. Candlemas is not strictly part of the Temporale, and is a relatively late addition to the medieval liturgy, but due to the general fervency of Marian devotion and the day's medial position in the Temporale, Candlemas becomes for late Anglo-Saxon England a sort of nodal point between the events of Christ's birth and those of his Passion. In particular, for the participants, Candlemas is a time when the promises of God to Simeon, and by proxy to them, that they would see Christ, are consummated in the reply of Simeon, the *Nunc Dimittis*, and in the presentation of the candle/Christ. It is by the dramatic assumption of the voice of Simeon and of his position in relation to the candle that the imperatives of the festival are realized.

The purification of Mary and the presentation to Simeon originally belonged to 1 January, adjunct with the reading for the circumcision. A separate feast-day for these events existed by the fourth century, on 14 February in the Eastern calendar, forty days after 6 January, and later on 2 February in some areas that used the Julian calendar. The Purification was introduced to Rome in the seventh century from Byzantium as a 2 February feast of Christ and Simeon, called either *Natale Sancti Symeonis* or, in Greek, *Hypapante*, 'the meeting,' and "the celebration of the Purification was solemnized by a procession."[1] The origin of this procession is uncertain. It might not be unexpected for a procession to develop by analogy with one on Palm Sunday, or any other major feast day, as processions were

---

[1] Mary Clayton, *The Cult of the Virgin Mary in Anglo-Saxon England* (Cambridge, 1990), p. 29.

Plate 1. The Presentation of Christ to Simeon, Benedictional of Æthelwold
London, BL MS Additional 49598, fol. 34v (by permission of the British Library)

often added to festivals, often for no explicit or obvious reason. However, medieval liturgists widely connect the procession for this day with a pagan procession for the expiation of the earthly empire. Bede makes this connection in what, according to Mary Clayton, is the "earliest evidence for the knowledge in England of the procession of 2 February:"

> But the Christian religion rightly changed this practice of expiating when in the same month on the feast day of St. Mary all the people together with their priests and ministers with devout hymns went into procession through the churches and suitable places in the city, and all carried in their hands burning wax candles given by the pope. With the growth of that good custom, he instructed that they do it also on the other feasts of the same Blessed Mother and Perpetual Virgin, not by any means for the five-year expiation of the earthly empire, but in perennial memory of the heavenly kingdom.[2]

According to Baumstark, the ancient pagan procession of the *Amburbale* had taken place at the beginning of February and had "set out from the ancient *curia* which was transformed into the Church of St. Adrian."[3] Baumstark postulates that the use of candles for the Purification procession, already known in Palestine before the introduction of the feast-day to Rome, may have been introduced by a Roman pilgrim in the fifth century, and then brought back to Rome with the introduction of the feast as a fitting replacement for the pagan procession in the seventh century. In any event, the Anglo-Saxon church understood the procession as a usurpation of a pagan one.

Clayton, in *The Cult of the Virgin Mary in Anglo-Saxon England*, describes the introduction into England and the spread of the Marian feasts, including the Purification. The evidence relating to the Purification, however, is less sure than that for the other feasts discussed by Clayton, as the Purification was not universally, in early Anglo-Saxon England, regarded as Marian. An early ninth-century poem by Æthelwulf seems to describe the Marian feasts, but apparently ignores the Purification, "since it could have been viewed as a feast of Simeon or of Christ, as it often was."[4] A ninth-century calendar in Bodleian Digby 63 refers to the feast of 2 February as *Ypapanti domini*, and some other early sources call it by its early Roman title, *Natale Sancti Symeonis*, or *Sancti symeonis patriarchie*.[5] The mass texts in the Gregorian Sacramentary for this day reflect its original function in celebrating the meeting of Christ and Simeon, and these texts are retained as the core of the mass in the late Anglo-Saxon witnesses despite the fact that, at least by the time of the *Concordia*, the

---

[2] Trans. Clayton, *The Cult of the Virgin Mary in Anglo-Saxon England*, p. 37. See also C. W. Jones, ed. *Bedae Venerabilis opera didascalica: De temporum ratione liber* (Turnhout, 1997), p. 323.

[3] Anton Baumstark, et al. *Comparative Liturgy* (London, 1958), p. 150.

[4] Clayton, *The Cult of the Virgin Mary*, p. 40.

[5] Of the manuscripts consulted by Wilson for his edition of the Gelasian Sacramentary, only his base text, Vat. Reg. 316, uses the more modern title. All others call the festival either *Sancti Sym(e)onis* or *Yppapanti*. See Wilson, *The Gelasian Sacramentary*, pp. 165–6.

festival is unilaterally referred to as *Purificatio Sanctae Mariae*. The Old English verse *Menologium*, written in the second half of the tenth century, illustrates the festival's duality: "We Marian mæssan healdað/ cyninges modor, forþan heo Crist on þam dæge,/ bearn wealdendes, brohte to temple."[6] Although the mass for the day is referred to as Mary's, what stands out in the mind of the composer of the *Menologium* is the fact that Christ was brought to the temple. As the most vivid aspect of Candlemas celebration is the procession of the lit candles through town to the 'temple,' this association makes sense, and dominates the participants' relationship to the festival. The focal point of the festival is, naturally enough, Christ, the candle, and those participating in the ritual will relate to the candle in accordance with the way the original figures in the gospel reading for the day related to Christ.

The procedure for the day is outlined in the *Concordia*, as follows:

> In Purificatione Sanctae Mariae sint cerei ordinati in ecclesia ad quam fratres ire debent, ut inde petant luminaria. Euntes autem silenter incedant, psalmodie dediti, et omnes albis induti, si fieri potest vel aeris permiserit temperies; et intrantes ecclesiam agant orationem cum antiphona et collecta ad venerationem ipsius sancti, cui eccelsia ipsa, ad quam itur, dedicata est. Deinde abbas, stola et cappa indutus, benedicat candelas et conspergat aqua benedicta et turificet et sic, accepto cereo ab aedituo,[7] psallentibus cunctis, accipiant singuli singulas acceptasque accendant. Inde revertentes canant antiphonas quae adsunt, usquequo veniant ante portam ubi, decantata antiphona *Responsum accepit Symeon*, dicatur oratio *Erudi, quaesumus, Domine*, post quam ingrediantur ecclesiam canentes responsorium *Cum inducerent Puerum*. Hoc decantato, dicant orationem dominicam. Dehinc sequatur tertia. Qua finita, si processionem induti non egerunt, induant se et, missam celebrantes, teneant luminaria in manibus, donec post oblationem ea sacerdoti offerant.[8]

The *Concordia*'s instructions outline four stages. The first, the approach to the church, is a preparatory procession, and is unremarkable, except for the

---

[6] Elliott Dobbie, ed. *The Anglo-Saxon Minor Poems* (New York, 1942), p. 49, lines 20–2. "We keep the mass of Mary, mother of the king, because she on this day brought Christ, son of the Ruler, to the temple."

[7] The Old English gloss here reads "cyrycwerde" (Kornexl, *Die Regularis concordia*, p. 64).

[8] Kornexl, *Die Regularis concordia*, pp. 63–5; see also Symons, *Regularis concordia*, pp. 30–1. "On the Purification of St. Mary candles shall be placed in the church to which the brethren must go to get their lights. The processors shall walk there in silence, occupied with psalms, and all shall be dressed in albs if this is possible and if the weather permits. Upon entering the church, they are to pray and say the antiphon and collect in honour of the saint to whom this same church is dedicated. Then the abbot, dressed in stole and cope, shall bless the candles, sprinkle them with holy water and incense them; when the abbot has received his candle from the church-warden, with everyone singing, they shall receive the candles one at a time and light them. During the return procession they shall sing the appointed antiphons until they reach the door of the church where, having sung the antiphon *Responsum accepit Simeon*, the prayer *Erudi quaesumus Domine* should be said, after which they shall enter the church, singing the respond *Cum induceruntt Puerum*. When this is sung, they shall say the Lord's prayer. Then Terce shall follow. After this is finished, if the brethren were not vested for the procession, they shall vest for celebrating Mass during which they shall hold their lighted candles in their hands until after the Offertory, when they shall offer them to the priest."

detail that those processing should sing the antiphon and collect for that church's saint, a detail that, according to Symons, is "peculiar to the *Concordia*."[9] The second, the blessing of the candles, is quite elaborate, and is one of the most fully treated ceremonies in liturgical books like the Canterbury Benedictional and the Missal of the New Minster. The third, the procession with the lit candles to the home church, featuring antiphons and readings at the door of the home church, just before entry, is the climax of the day and is treated along with the blessing of the candles in liturgical books. The fourth, the Mass of the Purification itself, is important mostly because of the offering of the candles after the Offertory of the Mass, heightening the relationship between Christ and the candles by conflating them with the Eucharistic offering.

Ælfric, in his Second Letter for Wulfstan, by way of asserting that the festival should be kept, breaks it down into its key elements:

> Ge sculon on þam mæsse-dæge þe is gehaton purificatio sanctae Mariae bletsian candela and beran mid lofsange, ge hadode ge læwede, to processionem, and ofrian hig, swa byrnende, æfter þam godspelle þam mæsse-preoste mid ðam offrum-sange.[10]

This passage is part of a set of three, flanked by otherwise non-liturgical material, giving skeletal descriptions of three ceremonies, Candlemas, Ash Wednesday, and Palm Sunday, followed by an assertion that "gyf hwa nyte hwæt þis getacnige, he leornige æt oðrum menn on leden oððe on englisc."[11] There are two points of particular interest in this set of passages. The first is the deliberate parallelism between the passage for Candlemas and that for Palm Sunday, as follows:

> Ge sculon on palm-sunnandæge palm-twigu bletsian and beran mid lofsange to processionem and habban on handa, ge gehadade ge læwede, and offrian hig æfter þam godspelle þam mæsse-preoste mid þam offrung-sange.[12]

That the ceremonies have come to reflect each other, at least in basic form, is again made clear in the *Concordia*, which explicitly instructs its readers that the Palm Sunday procession should be held 'as we have said above' in the directions for Candlemas.[13] This reflection is especially important in regards to the Christ totems, the candle and the palm-twig.

The phrase "ge hadode ge læwede" is particularly noteworthy, and

---

[9] See Symons, *Regularis concordia*, p. 31, n. 1. Ælfric includes this detail in his instructions for the monks of Eynsham (*LME*, p. 119).

[10] Fehr, *Die Hirtenbriefe Ælfrics*, p. 215. "You must on the mass day that is called the Purification of St. Mary bless candles and bear them with praise-singing, both monks and laity, in procession, and offer them, so burning, after the gospel to the masspriest with the offering song."

[11] Ibid. "If someone does not understand what this means, let him learn it from others, in Latin or in English."

[12] Ibid. "You must on Palm Sunday bless palm-twigs and bear them with praise-singing in procession and have them in hand, both monks and laity, and offer them after the gospel to the masspriest with the offering song."

[13] Kornexl, *Die Regularis concordia*, p. 72; Symons, *Regularis concordia*, pp. 34–5.

reflects the more implicit recognition of a mixed audience presented in Ælfric's First Series sermon for Candlemas:

> Wite gehwa eac þæt gesett is on cyriclicum ðeawum þæt we sceolon on ðisum dæge beran ure leoht to cyrican 7 lætan hi ðær bletsian, 7 we scolon gan syððan mid þam leohte betwux Godes husum 7 singan þone lofsang þe ðær to geset is; þeah ðe sume men singan ne cunnon hi beron þeahhwæðere þæt leoht on hyra handum, for ðy on ðysum dæge wæs þæt soðe leoht Crist geboren to ðæm temple, se ðe us alysde fram þeostrum 7 us gebrincð to ðam ecan leohte.[14]

Ælfric's assumption that some of the participants might not be able to sing but could still hold candles certainly seems to be targeted at the laity, as is his assertion that on Palm Sunday the palms are distributed to "þam folce."[15] The description used by Ælfric in his Second Letter for Wulfstan urges us to think of Anglo-Saxon liturgical participants as a juxtaposition of at least two more or less separate groups, interacting with and understanding the same rituals in potentially distinct ways. Particularly when using evidence from the monastic liturgy, one wonders how fully the laity might have related to the themes and images of the festivals (and, of particular concern for this discussion, to liturgical attempts at establishing identification with biblical figures) and to what extent they were intended to, throughout the church year. First, how much of the Latin liturgical formulae could the laity have been expected to understand? Even some secular priests clearly had difficulty with Latin, as the vernacular Easter tables and liturgical rubrics of Corpus 422, the Red Book of Darley, seem to assume. Second, how much were the laity expected to participate in a liturgy developed most fully for a monastic context? Within Holy Week, the most important witness for Anglo-Saxon ritual, the *Concordia*, is a monastic document, and it outlines the rituals such that one tends to envision monastic participants. Against this predisposition, however, discussion of the Deposition of the Cross on Good Friday stands out starkly. After describing the *Adoratio* ritual and its accompanying prayers, the *Concordia* outlines a practice "imitabilem ad fidem indocti vulgi ac neofitorum corroborandum."[16] This ceremony is particularly visual, and as described

---

[14] CH I.ix, pp. 256–7. "Everyone also should know that it is set in ecclesiastical customs that we must on this day bear our lights to church and let them be blessed there, and we must go afterwards with the lights between/among God's houses and sing the song of praise that is set for that occasion. Although some men cannot sing they can nevertheless bear those lights in their hands, because on this day that true light, Christ, was carried to the temple, who freed us from darkness and will bring us to eternal light."

[15] CH I.xiv, p. 297.

[16] Kornexl, *Die Regularis concordia*, p. 94; see also Symons, *Regularis concordia*, p. 44. "Worthy to be followed for the strengthening of the faith of unlearned common persons and neophytes." The Old English gloss here is perhaps even more proletarian, glossing 'neophytes' as 'heretics': ". . . fyligendlicne to geleafan ungelæredes folces 7 gedwolena to gestrangienne." Kornexl discusses possible meanings of "gedwolena," expressing reservations about suggestions that this use of 'gedwola' might mean simply 'ignorance' rather than 'heretical error.' In particular, she suggests that "gedwolena" might be semantically attached to the words "indocti vulgi," and therefore be

in the *Concordia*, its "getacnung" would come across quite well without the accompanying antiphons. One wonders at what point in the description of the Holy Week rituals the 'unlearned common person' has entered and at which points he might not be present. Much of this question depends, of course, on venue, for the differences between Holy Week commemoration in Winchester or in Canterbury and that in a more parochial context would depend somewhat on the presence of a large monastic community and its relationship to the surrounding people, and evidence for the Anglo-Saxon liturgy is generally too scattered and uncertain to say much about liturgical practice at a particular place and a particular time. Perhaps the authors of the *Concordia*, recognizing the inconsistent possibility of lay participation in certain places, and perhaps not others, have left it an open question in constructing a document usable throughout the country. As such, even this clear reference does not necessarily indicate lay participation at the ritual in Winchester or Canterbury (although these are two of the more likely sites for mixed participation), or anywhere in particular. More generally, the *Concordia*'s instructions indicate an understanding that the appreciation of the laity in regards to one of the most dramatic ceremonies in the Anglo-Saxon liturgy might be somewhat limited, that the visualization of what the liturgy is vocally proclaiming in the *Depositio* ceremony is often necessary, and is a conscious dynamic, an intended development of the images and associations expressed otherwise in the liturgical texts. It is this gap between the ideal of sympathetic identification with biblical figures established in the liturgy and the limited ability of the laity to appreciate what is being said that is addressed both by this sort of dramatic visualization and by the attempts of Ælfric and others to highlight and explain the dramatic role of the liturgical participants.

This dramatic visualization is given for the purpose not just of amazing and awing the common folk, but specifically for the 'strengthening of the faith,' which implies some kind of meaningful relationship to what is happening in the ceremony, but does not tell us what that relationship might be, and how it might correlate with that of the monastic community. In any case, for Candlemas, it would seem that the laity and the monastic community were meant to participate in and relate to the day's liturgy in fundamentally the same way. Of course, from this sole reference, one cannot be entirely certain when the laity would have joined the festivities. Ælfric's mention of it only specifies that the two would be together to 'bear with praise-singing,' and one wonders whether the laity would have participated in the first procession and in the ceremony in the visited church. Still, the passage seems to say that the laity would have been holding candles "swa byrnende," meaning that they must have received

part of a phrasal translation rather than a simple gloss of "neofitorum" (see Kornexl, *Die Regularis concordia*, pp. 307–8, n. 1111).

them during the blessing *Ordo*, as the candles had been lit at this time, and that they would have been present for the offering at Mass.

Outside of Holy Week, there is little overt indication of the involvement of the laity, making their specific mention here all the more important.[17] Ælfric's Second Letter for Wulfstan establishes a set of three festivals, Candlemas, Ash Wednesday, and Palm Sunday, the three highlights of the liturgical calendar between Epiphany and Holy Week, between which the events of his life, as commemorated liturgically, are specifically public.[18] In particular, these three ceremonies, as specified in Ælfric's letter, are marked by processions. As the directions for the *Concordia* tell us, Lent was a time of frequent processions, initiated by the procession of Ash Wednesday and finding its climax at Palm Sunday and, for the public penitents, on Maundy Thursday. By the time of Palm Sunday and Holy Week, we have several strata of liturgical participants relating to the liturgy in different ways and accepting different associations based on their particular relationships with the church. At Candlemas, however, between the blessing of the candles and the offering at Mass, they are all together. Some may have participated more than others in the observances of Christ's birth and revelation at Christmas and Epiphany, and many will have different experiences over Lent as they prepare themselves, as each needs, for commemoration of Christ's death and resurrection. Yet at Candlemas, they all, having received the promise of God, see and hold aloft Christ, a light to drive away ignorance and an offering to God. In this way, for the entire Anglo-Saxon Christian community, Candlemas becomes a focal point of the liturgical year, a communal celebration before the stratification necessary during Lent. As Ælfric makes clear both overtly and more subtly in his sermon composition, it is important that all those participating, consecrated or lay, whenever they might be present, be trained to understand fully the significance of their liturgical action.

There is a general difficulty in comparing forms for festivals like Candlemas from Anglo-Saxon sources in that service books often, and inconsistently, leave out whole classifications of texts, assuming that they will be supplied by accompanying books, such that one cannot generally place two full *ordines* side by side. Still, granted that differences between sources are often due to omissions that reflect only the nature of the particular liturgical books, and not necessarily omissions in practice, the differences are few and, for the purposes of this discussion, largely unimportant, with two interesting exceptions, discussed below. Witnesses differ most in terms of placement of the forms for the day. Not strictly part of the Temporale, the forms for

---

[17] See however Ælfric's discussion of the occasions during which the laity should partake of the Eucharist in his sermon *De Doctrina Apostolica*. He mentions specifically the Sundays in Lent, the three 'Swigdagum' (the three days before Easter), Easter day, Ascension Thursday, Pentecost, and the Sundays after the Ember days. See Pope, *Homilies of Ælfric*, p. 628.

[18] See Fehr, *Die Hirtenbriefe Ælfrics*, pp. 214–17.

Candlemas were sometimes placed within the Sanctorale, along with the other saints' days. Often, however, Candlemas has been placed within the Temporale, after Epiphany. Perhaps this inconsistency reflects the day's duality as both a Mass for Mary and a Mass commemorating a pivotal moment in the life of Christ.[19] The Mass forms for the day are more distinct than the forms for the blessing of the candles and the procession (probably because we have more evidence for these, covering a much larger period of time). Generally, the forms are those of the Gregorian Sacramentary, and, when used, are largely identical in the three witnesses for the processional liturgy on which I will focus here – the Robert Missal, the Leofric Missal (where they form part of Leofric C), and the Missal of the New Minster.[20] For the elaborate *Benedictio Ignis*, including the procession through town[21] and

---

[19] Among the witnesses that place Candlemas within the Temporale is the Leofric Missal, which puts it between the sixth Sunday after Epiphany and Septuagesima Sunday. The Leofric Collectar, which has it between the Octave of Epiphany and the first Sunday after Epiphany (the latter as part of a general set of texts for use between Epiphany and Septuagesima), generally mixes Temporale festivals and saints' days. In each case, interestingly, the Annunciation of Mary, celebrated on 25 March, directly follows the Purification, giving the sense that the two were inserted together. The Missal of the New Minster, the Robert Missal, the Canterbury Benedictional, and the Winchcombe Sacramentary keep both festivals in their proper places in the Sanctorale.

The Durham Collectar (late ninth to early tenth century, based possibly on a continental exemplar) has the Purification in the Temporale, between Epiphany and Lent (without the Annunciation). Hohler believes the transferral of this festival to the Temporale to be a 'highlighting' of an important feast, and Corrêa, besides calling this tendency (here and in Leofric) a sign of Continental influence, seems to concur (See Corrêa, *The Durham Collectar*, pp. 83ff, 103ff). As important as this festival is, its practical focus on an event in Christ's life rather than, primarily, a commemoration of a saint probably helped facilitate this shift.

[20] As Turner notes in the introduction to his edition, the Missal of the New Minster generally shows some innovation compared to the standard Gregorian family of Missals represented by Robert and Leofric (this innovation is usually a matter of replacing Gregorian forms with Gelasian and, occasionally, composing apparently new forms. See Turner, *The Missal of the New Minster*, pp. v–xxviii). These three Missals differ only, for Candlemas, in the Preface. Of these, against the generally correct classification made by Turner, only the Missal of the New Minster follows the original Gregorian form. The Leofric Missal, for some reason, has repeated here the Preface for Epiphany (which, as it deals with light and revelation, cannot necessarily be considered a mistake), and Robert has a much longer Preface, which mentions both Simeon and the prophetess Anna. Otherwise, all three use the Gregorian forms.

[21] That the Canterbury Benedictional describes a procession through town is likely, and while we have no mention of specific destinations in the Candlemas *ordo*, we do for Palm Sunday, which leaves at some point after the blessing of the Palms from the church of St. Martin (presumably back to Christ Church) (see Woolley, *The Canterbury Benedictional*, p. 26, and see ch. 5 below, "Palm Sunday"). At key centres like Canterbury and Winchester, where a range of Christians would be expected to participate, a procession through town is probable. Beyond this, however, little can be said. In his Letter for the Monks of Eynsham, Ælfric uses the same general language as did the *Concordia*, not mentioning anything that would help us define the procession within Eynsham, or tell us whether or not the procession left the monastery at all. Jones suggests that Ælfric's lack of particulars here "suggests either a very mechanical method of using a source or, perhaps, his foreknowledge that the text would be read and used beyond the walls of Eynsham" (*LME*, p. 170, n. 98). Of course, in a given place, a procession might simply proceed from a side chapel, or from another sanctuary in the same compound (see Mark Spurrell, "The Architectural Interest of the *Regularis Concordia*," *ASE* 21 (1992), p. 167, and below, "Palm Sunday," pp. 98–9), but we have no specific reason to apply this sort of arrangement to Candlemas or Palm

the entry into the home church, I will discuss three main witnesses, the Missal of the New Minster, the Robert Missal (incomplete), and the Canterbury Benedictional. Despite Turner's conclusion that the Missal of the New Minster represents a more or less independent strand of Missals from that represented in the Leofric and Robert Missals, all three largely agree. The most interesting presentation of the ceremonies for the day is in the Canterbury Benedictional. As opposed to the Benedictional of Robert (not the Robert Missal discussed above), which, for the Purification, has only the benediction for the blessing of the candles and those for the mass itself, the Canterbury Benedictional presents the full *ordo*, with rubrics, antiphons, collects, psalms, and readings, even the beginning of the canon of the Mass (for the blessing of the candles, not for the main Mass of the day, for which it reverts to its usual form of simply providing the benedictions). Outside of Holy Week, the Canterbury Benedictional is so complete only for Candlemas, Ash Wednesday, and Palm Sunday.

The Canterbury Benedictional, the most complete Anglo-Saxon witness for the Candlemas liturgy, does not include any forms for the Vigil ceremony,[22] but several other texts do, including the Leofric Collectar, and the forms are largely the same wherever they occur. The purpose of the Vigil is to present the images and associations that will be developed the following day. The Vigil Preface and the *Secreta* both refer to the upcoming festival as a festival of the Virgin, and two responses in the Leofric Collectar refer to Mary's ever-virgin status. Dominating the Vigil, however, is Simeon, specifically the raising up of Christ by Simeon. The chapter reading for the day establishes the link between Christ and the candle that will be repeated and developed throughout the festival and describes Simeon carrying about the lit Christ.[23] Chapter ends with the antiphon that on the next day will be read as the candle-bearing participants enter the home church:

> Cum inducerent puerum ihesum parentes eius, accepit eum symeon in ulnas suas et benedixit deum, dicens, "Nunc dimittis, domine, servum tuum in pace."[24]

With the *Nunc dimittis*, the celebrants assume the position and voice of Simeon, and this conjunction will be of particular importance in the

---

Sunday. In any event, even in documents written purportedly for a monastic audience, as are the *Concordia* and Ælfric's Eynsham Letter, a more public procession is allowed for, and perhaps expected. See also John Blair, *The Church in Anglo-Saxon Society* (forthcoming), who postulates that minsters in the late Anglo-Saxon period may have used processions like these to encourage the affiliation of the surrounding layfolk, in response to the growth of local parish churches. As Blair explains, the processions are especially important because they are often associated with financial and material support for the minster by the laity.

[22] See Clayton's discussion of the gradual introduction of vigil and octave services for the Marian feasts during the Anglo-Saxon period, Clayton, *The Cult of the Virgin Mary*, pp. 25ff.

[23] See Dewick and Frere, *The Leofric Collectar*, p. 45.

[24] Ibid. "When his parents were bringing in the boy Jesus, Simeon took him in his arms and blessed God, saying, 'Now you are dismissing, Lord, your servant in peace.'"

ceremonies for the next day. In the mass for Vigils (here from the Leofric Missal), the *Ad complendum* further hints at this relationship, as Simeon's action of 'raising up' is applied to the beseechers – "Da nobis, quaesumus, misericors deus, ipsius superveniente festivitate vegetari, cuius integra virginitate salutis nostrae auctorem suscepimus"[25] – and its significance is explained in a key collect for Vespers in the Leofric Collectar (taken from an alternate collect for the day itself from the Gregorian Sacramentary, and from the *Ad populum* in the Leofric Missal):

> Perfice in nobis, domine, gratiam tuam, qui iusti Symeonis expectationem implesti, ut sicut ille mortem non videt priusquam christum dominum videre mereretur, ita et nos vitam optineamus aeternam.[26]

If the purpose of the vigil is to get the participants into the proper frame of mind for the commemoration of the festival day, that frame of mind involves a sympathetic relationship with Simeon, holding up Christ with him, and reaping the benefits of seeing Christ in a way specifically compared to Simeon's reward.

Particularly strange, in a nominally Marian feast, called in every substantive Anglo-Saxon witness *In Purificatione Sanctae Mariae*, is the lack of discussion or development of Mary's purification. This is due not so much to the fact that the day was originally a festival of Christ and Simeon as to the fervency of the Marian cult. The mythos of Mary, fully developed in Anglo-Saxon England (the history of which Mary Clayton summarizes), no longer allows for the idea that Mary might need purification. The author of the Vercelli sermon for this occasion is greatly concerned that his audience understand this, reminding them that Mary had no need to be made clean, as she lived always in cleanness,[27] but that she brought the child to the temple to fulfill the law, much as Christ did not need baptism, but submitted to it so as to fulfill the law. As a consequence, the only overt treatment of Mary in the festival consists of assertions of her ever-virgin status and her role as the mother of Christ. In that context, the title for the festival can be understood less as a signal that Mary is being commemorated than as a statement of the occasion that gave rise to the meeting of Christ and Simeon.

The anticipation of Simeon's acceptance of Christ comes to fruition in the blessing of the candles in the away church. The candles are asperged, incensed and handed out one at a time (and, according to the apparent

---

[25] Warren, *The Leofric Missal*, p. 70. "Grant for us, we pray, merciful God, to be invigorated in this upcoming festivity of this same one [Mary], by whose pure virginity we have raised up the author of our salvation."

[26] Dewick and Frere, *The Leofric Collectar*, p. 46. "Perfect in us, Lord, your grace, you who fulfilled the expectation of just Simeon, that just as this one did not see death before meriting to see Christ the Lord, so also we may obtain eternal life."

[27] Scragg, *The Vercelli Homilies*, p. 282.

order in the *Concordia*, lit after dispersal), while the participants sing three antiphons (from the Canterbury Benedictional):

Puer Ihesus proficiebat aetate et sapientia coram deo et hominibus.
Nunc dimittis, domine, servum tuum in pace, quia viderunt oculi mei salutare
    tuum.
Lumen ad revelationem gentium et gloriam plebis tuae Israhel.[28]

The last two of these are in the voice of Simeon, from the dramatic declaration of Simeon upon seeing and raising up the Christ child. In the gospel speech, the last antiphon above is fairly under-emphasized, a more or less tacked-on, appositive metaphor. Its use here and in other places as an independent antiphon reflects how the dominance of the liturgical form, in which the idea of Christ as a light is much more important than it would have been to Simeon, has moulded use of the scriptural story. What is important here is not that the participants see in the ceremony a direct parallel to the events recounted in Luke 2:22–32, but rather that they see Christ in the lit candles and that they, like Simeon, accept him, raise him up, and praise God that they have been allowed to see him. The benediction directly following the dispersal of the candles, the first moment at which all participants would be holding a lit candle, makes this connection overt:

Omnipotens sempiterne deus, qui hodierna die unigenitum tuum in ulnis sancti Symeonis suscipiendum in templo sancto tuo praesentasti, te supplices depreca-mur, ut hos cereos, quos nos famuli tui in tui nominis magnificentia suscipientes gestamus, luce accensos, benedicere et sanctificare, atque lumine superne bene-dictionis accendere digneris, quatinus eos tibi domino deo nostro offerendo, digni et sancto igne tuae dulcissimae caritatis accensi in templo sancto gloriae tuae representari mereamur.[29]

The conflation of Christ with the candle is explicit here in the idea that the offered candles make present the light of Christ at the presentation to Simeon. Similarly, the conflation of the candle-raising celebrants with the infant-raising Simeon makes clear how the participants should relate to the Christ-candle, and makes their usurpation of Simeon's voice all the more real.

The procession begins, still in the away church, with an antiphon addressed first to Mary, and then to Simeon:

---

[28] Woolley, *The Canterbury Benedictional*, p. 83. "The boy Jesus grew in age and in wisdom in the sight of God and of men./ Now you are dismissing, Lord, your servant in peace, because my eyes have seen your salvation./ A light for the revelation of men and the glory of your people Israel." The Missal of the New Minster has only the latter two of these here (Turner, *The Missal of the New Minster*, p. 70).

[29] Woolley, *The Canterbury Benedictional*, p. 83. "Almighty eternal God, who on this day presented your only-begotten in your holy temple, raised up in the arms of holy Simeon, we beg you humbly that you bless and sanctify these candles, which we your servants carry, burning with light, raising them up in your glorious name, and that you will deign to kindle them with the heavenly light of benediction, in so far as with this our offering to you, Lord God, by the worthy and holy fire of your most precious love, we may merit to display your glory in the holy temple."

Ave gratia plena dei genetrix virgo ex te enim ortus est sol iustitiae illuminans quae in tenebris sunt; letare tuum senior iuste suscipiens in ulnas liberatorem animarum nostrarum donantem nobis et resurrectionem.[30]

Mary, here, is lauded as the mother of Christ, she who brought forth this light that the participants now carry, and that Simeon is receiving. Another antiphon, sung as the procession exits the church, praises Mary as both the door of heaven (*porta*) and she who carries the new light (*portat*) and this, along with the antiphon *Cum inducerent puerum*, makes one want to look for a more established association between the participants and Mary, parallel to the scriptural account in which Mary (with Joseph) carries the Christ child into the temple. This is not to be found, however, as both antiphons end with, and are dominated by, Simeon taking the child in his arms. The primary oration for the procession resolidifies this emphasis:

Domine Ihesu christe, qui hodierna die in nostrae carnis substantia inter homines apparens a parentibus in templo es praesentatus; quem Simeon uenerabilis senex, lumine spiritus sancti irradiatus, agnovit, suscepit, et benedixit; praesta propitius, ut eiusdem spiritus sancti gratia illuminati atque edocti, te veraciter agnoscamus.[31]

The propitiation for which the participants beg, described in terms of illumination, is parallelled to the irradiation of Simeon upon holding Christ aloft. The visual correlation here, as the processors are irradiated by their candles, solidifies the sympathetic relationship between them and Simeon.

The liturgy for Candlemas is dominated by descriptions of Simeon as 'just and timorous,' repeated assertions that he, expecting Christ, received the promise of God, and his own words, recognizing and proclaiming Christ as a light to drive away the darkness. Of particular interest in this vein is the first trope in the Winchester Troper for the day, placing in opposition, by response, Simeon raising Christ with the singers:

Adest alma virgo parens,
adest verbum caro factum
proclamemus omnes laudes,
in excelsis deo patri: *Suscepimus deus misericordiam tuam*
Lumen aeternum christum dominum: *In medio templi tui*:
In brachiis sancti Symeonis regem regum adesse,
    de quo propheta cecinit ovans   *Secundum nomen tuum deus*
Gloria salus et honor,   *In fines terrae*:
In saeculum saeculi   *Iustitia plena est dextera tua.*[32]

[30] Woolley, *The Canterbury Benedictional*, p. 83. "Hail virgin mother of God, full of grace, from you indeed the sun of justice has risen, illuminating those who are in darkness; rejoice, you aged just one, raising up in arms the liberator of our souls, given for us, who also gives us resurrection."
[31] Ibid. p. 84. "Lord Jesus Christ, you who on this day in the substance of our flesh appearing among men were presented by your parents in the temple; whom venerable old Simeon, irradiated by the light of the Holy Spirit, recognized, raised up, and blessed; remain gracious unto us so that, illuminated and instructed by the grace of this same Holy Spirit, we may recognize you truly."
[32] Frere, *The Winchester Troper*, p. 13. "Here is the kind virgin mother/ Here is the word made

Here again, as in the Vigil Mass, the action of 'raising up' is attributed, antiphonally, to Simeon and to the singers. This association dominates both the monastic liturgy and the mixed procession, which ends before the home church with an oration explaining its intended result, the *Perfice in nobis* quoted above.[33] They then sing the *Cum inducerent* and the *Nunc dimittis*, in Simeon's voice, as they enter the church for the offering of the candles at the Offertory of the Mass.

Powerful as the liturgy's attempts to make present the light of Christ and the experience of Simeon are, for Candlemas, it is particularly

flesh/ We cry out all praise/ to God the father on high (We have raised up, God, your mercy)/ The eternal light, Christ the Lord (In the middle of your temple)/ In the arms of holy Simeon here is the king of kings, of whom the prophets cried out, rejoicing (In accordance with your name, God)/ Glory, salvation, and honour (To the end of the earth), Forever and ever (Your right hand is complete justice)."

[33] As mentioned above, this text appears as a collect in the Leofric Collectar for Vespers on the Vigil and as the *Ad Populum*, the final reading for the main Mass, in the Leofric Missal and in the Missal of Robert (in the Gregorian Sacramentary, it rests in the same position, after the *Ad complendum*, but is simply labelled *Alia*, which does not necessarily mean that it would have followed liturgically, but simply that it could be considered as an alternate collect). In the Missal of the New Minster, which, unlike the other Missals, has the *Ordo* for the Blessing of the Candles and the procession, it appears only in the same position as that discussed here from the Canterbury Benedictional, having been moved from the end of the Mass to the end of the procession. The placement of this text in our two main witnesses reveals a discrepancy between them and the summary account in the *Concordia*. For the set of forms proclaimed just before and during the entrance into the home church, the *Concordia* prescribes the antiphon *Responsum accepit Simeon*, the collect *Erudi quaesumus Domine* (the Gregorian collect for the main Mass, also in the Leofric Missal), and, concurrent with the entrance, the *Cum inducerent puerum*, followed by Terce (focused thematically, in the Leofric Collectar, on the expectation of 'just and timorous' Simeon), and then the Mass (see Kornexl, *Die Regularis concordia*, pp. 64–5; Symons, *Regularis concordia*, p. 31). The Missal of the New Minster and the Canterbury Benedictional have replaced the collect *Erudi quaesumus* (which now follows the *Cum inducerent*, inside the church) with the passage that had ended the Mass, the *Perfice in nobis* (see Turner, *The Missal of the New Minster*, p. 71; Woolley, *The Canterbury Benedictional*, p. 84). (There is no indication of a break for Terce in either text, and Symons tells us that this detail is peculiar to the *Concordia*.) It might be that this placement of the *Perfice in nobis*, directly before the entrance into the church, is a later development, a deliberate shift of this passage to this position rather than just an anticipatory echo of the *Ad populum* of the Mass, as the only witness to provide both the processional forms and the forms for the Mass, the Missal of the New Minster, has no *Ad populum*, ending with the old Gregorian *Ad complendum* as its *Postcommunio*, such that the *Perfice* is not repeated. The Robert Missal has the *Perfice* as the final Mass text, called *Ad vesperum*, but the leaf of the manuscript that had dealt with the entrance to the church is lost (see Wilson, *The Missal of Robert of Jumièges*, p. 160). The Winchcombe Sacramentary gives only a few forms for the day, but it does have *Erudi quaesumus* as a *Collect Ad Processionem* and *Perfice* as its *Ad Vesperas* (see Davril, *The Winchcombe Sacramentary*, pp. 146–7). This seems to be more in agreement with the account in the *Concordia* (as the account in Robert might be), and the early date of this book (late tenth century) may be important in this regard. However, the Dunstan Pontifical, dated probably between 960 and 973, has the same order as the Canterbury Benedictional (as far as the *Perfice in nobis* before the entrance into the church, at which point the text breaks off), as does the early eleventh-century Samson Pontifical, which also has ties to Canterbury (see Conn, *The Dunstan and Brodie (Anderson) Pontificals*, p. 171; Woolley, *The Canterbury Benedictional*, pp. 158–9). The mid- to late eleventh-century Corpus 422 (the Red Book of Darley), pp. 285–8, follows CB's arrangement as far as it goes, including the placement of the *Perfice* (at which the *ordo* in Corpus 422 cuts off). Ælfric, in his Eynsham Letter, repeats the *Concordia*'s arrangement (*LME*, pp. 119, 170 n. 101).

difficult to see, in the general form of the rituals, a realistic commemoration of the events presented in the gospel for the day, Luke 2:22–32 (NRSV):

> When the time came for their purification according to the law of Moses, they brought him up to Jerusalem to present him to the Lord (as it is written in the law of the Lord, "Every firstborn male shall be designated as holy to the Lord"), and they offered a sacrifice according to what is stated in the law of the Lord, "a pair of turtledoves or two young pigeons."
>
> Now there was a man in Jerusalem whose name was Simeon; this man was righteous and devout, looking forward to the consolation of Israel, and the Holy Spirit rested on him. It had been revealed to him by the Holy Spirit that he would not see death before he had seen the Lord's Messiah. Guided by the Spirit, Simeon came into the temple; and when the parents brought in the child Jesus, to do for him what was customary under the law, Simeon took him in his arms and praised God, saying, "Master, now you are dismissing your servant in peace, according to your word; for my eyes have seen your salvation, which you have prepared in the presence of all peoples, a light for revelation to the Gentiles and for glory to your people Israel."

The gospel narrative discusses only Simeon's entrance into the temple, that of the parents with the child, the acceptance and 'raising up' of Christ by Simeon, and his response, the *Nunc dimittis*. The liturgy for Candlemas, instead, has a procession away, a blessing of the candles in another church, a procession home, an entry into the church, and the offering at Mass. If one were looking for mimetic correlation, one would point to the *Cum inducerunt* at the entry to the church, describing the parents bringing in the child, and expect a Simeon-based climax in the main Mass, in particular at the Offertory. However, presentation of this Mass in the liturgical witnesses is relatively understated, and the texts are, for the most part, either general or simply repeating passages and chants from earlier stages. In every way, the highlight of the festival is the blessing of the candles and, in particular, the procession through town, up to the entry into the church, as both the care given this part of the liturgy for the day in liturgical books and the force given this part of the festival in the descriptions in the *Concordia* and Ælfric's letters seem to indicate. This is probably due, in large part if not entirely, to the influence of the Palm Sunday services, which follow the same format. For Palm Sunday, the format makes particular sense, as the focus of the day is the procession to Jerusalem and the entry. Candlemas, because of the importance and visual dominance of the candle-lit procession, shifts commemorative focus from the main Mass and the Offering to a procession that has no meaningful antecedent. As such, one cannot look for associative antecedents based on correlation with the gospel narrative. Simeon holds up and proclaims Christ at several points, most notably as the candles are received and lit, during the procession, and before entry into the home church. This failure of the liturgy to correlate mimetically with the commemorated event, however, should not be used as an argument that the ceremonies are 'undramatic.' What is important is not whether the liturgical reenactment is accurate, but whether the participants think of themselves as taking the part of Simeon carrying in the Christ child. The liturgy has reshaped the biblical arrangement to highlight this aspect of the story, as it is in this way that the congregation can most directly participate in the revelation of Christ. The participants relate to the candle as Simeon did to Christ, seeing and recognizing in it the light of the Holy Spirit, holding it aloft, and proclaiming, 'now you are dismissing your servant in peace.'

As such, one finds identifications with Simeon not so much at points at which Simeon, in the biblical story, would have related to Christ, but at highlights of the liturgical services, the dispersal of the candles, the procession, and in particular the entry into the church, at which time the events of the bible story might be usurped in favour of establishing an edifying relationship between the participants/Simeon and the candle/ Christ. Perhaps the transposition of the *Perfice in nobis* collect to its position in the Canterbury Benedictional and the Missal of the New Minster is a reflection of this dynamic. After the antiphon *Responsum accepit symeon*, at the point at which the procession has drawn together before the home church, pausing before entering, the participants pray the *Perfice in nobis*, which begs God to fulfill the expectation of eternal life in the same way that he fulfilled Simeon's expectation. At the point of entry, the candle-bearers think of their potential reward, meriting eternal life, as analogous to Simeon meriting to see Christ. Flanked by the *Nunc dimittis* (the second part of both the preceding and the entrance antiphons), the participants might well see themselves as Simeon carrying the Christ child into the temple.

As was the case with Christmas and Epiphany, this sort of participation in the liturgy requires an appreciation of what is being said in the liturgy. This poses obvious difficulties for the lay people, most of whom probably did not have a firm grasp of Latin, especially when many of the prayers and chants are performed in ways that belie easy apprehension (in a low voice, broken up over a musical line, etc.). To describe not just dramatic potential in the liturgy but rather a dramatic, participatory experience, we have to look for some attempt to close this gap between the difficulty of understanding the Latin forms and the desire exhibited by Anglo-Saxon liturgical redactors for sympathetic participation. It is this gap that Ælfric is addressing, both subtly and overtly, in his First Series sermon for the day. Ælfric, in his attempt to explain "hwæt þis getacnige," presents a narrative order that seems to reflect the liturgical construction. Ælfric's rendering of the biblical narrative is rather free, and his elaborated presentation of Simeon is remarkably expressive. Rather than simply "looking forward to the consolation of Israel," Simeon is "swiðe oflyst þæs hælendes tocymes, 7 bæd æt Godes dæighwamlice on his gebedum þæt he moste Crist geseon ær he deaðes onbyrigde."[34] Rather than simply relating that Christ's coming had been revealed to Simeon, Ælfric makes it causal, explicitly the result of devout worship, of 'meriting,' and adds that "he wæs þa bliðe þæs behates."[35] In contrast to the terse biblical account, Ælfric sets up Simeon as a protagonist, with whom the faithful should sympathise. His description of Simeon's acceptance of Christ is particularly telling, both as a model of how the Candlemas participants should accept Christ and as a reflection of the liturgical order:

> And seo halige Maria com þa to ðam temple mid þam cylde, 7 se ealda man Symeon eode togenes þam cylde 7 geseah þone hælend 7 hine georne gecneow, þæt he wæs Godes sunu, alysend ealles middaneardes. He hine genam ða on his earmum mid micelre onbryrdnesse 7 hine geber into ðam temple 7 þancode georne Gode þæt he hine geseon moste. He cwæð þa, "Min drihten þu forlætst me nu mid sybbe of þysum life æfter þinum worde, for ðon þe mine eagan gesawon þinne halwendan, þone þu gearcodest ætforan ansyne ealles folces, leoht to onwrigenysse þeoda 7 wuldor þinum folce Israhele."[36]

The extra-biblical insight that Simeon took the child in his arms 'with great feeling' and 'fervently thanked God' is sympathetically reflective, and therefore instructive, of how the participants should take the candle and relate to it during the procession.

More striking here, however, is the order of Ælfric's presentation, particularly in that it seems to contradict the account in Luke. In Ælfric, Simeon enters the temple by the direction of the Holy Spirit (after having prayed, been diligent, etc), sees and recognizes the Christ child, exits the temple to get to the child, takes it fervently in his arms, and bears it into the temple, all the while giving thanks fervently and praying the *Nunc dimittis*.[37] Again, in Ælfric's explication, after a somewhat rhapsodic expansion of the anticipatory prayers of Simeon (which is reflective of the dynamic laid out in the *Perfice in nobis*, 'that he should not see death before he had seen Christ'), Ælfric repeats this order:

[34] CH I.ix, p. 250. "Very desirous of the Saviour's advent, and begged God daily in his prayers that he might see Christ before he tasted death."

[35] Ibid. "He was then happy for that promise."

[36] Ibid. "And the holy Mary came then to the temple with the child, and the old man Simeon went towards the child and saw the Saviour and knew him gladly, that he was the son of God, the redeemer of all the earth. He took him then in his arms with great ardour, and bore him into the temple and eagerly thanked God, that he could see him. He said then, 'My Lord, now let me go with peace from this life according to your word, because my eyes have seen your Healing One, the one you have prepared before the sight of all people, a light for revelation to the people, and glory for your people Israel.'"

[37] Actually, this is a slightly converted version of the *Nunc dimittis*. "Now you are dismissing your servant in peace" has become "My Lord, now you are letting me go in peace from this life," "my eyes have seen your salvation" is now "my eyes have seen your Healing-One/Saviour," and "a light for the revelation of the Gentiles" has been recast with the unspecific "þeoda" (although this word is not uncommonly used to translate 'Gentiles'). Particularly in the shift from 'salvation' to the actual figure that is represented in the seen candle, and in the addition of 'from this life,' perhaps an echo of the end of the *Perfice in nobis*, this version of Simeon's words seems to be influenced by the weight of the liturgical forms.

Maria Cristes moder bær þæt cild, 7 se ealda symeon eode hyre togeanes, 7 gecneow þæt cyld þurh Godes onwrigennesse, 7 hit beclypte 7 bær into ðam temple.[38]

From the biblical account, as expressed in the *Cum inducerent* entrance antiphon, it would seem that Mary and Joseph were the ones to carry the child into the temple, inside of which Simeon accepted him, and the illumination of the scene in the Benedictional of St. Æthelwold seems to show Mary handing the child to Simeon over the altar (see plate 1). What it actually shows, however, is both Mary and Simeon holding the child aloft, with Joseph and Anna on either side, over an altar that, according to Deshman, has been drawn to resemble the waiting arms of Simeon.[39] The importance of illumination like this is in its symbolic expression, and this illustration can represent both Mary and Simeon holding the child aloft, and the presentation to the altar of Simeon's arms, without trying to make a statement about the details of the historical account. In any case, the point of the illustration is Christ held aloft, the focal point of a circle of figures including Mary, Joseph, Simeon, and Anna, and it need not contradict the liturgically resonant idea of Simeon leaving from the temple, accepting the child outside, and bearing him, recognized, lit and praised, into the temple.

After a rhetorical discussion on the theme 'he bore that child, and that child bore him' (an expression of patristic origin but similar in tone to an antiphon for Matins for the day in the Leofric Collectar, *Senex puerum portabat puer autem senem regebat*[40]), Ælfric mentions Mary's offering of two turtle-doves and explains the offerings of the lamb and of the doves with the idea that we too should make offering. Again, however, the potential identification is avoided, as Ælfric's audience is told, not be like Mary, but be like the birds. He then returns to Simeon. The remainder of his discussion of Simeon pertains to the idea of seeing, explaining that he "ne gyrnde na þæt he moste Crist gehyran sprecan"[41] (although Christ certainly could have spoken had he wanted to),[42] because Christ was prepared 'before the sight of all people.' In his explication of this phrase, he explains what had been beseeched in the *Perfice in nobis*, what it means to 'see' him in contemporary terms:

Hine ne gesawon na ealle men lichomlice, ac he is gebodod eallum mannum, gelyfe se ðe wylle. Se ðe on hine gelyfð he gesyhð hine nu mid his geleafan, 7 on ðan ecan life mid his eagum.[43]

---

[38] Ibid. "Mary Christ's mother bore that child, and the old Simeon went towards her, and knew that child through God's revelation, and embraced it, and bore it into the temple."

[39] See Robert Deshman, *The Benedictional of Æthelwold*, p. 39.

[40] See Dewick and Frere, *The Leofric Collectar*, p. 46. "The old man carried the boy, but the boy ruled/guided the old man."

[41] CH I.ix, p. 253. "Did not beg that he might hear Christ speak."

[42] Ælfric mentions that Christ was as capable of speech, etc., as a child as he was at age thirty, and illustrations of Christ at the Presentation to Simeon like that in the Benedictional of St. Æthelwold bear this out, with a dressed Christ child, held aloft, blessing the old man.

[43] Ibid. "Not all men saw him physically, but he is proclaimed to all men, believe he who will. He who believes in him he sees him now with his faith, and in that eternal life with his eyes."

The rest of Ælfric's explication of the gospel for the day deals with Christ as 'a light,' and to build on this he pulls in Christ's own assertion that 'I am the light of the world . . .' The reward of being allowed to see this light is the fruit of diligent participation in the Candlemas liturgy, and it is through sympathetic association with Simeon that it is achieved for the participant.

Interestingly, Ælfric doesn't stop here, but gives exposition for the rest of the biblical story, not part of the reading for the day, and thus largely absent in the liturgical forms. The passage includes Simeon's prophecies concerning Christ, and then his address to Mary, "His sword shall pierce thy soul." Ælfric explains what this means, but relatively briefly, and it seems to have no real bearing on the themes and images of the day. It does, however, allow for his discussion of Anna. Anna has no place in the reading for the day, for according to the gospel narrative (and to Ælfric), she did not appear until after Simeon's speech. In the illustration in the Benedictional of St. Æthelwold, however, she is there, behind Simeon, as he holds the child. This detail is clearly out of sequence with the gospel narrative (if we are to take this illustration as depicting the transfer of Christ from Mary to Simeon), and one wonders what her symbolic function might be or whether, as may be the case with the maidservant standing behind Mary and next to Joseph, she might be there simply to fill out the picture. Possible insight into her function here may come from the one liturgical form for the day to include her, a Preface for the Mass in the Missal of Robert, as follows:

> . . . Grandeui Symeonis invalidis gestatur in manibus a quo mundi rector et dominus praedicatur. Accedit etiam oraculum viduae testificantis. quoniam decebat ab utroque sexu adnuntiaretur utriusque salvator . . .[44]

If Simeon provides the male model for the recognition and proclamation of Christ, Anna provides the female model. Mary is unattainable, as is Christ, and so discussion of her, in the liturgy or in preaching like that of Ælfric, discusses her only by way of explanation, not identification. But in his sermon, as in the above Preface, Ælfric explicitly sets up Anna as a model for women, the representative of the sex at this occasion, someone for women in his audience to sympathize and identify with. As with Simeon, Anna has merited to see and proclaim Christ because of her chastity in widowhood, which example Ælfric exhorts his female listeners to emulate, "Behealde ge wif 7 understandað hu be hyre awriten is . . . nime heo bisne be þisre wudewan."[45] Her function in Candlemas is understated, largely because the role of women in Candlemas is not specified, but Anna is presented as, symbolically, a female counterpart to Simeon, making sense of

[44] See Wilson, *The Missal of Robert of Jumièges*, p. 160. "He is borne in the arms of the aged and infirm Simeon, by whom he is declared Ruler and Lord of the world. There followed also the prophecy of the widow bearing witness. For it was right that he, the Saviour of both sexes, should be announced by each."
[45] CH I.ix, p. 255. "You women should behold and understand how it has been written concerning her . . . [and] take the example of this widow."

the Benedictional of Æthelwold's bunching of her with Simeon at the time of the Presentation.

Ælfric's establishment of Simeon's bearing of the lit Christ into the temple informs his final passage, describing the plan for the day.[46] It is not certain from this text whether Ælfric is saying that the candles were brought in the initial preparatory procession to the visited church (the *Concordia* seems to suggest that they were already set out there), such that "betwux Godes husum" means back to the home church, or whether the initial bearing mentioned here is to the home church, and the blessing means the blessing of the main Mass (which would then seem to indicate that the lights were carried again 'among God's houses'). A comparison of the language of this passage and that of his description of the day in his Second Letter for Wulfstan seems to suggest the former,[47] and the initial bearing of the lights to the visited church, where they are then blessed, need not mean that they had already been dispersed, but simply that they were transported there before the blessing.[48] In any event, dominant here is the idea of bearing 'Christ, the true light' to the temple, demonstrating both the centrality of the procession in the liturgy for the day and the importance of Simeon's role as bearer of the child to the temple.

The liturgical forms for Candlemas also explain, somewhat, the seventeenth Vercelli homily. This homily is, according to Scragg, "superficially exegesis,"[49] but mostly just general exhortation. His impression of the homily is rather poor, concluding that "[the author's] concentration on a very basic message, and his use of only very obvious and familiar Gospel quotations to support it . . . suggest that this homily was composed in an intellectually impoverished climate."[50] While the author here does seem to have some problems with the Latin, not all of the discrepancies that Scragg points to are necessarily mistakes (as he points out in a couple of instances), and his choice of explication is perhaps not so haphazard. While this text

---

[46] See above, from CH I.ix, pp. 256–7: "Wite gehwa eac . . ."
[47] See Fehr, *Die Hirtenbriefe Ælfrics*, p. 215.
[48] Malcolm Godden, in his commentary on this homily, sees in Ælfric's description a difference in practice from the *Concordia*, arguing that "possibly the extension beyond the monastic sphere involved a difference of practice" (*Ælfric's Catholic Homilies: Introduction*, pp. 76–7). His argument is based on the fact that Ælfric's summary account seems to imply that lights are borne to the home church, blessed there, and then carried 'between [or among] the houses of God.' All of the relevant liturgical witnesses seem to indicate that the candles are blessed at a visited church, but these witnesses are based on Winchester and Canterbury models, and perhaps practice does differ in smaller or in less monastic communities. It could be that by 'carry our lights to church' Ælfric means the visited church, as his account includes very little detail. It could also be that, for whatever reason, Ælfric is translating the rite in such a way as to leave optional the place of the candle blessing. Whatever the specific meaning of Ælfric's ambiguous description, all of the above accounts (the *Concordia*, Ælfric, and the liturgical witnesses) are structurally consistent in that they emphasize for the participants an outdoor procession, culminating in a dramatic entry into the church, as Simeon, before offering up the candles at Mass.
[49] Scragg, *The Vercelli Homilies*, p. 279.
[50] Ibid. p. 280.

would have been written a good deal earlier than the services in the Canterbury Benedictional and the Missal of the New Minster, such that one must be careful about using one to explain the other, some form of these services would have been practised at the time and place at which this sermon might have been preached, and whatever the peculiarities of that form, it surely would have featured the *Nunc dimittis* and the *Perfice in nobis* (either at the end of the procession or at the end of the main Mass), as does every extant Gregorian-based form of the service. The imperatives set forth in these forms, and generally in the liturgical identification between Simeon and the candle-bearers, lie at the heart of this homily.

The rendering of the gospel, as in Ælfric's sermon, is somewhat free, and likewise expands the actions and emotions of Simeon, in this case in the acceptance of the Christ child:

> þa genam se halga Simeon þone hælend on his earmas, 7 he hine mid bam handum beclypte, 7 he hine mid eallre modlufan sette to his breostum, 7 he bledsode 7 wuldrade Godfæder ælmihtigne . . .[51]

The author's first version of the *Nunc dimittis*, as part of the 'translation' of the gospel, is much closer to the gospel text than that in Ælfric.[52] After an explanation of why Christ's parents were there (and, most importantly, that Mary did not need purification), he seems to break away from straightforward exegesis. He goes into an explanation of the name "Jerusalem," interpreting it as "sibbe gesyhðe" ("vision of peace"). The point of the passage is 'peace,' Simeon's self-proclaimed state of mind after having seen Christ, and his explanation links this peace with eternal rest, calling Christ the "soðan sybbe gesyhðe." This interpretation amounts to an exploration of the importance of the *Nunc dimittis* passage and its meaning for his audience.

The next section, discussing the birds offered to God, symbolizing life's cleanness and innocence, is overtly funnelled into a description of Simeon's cleanness:

> Eac we sculon habban mid us Godes soðfæstnesse 7 his rihtwisnesse 7 eaðmonesse, swa we ær gehyrdon secgan þæt se eadiga Simeon wæs soðfæst 7 clæne 7 godfyrht on his life. Soðlice he hæfde lifes clænnesse gehealden, ge in wordum ge in dædum ge in geðohtum 7 eac in gesiehðe, for ðan him sægde se halga gast þæt he ne moste deaðes byrian ær þan þe he meahte mid his eagan dryhten geseon.[53]

---

[51] Scragg, *The Vercelli Homilies*, p. 282. "Then the holy Simeon took the Lord in his arms, and he grasped him with his hands, and he placed him at his breast very lovingly, and he blessed and glorified Almighty God the Father."

[52] Still, his version here is distinct, and shorter. The indicative "forlætst" is here the imperative "forlæt," and instead of seeing "þinne halwendan þone þu gearcodest ætforan ansyne ealles folces" (CH I.ix, p. 250), Simeon here sees "þa hælo þe ðu gearwadest to onsyne eallra folce" (Scragg, *The Vercelli Homilies*, p. 282).

[53] Ibid. p. 284. "Also we must have with us God's truth and his righteousness and his humility, as we previously heard it said that the blessed Simeon was true and clean and god-fearing in his life. Truly he had kept cleanness in life, in words and in deeds and in thoughts and also in vision,

There is no particular reason to interpret discussion of the birds in terms of Simeon except to explain the relationship between the crowd and Simeon in terms of meriting to see Christ, and this relationship is solidified in his assertion that, in praying for "ealles folces hælo" ("the salvation of all the folk"), Simeon "getacnode þæt we sceoldon beon swylces modes 7 swylces gewittes 7 on swylcre willan."[54]

The result of this similarity with Simeon is 'eternal salvation and eternal life,' and this echo of the *Perfice in nobis* is developed in his treatment of the *Nunc dimittis*. He quotes the Latin as extant in the liturgy, but his free rendering both expands and changes the passage, either by inept translation (as Scragg believes) or on purpose (or, possibly, a little of both):

> He swa cwæð: "Læt nu, dryhten, faran in sybbe þine þegnas æfter þinum wordum swa ðu him ær gehehtest." Efne swa he cwæde: "Læt me faran of þære tyddernesse þysses meniscan lichaman þe ic nu git on eom; læt me geendian þis deaðlic lif, 7 læt me becuman to þam ecan life 7 to þære ecan reste þe ðu þinum þam gecorenum 7 þam halgum gegearuwad hafast. For ðan þe ic þære andsware onfenc þæt ic ne moste deaðes byrian ær þan ic ðe, dryhten, mid minum eagum gesege. And nu gesegon mine eagan þine hælo ða ðe ðu geearuwadest to leohte 7 to frofre manigum þeodum 7 to wuldre þines folces." Soðlice ure hælend is ðæt soðe leoht . . .[55]

It is tempting to take the plural "þine þegnas" as a reflection, conscious or unconscious, of the symbolic transposition of Simeon's words onto the candle-bearers, although Scragg considers this a confusion of gender, or an error in copying (*þine* for *þinne*, and *þegn* made plural to agree). More important here is the conflation of the *Nunc dimittis*, the words of Simeon, with the idea expressed in the *Perfice in nobis*, in which Simeon's seeing translates into eternal life. In taking over Simeon's voice, the author here seems to recognize the mixing of his original words with ones more applicable to the candle-bearers, as explained in the *Perfice in nobis*. The author ends his sermon by drawing together his opening and closing Simeon themes, 'true peace' and 'eternal glory.' His sermon is short, compared to Ælfric's his choice of exegesis more selective, but it is selective in such a way as to develop the primary focus of the Candlemas liturgy, the assumption of Simeon's voice and Simeon's role in the events of the day by the participants, and to explain "hwæt þis getacnige."

---

because the Holy Ghost said to him that he would not taste death before he could see the Lord with his eyes."

[54] Ibid. p. 284. "Signified that we must be of such a mind and of such an understanding and with such a desire."

[55] Ibid. p. 285. "He said thus: 'Let now, Lord, your servant(s?) depart in peace, according to your words as you previously promised him (them?).' Even so he said, 'Let me fare from the frailty of this human body in which I now am; let me end this mortal life, and let me come to that eternal life and to that eternal rest which you have made ready for your chosen ones and for the saints. Because I have received the answer, that I could not taste death before I saw you, Lord, with my eyes. And now my eyes have seen your salvation, which you had prepared for light and for comfort for many nations and for the glory of your people.' Truly our Lord is that true light . . ."

Again, we do not know exactly what form the Candlemas liturgy might have taken in the earlier part of the tenth century, when the Vercelli homily was likely composed. There was a Candlemas celebration, with a procession, already in Bede's time, and what we see in the *Concordia* and in the later liturgical manuscripts may or may not have been as developed before the 970s. However, at least from the tenth century, and certainly by Ælfric's time, we can see conscious attempts to package the liturgy in such a way that this relationship with Simeon is enhanced. Whatever the logistics of the procession, whatever the respective roles of monastic and lay folk, the audiences of the Vercelli homilist and of Ælfric would have been trained to treat the Candlemas liturgy as a reenactment of Simeon's acceptance of Christ, embraced concurrently by Simeon and the celebrants to light the way to salvation.

4

Ash Wednesday and Lent

THE HOLY SEASON (from Septuagesima to Easter) is the climax of the year, ending with the Resurrection, the event that makes possible the place of the faithful in the heavenly kingdom. The Old English verse Menologium, describing the festivals of the year, pays homage to the importance of this period by taking the time to announce it with prophetic direct speech.[1] Lent and Easter week likewise are the focal point of the *Concordia*. After a chapter on year-round rituals like the Eucharist[2] and the weekly Maundy, the *Concordia*'s instructions for ritual begin with Christmas Vigils, move on to Candlemas, and then devote a remarkable amount of space to Lent and Easter. The ritual importance of this period is evident in the fact that ceremonies for other times of year come to reflect those of Easter; the *Concordia* makes explicit links between Christmas Vigils and Easter Vigils, and between Candlemas and Palm Sunday. As the Easter rituals, along with vernacular preaching texts for this time of year, indicate, Holy Season is treated as something of a mini-model of the year. Moving from the Fall of Adam to the Resurrection (often, like Advent, conflated with the Last Judgement), Holy Season encompasses Christian history, but in a specific way. The rituals and preaching of the church together allow the faithful to relive the progress of Adam from sin-based ejection from God's presence to the reconciliation made possible by Christ's sacrifice and Christian penance, providing them a way into God's heavenly kingdom (symbolized by the church), making them again citizens of heaven. These themes dominate both the ritual and the preaching for the period.

By the time of the tenth-century English liturgy, the forty-day Lent as it is known today, stretching from Ash Wednesday to just before Easter, was not ancient. In the earliest centuries of the Christian church there was often a pre-paschal fast lasting from only one or two days to the six days of Great Week, or (unusually) longer. Although Leo and Jerome in the fifth century asserted that the forty-day fast before Easter was of apostolic origin, the first certain reference to it is in the Canons of Nicaea in AD 325 (canon 5). Baumstark notes an ante-Nicene Egyptian fast of forty days

---

[1] See Dobbie, *The Anglo-Saxon Minor Poems*, p. 50, lines 60–2.
[2] The *Concordia* is peculiar in its time in prescribing daily Eucharist. See Symons, *Regularis concordia*, p. xxxix.

beginning after Epiphany,[3] and Talley tries to connect scattered early fourth-century references in other Eastern churches to a forty-day fast separated at times by a week or two from a six-day Paschal fast.[4] This fast seems to have been a commemoration of Christ's forty days in the wilderness, and Christian tradition in the West held that the origin of the pre-paschal Lent was similarly connected with Christ's fast. The weight of modern criticism, however, holds that this association between Christ's fast and the pre-paschal *quadragesima* was made later, and that the period had its origins in the preparations of the catechumens for baptism,[5] although Christ's period in the wilderness, as well as the examples of Moses and Elias, was surely a conscious part of the background in deciding that a forty-day fast was appropriate. In any event, there was for centuries a tremendous variety in how the *quadragesima* was constituted. Much of this variety stemmed from uncertainty as to whether the fast called for irregular fasting during a forty-day period or forty actual days of fasting. It seems likely that much of the impetus for fasting during this period was related to the encouragement to fast along with catechumens in the weeks before Easter, which, with the exclusion of Saturdays and Sundays, could amount to less than forty days of actually fasting. On the other hand, Egeria reports a Jerusalem Lent of eight five-day weeks, and Talley discusses other Lenten arrangements through the sixth century. By the time of Gregory the Great (end of the sixth century), Lent in Rome consisted of six weeks of six fasting days, or thirty-six days, not forty. Gregory discusses Lent as the 'tithe of the year,' and does not seem concerned with making up the extra four days, although in other contexts he speaks of Lent as a forty-day period. Probably by the seventh century, and possibly a good deal earlier, the four days preceding the accepted *initium quadragesima* on the First Sunday accrued something of a preparatory nature, until the establishment of Ash Wednesday as the beginning of Lent. Ash Wednesday is first attested in the Gelasian Sacramentary as *caput ieiunii*, although the First Sunday is still referred to here as *initium quadragesima*. Anglo-Saxon liturgical books still tend to retain this distinction, and Ælfric in many instances still seems to regard the First Sunday as properly the beginning of Lent.[6]

The word Lent originally referred more generally to springtime, as seen in the Anglo-Saxon 'lencten' or 'lenctentid,' but the imperatives of Lent extended well back into the winter months. The mood for the Lenten season was established on Septuagesima Sunday with the removal of the

---

[3] Baumstark, *Comparative Liturgy*, p. 194.
[4] See Talley, *The Origins of the Liturgical Year*, pp. 193ff.
[5] Even the Coptic forty-day fast beginning 7 January had baptismal associations. Talley notes that the sixth day of the sixth week after Epiphany was, in Coptic tradition, a baptismal day.
[6] See for example Ælfric's explanation of the relationship between Ash Wednesday and Lent in Skeat, *Ælfric's Lives of Saints*, vol. I, pp. 260ff.

Hallelujah and the *Gloria in excelsis Deo* from the liturgy. In his Second Series sermon for the day Ælfric explains, with reference to Amalarius, the significance of the omission. The seventy day period "gefylð ða getacnunge þæra hundseofontig geara þe Israhela folc on hæftnede Babiloniscum cyninge þeowde."[7] The removal of the hymns was in imitation of Jeremiah's prophecy that the people of Israel "sceoldon . . . geswican blisse stemne and fægnunge brydguman stemne and bryde."[8] A direct contrast is established between the present world and the expected divine one in Ælfric's explanation that the Hallelujah, a "heofonlic sang," in the 'sublime tongue' of Hebrew, is replaced by *Laus tibi, Domine* in the humbler Latin. Similarly, the *Gloria* is replaced by the song *Circumdederunt me gemitus mortis*. Like the captive Israelites, the congregation are told to bemoan their sins during the "bereowsungtid" and pray "þæt we moton geseon his heofenlican eastertide, æfter þam gemænelicum æriste, on ðam we him singað ecelice alleluian butan geswince."[9] Ælfric's audience is taught to see the period before Easter as a time of alienation from God, a dismissal from God's divine presence, and a time of mourning and penance. Similarly, Easter is to be seen as the time of reconciliation with God and reinstitution into God's holy presence, signified by the renewal of the 'heavenly songs' that the participants will be able to sing 'eternally' and 'without weariness,' as if in heaven. This context prepares the participants for association with Adam cast out of Paradise and prefigures the conflated expectations of both the Resurrection and the Second Coming at Easter.

This dichotomy between present exile and future reconciliation at Easter/ Doomsday was exploited by the tenth-century homilist represented in the Blickling collection. The Blickling homilist casts his Shrove Sunday (the Sunday before Ash Wednesday) exposition of the blind man restored by Christ in terms of the present human condition represented in Lent. He exhorts,

> Eal þis mennisc cyn wæs on blindnesse, seoððan þa ærestan men asceofene wæron of gefean neorxna wanges, 7 þa beorhtnessa forleton þæs heofonlican leohtes, 7 þisse worlde þeostro 7 ermða þrowodan.[10]

Christ came to restore this light to his people, and this light, equated with "þæs ecan lifes," is regained by perceiving the 'darkness of our sins' and making amends. It is specifically this light, in the model set up by the Blickling homilist, that separates the present world from the heavenly:

[7] CH II.v, p. 49. "Fulfills the signification of the seventy years that the people of Israel lived in captivity by the Babylonian king."
[8] Ibid. p. 50. "Must . . . abandon the sound of joy and the sound of the rejoicing bridegroom and the bride."
[9] Ibid. p. 50. "That we may see his heavenly Eastertide, after the universal resurrection, in which we will sing to him eternally the Alleluia without toil."
[10] Morris, *The Blickling Homilies*, p. 17. "All this humanity was in blindness, after the first people were cut off from the joys of paradise, and they abandoned the brightnesses of the heavenly light, and suffered the darknesses and miseries of this world."

þis leoht we habbaþ wið nytenu gemæne, ac þæt leoht we sceolan secan þæt we motan habban mid englum gemæne, in þæm gastlicum þrymmum.[11]

Developing the association with Adam and his separation from the 'light,' the homilist sets forth the Lenten imperatives for his audience:

Forþon we habbaþ nedþearfe þæt we ongyton þa blindnesse ure ælþeodignesse. . . . We synd on þisse worlde ælþeodige, 7 swa wæron siþþon se æresta ealdor þisses menniscan cynnes Godes bebodu abræc. And forþon gylte we wæron on þysne wræcsiþ sende, 7 nu eft sceolon oþerne eþel secan, swa wite swa wuldor, swe we nu geearnian willaþ.[12]

Lenten observance begins with a recognition of the fallen state, that the audience are in the mould of Adam, having fallen from paradise and seeking readmittance from exile.[13] In fact, the Paradise of Genesis and the heavenly kingdom described in Revelations are conflated for the Blickling homilist, who explains that Christ suffered so that we might "þæt heofenlice rice onfengon, þæt þa ærestan men forworhtan þurh gifernesse 7 oferhygde."[14] Through true penitence, demonstrated by weeping, we may be brought into the kingdom. The homilist ends with a description of the joys of this kingdom, a rather rhapsodic string of clauses establishing the correct Lenten destination firmly in the minds of his audience:

þær is ece blis 7 þæt ungeendode rice; nis þær ænig sar gemeted, ne adl, ne ece, ne nænig unrotnes; nis þær ege, ne geflit, ne yrre, ne nænig wiþerweardnes; ac þær is gefea, 7 blis, 7 fægernes, 7 se ham is gefylled mid heofonlicum gastum, mid englum 7 heahenglum, mid heahfæderum 7 apostolum, 7 mid þy unarimedan weorode haligra martyra þa ealle motan wunian mid Drihtne in eallra worlda world.[15]

---

[11] Morris, *The Blickling Homilies*, p. 21. "This light we have in common with the animals; but that light we must seek so that we may have it in common with the angels, in the spiritual company."

[12] Ibid. p. 23. "Therefore it is necessary for us to perceive the blindness of our exile. . . . We are foreigners in this world, and so we have been after the first ancestor of this mankind broke God's commands. And for that guilt we were sent into this exile, and now afterwards must seek another homeland, either in punishment or in glory, as we now will earn."

[13] The elaborated account in Genesis B of the penitential state of Adam and Eve at the recognition of their sin, before being cast out, might serve as a model to the penitent on Ash Wednesday: "hwilum to gebede feollon/ sinhiwan somed and sigedrihten/ godne gretton and God nemdon,/ heofones waldend and hine bædon/ þæt hie his hearmsceare habban mosten,/ georne fulgangan þa hie Godes hæfdon/ bodscipe abrocen" (A. N. Doane, ed. *The Saxon Genesis* (Wisconsin, 1991), p. 228, lines 777–83. "At times they fell into prayer, the couple together, and cried out to the good Lord of Victory, and addressed God, the ruler of heaven, and bade him that they might have his punishment, eagerly to obey the command of God which they had broken").

[14] Morris, *The Blickling Homilies*, pp. 23–5. "Receive that heavenly kingdom that the first people lost through avarice and pride."

[15] Ibid. p. 25. "There is eternal bliss and the unending kingdom; there is no sorrow found, no sickness, no pain, nor any sadness; there is no fear, no conflict, no anger, nor any antagonism; but there is joy, and bliss, and beauty, and the home is filled with heavenly spirits, with angels and archangels, with patriarchs and apostles, and with the innumerable host of holy martyrs who all may dwell with the Lord forever."

This description may be compared to a list of the tortures of hell and another description of heaven that ends the Lenten collection.[16] Together they make vividly clear what is at stake. As the Blickling homilist warns again and again, proper Lenten observance will lead to heaven, and negligence or apathy to hell.

One of the most dominant characteristics of Anglo-Saxon treatment of Lenten themes is its constant eschatological focus. Whatever moral is being put forth in Anglo-Saxon Lenten sermons, the concern is not so much for this life, or even for a heavenly life that will be reached eventually, but rather for a Doomsday that is frighteningly imminent. In repeatedly describing Lent as a life of laborious exile caused by our sin-inspired expulsion from Paradise and targeting reinstitution in the heavenly kingdom, it is not surprising to see the events of the Passion and Resurrection, for which Lent is a preparation, conflated with the coming of the heavenly kingdom on Doomsday. The homilist of the Blickling sermon for the First Sunday in Lent has taken this conflation much further than a more conservative man like Ælfric would have been willing, claiming that:

> þa gesetton halige fæderas 7 Godes folces lareowas þa tid þæs fæstenes foran to Cristes þrowunga, 7 hie sweotollice cyþdon þæt se egeslica domes dæg cymeþ on þa tid þe Godes sunu on rode galgan þrowode. . . . Hwæt we gehyrdon þæt þæt fasten þyses feowertiges daga ongunnen wæs instepes þæs þe he of þæm fulwihte astag, 7 þa eode sona on þæt westen; 7 þa gesetton cyricena aldoras þæt fæsten foran to his þrowunga, 7 eac foran to þon tocyme þæs egeslican domes dæges.[17]

Connecting the origin of Lent with Christ's fast, the homilist describes Lent as the interim between Christ's baptism and his Passion (directly conflated with the Last Judgement) during which he fasted and was tempted. The temptation of Christ is a direct parallel to that of Adam, and therefore that faced during Lent by the faithful:

> Rihtlic þæt wæs þæt he eode on westen þær ær Adam forwearþ. For þrim þingum Hælend eode on westen; forþon þe he wolde deofol gelaþian to campe wiþ hine, 7 Adam gefreolsian of þam langan wræce, 7 mannum gecyþan þæt se awyrgda gast æfestgaþ on þa þe he gesyhþ to Gode higian.[18]

---

[16] Ibid. p. 61, 65. See below, pp. 204–5, for discussion of this topos of the 'Joys of Heaven' in relation to Rogationtide and the Ascension.

[17] Ibid. pp. 27, 35. "The holy fathers and teachers of God's folk established the time of the fast, before Christ's passion, and they have clearly demonstrated that the terrible doomsday will come at the time when God's son suffered on the Cross. . . . Lo, we have heard that that fast of this forty days began directly after he rose from baptism, and then went immediately to the wasteland; and therefore the elders of the church set the fast before his passion, and also before the coming of the terrible doomsday."

[18] Ibid. p. 29. "It was fitting that he went into the wasteland where Adam was previously undone. Christ went into the wasteland for three things: because he desired to invite the devil to fight with him, and to free Adam from his long exile, and to demonstrate to people that the cursed spirit assaults those whom he sees hastening to God."

There is at work here a juxtaposition of Adam with the audience in the homilist's development of the nature of Lent. The need for forgiveness was caused by Adam's first sin, described in terms of "gifernesse" and "ofer-hygde," both from the list of eight capital sins that would have been used by Anglo-Saxon confessors to categorize the sins committed by their congregations. It was Christ's ability to overcome the temptations that overcame Adam which allowed the contemporary faithful to conquer these sins by Lenten confession and penance. This is the task of the faithful in life, to regain Paradise by conquering sins, and this is in a more focused and urgent way the purpose of Lent, as the homilist makes explicit:

> þas dagas þyses feowertiges nihta tacnaþ þas ondweardan weorld, 7 þa Easterlican dagas tacniaþ þa ecean eadignesse; 7 swa we nu on maran forhæfdnesse lifiaþ þas dagas, 7 on andrysnum þingum beoþ on þysse worlde, swa magon we þe maran blisse habban þa Easterdagas, 7 swa we sceolan þa hwile þe we lifgaþ her on worlde. Don we urum Drihtne soþe hreowe 7 bote, þæt we þurh þæt gegearnian ura synna forlætnesse, 7 ece lif æfter þisse worlde on þære ecan eadignesse.[19]

The Lenten themes developed by the Anglo-Saxon homilists are all founded on this comparison of Lent/the present world versus Eastertide/the future world, and all of Lent is dominated by this eschatological thrust.

Although Ælfric's tone is more restrained[20] and his theology more orthodox than that of the Blickling homilist, the same themes and imperatives set forth above reappear in a more developed form in Ælfric's many sermons for Lent. As did the Blickling homilist, Ælfric describes in his First Series sermon for Shrove Sunday the correct mindset for the faithful in the approaching time:

> Nis þeos woruld na ure eþel, ac is ure wræcsið; for ði ne sceole we na besettan urne hiht on ðisum swicelum life, ac sceolon efstan mid godum geearnungum to urum eðele.[21]

---

[19] Morris, *The Blickling Homilies*, pp. 35–37. "The days of this forty-night period signify the present world, and the Easter days signify the eternal blessedness; and as we now in great abstinence live these days, and as we are involved in fearful things in this world, so may we have the greater bliss during the Easter days, and so we must all the time that we live here in this world. Let us do for our Lord true repentance and penance, so that we through that may merit forgiveness of our sins, and eternal life after this world in the eternal blessedness."

[20] An instance in which Ælfric's tone is not so restrained is his Mid-Lent homily on the Prayer of Moses in the Lives of Saints. In exhorting his audience to constancy, he compares England "when the monastic orders were held in honour" to England at the time, asking, "Hu wæs hit ða siððan ða þa man towearp munuc-lif, and Godes biggengas to bysmore hæfde, buton þæt us com to cwealm and hunger, and siððan hæðen here us hæfde to bysmre" ("How was it that afterwards when one cast down monastic life, and treated God's observances shamefully, after that torment and hunger came to us, and afterwards a heathen army treated us shamefully") and concluding that "þes tima is ende-next and ende þyssere worulde" (Skeat, *Ælfric's Lives of Saints*, vol. I, pp. 294, 304). Perhaps recent troubles have lent Ælfric the same sense of urgency seen in Wulfstan's *Sermo Lupi ad Anglos* (see Dorothy Bethurum, ed. *The Homilies of Wulfstan* (Oxford, 1957), pp. 255–75).

[21] CH I.x, p. 264. "This world is not our homeland, but it is our exile; therefore we must not set our joy in this false life, but must hasten with good works to our homeland."

As before, it is an approaching heaven for which the penitents are aiming, and during these forty days they will follow either the 'narrow and steep' road to heaven or the 'wide and smooth' way, described as slackness in Lenten piety, to hell. Ælfric illustrates this imminent tension in his long recounting of the judgement given out by Christ on the sheep and the goats, with which he ends his Second Series sermon for the First Sunday in Lent.[22] Although Ælfric is too orthodox to repeat the sorts of superstitions held by the Blickling homilist that the End will come at Passiontide (as such a prognostication would work against the injunction in Matthew 24 to expect the End at any time), he thoroughly establishes the counterpoint between the present world and the eternal in Lent, illustrating this counterpoint with a number of themes on this model, exhorting that "we her sume hwile swincon, to ðy þæt we ecelice beon buton geswince," and "se ðe nan þincg nele on ðisum life þrowian, he sceal þrowian unðances wersan þrowunge on ðam toweardan life."[23] Ælfric takes delight in these sorts of doublets, and in his Lives of Saints homily for Ash Wednesday tells the story of a man who spurned the ashes and "wearð ða bebyrged, and him læg on-uppan fela byrþena eorðan binnon seofon nihton þæs ðe he forsoc þa feawa axan."[24] A motif on this model that Godden considers "peculiarly Anglo-Saxon"[25] in the same sermon preaches confession by reminding that "seðe ne mæg for sceame his gyltas anum menn ge-andettan, him sceal þonne sceamian ætforan heofon-warum and eorð-warum and hel-warum, and seo sceamu him bið endeleas."[26] Each of these themes works because the penitents are trained to equate the present life with Lenten piety.

As before, their place in this life is that of Adam. Ælfric, in a First Series sermon, explains the three sins with which Adam was tempted and which Christ conquered, allowing the contemporary faithful to defeat them as well. As before, the sins are from the list of capital sins used by the confessionals, specifically "gifernesse," "ydelum wuldre" (often called 'idelgylp'), and "gitsunge."[27] The conflation of Adam with the contemporary penitents is implicit in Ælfric's summation of this idea:

> Ac se deoful wæs ða oferswiðed þurh Crist on ðam ylcum gemetum þe he ær Adam oferswiðe, þæt he gewite fram urum heortum mid ðam infære gehæft mid ðam ðe he in afaren wæs 7 us gehæfte.[28]

---

[22] CH II.vii. This is properly the reading for Monday after the First Sunday, which in Gregory the Great's time was the occasion for the dismissal of the public penitents.

[23] CH I.x, p. 265. "We toil here for awhile, so that we may be eternally without toil. . . . he who is not willing to suffer anything in this life, he must suffer unwillingly a worse suffering in the coming life."

[24] Skeat, *Ælfric's Lives of Saints*, vol. I, p. 264. "Was then buried, and many burdens of earth lay upon him within seven nights of the one on which he forsook those few ashes."

[25] M. R. Godden, "An Old English Penitential Motif," *ASE* 2 (1973), p. 238.

[26] Skeat, *Ælfric's Lives of Saints*, vol. I, p. 274. "He who cannot because of shame confess his faults to one man, then it must shame him before the heaven-dwellers and the earth-dwellers and the hell-dwellers, and the shame for him will be endless."

[27] CH I.xi, p. 272. "Gluttony," "vain-glory," and "covetousness."

[28] Ibid. "But the devil was then overcome by Christ in those same respects in which he previously

This association with Adam is the key for the contemporary penitents in understanding what Christ did for them in the wilderness, and what it means for their place at Doomsday.

It is interesting to note what seems to be an ambiguity on the part of both the Blickling homilist and Ælfric concerning the length of Lent. In their related homilies for the First Sunday, both homilists move from a discussion of the origin of Lent as a forty-day period (based on the fasts of Moses, Elijah, and, especially, Christ) to Gregory's description of his thirty-six days of fasting (six weeks of six days) as "teoðing-dagas."[29] The Blickling homilist seems to smooth out the problem by describing Gregory's tithing-days as "þara fæstendaga . . . syx 7 þritig," such that we might imagine forty fast days, thirty-six of which we consider the tithe. Ælfric, however, seems to create a problem by prefacing Gregory's calculations with the question, "Hwi is þis fæsten þus geteald þurh feowertig daga"[30] and then explaining only the thirty-six. Perhaps this passage reflects a lingering tendency to ascribe the *initium quadragesima* to the First Sunday and the *caput ieiunii* to Ash Wednesday, as illustrated in the Gelasian Sacramentary, and occasionally in Anglo-Saxon service books (the Leofric Missal, Lanalet, and the Robert Benedictional, among others). In his later homily for Ash Wednesday in the Lives of Saints, he begins with a rubric specifying that "þis spel gebyrað seofon niht ær lenctene,"[31] which must refer to Shrove Sunday, one week before the First Sunday in Lent (although only the rubric in the Corpus 303 copy of this sermon specifies *Dominica in Quinquagesima*), and certainly not to the preceding Wednesday.[32] Further, despite defining 'caput ieiunii' as "heafod lenctenes fæstenes" ("the head of the Lenten fast"), Ælfric explains:

> Nu ne beoð na feowertig daga on urum lenctenlicum fæstene gefyllede, buton we fæsten þær-foran to þas feower dagas, wodnes dæg and þunres dæg and frige dæg and sæternes dæg, swa swa hit gefyrn geset wæs þeah ðe we hit eow nu secgan.[33]

Whether or not Ash Wednesday as the beginning of Lent was "gefyrn geset," there is a recognition here of a need to make a distinction between Ash Wednesday and the First Sunday, and the four days preceding the First Sunday are put forth as more recent additions, as something that goes

---

had overcome Adam, so that he departed from our hearts, bound by the entrance through which he had entered and bound us."

[29] Morris, *The Blickling Homilies*, p. 35.

[30] CH I.xi, p. 273. "Why is this fast thus reckoned as forty days?"

[31] Skeat, *Ælfric's Lives of Saints*, vol. I, p. 260. "This sermon belongs to the seventh day before Lent."

[32] As Scragg points out, a later version of this sermon (altered by a "Wulfstan-imitator") in Corpus 162 "makes clearer than the opening of . . . Skeat's base text that the piece is preached on Quinquagesima, the Sunday before Ash Wednesday" (Scragg, "Cambridge, Corpus Christi College 162," p. 77).

[33] Skeat, *Ælfric's Lives of Saints*, vol. I, p. 262. "Now there are not forty days completed in our lenten fast unless we attach to it beforehand four days, Wednesday and Thursday and Friday and Saturday, just as it has been firmly established, although we are now telling it to you."

"þær-foran to" the Lenten fast (an explanation given by Amalarius in the ninth century).

Ælfric then describes the liturgy for the application of the ashes and explains its significance:

On þone wodnes dæg wide geond eorðan,
sacerdas bletsiað swa swa hit geset is,
clæne axan on cyrcan, and þa siððan lecgað
uppa (sic) manna heafda, þæt hi habban on gemynde
þæt hi of eorðan comon, and eft to duste gewendað,
swa swa se ælmihtiga God to Adame cwæð
siððan he agylt hæfde ongean Godes bebod,
"On geswincum þu leofast and on swate þu etst
þinne hlaf on eorðan, oðþæt þu eft gewende
to þære ylcan eorðan þe þu of come,
forðan þe þu eart dust and to duste gewendst."[34]

Ash Wednesday is also described, between descriptions of Candlemas and Palm Sunday, in Ælfric's Second Letter for Wulfstan:

Ge sculon bletsian axan on *caput ieiunium* and mid halig wætere besprencgan. Do þonne se mæssepreost on ufe-weardum his heafde myd ðære haligan rode tacne and on ealra þara manna, þe æt þære mæssan beoð, ær-ðam-þe he mæssige and gan to processionem.[35]

Those receiving the ashes receive the same words given Adam at the time of the fall, that they were created from ashes, and to ashes would return. The curse is coupled with a promise, however, that looks forward to Easter. After having returned to the earth, he tells his audience, they will all arise at doomsday "swa swa ealle treowa cuciað æfre on lenctenes timan."[36] Ælfric discusses the application as quite ancient, and references to the *dies cinerum* go back to the earliest copies of the Gregorian Sacramentary.[37]

However, while several Anglo-Saxon liturgical manuscripts provide prayers for the blessing of the ashes, there is no clearly datable liturgy for the application of ashes, in terms of a complete *ordo*, until the tenth-century Romano-German Pontifical, a later copy (mid-eleventh century) of which was known in England in Cambridge, Corpus Christi College

[34] Ibid. "On Wednesday, widely across the earth, priests bless clean ashes in church, just as it is established, and afterwards place them upon men's heads, that they may have in mind that they came from earth, and afterwards will return to dust, just as the Almighty God said to Adam after he had transgressed against God's command, 'Through labours you shall live and through sweat you shall eat your bread on earth, until you afterwards return to the same earth from which you came, because you are dust, and to dust will return.'"

[35] Fehr, *Die Hirtenbriefe Ælfrics*, p. 216. "You must bless ashes on *caput ieiunium* and sprinkle them with holy water. The masspriest should then apply them to his forehead with the sign of the holy Cross, and also onto the heads of all of the people who are at the mass, and go in procession before he gives mass."

[36] Skeat, *Ælfric's Lives of Saints*, vol. I, p. 262. "Just as all trees always quicken in Lenten time."

[37] See Cross and Livingstone, eds. *The Oxford Dictionary of the Christian Church* (Oxford, 1997), p. 966; Talley, *The Origins of the Liturgical Year*, p. 222; K. W. Stevenson, *Worship* (Washington, 1992), pp. 159–87.

MS 163.[38] The practice of applying ashes to the penitents (along with the sympathetic association between the penitents and Adam) is derived from the orders for admitting sinners into the class of public penitents. It is this liturgy, rather than the general application of the ashes discussed by Ælfric, that is reflected in an Ash Wednesday sermon by Wulfstan. After general exhortations to prayer, churchgoing, and almsgiving during Lent, addressed to all, Wulfstan discusses what is to be done with those guilty of 'high' sins:

> And sume men syndon eac þe nyde sculan of cyricgemanan þas halgan tid ascadene mid rihte weorðan for healican synnan, ealswa Adam wearð of engla gemanan þa ða he forworðe þa myclan myrhðe þe he on wunode ær ðam þe he syngode. . . . Leofan men, on Wodnesdæg, þe byð *caput ieiunii*, bisceopas ascadað on manegum stowan ut of cyrican for heora agenan þearfe þa ðe healice on openlican synnan hy sylfe forgyltan. And eft on Ðunresdæg ær Eastran hy geinniað into cyrican þa ðe geornlice þæt Lencten heora synna betað, swa swa hym man wissað; þonne absolutionem bisceopas ofer hy rædað 7 for hi þingiað 7 mid þam heora synna þurh Godes mildheortnesse myclum gelyhtaþ.[39]

The central element of this penitential practice is the formal expulsion from the church on Ash Wednesday and the episcopal absolution on Maundy Thursday. This type of penance is designed for those who have committed especially heinous, and often public, sins. That the practice described by Wulfstan stems from the Roman system of canonical penance is clear, and *ordines* for public penance are extant in more than a few Anglo-Saxon liturgical texts.[40] Of the liturgy for Lent, it is to public penance that critics of medieval drama look for the dramatic sensibilities demonstrated in the liturgy, and some of the most powerful sermons written for this time of year were those composed for this occasion by Wulfstan. Because of the fluidity in usage between public penance, as represented in Anglo-Saxon manuscripts, and more general Lenten penitential practices, the themes and identifications of public penance are extended to the larger Christian community.

---

[38] See Nelson and Pfaff, "Pontificals and Benedictionals," pp. 96–8, for analysis of the knowledge of the RGP in eleventh-century England.

[39] Bethurum, *The Homilies of Wulfstan*, pp. 234, 235. "And there are some men also who rightly must in this holy time be expelled from the church community for high sins, just as was Adam from the community of angels when he forsook the great joy in which he dwelt before he sinned . . . Dear men, on Wednesday, which is *caput ieiunii*, bishops expel in many places out from the church for their own need those who have made themselves highly guilty in open sins. And afterwards on Thursday before Easter they reenter the church, those who zealously during Lent atone for their sins, just as one instructs them. Then bishops read the absolution over them, and pray for them, and with that alleviate their sins through God's great mercy."

[40] See Bedingfield, "Public Penance in Anglo-Saxon England," *ASE* (forthcoming), for a survey of the evidence for the knowledge and use of public penance in pre-Conquest England. I argue that, while the English derived their principle understanding of this rite from Carolingian practice, we can discern distinctly Anglo-Saxon strains of the liturgy for public penance. Anglo-Saxon manuscripts often tend to recast this liturgy in such a way that the forms may be used for strict canonical penance, for something more improvisational, or as a basis for the general Lenten liturgy described by Ælfric.

The central theme is the identification between the penitent, who is being cast out of the church for the duration of Lent, and Adam cast forth from paradise, and this dynamic is central to all of the extant *ordines* for public penance. *Ordines* for the Dismissal of penitents on Ash Wednesday relate the sinful state of those about to undergo public penance to Adam's exile. In the ceremony in the Claudius Pontifical I (a manuscript of c. 1000, and possibly that used by Wulfstan at Worcester[41]), after a series of prayers and blessings for the ashes, which express sin in these terms, is an instruction for the application of the ashes and the Dismissal:

> Hic mittuntur cineres super capita eorum cum aqua benedicta et expellantur extra ecclesiam, incipitur, *In sudore vultus tui*; et prosternens se ante hostium canit episcopus, *Inclina domine*.[42]

The expulsion from the church, with the words of God to Adam that he must earn his bread from the sweat of his brow, includes physically escorting the penitent to the doors of the church, expelling him, and barring him from returning until Maundy Thursday. The prayers of the penitents acknowledge that they, like Adam, have been cast out of paradise into the earthly valley, and are undertaking the ashes in hopes of attaining mercy. During Lent, the penitent is to bewail his situation as one removed from the joys of paradise (specifically the Eucharist, the action that most clearly symbolizes unity with the spiritual community). The absolution prayers for the Reconciliation on Maundy Thursday, similarly, describe the penitent as Adam changing from an exile, weak with hunger, to an adopted son of God's Kingdom, splendidly clothed.[43] Absolved from all grave sins, the penitent's reconciliation with the church is described as a processing into heaven, where he will be given over to the custody of angels. The actions and words of those subjected to public penance centre on this connection with Adam, lending both ceremonies (the Dismissal and the Reconciliation) dramatic propensities.

There are three extant vernacular sermons that give explicit instructions for public penance, all of which are connected to Wulfstan, and all of which pick up on the dramatic possibilities afforded in the liturgy's promotion of Adam as a sympathetic model for the penitential experience.[44] Wulfstan's

---

[41] See Nelson and Pfaff, "Pontificals and Benedictionals," p. 91.

[42] Turner, *The Claudius Pontificals*, p. 85. "Here let ashes be applied to their heads with blessed water and let them be expelled from the church, beginning, *In sudore vultus tui* [from the sweat of your brow]; and prostrating himself before the crowd the bishop sings, *Inclina domine*." See also CB, p. 17, for examples of prayers that describe the experience in terms of Adam's expulsion.

[43] For example see Woolley, *The Canterbury Benedictional*, pp. 32–3.

[44] Two are Wulfstan's own sermons for Ash Wednesday and Maundy Thursday (Bethurum, *The Homilies of Wulfstan*, pp. 233–8), written probably around the year 1000, or just before. The third, an earlier sermon and possibly a source for Wulfstan's, is a translation of a Latin sermon for Ash Wednesday. Both the original Latin sermon and the Old English one are extant in Corpus 190 (pp. 247–9; pp. 351–3), one of the family of manuscripts often referred to as

sermon for the Reconciliation is a reworking of a sermon by Abbo of St. Germain. The changes made by Wulfstan reveal an interest in clarifying and intensifying the established relationship between Adam and the Lenten penitent. Abbo's sermon appears in four Anglo-Saxon witnesses. Two of these manuscripts have the longer version printed by Migne, and two, including Corpus 190, have a condensed version. Corpus 190 also provides a hyperliteral translation into Old English, and Bethurum prints both the shorter Abbo sermon and the translation as her Appendix I.[45] The translation was not Wulfstan's, and was probably commissioned by him as an exercise, but the shortening of Abbo's sermon in preparation of his creation of his own may have been his, an idea that Bethurum believes to be "quite likely."[46] Bethurum outlines the nature of this translation and a few of its peculiarities. Abbo's sermon originally began with a passage describing the significance of the day and outlining the day's liturgy, including the Maundy, the blessing of the chrism in preparation for baptism, the washing of the church, and the reconciliation of those who had been expelled for their crimes. The shorter version picks up here, with the explanation of public penance. Wulfstan begins his sermon with "Leofan men," replacing *fratres karissimi* in Abbo (and "Mine gebroðru ða leofestan" in the Corpus translation) and a short introduction which lasts only a few lines and reminds the participants of the reason that they are present, to "æfter geornfulre dædbote into cyrican lædað" ("after zealous penance be led into the church") just as previous participants had been. Wulfstan then gives his rendition of the spiritual journey of Adam. This rendition begins with a generic description of the creation of Adam and his initial sinless state. After a repeated "Leofan men," he describes Adam's placement in Eden, his ejection from paradise, his life away from paradise, and his eventual salvation and reinstitution into the heavenly company. Adam's life in Eden is particularly significant:

> . . . for Adames godnesse 7 for his halignesse God hine gelogode on fruman in paradyso on ealre myrhðe 7 on ealre mærðe, ðær he geseah Godes englas 7 wið spæc, 7 wið God sylfne he spæc; 7 næfre he ne swulte ne deað ne þolode ne sar ne sorge næfre ne gebide, nære þæt he ne syngode. Ac sona swa he syngode . . .[47]

This passage has a different character than that in Abbo. Wulfstan is here replacing (both in the long and the short Abbo):

Wulfstan's 'commonplace book.' This Old English sermon is unedited (OEC designation HomS9, Cameron number B3.2.9).

[45] The longer version of Abbo's sermon can be found in Migne, PL 132, 765ff. The shorter Abbo, along with the literal translation, are edited in Bethurum, *The Homilies of Wulfstan*, pp. 366–73.

[46] Bethurum, *The Homilies of Wulfstan*, p. 346.

[47] Ibid. "For Adam's goodness and for his holiness God placed him at first in paradise in all joy and in all glory, where he saw God's angels and spoke with them, and with God himself he spoke; and he would never perish or suffer death or experience pain or sorrow, as long as he did not sin. But as soon as he sinned . . ."

In ipso autem paradiso dedit ei Dominus omnem gloriam. Ibi videbat angelos et loquebatur cum illis, et nunquam moreretur si non peccasset. Ibi audiebat Dominum secum loquentem, et talem obedientiam sibi commendantem, ut numquam comederet de ligno scientie boni et mali. In ipsa vero hora qua peccavit Adam, eiecit eum Dominus . . .[48]

God is then described as *Episcopus episcoporum* ("bisceopa bisceop" in Wulfstan), driving him out from paradise and saying *In sudore vultus tui.* Abbo explains that Adam then did a long penance of 6000 years and more, *in carcerem infernalem*, until Christ, *qui est pontifex pontificum*, absolved him and brought him back to paradise. Abbo here sets forth clearly the model established in Adam, but Wulfstan more powerfully connects that model with the listening penitents. His expansion of the joys of heaven is somewhat more emotional, and is similar to descriptions of Heaven in the Blickling homilies,[49] and to the descriptions of Eden/Heaven in *The Phoenix*, more descriptive of the joys of heaven than of the Paradise of Genesis. Of particular interest is his translation of Abbo's *paradyso.*[50] Whereas Abbo tells us that "[Christ] liberavit eum de poenis tenebrarum et reddidit ei paradisum,"[51] Wulfstan relates instead that "þurh his mildheortnysse of yrmðum brohte, 7 hine into þære heofonlican cyrican syððan gelædde, þe he a syðþan inne on wunode mid Godes englum 7 mid his halgum on ecan wuldre."[52] Wulfstan here conflates Adam, entering 'the heavenly church,' with the penitents about to enter the earthly church, and reminds them that they will be in the company of angels, and in the midst of God's glory. The account is more circular than linear; rather than moving from paradise to the world to heaven (or back to paradise, as Abbo specifies), he is cast out from the heavenly company into the world and then, after a period of penance, reestablished in that heavenly company (actually the 'heavenly church'). Adam's story is important insofar as it provides for all Christians the archetype of punishment for sin and forgiveness attained through penance by Christ's power. As such, the story is subjugated to the experience of the penitents. The altered structure of the biblical account, and Wulfstan's adaptation of that structure taken from Abbo, mimics the arrangement of the *ordines* for public penance, and

[48] Ibid. pp. 369–7. "In this same paradise, however, the Lord placed him in all glory. There he saw angels and spoke with them, and would not at all have died if he had not sinned. There he heard the Lord speaking with him, and entrusting to him such a great obedience, that he might never eat of the tree of the knowledge of good and evil. Truly at the same time that Adam sinned, the Lord ejected him."
[49] See Morris, *The Blickling Homilies*, pp. 25, 65.
[50] The Corpus translation uses "neorxnawange" throughout, the same word used in the Blickling homilies. Wulfstan instead uses "paradyso" in describing Adam in the Garden of Eden.
[51] Bethurum, *The Homilies of Wulfstan*, p. 369. "Christ freed him from the punishments of darkness and reestablished him in paradise."
[52] Ibid. p. 236. "Through his mercy he brought him from miseries, and afterwards led him into the heavenly church, in which he always afterwards dwelt with God's angels and with his saints in eternal glory."

allows the participants to see more clearly Adam's fall and salvation as theirs.

This relationship between Adam and the Lenten penitents is made explicit in the remaining paragraph. Wulfstan recreates the progression established in the earlier liturgically influenced, biblical account, this time replacing Adam with the penitents. The following passage contains the most explicit thrust towards this identification:

> And gif hwylc man þonne Godes lage swa swyðe abrece þæt he hine sylfne openlice wið God forwyrce mid healicre misdæde, þonne be þære bysene þe God on Adame astealde þa þa he hine nydde ut of paradiso, be ðære bysne we eac nydað ut þa forsyngodan of Godes cyrican oð þæt hi mid eadmodre dædbote hi sylfe geinnian to þam þæt we hy þyder in eft lædan durran.[53]

In this paragraph, Wulfstan specifically identifies the participants with Adam in respect to their initial placement in the church, their sinful state and expulsion, and their necessary period of repentance. The hearers are coincident with Adam so that his desire, to find reunification with God and the heavenly church, becomes the desire of the participants. That the ceremony was taken as coincident (or, at least, was intended to be) is implied in Wulfstan's description of the participants' mindset during the ordeal,

> ... swa he geornor 7 gelomor Godes hus sece dæges 7 nihte 7 cneowige þær ute oft 7 gelome 7 clypige to Criste geomeriendum mode 7 talige hine sylfne wið God swa forworhtne þæt he wyrðe ne sy þæt he gan mote into Godes huse.[54]

Wulfstan concludes this description by asserting that only after such alienation may the bishop help the sinner find forgiveness. The second half of this sermon is greatly condensed and altered from Abbo. Abbo explains that, as Adam was given the law not to eat from the tree of the knowledge of good and evil, so was mankind given a law, that from Exodus 20:13. It is for these sins, "quae nos supra nominavimus"[55] that the penitents have been ejected from the church. At the beginning of the part of Abbo that corresponds with Wulfstan, Abbo mentions simply "peccatores homines" as those cast out of the church. Wulfstan has changed this to "þe men þe mid openan heafodgyltan hy sylfe forgyltað,"[56] and in his explication, instead of the description from Exodus, he refers only to the

---

[53] Bethurum, *The Homilies of Wulfstan*, p. 237. "And if anyone then should break God's law so egregiously that he has undone himself in relation to God with high sins, then by the example that God established in Adam when he expelled him from paradise, by that example we also expel from God's church the seriously sinful until they, with humble penance, restore themselves to the point that we thereafter dare to lead them (back) there."

[54] Ibid. pp. 237–8. "So he more eagerly and constantly seeks God's house day and night and kneels there outside often and frequently and cries out to Christ with a sorrowful mind and reckons himself so guilty against God that he is not worthy that he might go into God's house."

[55] "Which we have named above." The phrase is in Migne, but not in the shorter Abbo.

[56] Ibid, p. 236. "Those who with open, capital sins make themselves guilty."

sinner who "hine sylfne openlice wið God forwyrce mid healicre mis-
dæde."[57] The description of the participants' mindset above is not in
Abbo, who instead asserts more generally that "vos similiter fecistis
poenitentiam in ista quadragesima, quo vos sitis digni intrare in ecclesiam."[58] Abbo, in the long version, concludes with a long description of the
capital sins. The shorter Abbo has compressed all this into "ullum criminale
vitium"[59] in a warning not to remain in or fall back into these sins, which
Wulfstan leaves alone, instead expanding the description of those trying to
get back into God's house by doing penance "swa biscop him tæce."[60] By
subjugating his source material to his interest in emphasizing the experience
of Adam, and the relationship between that and what is happening
liturgically over Lent to those engaged in public penance, Wulfstan trains
his audience to assume this sympathetic role.

This sort of relationship with the Lenten liturgy, however, is not
constrained to the public penitents. As the themes (along with some of
the liturgical forms) of public penance are taken up by redactors of the
more general ashing, this identification is extended to all those involved in
the Ash Wednesday liturgy (not just those few who have committed serious
sins), as reflected in Ælfric's explanation of the day. This inclusiveness is
evident in the fact that, in the two vernacular sermons which describe public
penance for Ash Wednesday (Wulfstan's and Cameron B3.2.9), a clear
effort is made to include the whole congregation in the Adam-like
experience. The first half of Wulfstan's sermon for Ash Wednesday is
addressed to all the folk, and is a general exhortation to observe Lent. All of
the faithful are penitents here, granting God a tithe of the year by making
up for those bad deeds done the rest of the year. He exhorts his audience to
search themselves zealously and confess their misdeeds. He then explains
the role and means of public penance, describing the toils and miseries of
Adam cast out of paradise. For those who need to be expelled in this way,
he goes on to temper this harsh picture with an assurance that God is very
mild, and will certainly forgive those with the right mindset. That mindset
centres on an appreciation that the works of penance, while hard, are as
necessary for obtaining mercy as it was that Adam work, "bescofen to
hefigum geswincum" ("cast into heavy toils"). However the fact that
Wulfstan addresses both these penitents and the larger public urges all
those entering Lent to submit according to the model of Adam, taking the
ashes and bewailing their sins as a means of reentering the community of
the church.

The anonymous homily Cameron B3.2.9, also for Ash Wednesday,

---

[57] Ibid. p. 237. "Openly against God ruins himself with high crimes."
[58] Migne, PL 132, 765ff. "You have similarly done penance in these forty days, because of which
you are worthy to enter the church."
[59] Bethurum, *The Homilies of Wulfstan*, p. 373. "All wicked vices."
[60] Ibid. p. 238. "As the bishop may teach him."

reveals this same duality. The first two-thirds of the sermon amounts to a string of general exhortation to "Bugað fram yfele and doð god" ("flee from evil and do good") and to do penance faithfully. About halfway through is a warning specifically against the capital sin of drunkenness, and against the danger of breaking the fast, followed by a warning against gluttony based on Adam:

> Forbugað æfre þa oferfille soðlice for ðære oferfille and for ðære gifernisse wæs Adam ascofen of neorxnawange and gif we willað ure yrfe and urne eðel, þæt is neorxnawang underfon, þonne is us þearf þæt we ðyder faron þurh oðerne weg, þæt is ðurh fæsten and forhæfednisse.[61]

The same parallel used by Abbo and by Wulfstan is used here, in the same way, but with a more general focus. Abbo and Wulfstan say that just as Adam was thrown out of heaven, so must be those who have sinned openly. This homilist says that just as Adam was thrown out of heaven (for capital sins), so must we find another way back through fasting. This applies to all in Lent, and the sermon would seem to be simply a nice adaptation of a Dismissal sermon for general penitential use, except that the rest of the sermon deals directly with public penance:

> Witodlice Adam forgægde his drihtnes æ þa ða he æt of ðam forbodenan treowe and forðon drihten hine sceaf ut of neorxnawange on wræcsið þisses lifes þær he ðolode mænigfealde geswinc and siþþan æfter ðisses lifes geswincum on helle susle lange heofode oðþæt Crist þe ðisne middaneard alisde hine þanon generede and hine eft ongean lædde to nerxnawanges blisse. Æfter ðære bisne we sind gelærede þæt we ut drifað þæge þe forgægdon Godes æ and þurh heafodgilt beoþ scildige wiðutan þis þerxwolde Godes huses. And heom biþ forwirnd cyrclic ingang oþ þæt hig geendodre openlicre dædbote eft beon onfangene mid bisceoplicre lefe on bosm þære modorcircan swa swa Adam wæs onfangen æfter langre behreowsunge and langre tyde heofunge into neorxnawange to halgra geferræddene. To ðære geferræddene us eac gebringe Christ se ðe leofað and rixað mid his efenecan fæder and þam halgangaste on ealra worulda woruld.[62]

In many respects, this sermon seems closer to the middle section of Bethurum XV than does the corresponding section of Abbo, or of its translation, and perhaps it had some influence on Wulfstan's sermon. In

---

[61] "Always flee drunkenness truly because for drunkenness and for gluttony was Adam cast out of paradise, and if we desire our inheritance and our homeland, that is to receive paradise, then it is very necessary for us that we travel there through another way, that is through fasting and abstinence."

[62] "Truly Adam forsook his Lord's law when he ate from the forbidden tree, and therefore the Lord cast him out of paradise into the exile of this life, where he suffered manifold toil, and after the toils of this life lamented for a long time in hell-torment until Christ, who freed this world, saved him from there, and afterwards led him back to the bliss of paradise. After this example we are taught that we drive out those who have forsaken God's law and through capital crime are guilty, outside the threshold of God's house. And for them entrance into the church is forbidden until they, having completed open penance, afterwards might be received with the bishop's leave into the bosom of the mother-church, just as Adam was received after long repentance and a long time of lamentation into paradise, into the holy company. To that company may Christ bring us also, he who lives and reigns with his eternal father and with the Holy Ghost forever and ever."

any event, the dual address, to the general penitential public who must find another way home and to the public penitents who must do "openlicre dædbote," makes the final prayer, to enter heaven and the holy fellowship, as did Adam after a long penance, a prayer for all Christians in Lent. As such, the identification with Adam that runs through the liturgy for Lent is extended powerfully to the entire Christian community. Both those formally subjected to public penance and those participating in the application of the ashes (with its subsequent procession) adopt the role of Adam, thereby adopting his objective, to find reconciliation with God, by means of Adam-like expulsion and Lenten penitential exile. Again citizens of the heavenly kingdom, allowed again into the full privileges of the church, they are prepared to mourn Christ's death and exult in his resurrection in the following days.

5

Palm Sunday

O NE OF the most overtly dramatic rituals in the Anglo-Saxon
calendar is the Palm Sunday procession. Its inclusive nature goes
back to its inception. Of the Jerusalem rituals described by Egeria in the
fourth century, those for Palm Sunday are perhaps the most dramatic,
involving a procession from the Mount of Olives into Jerusalem. The
faithful, many of them pilgrims, would act as the crowd at the triumphal
entry, accompanying the bishop, who took Christ's position, into the city.
As strong an impression as this procession evidently made on Egeria, and
surely on other pilgrims like her, however, we can find no evidence of a
Palm Sunday procession in the West before the eighth century, and
possibly the ninth. As with most of the liturgy, due to the spotty
nature of the evidence, its origins and history are uncertain. Standard
liturgical history, on the weight of Egeria's account, attributes the origin
of the procession to Jerusalem. Duchesne believes that the Palm Sunday
procession was

> at first peculiar to Jerusalem. It was introduced into the West at a relatively late
> date, that is, about the eighth or ninth century. The ancient Latin liturgical books
> make no mention of it whatever. Amalarius speaks of it, but in terms showing that
> the custom of observing it was not universal.[1]

Talley, however, following a rather elaborate string of conjecture, argues
for an origin at Constantinople, which in turn, he believes, borrowed much
of its Palm Sunday commemoration from ante-Nicene Alexandria.[2] For
Talley, many of the Jerusalem processions involving visitation to commemorated sites constituted a second tier of the Jerusalem liturgy, not
native but developed in response to the expectations of pilgrims, in
particular those from Constantinople. Whatever its origins, from the
beginning the procession strove to establish an identification between the
processors and the original palm-carrying, singing crowd.

Its practice in the West before the ninth century, however, is untestified.
As Duchesne points out, the earliest liturgical books have no forms for the
blessing of the palms and no hint of a procession. The Gelasian and
Gregorian sacramentaries each have forms for Palm Sunday, and they

---

[1] Duchesne, *Christian Worship*, p. 247.
[2] Talley, *The Origins of the Liturgical Year*, pp. 181ff.

Plate 2. The Entry into Jerusalem, Benedictional of Æthelwold
London, BL MS Additional 49598, fol. 45v (by permission of the British Library)

refer to the day as Palm Sunday, a title that has particular resonance in conjunction with a palm-carrying procession. However, the forms make no mention of palms, and indeed seem to have no particular relation to the story of the triumphal entry as presented in the gospels. Rather, these forms pertain to this Sunday's other, and perhaps more central, function. Over the course of Holy Week, the Passions of each of the four gospels are read. The gospel of Matthew is read on Palm Sunday, and much of the day's liturgical emphasis looks forward to the events of the following weekend. Ælfric's First and Second Series sermons for Palm Sunday reflect this focus. His second is a composite account of the Passion, and the triumphal entry is glossed over in less than a sentence.[3] At the beginning of his First Series sermon, he mentions that the Passion (presumably from Matthew) has been read, and seems to present his upcoming exegesis of the triumphal entry as something of a tangent to the day's central purpose:

> Cristes þrowung wæs gerædd nu beforan us, ac we wyllað eow secgan nu ærest hu he com to ðære byrig Hierusalem 7 genealæhte his agenum deaðe, 7 nolde þa þrowunge mid fleame forbugan.[4]

The theological highlight of the triumphal entry, that Christ went willingly to his own Passion, looks forward to Good Friday. Throughout Anglo-Saxon treatment of Palm Sunday, both in preaching and in the liturgy, the point of the day is its relationship to Easter weekend, and this focus imbues

---

[3] By tradition, for the Sunday, Tuesday, and Wednesday before Easter were read the Passions of Matthew, Mark, and Luke respectively. The Passion of John was reserved for the Fore-Mass on Good Friday. Some later rubrics for Ælfric's Second Series compilation, however, refer to the account in John, which would not strictly befit Palm Sunday. Ælfric's account owes no more to John than to the synoptic gospels, but these rubrics might reflect confusion concerning how consonant this composite Passion might have been with the liturgical scheme. Two manuscripts collated by Godden, N and O (Clemoes' sigla), include both of Ælfric's Palm Sunday sermons, reserving his Second Series compilation for Monday of Holy Week, which had no liturgically prescribed Passion reading. The rubrics applied to this compilation in two closely related manuscripts, C, *De passione domini nostri iesu christi Secundum Iohannem*, and F, *Dominica in Ramis Palmarum. Passio Domini Nostri Ihesu Christi Secundum Iohannem*, are intriguing. The *Concordia* clearly prescribes the *Passio Domini nostri Ihesu Christi secundum Iohannem* for reading on Good Friday, including a dramatization, during which, at the point in the reading at which the crucified Christ's garments are taken from him, two deacons are instructed to strip away the altar cloth (Ælfric's version, as do the synoptic gospels, leaves out the actual stripping of the clothes). Both manuscripts (as Ælfric adamantly would not, having forbidden preaching on the three days before Easter, on which see J. Hill, "Ælfric's 'Silent Days,'" *LSE* 16 (1985), pp. 118–31) already supply a homily for Good Friday, Vercelli I, and clearly intend this one for Palm Sunday. Manuscripts C and M supply for Palm Sunday Ælfric's First and Second Series sermons in reverse order (CH II.xiv, CH I.xiv), such that Ælfric's version of the Passion might be read before his discussion of the triumphal entry. This may at least indicate that someone thought Ælfric's collated and rather interpretive Passion narrative a suitable companion to the liturgically prescribed Passion from Matthew.

[4] CH I.xiv, p. 290. "Christ's suffering was now read before us, but we desire to tell you first how he came to the city of Jerusalem and drew near to his own death, and did not desire to escape with flight that suffering."

the commemoration of the entry itself with a range of anticipatory and eschatological overtones.

That the early continental sacramentaries have no forms indicating a procession with palms does not of course necessarily mean that there was none. By its nature, a sacramentary tends to give only the core readings of the mass, and there are sacramentaries from Anglo-Saxon England that give no more. Still, the first indication we have in the West of any forms for the blessing of palms is from the eighth-century Bobbio Missal. This heavily Gallican massbook gives, without context, a *Benedictio Palmae et Olivae super Altario*, which invokes the following crowd, connects the branches to be blessed (olive branches are specified) with the palms held at Christ's entry, and equates the commemoration with victory over the devil and the promise of participation in Christ's resurrection.[5] With its recollection of the original crowd at the entry, its emphasis on the conquering power of the palm, and its eschatological thrust, this blessing has many of the elements that characterize the later Anglo-Saxon forms, and it is easy to envision a full commemoration, with a procession, surrounding it. However, although the wording of the Bobbio Missal's benediction seems to imply one, we have no certain indication that these palms were taken in procession until the Frankish witnesses of the ninth century. In the early ninth century, Amalarius writes of it in his description of the liturgy:

> Quarta varietas est quae dicitur diei palmarum. Eadem die Dominus de Bethania descendit Hierusalem, quando obviam venit ei turba. Ioannes narrat: "In crastinum autem turba multa, quae venerat ad diem festum, cum audisset quia venit Iesus Hierusolimam, acceperunt ramos palmarum, et praecesserunt obviam ei, et clamaverunt, 'Osanna, benedictus qui venit in nomine Domini, rex Israhel.'" In memoriam illius rei nos per ecclesias nostras solemus portare ramos et clamare, "Osanna."[6]

Although Duchesne believes that the procession may not yet be "universal" by this time, Amalarius treats it as at least customary, with its core elements of carrying palms and singing *Hosanna* presented as parallel to the biblical account. We get no indication from Amalarius as to how ancient the procession might be, but from the extant liturgical evidence it might seem more reasonable to attribute the elaborate blessings and dramatic procession to the earlier Gallican liturgy as reflected in the Bobbio Missal than to

---

[5] See Lowe, *The Bobbio Missal*, p. 170.

[6] Hanssens, ed. *Amalarii episcopi opera liturgica omnia*, vol. 2, p. 58. "The fourth variety is what is called the day of the palms. On this same day, the Lord was descending from Bethany to Jerusalem, when a crowd came to meet him on the way. John narrates: 'On the next day, however, a great crowd, which had come because of the festal day, having heard that Jesus was coming to Jerusalem, took up the branches of palms, and preceded him on the way, and cried out, "Hosannah, blessed is he who comes in the name of the Lord, king of Israel."' In memory of this event, we have the custom of carrying branches through our churches and proclaiming, 'Hosannah.'"

the Romanizing Carolingians.[7] By the time of the Anglo-Saxon witnesses, in any event, the early mass forms represented in the Gregorian and Gelasian books, focused entirely on the upcoming Passion and set in their forms from the earliest recorded stages, have been supplemented by a body of benedictions and blessings showing a tremendous degree of variety and originality, surrounding a procession of the palms into 'Jerusalem.' Talley speculates that the commemoration of the entry may have come from the East through the Irish liturgy to the rest of Western Europe. The development of this procession and its surrounding blessings seems, for the West, indebted to Frankish innovation, and probably gained general currency as the Romano-German Pontifical became established in Rome in the tenth century.

From an early stage, the blessings of the palms seem to reflect practice in an area in which palms were not profligate, most commonly specifying 'branches of palms and other various trees.'[8] For the Anglo-Saxon liturgy, standing in stark contrast to the core mass texts, which seem to be universal and unchanged from those in the earliest Gregorian books, are these divergent, and often originally composed, blessings, reflecting

---

[7] Although, as Rosamond McKitterick (*The Frankish Church and the Carolingian Reforms, 789–895* (London, 1977), pp. 134–7) demonstrates, both the Gallican and the Roman liturgical forms had residing value for the Carolingians in the resistance of some to the expressed need for a new Roman Sacramentary.

[8] The Winchcombe Sacramentary asks God to bless "hanc creaturam olivae, vel palmae, sive arborum quam ex ligni materiae producere iussisti" (Davril, *The Winchcombe Sacramentary*, p. 72: "this creature of olive, or of palm, or of the trees which you have appointed to be produced from the matter of wood"). Generally speaking, all forms of these blessings seem to assume that, while palms would be ideal, other sorts of branches would have to be used, as available. Flowers were probably used in some places in England, as they are specified on occasion. John is the only evangelist to specify that palms were involved, Matthew and Mark telling of only "leafy branches," and Luke mentioning no foliage whatsoever. An Old Latin reading of John 12:13, however, apparently read "flowers and the branches of palm trees" (see Deshman, *The Benedictional of Æthelwold*, p. 79), and the influence of this tradition is at times evident in the Anglo-Saxon liturgical forms. An antiphon in the Canterbury Benedictional asserts that "Occurrunt turbae cum floribus et palmis" (Woolley, *The Canterbury Benedictional*, p. 26: "the crowds came together with flowers and palms"). References to flowers can also be found in Palm Sunday forms from Corpus 422 (pp. 291–2) and from the mid to late eleventh-century Exeter book, London, BL MS Additional 28188 (fols. 89v–98v), among others. In his detailed directions for Palm Sunday, Lanfranc (c. 1078) instructed that the processors receive "flores, et frondes caeteris" (see Woolley, *The Canterbury Benedictional*, p. 148: "flowers, and various branches"). The Blickling homilist, in his account of the entry, recasts the palms as "blowende palmtwigu" (Morris, *The Blickling Homilies*, p. 69: "blooming palmtwigs"), which may be a reflection of the role of blooms in Anglo-Saxon liturgical practice. The Anderson Pontifical has in its blessings perhaps the most complete range of branches. Besides general blessings for 'branches of various types,' Anderson has specific prayers for olive branches and for flowers, and refers to branches of willow-trees: "quaesumus ut has arbores palmarum sive salicum, sive aliarum arborum, sanctifices atque benedicas, et sicut populus ille Israeliticus cum clamoribus excipientibus praedicabant gaudium, et dicebant, 'Benedictus qui venit in nomine domini,' ita et nos precamur indigni famuli tui . . ." (Conn, *The Dunstan and Brodie (Anderson) Pontificals*, p. 329: "we pray that you will sanctify and bless these branches of palms or of willows, or of various trees, and that just as those Israelites with clamouring proclaimed joy to those following, and said, 'Blessed is he who comes in the name of the Lord,' so also we, your unworthy servants, may pray . . .").

respectively an established liturgy anticipating the approaching Passion and a newer, freer symbolic reenactment of the entry. As such, the Palm Sunday procession, with its elaborate and seemingly less codified blessings, seems still to be at a relatively early, experimental stage when we see it in Anglo-Saxon witnesses of the tenth and eleventh centuries, although Ælfric, as did Amalarius, indicates in his sermon for the day that it was general, "þurh lareowum geset . . . gehwær on Godes gelaþunge."[9] Bede gives no clear indication that he knows of it. The reading for the main Palm Sunday mass had, of course, always been Matthew's account of the entry, and Bede, in his explication, urges his readers to cry *Hosanna*, to lay down cloaks, and to cut branches, but explains these actions only in terms of fulfilling their Lenten obligations in preparation for participation in Christ's resurrection.[10] This traditional paschal focus remained as the commemoration of the triumphal entry developed, picking up patristically established connections between the faithful and the crowd at the entry reflected in Bede and basing around them a procession that became one of the highlights of the liturgical year, as the participants took on the actions and imperatives of the Jerusalemites welcoming Christ as he approached his Passion.

The mimetic propensity of this procession is much clearer than that for Candlemas. The participants go out to get branches, come together to meet Christ on the way, and escort him into the city. Any sense of clear impersonation, however, is complicated by the fact that the starring role of the entry, Christ himself, is missing from the reenactment. In the later Middle Ages, Christ was represented in a number of ways, ranging from the consecrated host that Lanfranc ordered for the procession (c. 1078)[11] to carved representations of Christ on a donkey. For the Anglo-Saxon ritual, however, we get no clear indication of anything taking the place of Christ, certainly not with such a dramatic arrangement as that ordered by Lanfranc. We might expect the procession to involve a cross, or a gospel book, or some other item that might serve as a Christ token, but if they

---

[9] CH I.xiv, p. 297. "Through teachers established . . . everywhere in God's church."

[10] See Martin and Hurst, trans. *Bede the Venerable: Homilies on the Gospels*, vol. 2 (Kalamazoo, 1991), pp. 27ff. See also D. Hurst, ed. *Bedae Venerabilis homeliarum evangelii* (Turnhout, 1955), pp. 226–7.

[11] At an early station in the procession from the away church, concurrent with an antiphon announcing that the crowds descended to meet Christ, Lanfranc instructs, "Cantore autem incipiente antiphonam, *Occurrunt turbae*, exeant duo Sacerdotes albis induti, qui portent feretrum, quod parum ante diem ab eisdem sacerdotibus illuc debet esse delatum, in quo et corpus Christi esse debet reconditum" (Woolley, *The Canterbury Benedictional*, p. 148: "With the cantor beginning the antiphon, *Occurrunt turbae*, two priests should proceed, dressed in albs, who should carry a bier, which by these same priests must be delivered there just before the day, in which the body of Christ must be concealed"). *Pueri* flanking the bier, followed by others, are then instructed to sing the *Osanna filio David*, the song of the crowd, to the host, genuflecting, and all accompany the bier into the home church. The mimetic resonance of the ritual promoted by Lanfranc is striking.

are present, they draw no emphasis. Rather, possibly in part due to the close relationship between the rituals for Candlemas and for Palm Sunday, the palms themselves seem to gather the aura of salvation and victory over death surrounding Christ at the entry, having absorbed much of the divinity warranted the Christ-representing candles in the Candlemas procession. While this emphasis might detract from the ritual's verisimilitude with the original event, it brings in a range of associations that help the participants directly and powerfully enter Christian history. These associations are emphasized in the vernacular homilies and sermons that deal with the Palm Sunday ritual, as well as other works that deal with the symbol of the palm-twig, and serve to make Christ present in the moment of commemoration. The presence of the divine Christ is particularly important as the participants reenact his entrance into Jerusalem, and, as we shall see, the dramatic dialogue prescribed for the entry, the *Gloria laus et honor tibi*, testifies to the ritual's success in establishing the idea of the liturgical participants, made one body with those at the entry by carrying the palms and singing the same song, accompanying Christ into the city/church as a prelude to his Passion and Resurrection.

The forms for the Palm Sunday (eve) Vespers betray the day's original function, looking forward to Christ's upcoming sacrifice, and only with Matins, right before the procession, do we get forms pertinent to the entry itself. The collect for the morrow mass is the old Gregorian one, which begs that God, who had his son submit to the Cross, allow the petitioners to participate in the approaching Resurrection. An antiphon for Prime, beginning with Christ's announcement that the time is nearing for him to approach his Passion, solidifies the pre-processional expectation:

> *Ant.* Magister dicit tempus meum prope est apud; te facio pascha cum discipulis meis.
> ℣. Ingrediente domino in sanctam civitatem, Hebreorum pueri, resurrectionem vitae pronuntiantes, cum ramis palmarum osanna clamabat in excelsis.
> ℣. Cumque audissent quia venit Ihesus Hierosolimam exierunt obviam ei, Cum ramis.[12]

The first versicle, the *Ingrediente domino*, will also be sung at the climax of the procession, as the crowd enters the home church. Its use here, and that of the following versicle, establishes in the minds of those participating in the monastic hours their role as the crowd in the upcoming procession in terms of palms and singing.

The *Concordia*'s instructions for the procession are intentionally similar

---

[12] Dewick and Frere, *The Leofric Collectar*, p. 123. "The master says, 'My time is almost at hand; I will fulfill with you the Passover with my disciples.'/ With the Lord entering into the holy city, the sons of the Hebrews, announcing the resurrection of life, cried out with palm branches, 'Hosannah in the Highest.'/ When they heard that Jesus was coming to Jerusalem, they came out to meet him on the way, with branches."

to those for Candlemas, and the *Concordia* invokes the Candlemas procession as it begins its instructions for Palm Sunday. It directs:

> . . . ut ad illam ecclesiam, ubi palmae sunt, sub silentio ordinatim eant, dediti psalmodiae, omnes, si fieri potest et aura permiserit, albis induti. Quo cum pervenerint, agant orationem ipsius sancti, implorantes auxilii intercessionem, cui ecclesia dedicata est. Finita oratione, a diacono legatur evangelium *Turba multa* usque *Mundus totus post ipsum abiit*, quod sequatur benedictio palmarum. Post benedictionem aspergantur benedicta aqua et tus cremetur. Dehinc, pueris inchoantibus antiphonas *Pueri Hebreorum* distribuantur ipsae palmae et sic, maioribus antiphonis initiatis, egrediantur. Venientes ante ecclesiam subsistant donec pueri, qui praecesserunt, decantent *Gloria laus* cum versibus, omnibus, sicut mos est, *Gloria laus* respondentibus. Quibus finitis, incipiente cantore *Ingrediente Domino* responsorium, aperiantur portae. Ingressi, finito responsorio, agant sicut supra dictum est et teneant palmas in manibus usque dum offertorium canetur et eas post oblationem offerant sacerdoti.[13]

As with Candlemas, the highlight of the day is from the blessing of the palms to the entrance into the church. Ælfric's skeletal instructions for Palm Sunday in his Second Letter for Wulfstan (Fehr, Brief III) focus on this part:

> Ge sculon on palm-sunnandæge palm-twigu bletsian and beran mid lofsange to processionem and habban on handa, ge gehadade ge læwede, and offrian hig æfter þam godspelle þam mæsse-preoste mid þam offrung-sange.[14]

His assertion, mimicking his instructions for Candlemas, that those involved included "ge gehadade ge læwede" again raises the question of demographics. One wants to assume that "ge læwede" refers to more or less everyone, and with Ælfric's use of it envision as wide a demographic sampling as possible acting as one group from the blessing of the palms to the offering at the home church. Liturgical witnesses, however, largely ignore "ge læwede," making it difficult to know exactly to what degree, and in what way, they might have been involved. Lanfranc lists the order of the return procession (following the blessing of the palms) during his time. The

---

[13] Kornexl, *Die Regularis concordia*, pp. 72–4; see also Symons, *Regularis concordia*, pp. 35–6. ". . . the brethren, dressed in albs, if this can be done and the weather permits, shall go to the church where the palms are, silently, in the order of procession and occupied with psalmody. When they arrive, they shall say the prayer of the saint to whom the church is dedicated, pleading for the intercession of his aid. When the prayer is finished, the gospel *Turba multa* shall be read by the deacon as far as *Mundus totus post ipsum abiit*; the blessing of the palms should follow. After the blessing the palms shall be sprinkled with holy water and the incense shall be burned. Next, while the antiphons *Pueri Hebraeorum* are begun by the children, these same palms shall be distributed, the greater antiphons shall be begun, and all shall go forth. As soon as the Mother church is reached all shall wait while the children, who had gone ahead, sing the *Gloria laus* with its verses, to which all shall answer, as is the custom, *Gloria laus*. When these have been finished, as the cantor begins the respond *Ingrediente Domino*, the doors shall be opened. When all have entered and the respond is finished they shall do as has been said above, holding their palms in their hands until the Offertory has been sung, and then offering them to the priest."

[14] Fehr, *Die Hirtenbriefe Ælfrics*, p. 216. "You must on Palm Sunday bless palm-twigs and bear them with praise-singing in procession and have them in hand, both monks and laity, and offer them after the gospel to the masspriest with the offering song."

Secretary distributes "palmas Abbati, et prioribus, et personis honest-ioribus."[15] The procession is then arranged, lining up behind pairs of priors carrying pairs of crosses, candelabras, and thuribles:

> Hos sequantur duo Subdiaconi portantes duos textus Evangelivorum. Post quos laici monachi, deinde infantes cum magistris. Post quos caeteri fratres praece-dentes Abbatem, qui ultimus procedit; duo et duo, sicut sunt priores.[16]

While specifically making a place for the "laici monachi," nothing else here indicates the presence of anyone outside the monastic community, at least at the blessing of the palms.

Lanfranc's instructions are, of course, post-Conquest, as is a decree by Osbern, Bishop of Exeter, to the monks of St. Nicholas which reads, "And for þyse leaua, twygys elce gere, þat is an Palmsunnendeg 7 Cristes upstigan deg, to processiun mid þam canunche hy gan sceule."[17] One wonders if it is significant that, if the procession was to have included the general populace, only the canons are mentioned here. Of course, we would not want to assume consistency in this sort of thing throughout Anglo-Saxon England, and various communities and monastic centres will surely have arranged the ritual distinctly, by necessity or by choice. Still, the paucity of specific evidence including the common people in the blessings and the procession has led some critics to see them as more insular and exclusionary. Some doubt whether the processions would even have been visible to the general public. Mark Spurrell, discussing the *Concordia*'s processional directions, points out that

> Nothing is stated as to whether the church so visited was within or outside the monastic enclosure; and since we know from archaeological evidence that there was often more than one church within the walls, these passages cannot be used as evidence for processions through the streets.[18]

Again, due to the spotty nature of liturgical evidence in Anglo-Saxon England, one cannot generally describe with any confidence how a particular liturgical feast would have been arranged at any particular time or place. The directions for Palm Sunday in the Canterbury Benedictional, however, are a welcome exception, supplying an *Oratio ad processionem in ecclesia sancti martini episcopi*. St. Martin's still stands outside Canterbury, and any procession involving both Christ Church Cathedral and St. Martin's would to some degree have involved the whole city, whether or not all were carrying palms distributed during the

---

[15] Woolley, *The Canterbury Benedictional*, p. 148.

[16] Ibid. "Two subdeacons should follow these, carrying two gospel books. After these, the canons, next the children with the masters. After these, the various brothers preceding the Abbot, who processes last; two by two, just as are the priors."

[17] John Earle, ed. *A Hand-book to the Land-charters, and Other Saxonic Documents* (Oxford, 1888), p. 260. "And by this leave, twice each year, that is on Palm Sunday and Christ's Ascension day, they should go in procession with the canons."

[18] Spurrell, "Architectural Interest," p. 167.

blessings. The monastery of St. Augustine stood between the two, and its denizens surely would have joined the procession of Christ Church (it may even have been the site for the blessing and distribution of the palms). The Canterbury instructions are consistent with those in the *Concordia*, and seem to be purposely so, as the Canterbury Benedictional cites "the greater part of the rubrical directions of the *Concordia*" for this occasion.[19] With a monastic-based ceremony processing through the streets of Canterbury, from Christ Church through the heart of the city and out the gates towards St. Martin's, it seems natural to imagine a wide demographic, at least by the time of the compilation of this book (c. 1030) at Canterbury. That the *indocti vulgi* were included in at least some of the monastic ritual of Easter weekend in the tenth century is specified in the *Concordia*'s directions for the Deposition of the Cross. It is surely even more natural to envision their participation here.

Such a view is further justified by rubrics for Palm Sunday in the Benedictional represented in MS Additional 28188. Generally speaking, the processional *ordo* in Additional 28188 (fols. 89v–98v) is structurally the same as that in the Canterbury Benedictional, albeit with much internal variation (especially reworking or replacing of liturgical forms). Both begin with a rubric outlining basically the instructions from the *Concordia*, that the participants, following the morning Mass, are to travel to the church where the palms or branches await consecration, singing antiphons in veneration of that church's saint. The one primary difference between these two rubrics refers to their participants. Where the Canterbury Benedictional instructs, "Dominica die palmarum post matutinalem missam fratres ad illam aecclesiam ubi palmae fuerint ordinate pergant,"[20] Additional 28188 refers to a wider group of processers: "Dominica die palmarum expleto, matutinalis missae sacramento, clerus et populus ad illam pergant ecclesiam ubi palmarum et arborum rami ad consecrandum sunt collocati."[21] This broader demographic is in line with Ælfric's reference to "ge gehadade ge læwede" and with his First Series assertion that the blessed palms are distributed to "þam folce."[22] Although Additional 28188 (from Leofric's Exeter) does not specify a visited church (referring only to the wildcard "sancti .iłł."), the evidence from these witnesses encourages us to see throughout the stages of the Palm Sunday liturgy outlined in the *Concordia*, explicated by Ælfric, and developed in Canterbury and Exeter the entire demographic spectrum of

[19] Symons, *Regularis concordia*, p. 35, n. 2.
[20] Woolley, *The Canterbury Benedictional*, p. 22. "On Palm Sunday after the morrow mass, the brothers should proceed to the church where the palms have been set out."
[21] "On Palm Sunday, when the sacrament of the morrow mass has been completed, the clergy and the people should proceed to that church where branches of palms and of other trees have been collected for consecration."
[22] CH I.xiv, p. 297.

late Anglo-Saxon society processing together, carrying palms and singing the Hosanna, thereby joining themselves with the original palm-waving, singing crowd.

This association is liturgically established in the blessings of the palms. While the core elements of the Palm Sunday liturgy seem to be set, and in harmony with the *Concordia*, the benedictions for the blessing of the palms show tremendous ingenuity, and there is little consistency between liturgical witnesses, though a few forms appear regularly (if at times in altered ways). With the large number of deviant forms, in the Canterbury Benedictional as well as between witnesses, one cannot help but think of this part of the liturgy as newer, such that the composers of these witnesses took advantage of the lack of firmly established benedictions to compose original ones. They tend, nevertheless, to follow more or less the same template, with many of the same elements. The fourth blessing for the palms given in the Canterbury Benedictional is nicely representative:

> Omnipotens deus, rex mundi, creator et redemptor, qui nostrae liberationis et salvationis gratia ex summa caeli arcae descendere, carnem sumere, et passionem subire dignatus es, quique sponte propria loco eiusdem propinquans passioni, a turbis cum ramis palmarum obviantibus benedici, laudari, et rex benedictus in nomine domini veniens clara voce appellari voluisti, tu nunc nostrae confessionis laudationem acceptare, et hos palmarum ac florum ramos benedicere et sanctificare digneris, ut quicumque in tuae servitutis obsequio exinde aliquid tulerit, caelesti benedictione sanctificatus, peccatorum remissionem et vitae aeterne premia percipere mereatur.[23]

The blessings, addressed to God, often invoke Christ's incarnation, his willing procession to his own Passion, and the response of the crowd, specifically their song, and then beseech God to bless the palms so that, like the original crowd, the petitioners may participate in these events. For the contemporary celebrants, as this blessing makes clear, being part of the crowd is a means to remission of sin and entry into heaven (the Resurrection is occasionally invoked here), grounding the Palm Sunday rituals both in Lent and in the events of Easter weekend. Some blessings extend the significance of the palm-branches, and several invoke the olive twig carried to Noah in the ark by a dove as an announcement of the restoration of peace to humanity.[24] The first benediction for the palms in the Lanalet

---

[23] Woolley, *The Canterbury Benedictional*, p. 24. "Almighty God, king of the world, creator and redeemer, you who deigned to descend from the summit of the arch of heaven for our liberation and salvation by grace, to assume carnality, and to undergo the passion, the same who by your own will, drawing near to the place of the passion, were willing to be blessed by the crowd that had come to meet you on the way with palm branches, to be praised, and, approaching, to be called in a clear voice King, Blessed in the name of the Lord, now accept the praise of our confession, and deign to bless and sanctify these branches of palms and flowers, so that whosoever in the submission of your service thence will have borne any such thing, with the holy blessing from heaven he may merit to obtain remission of sins and the gift of eternal life."

[24] The olive twig figures to a surprising degree in the Palm Sunday forms, and some blessings, including that quoted above from the Winchcombe Sacramentary, list olive branches among

Pontifical cleverly works Matthew's gospel account of the entry into a prayer, attributing the song of the Jews in Matthew to the original crowd and the song in John to the contemporary petitioners while making the connection between the two groups:

> Omnipotens sempiterne deus, qui de caelis ad terram descendere dignatus es, et ad passionem voluntatis tuae venire voluisti, ut humanum genus per tuum sanguinem liberares, qui in monte oliveti misisti discipulos tuos, et praecepisti tibi asinam et pullum cum ea adducere, quia tu, deus, dignatus es super eam ascendere, et pueri Hebrorum cum ramis palmarum in occursum tibi venerunt, te laudantes et dicentes, *Osanna fili David, benedictus qui venit in nomine domini rex Israhel, osanna in excelsis*; qui Noe in arca super undas diluvii gubernasti, et ipse ex ea columbam dimisit, ut prospiceret mundum, et revertus ipsa ad eum in ore suo ramum olivae proferebat . . . proinde rogamus te, omnipotens deus, ut benedicas hos ramos quos tui famuli in suis manibus sunt suscepturi, venientes in occursum tuum, te benedicentes, et dicentes, *Benedictus qui venit in nomine domini, rex Israhel.*[25]

Many blessings give recognition to the temporal juxtaposition of the original crowd and the reenacting processors. The song of the crowd is, for the reenactors, a song of confession, and participation in the festival will allow them to run to meet Christ in the heavenly Jerusalem. This eschatological overtone is repeated throughout these forms.

The final blessing given by the Canterbury Benedictional, the *Praephatio in consecratione palmarum*, explains the cutting of branches and the strewing of cloaks as a declaration of triumph over death, which segues well into the following antiphons prescribed universally for the distribution of the palms:

> *Ant.* Pueri ebreorum tollentes ramos olivarum obviaverunt domino, clamantes et dicentes, "Osanna in excelsis."
> *Ant.* Pueri ebreorum vestimenta prosternebant in via et clamabant, dicentes, "Osanna filio David, benedictus qui venit in nomine domini."[26]

those potentially being blessed. In addition, a key antiphon for the distribution of the palm, the first of the *Pueri ebreorum* antiphons below, has the sons of the Hebrews at the original entry carrying "ramos olivarum." Perhaps the frequent references to olive branches points to the influence of liturgical forms, such as that represented in the Bobbio Missal, from an area in which olive trees are somewhat more common than they are in England.

[25] Doble, *Pontificale lanaletense*, pp. 73–4. "Almighty everlasting God, you who from the sky deigned to descend to the earth, and desired to approach the passion by your own will, so that you might free mankind with your blood, you who sent your disciples to the mount of olives, and instructed them to bring back to you the ass and her foal with her, because you, God, deigned to sit atop her, and the sons of the Hebrews came to you on the way, praising you and saying, *Hosannah to the son of David, blessed is he who comes in the name of the Lord, king of Israel, Hosannah in the highest*, you who steered Noah in the ark over the surgings of the flood, and this same one [Noah] sent from himself a dove, so that it might survey the world, and this same one returning to him carried in its mouth an olive branch . . . so, we beseech you, Almighty God, that you bless these branches which your servants have accepted in their hands, coming to meet you on the way, blessing you, and saying, *Blessed is he who comes in the name of the Lord, King of Israel.*"

[26] Woolley, *The Canterbury Benedictional*, p. 25. "The sons of the Hebrews, carrying olive branches, came to meet the Lord, crying out and saying, 'Hosannah in the highest.'/ The sons

Liturgical antiphons tend to be loosely based on the biblical texts, and often feature composite or interpretive readings. A set of antiphons for the beginning of the procession from the away church, the 'greater antiphons' mentioned by the *Concordia*, demonstrates the interpretive freedom of these antiphons:

> *Ant.* Ante sex dies sollempnis pascae, quando venit dominus in civitatem Hierusalem, occurrerunt ei pueri et in manibus portantes ramos palmarum et clamabant voce magna, dicentes, "Osanna in excelsis, benedictus qui venisti in multitudine misericordiae, osanna in excelsis."
>
> *Alia. Ant.* Cum audisset populus quia Hiesus venit Hierosolimam, acceperunt ramos palmarum et exierunt ei obviam et clamabant pueri, dicentes, "hic est salus nostra et redemptio Israhel; quantus est iste cui throni et dominationes occurrunt; noli timere, filia Sion, ecce, rex tuus venit tibi, sedens supra pullum asinae, sicut scriptum est; salve, rex, fabricator mundi, qui venisti redimere nos."
>
> *Alia. Ant.* Occurrunt turbae cum floribus et palmis redemptori obviam, et victori triumphanti digna dant obsequia; filium dei ore gentes praedicant, et in laudem christi voces sonant per nubila, "osannah."[27]

The third of these includes the flowers, not found in any of the gospel accounts, except for the Old Latin reading for John. Of particular interest here, however, is the role given the *pueri*. They are inserted into the loose gospel accounts in the first two antiphons (both based on John), and are the focal point of the distribution antiphons. Regularly throughout the forms for the day, there are *pueri* at the original entry carrying palm twigs and singing *Hosanna* to Christ. None of the gospel accounts, however, make any mention of children here. Matthew mentions children singing praises in the temple, but only after the entry and the scourging of the money-changers by Christ, and there is no biblical reason for connecting these children with the entrance through the gates into the city. Liturgically, the *pueri* are used to represent those in the city who sing to those approaching with Christ, and their prominence in the liturgical forms allows them to be retrofitted into accounts of the original entry.[28] The Blickling homilist does so, in a reinvented gospel account that greatly

---

of the Hebrews spread out their cloaks on the way and cried out, saying, 'Hosannah to the son of God, blessed is he who comes in the name of the Lord.'"

[27] Ibid., pp. 25–6. "Six days before the Passover, when the Lord came into the city of Jerusalem, the children came together carrying in their hands palm branches and they cried out in a loud voice, saying, 'Hosannah in the highest, blessed is he who has come with mercy to the people, Hosannah in the highest.'/ When the people heard that Jesus was coming to Jerusalem, they took up palm branches and went to meet him on the way and the children cried out, saying, 'This is our salvation and the redemption of Israel; how great is the one for whom thrones and dominions come together; do not be afraid, daughter of Zion, lo, your king comes to you, sitting on the foal of a donkey, just as is written; hail, king, maker of the world, who came to redeem us.'/ The crowds come together with flowers and palms on the way of the redeemer, and give worthy service to the triumphant victor; the people proclaim with their mouths the son of God, and voices sing about the glory of Christ through the clouds, 'Hosannah.'"

[28] The role of the *pueri* in regards to the entrance into the city/church is specified in the *Concordia*, in CB, and in MS Additional 28188.

reflects this liturgical emphasis and illustrates the interrelationship between liturgical forms and vernacular preaching. In Matthew, after the entry and the scourging of the temple, Christ reminds the pharisees of the prophecy that he would be praised by children. The entry itself has no children, but rather features a dialogue between those in the city and those in the crowd (Matthew 21:10–11):

> When he entered Jerusalem, the whole city was in turmoil, asking, "Who is this?" The crowds were saying, "This is the prophet Jesus from Nazareth in Galilee."

In the Blickling homilist's rendering of the entry, the mention of the children is shifted to the entry itself, proclaimed in this rather ritualistic dialogue:

> Mid þy þe Hælend þa eode on þa ceastre, eal seo burh wæs onstyred, 7 þa ceasterware cegdon 7 cwædon, "Hwæt is þes mihtiga þe her þus mærlice fereþ?" þæt folc him ondswarode 7 cwæþ, "Hit is se Nadzarenisca witga of Galileum, se sceal beon gehered ofor ealle þeoda, 7 geweorþod ge of cilda muþe meolcsucendra."[29]

More important than a realistic account of the actual entry are the symbolic functions of the meeting between the crowd and the citizens of the city, through which the city becomes infected with the crowd's enthusiasm, and of the praising children. Praising children, at times carrying palms, are common elements in descriptions of heaven, and their symbolic use in this sort of ritual has overtones of divine victory, making the home church at the point of entry both the historical Jerusalem and the Heavenly Jerusalem that the church prefigures. Those who developed the liturgical forms, at the expense of accuracy, have transformed a later, almost off-hand reference by Christ to the praising children into a powerful symbol of Christ's victory upon entering Jerusalem, made present in the liturgical entry into the home church.

The ritual importance of the dialogue between those in the city and those following Christ is established in the liturgical instruction that *pueri* be sent ahead of the procession to the gates of the home church, representing Jerusalem. The children were to wait within the closed gates until the procession had come together on the other side and sing an exchange with those outside, reflecting Matthew's account of the splitting of the crowd into those who went before and those who went behind (Matthew 21:8–9a):

> A very large crowd spread their cloaks on the road, and others cut branches from the trees and spread them on the road. The crowds that went ahead of them and that followed were shouting, "Hosannah . . ."

In his First Series sermon, Ælfric makes much of this split crowd, explaining those who went before as the patriarchs and prophets who

---

[29] Morris, *The Blickling Homilies*, p. 71. "When the Lord then rode towards the city, all of the city was stirred up, and the city-dwellers called out and said, 'What is this great one who here so gloriously approaches?' The folk answered them and said, 'It is the Nazarene prophet from Galilee, who shall be proclaimed over all nations, and praised from the mouths of suckling children.'"

lived before Christ, and the crowd following as those who have inclined, and continue to, after his incarnation, all singing the same song. He seems to draw somewhat more focus to it in his rather free version of the gospel narrative, changing a subordinate clause ('The crowds that went ahead and that followed') into a coordinate ("7 eodon þa sume beforan, sume bæftan"[30]). Perhaps the liturgical importance of the splitting of the crowd, all singing together, has coloured his description of their actions, giving extra weight to what, for his audience, might be taken as liturgical instruction.

Robert Deshman notes that, for the Palm Sunday illustration in the Benedictional of Æthelwold (see plate 2), the following crowd are not, as was traditional in Palm Sunday illustration, the apostles, but are rather a body of palm-bearing townspeople (one of which is a woman). He argues that "these figures must be citizens, who seem to have displaced the apostles from their customary place . . . the apostles were simply omitted, the adult citizens before Christ were shifted into their place, and the youths spreading garments were moved back into the vacated space in the gate."[31] As such, this illustration too is focused on the split crowd, those who went before and those who follow behind, surrounding Christ at the gates of Jerusalem. In particular, it sets up an opposition between the adult crowd of townspeople behind and the youths before, with two youths in the city gates spreading garments, three in trees harvesting branches, and two in the city above the gates holding flowers out directly to Christ. This splitting of the crowd, symbolized by the sending forth of the *pueri* and dramatized in their exchange with the following crowd, the *Gloria laus et honor tibi*, is the climax of the Palm Sunday procession.

The *Gloria laus* was written by Theodulph, Bishop of Orléans (d. 821), but original verses have been composed for the Canterbury Benedictional. The *pueri* sing the refrain, at the beginning and again after each verse:

Gloria laus et honor tibi sit, rex, christe, redemptor,
    cui puerile decus prompsit "osanna" pium.
Cant. Quis rex hic equitat, cui gloria redditur ista,
    cui pueri cantant, cui sola cuncta boant. *Gloria.*
Ver. Hic rex, descendens caelorum culmine, venit
    atque suum proprium dixit ab arce decus. *Gloria.*
Ver. Videmus ante alios reges non talis honoris,
    cui pleps posternit tegmina cuncta sua. *Gloria.*
Ver. Debuerant ipsi mortis iam damna subire;
    hic, calcans mortem, sponte sua moritur. *Gloria.*
Ver. Cur igitur venit, querens per vulnera palmam;
    cum sibi semper sit gloria laus et honor. *Gloria.*
Ver. Mercari venit proprio de sanguine mundum,
    patris oves secum ducere in astra volens. *Gloria.*

---

[30] CH I.xiv, pp. 290–91.
[31] Deshman, *The Benedictional of Æthelwold*, pp. 77, 78.

Ver. Hicne est cui quondam nostri cecinere prophetae,
 laudem lactantes ore proferre pio? *Gloria.*
Ver. Hic rex est regum; nunc portas tollite vestras
 cumque introveniat dicite "osanna" sibi. *Gloria.*[32]

The song portrays Christ, descended from the heavens and about to trample death by submitting to it. The focus is on his worth to enter the city, and through the song we see something of a double Christ standing before the gates, the king worthy of more honour than any who has come before and the suffering Christ approaching his sacrifice. After the song has finished, the doors are asperged and opened and all go in singing in a high voice the entrance antiphon, *Ingrediente domino in sanctam ciuitatem hebreorum pueri resurrectionem uite pronuntiates cum ramis palmarum osanna clamabant in excelsis.* Although the reenactment of the Palm Sunday entry has nothing explicitly prescribed to represent Christ, the Canterbury version of the *Gloria laus* allows the participants to see him entering the city before them, praised by palm-waving children. The dramatic mixing of past and present here in the welcoming praise of the crowd and the expectation of the upcoming Passion casts the participants into the midst of the triumphal entry, or rather brings the triumphal entry to the contemporary celebrants, to such a degree that the liturgical forms actually reshape the narrative and homiletic portrayals of the biblical event. The very ritualistic elements that ruin its verisimilitude with the gospel account, such as the elaborated significance of the palm and the children's substitution for the citizens of the city, serve to juxtapose the processors with Christian history, so that the objective of those on the original Palm Sunday, to praise the victorious Christ, becomes theirs.

The final reading for the procession, after all have entered, brings these themes together, and reminds the processors of their spiritual reward:

Deus qui dispersa congregas, et congregata conservas, qui populis obviam Ihesu ramos portantibus benedixisti, benedic etiam hanc fidelium tuorum turbam, in honore tui nominis congregatam, ut omni infirmitatis valetudine effugata, tua ab omni incursu inimici protegatur dextera, et cum caelestium donorum palma glorietur victorifera.[33]

---

[32] Woolley, *The Canterbury Benedictional*, pp. 27–8. "Let there be glory, praise, and honour for you, King, Christ, Redeemer, to whom youthful grace brings forth a holy 'Hosannah.'/ Who is this king who rides, to whom such glory is given, to whom the children sing, to whom alone they all cry aloud, *Gloria.*/ This king, descending from the roof of the heavens, comes and his own glory has spoken from the heights, *Gloria.*/ We have not seen other kings of such glory, before whom the people have laid down their cloaks together, *Gloria.*/ They were obligated now to submit to the damnation of death; this one, trampling death, died of his own free will, *Gloria.*/ Wherefore he comes, protesting by means of the palm–wounds; with him always will be glory, praise, and honour, *Gloria.*/ He comes to buy the world with his own blood, desiring to lead the father's sheep with him into the skies, *Gloria.*/ Is this not the one about whom formerly our prophets foretold, inducing to bring forth praise with holy speech? *Gloria.*/ This is the king of kings; now lift up your gates when he would enter and say to him, 'Hosannah.' *Gloria.*" MS Additional 28188 gives the first, second, third, and last of these.

[33] Ibid. p. 28. "God, you who bring together the scattered, and preserve those who have come

The request that God bless the contemporary participants just as he did the palm-carrying people who met Jesus on the way highlights the union of biblical history and liturgical reenactment established in the procession. Their reward, thanks to the victorious palm, is the ability to glory in heavenly gifts. With the Passion reading from Matthew and the constant liturgical reminders of the upcoming Passion and Resurrection, the Palm Sunday celebrants are always looking beyond the fact of Christ entering the city to exactly where he is going six days later, and what it means for them. More than just participation in the events of Easter week, the celebrants look forward to the ultimate significance of those events, the opening of heaven to them, and many of the forms for the day end with this sort of eschatological focus. Participation in the events of Christ's life allows participation in his ultimate victory, and meriting the right to enter the Heavenly Jerusalem at the end of the world is the ultimate goal of the liturgy for Palm Sunday through Easter.

Granted the central place explicitly given the laity in the liturgy for Palm Sunday, the role of the vernacular preaching in explaining the meaning of the ritual for its participants is particularly important. The Latin antiphons and benedictions prescribed by Anglo-Saxon liturgical books imbue the elements of the ritual with a range of nuance, as when the blessed branches are connected to the olive twig given Noah, and surely the laity would have been at something of a disadvantage in taking in all of their liturgical richness. All the laity truly need to understand, however, to harvest spiritual edification from the day's liturgy is its core element, the same for Ælfric as for Amalarius, that they 'carry branches and cry *Hosanna*.' Its purpose is to unite the processors with the original crowd at the entry, and the rest of the liturgy is in one way or another a development of this association. The power of the palm-twig to make present the divine power of Christ, the splitting of the crowd and their dialogue at the city gates, and the expectation of entry into the Heavenly Jerusalem are all explained and developed in the vernacular preaching specifically in terms of the intended juxtaposition of the processors and the biblical crowd.

Whether or not the Palm Sunday procession was firmly established in Anglo-Saxon England, the divine mystique of the palm itself surely was, and figures largely in discussions of the liturgy and in hagiography. The Blickling Palm Sunday sermon demonstrates the ritualistic importance of the palm-twig. The palm is, of course, primarily a symbol of victory. The Blickling homilist explains:

together, you who blessed the branches carried by the people on Jesus' way, bless now this crowd of your faithful ones, come together in honour of your name, so that the one who has escaped from the illness of all infirmities may be protected by your right hand from every attack of the enemy, and may glory with the victorious palm of heavenly gifts."

þa bæron hie him togeanes blowende palmtwigu; forþon þe hit wæs Iudisc þeaw, þonne heora ciningas hæfdon sige geworht on heora feondum, 7 hie wæron eft ham hweorfende, þonne eodan hie him togeanes mid blowendum palmtwigum, heora siges to wyorþmyndum.[34]

The victory, in this case, is Christ's victory over death in the raising of Lazarus which, as the Gospel of John indicates, drew the people to the event. The Blickling homilist then extends the significance forward to Christ's victory over death by means of his own death and his Harrowing of Hell, paving the way for the use of the palm-twig in the *Concordia*'s *Visitatio* ceremony (held by the 'angel' at the tomb). It is the raising of Lazarus that begins the miracles of Holy Week, culminating in the Crucifixion and Resurrection. The palm-twig symbolizes both of these events.

Other uses of the palm-twig in vernacular homilies extend its significance. Ælfric's homily on the Innocents, the infants slaughtered by Herod, describes them as "þa ða Criste folgiað on hwitum gyrlum swa hwider swa he gæð, 7 hi standað ætforan his þrymsetle buton ælcere gewemmednysse, hæbbende heora palmtwigu on handa 7 singað ðone niwan lofsang þam ælmihtigum to wurðmynte."[35] The palm-twig is a commonplace in descriptions of the victorious faithful in heaven, and it is hard to find an assumption narrative that does not feature them. Their common appearance in heaven imbues their appearances on earth with divinity, and at times they glow "swa se scinenda mergensteorra," or otherwise serve as a conduit for God's power. This mystique is connected to traditions that the Cross was made from a palm-tree, as reflected in the Old English Life of St. Machutus:

Nis nan mon þæt wite þæs treowes cynren, managa þeah wenaþ þæt hit of palmtrywa sy, 7 þæt treow for his mycelnesse mycle wafunge gegearwaþ, eallum þam þe hym to cumaþ.[36]

This mystical power accrued by the palm makes it something more than just a symbol of victory, and at times it takes a far more active role. One of the most compelling uses of the palm-twig is featured in the Blickling Assumption of the Virgin Mary. The story begins with the angel's presentation to Mary of the glowing palm-twig, which "wæs soþlice swiþe scinende palmtwig 7 hit wæs þa swa leoht swa se mergenlica steorra, þe heo þær onfeng of

---

[34] Morris, *The Blickling Homilies*, p. 67. "Then they carried flowering palm-twigs towards him, because it was a Jewish custom, when their kings had achieved victory against their enemies, and they were afterwards turned towards home, then they went towards him with flowering palm-twigs to commemorate their victory."

[35] CH I.v, p. 223. "Those who follow Christ in white robes wherever he goes, and they stand before his throne without any corruption, having their palm-twigs in hands and they sing a new song of praise to the Almighty to honour him."

[36] David Yerkes, ed. *The Old English Life of St. Machutus* (Toronto, 1984), p. 31. "No one knows the type of the tree, but many think that it is from a palm tree, and that tree for his greatness prepares a great spectacle, for all those who come to him."

þæs engles handa."[37] The palm-twig symbolizes Mary's victory in such a direct way that the belligerent Jew feels compelled to steal and desecrate it as a way to defeat Mary. Protected by God, it is then held aloft as the Jew processes around town, healing the blindness of the other Jews. The conflation of the palm-twig with Moses' healing serpent in the wilderness, which is itself a prefigure of the Cross, certainly colours the Palm Sunday ceremony and increases the power of the ceremony's ritualistic use of the palm. The divinity bestowed upon the palm (as upon the candle, the staff, and the Cross) serves as a ritualistic substitution for the presence of the divine Christ.

The power of the palm-twig is central to its ability to juxtapose the liturgical participants with the crowd at the entry. Both the Blickling homilist and Ælfric centre their sermons on this juxtaposition. As had Bede, the Blickling homilist describes those who went before Jesus as betokening "þæt Iudisce folc on þæm wæs se halga heap hehfædera 7 witgena, þa þe Cristes tocyme wiston 7 forsægdon, 7 þa wundro þe he worhte, 7 his þrowunga . . ." and the crowd that followed as "ealle þaþe seoþþan æfter Cristes cyme wæron to Gode gecyrrede."[38] He emphasizes that "Ealle hie cleopodan 7 cwædon anre stefne, 'Hælend, Davides sunu, þu eart gebletsod, þu þe come on Drihtnes naman, hæl us on þæm hehstan.'"[39] Then, in a mixing of past and present voices, the Blickling homilist explains the meaning of the songs for Palm Sunday, relating them to what was originally said, and relating singers now to the singers at the triumphal entry. Noting that those who went before had sung "Hæl us on þæm hehstan" and had been saved through his Passion and Resurrection, he makes clear how his audience should relate to the Palm Sunday narrative, highlighting the importance of this mindset with an invocation of the Last Judgement:

> We þonne synt þe þær æfter fylgeaþ; 7 we witon eall þis þus geworden, forðon we sceolan on hine gelyfan, 7 hine gelufian, 7 we eac witon þæt he is toweard to demenne, 7 þas world to geendene. Nu we habbaþ mycele nedþearfe þæt he us gearwe finde. We witon ful geare þæt we sceolan on þisse sceortan tide geearnian ece ræste, þonne motan we in þære engellican blisse gefeon mid urum Drihtne . . .[40]

---

[37] Morris, *The Blickling Homilies*, p. 137. "Truly, the palm-twig was shining brightly and it was then as light as the morning star, what she received there from the angel's hands."

[38] Morris, *The Blickling Homilies*, p. 81. "The Jewish folk in whom was the holy company of patriarchs and prophets, those who knew and prophesied about Christ's coming, and the wonders that he wrought, and his suffering . . . all those who after Christ's coming were turned to God." Liturgically, the ultimate purpose of the split crowd is that it allows for the dialogue between those in the city and those following Christ. The Blickling homilist, while recasting the account of this dialogue from Matthew to include the *pueri*, has changed the question of the city-dwellers from a simple "Who is this?" to "Hwæt is þes mihtiga þe her þus mærlice fereþ?" a question that seems more consonant with the sorts of replies given in the versicles of the *Gloria laus et honor tibi* than with the biblical response.

[39] Ibid. "They all cried out and spoke with one voice, 'Lord, son of David, you are blessed, you who came in the Lord's name, save us in the highest.'"

[40] Ibid. pp. 81, 83. "We then are those who follow after, and we know all this which has thus

The power of Christ's entry into Jerusalem for 'those who went ahead' was that those who welcomed Christ into the city, crying out for salvation, were indeed saved that next weekend through Christ's Passion and Resurrection. The Blickling homilist makes clear that his audience should on Palm Sunday partake of that original power by considering themselves part of that crowd, singing the same song and expecting imminent salvation in the events of the upcoming week. The time is short, and joining this Palm Sunday crowd has direct bearing on one's place in heaven. The participants in the festival's events are encouraged to cry, with the voices of the crowd, for salvation to the entering Christ, and expect to see the fruits of it soon. This is the heart of the liturgical forms, and it is made accessible to the audience of the Blickling homilist by his development of the link between the biblical figures who went ahead and the contemporary faithful who follow behind. While we do not know the exact makeup of the Palm Sunday liturgy at the time of the composition of this homily, the Blickling homilist's response to the festival indicates that appreciation of the use of identification with the original crowd to encourage a sympathetic relationship with the events of the day, for the sake of contemporary edification, was already at work in England by the time of the *Concordia*.

Ælfric, in his First Series sermon for the day, discusses the ceremony more directly and describes this association explicitly as liturgical instruction:

> se gewuna stent on Godes cyrican þurh lareowum geset þæt gehwær on Godes gelaþunge se sacerd bletsian scule palmtwigu on ðisum dæge, 7 hi, swa gebletsode, þam folce dælan, 7 sceolon þa Godes þeowas singan þone lofsang þe ðæt Iudeisce folc sang togeanes Criste þa ða he genealæhte his þrowungæ. We geefenlæcað þam geleaffullum of ðam folce mid þysre dæde, for ðan þe hi bæron palmtwigu mid lofsange togeanes þam hælende. Nu sceole we healdan urne palm oð þæt se sangere onginne þone offringsang, 7 geoffrian þonne Gode þone palm, for ðære getacnunge. Palm getacnað sige. Sigefæst wæs Crist þa ða he ðone miclan deoful oferwan 7 us generode; and we sceolon beon eac sigefæste þurh Godes mihte, swa þæt we ure unþeawas 7 ealle leahtras 7 þone deoful oferwinnan 7 us mid godum weorcum geglengan, 7 on ende ures lifes betæcan Gode þone palm þæt is ure sige.[41]

happened, because of which we must believe in him, and love him, and we also know that he is coming as a judge, and to put an end to this world. Now we have great need that he find us ready. We know certainly that we must merit in this short time eternal rest, when we may rejoice in angelic bliss with our Lord."

[41] CH I.xiv, p. 297. "The custom stands in God's church, established through wise teachers, that everywhere in God's church the priest shall bless palm-twigs on this day, and distribute them, so blessed, to the folk, and God's servants shall sing the song of praise that the Jewish folk sang to Christ when he drew near to his Passion. We imitate the faithful of that folk with this deed, because they bore palm-twigs with praise-singing to the Lord. Now we must hold our palm until the singer begins the offering song, and then offer the palm to God, because of its signification. The palm betokens victory. Christ was victorious when he conquered the fearsome devil and rescued us; and we must also be victorious through God's might, so that we conquer our wicked deeds and all sins and the devil, and adorn ourselves with good works, and at the end of our life deliver to God the palm which is our victory."

Again, the liturgical participants are to think of themselves as one with those following behind Christ, carrying palms as totems of victory over the devil and singing *Hosanna*. Ælfric's exegetical description of the split crowd, however, is more complex, as was Bede's, whom he is following. As do the biblical texts and illustrations of the event like that in the Benedictional of Æthelwold, Ælfric presents four groups of people surrounding Christ at the entry. Those who cast garments under the feet of the ass represent the martyrs trampled for the faith. Those who hewed branches to prepare Christ's way are "þa lareowas on Godes cyrcan, þe plucciað þa cwydas þæra apostola, 7 heora æftergengena."[42] Those who went before are "þa heahfæderas 7 þa witegan" before Christ's incarnation, and those behind are "þa ðe æfter Cristes acennednysse to him gebugon, 7 dæghwomlice bugað,"[43] all singing one song. This partition might be problematic if one were to consider those who hewed branches as the same people who carried them at the entry, as seems to be the case in the gospel accounts. It could be confusing to Ælfric's audience, presumably not made up predominantly of teachers, to be told that they are to go out and hew branches as teachers. Indeed, this partition points to a more interesting problem in unifying the liturgy with the biblical accounts, and the gospel accounts with each other. Nowhere in the gospels do we get any indication that the people waved palm branches over their heads as they accompanied Christ into the city. Matthew and Mark say that branches were spread on the road, not held aloft. John is the only evangelist to mention palms at all, and he makes no mention of what was done with them. One could easily imagine, given the syntax of John's account, that the branches were taken up and carried aloft to meet Christ, but it seems more natural, when taking the gospel accounts together, to assume that they would have been spread on the road, unless we are to assume that the branches in Matthew and Mark are distinct from the palms carried in John, and that each gospel simply leaves the other type of foliage out of the account. For whatever reason, possibly because the divinity bestowed upon the palm encourages processors to hold it as an honoured totem, as they would the Cross, the candle, and the gospel books, the liturgical forms, described and enforced by vernacular treatments, demand that the palms be held aloft. As such, treatment of the branches in witnesses surrounding the liturgy has settled into something of a fractured account of these branches. In Ælfric's account, both in his gospel rendering and in his exegesis, he discusses the branches hewn and thrown on the way as "treowa bogas," not as palms, such that the palms carried by those following Christ are distinct. The illustration of the entry in the Benedictional of Æthelwold depicts the four groups described by Ælfric

---

[42] CH I.xiv, p. 294. "The teachers in God's church, who pluck the sayings of the apostles, and their followers."

[43] Ibid. p. 295. "The patriarchs and the prophets . . . those who after Christ's birth submitted to him, and daily submit."

surrounding Christ. Behind Christ are the only adults in the picture, holding aloft palms and following him into the city. Before him is one group of youths (signified by their shorter tunics), casting down a cloak under the feet of the ass.[44] In the city, above the gate, are two youths holding out flowers towards Christ. Above are three youths harvesting branches that are quite distinct from the palms held by the following adults. The importance of this sort of illustration is typological. As such, the youths may be harvesting one type of branches, signifying the harvesting of Christian teaching, while another group (the adults) holds palms of victory behind Christ. There is no relationship between the two groups, and this is only a problem if one is overly concerned with a highly accurate accounting of the gospel story, in illumination or in the liturgy. In his rendering of the gospel account and in his exegesis, Ælfric has separated them, as the liturgy demands. Just as the only adults in the entry illumination are those carrying palms behind Christ, so the only liturgical role prescribed by Ælfric for his audience is that of the following crowd. It is not unusual, both in illumination and in the liturgy, to have *pueri* stand for roles supporting those established for the bulk of the liturgical participants, as they do for those who have gone ahead of Christ and for the harvesters. In the liturgical forms, the harvesters have no specified role. Those processing to the away church are going to collect branches that are clearly meant to represent the palms, but there is no sense that they are going to 'harvest' them. Nowhere in the liturgical witnesses do we get any indication of just how the palms get to the altar of the away church.[45] As with the candles on Candlemas, it doesn't seem to be important. They have no real significance until the blessing of the palms, with which the liturgical forms for the procession begin. As such, one can imagine them previously harvested by the teachers of the church and prepared on the altar, although the harvesting of the branches has no place in the liturgy any more than the casting of the cloaks. What is pertinent in all of these witnesses, and what is emphasized in all of them, is the following crowd, and Ælfric makes abundantly clear that this is what his audience must join to reap the rewards of the Resurrection.

Participating in the events of Christ's life allows participation in his victory, and Ælfric in his instructions for Palm Sunday, illustrating the liturgical resonance between the original entry, the commemoration, and entry into the Heavenly Jerusalem, urges his flock to 'at the end of our life deliver the palm to God, that is, our victory.' He ends his sermon describing how, at the End,

---

[44] As Deshman, *The Benedictional of Æthelwold*, pp. 77ff, points out, the donkey, while walking on the cloak, seems to be higher than those before or after him, as if it were stepping onto a bridge between him and the city gate. Ælfric, in his rendering of Matthew's account of the entry, has added the fact that those casting cloaks "under þæs assan fet . . . bricgodon þam hælende" ("under the the feet of the ass . . . made a bridge for the Lord") (CH I.xiv, p. 290).

[45] The opening rubric for the *ordo* in Additional 28188 indicates that the branches had been gathered together at the away church beforehand, referring to the church "ubi palmarum et arborum rami ad consecrandum sunt collocati" (fol. 89v).

the faithful will arise, and "scinað þa rihtwisan, swa swa sunne, on heora fæder rice."[46] This eschatological focus is even more elaborate in the Blickling homily for Palm Sunday. One of the most striking characteristics of the Blickling Lenten homilies is their emphasis on the Last Judgement. If, as was claimed in the Blickling sermon for the first Sunday of Lent, the forty days of Lent are to be seen as representative of the world, it is natural to see Good Friday or Easter as its end. Consequently, as we have seen in homiletic treatments of Palm Sunday, the events of Easter weekend tend to become conflated with those of the Last Judgement. The author of the Blickling homily for the First Sunday in Lent claims that the day of Judgement will come at the time that Christ was hanging on the Cross.[47] A Vercelli homily (Scragg II) reflects this idea; "on þam dæge bið dryhtnes rod blode flowende betweox wolcnum, 7 in þam dæge bið dryhtnes onsyn swiðe egeslicu 7 ondryslicu 7 on þam hiwe þe he wæs þa hine Iudeas swungon 7 ahengon 7 hiora spatlum him on spiwon."[48] Others apparently felt that the End would come at Easter Vigils, symbolically the time of the Resurrection. While Ælfric and others would surely have objected to such a prognostication, the compelling connection between the Second Coming and the Crucifixion and Resurrection intensifies the rituals of the season. If the participants expect that their relationship to these ceremonies could determine their place in a Judgement that is waiting at the dramatic pinnacle towards which these ceremonies are pointing, they will certainly be more predisposed to experience them fully. In this vein, the author of the Blickling Palm Sunday sermon includes a discussion of the destruction of Jerusalem, forty years after Christ's death. Marcia Dalbey discusses his use of this image:

> . . . with many doublets and parallel structures, the homilist develops his description in an almost epic style that heightens the sense of awe inspired by the physical appearance of the city and that underlines by contrast the terrible destruction to come. . . . The appeal is to the emotion rather than to the intellect.[49]

The congregation are reminded of the consequences of failing to repent during their forty-day period. They are then given the contrasting positive example of those who followed Christ at the triumphal entry. Dalbey calls this contrast "the typical pattern of Anglo-Saxon exhortation in which a description of hell precedes a final view of the joys of heaven." The dual tone established in this homily prepares the participants for the contrasting moods of sorrow and exultation that the ceremonies of Holy Week will engender and ensures that they are in the correct frame of mind to relate

---

[46] CH I.xiv, p. 298. "The righteous will shine, just as the sun, in their father's kingdom."

[47] Morris, *The Blickling Homilies*, p. 26.

[48] Scragg, *The Vercelli Homilies*, p. 54. "On that day the Lord's Cross will be flowing with blood among the clouds, and on that day the image of the Lord will be very awful and terrible and in the appearance that he was in when the Jews beat him and hung him and spewed him with spittle."

[49] Marcia Dalbey, "Themes and Techniques in the Blickling Lenten Homilies," in *The Old English Homily and its Backgrounds*, ed. Szarmach and Huppé (Albany, 1978), p. 230.

personally to the upcoming commemorated events, looking forward in particular to their place in heaven, the road to which is at the heart of the Holy Season liturgy. This road is embarked upon by joining Christ's entry into Jerusalem, reenacting the exultation of the following crowd as Christ approaches his Passion.

6

Holy Week and Easter

THROUGHOUT the Temporale liturgy has developed a growing expec-
tation of the events of the Passion. After the first Passion reading on
Palm Sunday, this anticipation has captured the full attention of the church.
Passiontide begins a week earlier, actually, on Passion Sunday, which
Ælfric introduces in his Second Series homily for the day:

> þeos tid fram ðisum andwerdan dæge oð ða halgan eastertide is gecweden Cristes
> ðrowungtid, and ealle Godes ðeowas on ðære halgan gelaðunge mid heora
> circlicum ðenungum wurðiað, and on gemynde healdað his ðrowunge, þurh ða
> we ealle alysede wurdon.[1]

The remembrance of Christ's Passion and Resurrection is the centre of
liturgical commemoration, celebrated in apostolic times with a single all-
night vigil and eventually extended by weeks before and after, and the rest
of the Temporale festivals focus on it, and on its eschatological expectations. As such, it is not surprising to find that the liturgy for Easter
weekend both retains some of the oldest practices of the church (as
described by Baumstark's Law of Organic Development[2]) and attracts
some of its most exciting accretions. The point of the commemoration has
always been to unite the celebrants with the saving events of Christ's
Passion and Resurrection, and the method used by the church throughout
the year for effecting this unity abounds here. At the beginning of Holy
Week, the faithful have been thoroughly integrated with the crowd at the
Entry. From Christmas through Lent, the associations established in the
liturgy have been quite specific, generally chosen to correspond with
particular characters in the gospel narratives. For Holy Week, we see,
alongside specific associations with the prisoners in Hell and the women at
the tomb, a return to the general association, developed in expectation of
Christmas in much the same way, whereby the faithful are the people of
God, at one with those actually before the Cross and explicitly extended,
in the *orationes sollemnes*, to all of Christendom, waiting in the terror of
sin-inspired darkness for the light of Christ on Easter morning. The

---

[1] CH II.xiii, p. 127. "This time from this present day until the holy Eastertide is called Christ's
Passiontide, and all of the servants of God in the holy church celebrate with their churchly
services, and keep in mind his suffering, through which we all were set free."
[2] Baumstark, *Comparative Liturgy*, p. 23.

liturgical exercises, concerned primarily with light and darkness, cultivate mood as well as narrative, reaching a climax on Good Friday with the *Adoratio* and another on Saturday evening with Easter Vigils before the joyful denouement of Eastertide, following the witnessing of the proof of the Resurrection.

The late Anglo-Saxon church was quite interested in the dramatic reenactment of the events of this holiest of times. Although there was certainly something new at work in the ninth and tenth centuries in England and France, where many of these dramatic elaborations of the liturgy developed, they represent not so much the 'growth of drama' as dramatic expressions of already present liturgical and narrative dynamics, using liturgical language and modes of expression to unify the faithful with Christian history. In this chapter, I will discuss the more dramatic liturgical or extra-liturgical rituals, placing them not in the context of the history of Western drama but in the liturgical and devotional setting from which they were never divorced. Together the light-based reflection of Christ's Passion (given currency most prominently in *Tenebrae*, the *Adoratio*, and Easter Vigils and reflected powerfully in accounts of Christ's Harrowing of Hell) and the *Visitatio*, connecting the participants with the women at the tomb, allow the faithful to appreciate first-hand the fact and the significance of Christ's death and resurrection.

MAUNDY THURSDAY

Formal preparation for the Passion begins with the Passion reading from Matthew on Palm Sunday, followed during the week (on Tuesday[3] and Wednesday) by Passions from Mark and Luke. The liturgical forms for the days preceding the *triduum* of Maundy Thursday, 'Long' Friday, and Holy Saturday are general, reiterating the fact of the Passion and its significance. The commemoration begins in earnest, however, on Thursday, with a particularly rich series of events, including the Reconciliation of Penitents, discussed above. In his Second Letter for Wulfstan, Ælfric outlines its major elements (except for the Reconciliation). In the morning are the washing and stripping of the altars:

> On þunres-dæg ge sculan aþwean eower weofodu, ær-þan-ðe ge mæssian . . . And æfter æfensange ge sculon unscrydan þa weofodu, and standan hi swa nacode oþ þone sæternes-dæg.[4]

---

[3] In the time of Leo the Great, the Mark Passion was read on Easter Sunday, but was later moved to the preceding Tuesday. (See Jungmann, *The Mass of the Roman Rite*, p. 261.)

[4] Fehr, *Die Hirtenbriefe Ælfrics*, p. 156. "On Thursday you must wash your altars before you go to mass . . . And after evensong you must strip the altars, and let them stand so unadorned until Saturday."

According to the *Concordia*, the pavement of the church is likewise scrubbed by unshod brethren.[5] This presumably applies to churches where unshod brethren might be about, and the *Concordia* makes explicit distinction between the brethren who wash the floors and the priests and ministers who wash the altars.[6] The key point, stressed in the *Concordia*, in Corpus 190, and in Ælfric's Letter, is that the Maundy Mass must not be held until after the altars have been washed.

Mass is held after Sext, and includes the Maundy, the washing of feet following Christ's example given at the institution of the first Communion. According to the *Concordia*, a group of needy folk will have been gathered together and prepared at the direction of the abbot.[7] Appropriate antiphons are sung[8] and the feet are washed, dried, and kissed. The poor are offered water for their hands, fed, and given money at the abbot's discretion. Ælfric also gives directions for the Maundy in his letter for Wulfstan. The description is more general, with nothing to specify a monastic context (although many of the directions for the rest of Holy Weekend do mention the brethren):

> Doþ on þam þunres-dæge, swa-swa ure drihten bebead. Aþweað þearfena fet and him fodan doð; scrud, gif eow to on-hagige. And eac eow betwynan eowre fet aþweað mid eadmodnysse, swa-swa Crist sylf dyde and us swa don het.[9]

The *Concordia* here describes only the washing and feeding of the poor, then goes onto None, the Blessing of the New Fire, the consecration of the chrism (only in passing, in conceding that the *Dominus vobiscum* will be said by the consecrating bishop), and the following Mass. Only after Vespers does the abbot, with his select group, carry out his own Maundy.[10] This ceremony (not reflected in Ælfric's Letter for Wulfstan but referred to in his Letter to the Monks of Eynsham[11]) is remarkably elaborate, featuring special garb, a procession, and a reading of John's account of the first Maundy. Besides the usual foot and hand washing, the abbot drinks to the health of each of the brethren. Symons claims that "this, the abbot's special Maundy, would seem to be peculiar to the *Concordia*."[12] The *Concordia* also prescribes a daily Maundy, assuming a stable of poor folk from whom three

[5] Kornexl, *Die Regularis concordia*, pp. 80–1; Symons, *Regularis concordia*, pp. 38–9.

[6] The same sentence, describing the split washing of the pavement and the altars, appears in the Corpus 190 manuscript (Fehr, *Die Hirtenbriefe Ælfrics*, p. 239). This passage specifies that the washing of the church occurs after Terce.

[7] Kornexl, *Die Regularis concordia*, p. 81; Symons, *Regularis concordia*, p. 39.

[8] Those prescribed by the Canterbury Benedictional explain the Maundy as a fulfilment of Christ's command to follow his example (Woolley, *The Canterbury Benedictional*, p. 43).

[9] Fehr, *Die Hirtenbriefe Ælfrics*, pp. 157–8. "Do on Thursday just as our Lord commanded. Wash the feet of the needy and give them food; clothe them, if it is possible for you. And also wash each others' feet with humility, just as Christ himself did and so commanded us to do."

[10] Kornexl, *Die Regularis concordia*, pp. 84–6; Symons, *Regularis concordia*, pp. 40–1.

[11] *LME*, p. 131.

[12] Symons, *Regularis concordia*, p. 40, n. 2.

might be chosen each day,[13] and perhaps the abbot's Maundy (along with the instruction to gather together many poor folk) is a means of making special and more personal the celebration of the Maundy on the actual day of its inception. In any event, the different accounts of the Maundy in the *Concordia* and in Ælfric may indicate something about the relationship between the monastic churches, through which the tenth-century regularization of the liturgy was effected, and other Christian communities to whom Ælfric, himself a monk but writing on behalf of an Archbishop, Wulfstan, was writing, which may or may not have had monks about.

In his vernacular writings, Ælfric mentions the consecration of the oils only briefly (though not as allusively as the *Concordia*), but he treats it much more fully than does the *Concordia* in his Eynsham Letter,[14] reflecting its true importance in the Anglo-Saxon liturgy. The *Consecratio Chrismatis* is one of the most sumptuously provided *ordines* in liturgical books. A full *ordo* is found in the Canterbury Benedictional. The interrelationship of extant *ordines* for the consecration of the oils is tricky, and a full accounting is outside the purview of this discussion.[15] Banting compares forms in the Lanalet Pontifical, in the Egbert Pontifical,[16] and in the Missal of Robert. Of particular interest, the Lanalet *ordo* seems to be of a kind more ancient than that even in the *Ordines Romani*, apparently reflecting the practice of seventh-century Rome (and may, indeed, descend from a direct importation from early Rome, retaining even mention of the Lateran).[17] The forms in the Canterbury Benedictional are distinct in another way. Generally, the oil is separated into three parts for different uses. The standard order of consecration is "oleum infirmorum, chrisma, oleum exorcizatum [for baptism]."[18] The Canterbury Benedictional reverses the last two, and displaces many of the forms from consecration of the baptismal oil to consecration of the 'true holy chrism,' which now attracts the bulk of the liturgical attention. Perhaps this shift reflects the diminished importance of Easter baptism.[19]

The most important rituals for the day, however, in terms of their relationship to the events of the weekend, are the *Tenebrae* and Blessing

---

[13] See Symons, *Regularis concordia*, p. xxxvii. As an indication of Oswald's piety, it is reported that he had a Lenten practice of giving the Maundy to twelve poor men daily. He passed away at the close of one such service, on the third Sunday in Lent 992 (p. xxvii).

[14] Jones speculates that Ælfric's inclusion here of an episcopal rite "probably reflects a scholarly interest in the rite itself and in the unusual exposition provided by his exemplar of the *Retractio prima* [of Amalarius]" (*LME*, p. 193, n. 196).

[15] For a thorough study of the types of chrism rites used in pre-Conquest England, and their relationships to continental sources, see Christopher A. Jones, "The Chrism Mass in Late Anglo-Saxon England." Jones describes peculiarities in the English rite, attributing special importance to the originality of the chrism mass in the Canterbury Benedictional.

[16] A text of c. 1000, possibly of West Country origin. On dating and provenance, see Banting, ed. *Two Anglo-Saxon Pontificals* (London, 1989), p. xxxvii, and Nelson and Pfaff, "Pontificals and Benedictionals," p. 90.

[17] See Banting, *Two Anglo-Saxon Pontificals*, p. xxvii.

[18] Woolley, *The Canterbury Benedictional*, p. 150.

[19] See below, "Baptism in Anglo-Saxon England."

of the New Fire ceremonies, some of the most dramatic rituals for Holy Week. The directions for *Tenebrae*, in particular, offer a wonderful glimpse at the Anglo-Saxon sense of just what it means to reenact a key biblical event through liturgical expression. The use of darkness and light in these rituals directly anticipates that in the upcoming Easter Vigils. It is through *Tenebrae* and the New Fire that many celebrants are prepared emotionally for the terror and joy of the Passion and Resurrection. The *Concordia*'s instructions for *Tenebrae* are peculiarly interesting, and give us a tantalizing glimpse into the philosophy and intentions of its compilers:

> Quinta feria, quae et cena Domini dicitur, nocturnale officium agatur secundum quod in antiphonario habetur. Comperimus etiam in quorundam religiosorum ecclesiis quiddam fieri, quod ad animarum conpunctionem spiritualis rei indicium exorsum est,[20] videlicet ut, peracto quicquid ad cantilenam illius noctis pertinet, evangeliique antiphona finita nichilque iam cereorum luminis remanente, sint duo ad hoc idem destinati pueri in dextera parte chori, qui sonora psallant voce *Kyrrieleison*, duoque in sinistra parte similiter, qui respondeant *Christe eleyson*, nec non et in occidentali parte duo qui dicant *Domine miserere nobis*; quibus peractis, respondeat simul omnis chorus: *Christus Dominus factus est obediens usque ad mortem*. Demum pueri dexterioris chori repetant quae supra, eodem modo quo supra, usquequo chorus finiat quae supra. Idemque tertio repetant eodem ordine. Quibus tertio finitis agant tacitas, genu flexo more solito preces. Qui ordo trium noctium uniformiter teneatur ab illis. Qui, ut reor, ecclesiasticae conpunctionis usus a catholicis ideo repertus est, ut tenebrarum terror, qui tripertitum mundum dominica passione timore perculit insolito, ac apostolicae praedicationis consolatio, quae universum mundum Christum Patri usque ad mortem pro generis humani salute oboedientem revelaverat, manifestissime designetur. Haec ergo inserenda censuimus, ut, si quibus devotionis gratia conplacuerint, habeant in his unde huius rei ignaros instruant. Qui autem noluerint, ad hoc agendum minime compellantur.[21]

---

[20] The Old English gloss for this line reads, "þæt to sawla onbryrdnysse gastlices ðincges beacn geswutelude ys" (Kornexl, *Die Regularis concordia*, p. 75).

[21] Kornexl, *Die Regularis concordia*, pp. 75–7; see also Symons, *Regularis concordia*, pp. 36–7. "On the fifth day, which is also called *Cena Domini*, the night Office shall be performed following what is set down in the Antiphonar. We have learned also that, in churches of certain religious people, a certain thing is done whereby, for the compunction of the soul, the outward presentation of a spiritual thing is arranged, specifically that when the singing for the night is completed, the antiphon of the gospel is finished, and no light from the candles remains, two children should be placed on the right hand side of the choir who shall sing *Kyrrieleison* with a loud voice; two more on the left hand side who shall respond *Christe eleison*; and, to the west of the choir, another two who shall say *Domine miserere nobis*; after which the whole choir shall respond together, *Christus Dominus factus est obediens usque ad mortem*. The children to the right of the choir shall then repeat the same thing once again in the same way. When this has been sung the third time the brethren shall say the preces on their knees and in silence, as is the custom. This same arrangement shall be observed by them in the same fashion for three nights. This manner of arousing religious compunction was, I think, devised by catholic men so that the terror of the darkness which struck the tripartite world with unusual fear, as well as the consolation of the apostolic preaching which revealed to the whole world Christ obedient to His Father even unto death for the salvation of the human race, may be signified most manifestly. Therefore it seemed good to us to insert these things so that, if they please any for the sake of devotion, they may find therein the means of instructing those who are ignorant of this matter. However, those who are not willing shall not in any way be compelled to follow this practice."

The extinguishing of the lights (the *Tenebrae* itself), occurring at the Night Office early on Thursday, Friday, and Saturday, is common, and is treated by Amalarius[22] and in *Ordo Romanus I*. Here, it is passed over, and attention is given, rather, to an elaboration that was apparently not universally favoured. The compilers of the *Concordia* used as their philosophy that shrewdly given Augustine by Gregory in the sixth century, to combine Roman usage with that which is best among local customs. For the tenth-century reformers, much of what the *Concordia* prescribes will have been imported from the continent, especially from Lotharingian and Cluniac centres. Perhaps the elaborations suggested here are of this category.[23] While familiarity with *Tenebrae* is assumed, this elaboration is something that the compilers have only heard about, "in quorundum religiosorum ecclesiis." The expression is used again in reference to the Deposition of the Cross, where it is suggested that some may want to follow "usum quorundam religiosorum,"[24] and in both instances, the descriptions of the rituals feel like new importations. Although Symons translates this phrase as "in churches of certain religious men," *religiosorum* could refer specifically to monastic houses (this usage is provided by Latham[25]), an expression that certainly might recall the experience of certain Anglo-Saxon reformers who spent time on the continent.[26] In any case, the attribution of the *Tenebrae* elaboration to "catholicis" gives it an aura of orthodoxy and authority.

It is strikingly unusual for the *Concordia* to feel the need to explain or apologize, as it has in both of these instances. The compilers state the intention of the ritual, to 'arouse compunction of soul.' Most uncharacteristically, they describe its effects, setting forth the terror that covered the whole world at the time of the Passion. The ritual certainly might be terrifying. Left in a darkened church, after a ritual that is to be understood as the extinguishing of the light of Christ, the celebrants, kneeling, hear, from three sides, cries to the Lord from pairs of clear, young voices, and then resounding from the entire chorus, in effect, "Christ is dead." This is done three times, after which the brethren remain on their knees, praying silently. Although the compilers of the *Concordia* suspected that some churches might find it objectionable, or perhaps too disturbing (and therefore do not force anyone to perform it), they felt it good to include it because of the way in which it so clearly set forth 'the terror of that darkness,' and they discuss its intention so that those participating in it can

---

[22] *De ordine antiphonarii*, PL, 105, 1293[b-c].

[23] Symons points out that the ritual for *Tenebrae* in the *Concordia* is related to that in Verdun custom. Symons, *Regularis concordia*, p. 36, n. 6, and "Regularis Concordia: History and Derivation," pp. 57–9.

[24] Kornexl, *Die Regularis concordia*, p. 94; Symons, *Regularis concordia*, p. 44.

[25] R. E. Latham, *Revised Medieval Latin Word-List* (London, 1989), p. 400.

[26] The Old English glossator has translated "religiosorum," in its two appearances, as "ægfæstra" and "æwfæstra" (Kornexl, *Die Regularis concordia*, pp. 75, 94).

be instructed as to its significance. Whether or not the practice was in use in England before the 970s, the fact that the central figures of the English church were so interested in practices that provided reenactments of biblical events, so that their celebrants could feel the terror felt by the disciples of the dead Christ on the Cross as darkness covered the earth, and understand by instruction just what is happening, reveals their sense of dramatic possibility in liturgical exercises. Ælfric at least liked it, as he includes it not as an option but as an integral part of the ritual in his Eynsham Letter.[27] The central theme of the ritual, the relationship between the death of Christ and darkness (and by extension between the resurrection of Christ and light) is one with which the Anglo-Saxon Christians were intimate, as seen clearly in their celebration of Easter Vigils and in both Latin and vernacular representations of the Harrowing of Hell. Their willingness to enhance the associations between the celebrants and those at the Cross demonstrates the strength, and the self-consciousness, of their use of dramatic association.

Although the *Concordia*'s *Tenebrae* elaboration may or may not have been established already in England, the *Tenebrae* itself, the ritual extinguishing of the lights, seems to have been quite general, and the *Concordia* passes it over as familiar, concerned only with what happens "when the singing for the night is over . . . and all of the lights put out." Ælfric, in his Second Letter for Wulfstan, describes the *Tenebrae* ritual that is the assumed core of the *Concordia*'s:

> *In cena domini et in parasceve et in sancto sabbato.* On þyssum þrym swige-nihtum ge sceolan singan ætgædere be fullan eowerne uhtsange, swa-swa se antifonere tæcð. And feower and twentig candela acwencan æt þam sealmum and æt ælcere rædingce oþ þone afte-mynsta antifon. And ge-endian þone æfter-sang swa, þæt ælc sing his pater noster on sundron and þa *preces* þærto butan ælcum leohte licgende on cneowum.[28]

It is between the extinguishing of the twenty-fourth candle and the *preces* that the *Concordia*'s elaborations would fit, and Ælfric ignores them here, instructing only the silent *pater noster*. This should not necessarily be seen as a rejection of the *Concordia*'s elaboration by Ælfric, for Ælfric's account is summary, and he seems to focus on those elements that he deems essential, whereas the extended *Tenebrae* and the Good Friday Deposition of the Cross (which he also ignores) are put forth in the *Concordia* as optional. It would be too much as well to argue that Ælfric ignores these elements (along with the *Visitatio Sepulchri*) in his letter for Wulfstan because they were purely for monastic observance, for the Deposition, as we shall see, had a definite role in lay celebration, and the innovations to

---

[27] *LME*, p. 127.
[28] Fehr, *Die Hirtenbriefe Ælfrics*, p. 154. "On these three silent nights you must sing together your matins entirely, just as the antiphonary instructs. And you should quench twenty-four candles at the psalms and at each reading until the last antiphon. And end the matins thusly, that each sing his *pater noster* separately and the *preces* thereto without any lights, remaining on knees."

Tenebrae highlight what was already there. What can be claimed is that the *Concordia*'s elaborations represent easily assimilated extensions to rituals whose themes and associations already had widespread currency in the Anglo-Saxon church.

As *Tenebrae* foreshadows the Passion, so the Blessing of the New Fire[29] foreshadows the Resurrection, as celebrated in Easter Vigils. Described as "ob archanum cuiusdam mysterii indicium," the 'brethren,' from the doors of the church, bear a staff "cum imagine serpentis." Warren believes that the use of the serpent in the New Fire ritual represents an Eastern influence, via the Irish.[30] Symons discusses parallels to the serpent staff.[31] The idea that much of the liturgy, particularly before the tenth-century reforms, was either of Irish origin or influenced by the Irish is probable. The Irish church had a particular interest in the use of light and darkness, and Duchesne connects the New Fire with sixth-century Irish accounts of great fires kindled at night on Easter Eve.[32] However, the New Fire, as with most of the central elements of Holy Week commemoration, was widespread by the tenth century.[33] In the *Concordia*, the fire is struck from flint (as were the Irish bonfires) in the mouth of the serpent, and a single candle is lit from it. This candle is then used to relight the other candles before *Tenebrae*. It is explicitly the New Fire that is used on Saturday to light the paschal candle at the Easter Vigil. The light in the mouth of the serpent, through which the lights are rekindled, therefore, holds the promise of Christ's resurrection.

The Anglo-Saxon instructions for *Tenebrae* and the New Fire reveal something about how those codifying the liturgy understood reenactment. It is a reenactment that requires all present to assume a role, as the compilers want the *Tenebrae* participants to feel the terror felt by those at the original death of Christ, while at the same time remembering the prophetic promise (also made clear in preaching for the week) that the Passion will inevitably lead to the Resurrection. The point could be made quite clearly (and often was) through simple instruction, explaining the meaning and promise of the lections and liturgical collects and prefaces for the time, but the compilers of the *Concordia* elaboration are looking to do something more, to make those watching the usual *Tenebrae* understand its

[29] See Kornexl, *Die Regularis concordia*, pp. 82–4; Symons, *Regularis concordia*, pp. 39–40. On the history and variety of the New Fire, see A. J. MacGregor, *Fire and Light in the Western Triduum: Their Use at Tenebrae and at the Paschal Vigil* (Minnesota, 1992).

[30] See Stevenson, *Worship*, p. 53.

[31] Symons, *Regularis concordia*, pp. 39ff. See also MacGregor, *Fire and Light*, pp. 259–66.

[32] Duchesne, *Christian Worship*, p. 250.

[33] Symons, "Regularis Concordia: History and Derivation," pp. 51–2, discusses the relationship between the *Concordia*'s instructions and those for Fleury. Lilli Gjerløw, *Adoratio Crucis* (Oslo, 1961), pp. 29ff, gives forms for the New Fire from fragments of an eighth-century English Missal, Mi I, and discusses the relationship of its central prayer with other English witnesses. As with *Tenebrae*, the New Fire was surely familiar in both England and on the continent in the tenth century, the ritual in the *Concordia* representing a fusion rather than an importation.

significance more directly by making them feel just what Christ's followers must have felt as darkness descended over the body of God on the Cross. Of course, we cannot possibly understand just what an Anglo-Saxon mind, monastic or lay, might actually have made of this pair of rituals, but we do know something about what their more learned spiritual leaders wanted them to make of it. Throughout the tenth-century Anglo-Saxon church, we can see a concerted and self-conscious effort, by means of elaborations and clarifications of the existing and familiar liturgical expressions, to bring their events and lessons to life by trying to make the faithful feel, for Easter, the terror of Christ's death and the joy in hearing the news of Christ's resurrection. The result is as aesthetically experiential as it is instructive. Because this reenactment is derived from the preexisting liturgy, the dynamic of temporal identification might be to some degree lost, as it must be to explore the Crucifixion in the early hours of Thursday morning. This is hardly a hindrance, however. It is a common character-istic of the liturgy that the commemoration of central Christian events casts forth ripples both before and after the central festival, so that the terror of the Crucifixion can be celebrated for days beforehand, and the joy of the Resurrection for days after. The dramatic elaborations of the liturgy were never attempts to represent historical events at historical times, but rather to make more directly experienced the yearly cycle of Christian history as developed over centuries in the liturgy. As such, *Tenebrae* is a reenactment of the Passion, and the *Visitatio* of the revelation of the Resurrection, in the same way that the Mass is a reenactment of Christ's self-sacrifice. There is little of 'representational' interest in the extended *Tenebrae* (in the dramatic sense posited by Young and Hardison), no 'costuming' or realistic stage-directions, but although the ceremony is thoroughly ritual-istic, its redactors expect the participants to feel that same 'terror' none-theless. There is no sense that the reenactment, in any of these cases, was in need of historical or representational accuracy, in part because the medieval conception of biblical history was itself largely formed by the liturgy, but mainly because the liturgical expressions were central to uniting the presence of Christ, and the glory of heaven, with the space and inhabitants of the church. In this liturgical context, the *Tenebrae* on Thursday, Friday, and Saturday mornings, in its reenactment of the darkness covering the world, is as 'dramatic' as the announcement of the angel to the women on Easter morning, as was the announcement of the birth to the shepherds at Christmas, the acceptance of Christ by Simeon at Candlemas, and the welcoming of Christ into the city/church on Palm Sunday.

GOOD FRIDAY: *ADORATIO CRUCIS*

Although temporal coincidence is certainly not necessary for reenactment, as we have seen in *Tenebrae*, and in the Eucharist almost every day, it is still a desideratum, and the Western liturgy generally demonstrates a tension between the desire to celebrate Christian events at the time of day when they might have happened and the practical need to, at times, rearrange (usually by anticipating earlier in the day) these commemorative Masses. The biblical Good Friday accounts, however, provide wonderful detail, and, as their readers knew exactly what happened at three of the liturgical hours, the liturgy takes advantage of the temporal opportunity. The collects for Terce, Sext, and None in the Leofric Collectar make reference to the events of each hour, and direct their prayers accordingly. Of particular interest is the collect for Sext, at the time when darkness fell over the earth:

> Domine Ihesu christe qui hora diei sexta pro redemptione mundi crucis ascendisti lignum, ut universus mundus qui in tenebras conversus est illuminaretur, illam nobis lucem in anima et corpore nostro semper tribue, per quam ad aeternam vitam pervenire mereamur.[34]

Ælfric describes the darkness at this time as an acknowledgment by the sun; "seo sunne oncneow þa ða heo wearð aþystrod on Cristes þrowunge, fram middæge oð non."[35] Already at the time of the darkness Christ is discussed as the light that soon will drive away that darkness. The two themes central to this collect, that Christ is a light to drive away the darkness and that this light emanates from the Cross, were quite native to the Anglo-Saxon liturgical audience, and the complex relationship between these themes and the reenactment of Christ's death on the Cross in the ancient *Adoratio Crucis* ceremony was explored in a variety of ways from at least the eighth century. The tenth-century liturgical forms provided by the *Concordia*, and reflected in Ælfric's Letter, present a reenactment of a different sort than that experienced at *Tenebrae*, whereby all of the faithful, both monks and common folk, confront the raised up, revealed, personified, and buried Christ on the Cross.

After *Tenebrae* at the night Office, according to the *Concordia*, the brethren approach at Prime barefoot 'until the Cross has been adored.' This instruction is reflected in Ælfric's Letter, "And ne beo hyra nan gesceod þæs dæges, butan he untrum sy, ær-þan-þe þis gefylled sy,"[36]

---

[34] Dewick and Frere, *The Leofric Collectar*, p. 131. "Lord Jesus Christ, you who on the sixth hour of the day mounted the wood of the Cross for the redemption of the world, so that the whole world which had dwelt in darkness would be illuminated, grant always this same light to us in spirit and in body, through which we may merit to come to eternal life."

[35] CH I.xv, p. 306. "The sun acknowledged when it became dark at Christ's Passion, from midday until None."

[36] Fehr, *Die Hirtenbriefe Ælfrics*, p. 168. "And no one should be wearing shoes on this day, unless he is ill, before this is fulfilled."

Plate 3. The Crucifixion, Dunstan Pontifical
Paris, Bib. nat. MS lat. 943, fol. 64v (by permission of the Bibliothèque nationale de France)

requiring that all those to whom Ælfric is speaking, presumably both monks and secular priests (unless they are somehow unhealthy), remain barefoot for the *Adoratio Crucis* and the Mass of the Pre-Sanctified. The *Adoratio*, "from which Western liturgical drama may take its origins,"[37] is the day's central event. It goes back at least to fourth-century Jerusalem and is described by Egeria. Developed in veneration of relics of the true Cross in Jerusalem (and a good deal later, by the early eighth century, in Rome), it spread throughout the church. Talley summarizes fourth-century accounts of Holy Week liturgy in Jerusalem, including the *Adoratio*.[38] From eight in the morning until noon, in the church of Golgotha, the wood of the Cross was venerated, followed by readings of the Passion narratives until three (or 'None,' the ninth hour), the time of Christ's death. The practice in some form was known throughout the church by the tenth century. Still, although the *Adoratio* is prescribed allusively in the Old Gelasian, no full *ordo* has survived from before the ninth. The prayers to the Cross that form part of the *ordines* in Anglo-Saxon witnesses are from the eighth and ninth centuries, and apparently stem from a variety of sources, including *Ordo Romanus I* (the primary source for the *Concordia*'s instructions)[39] and the devotional forms of the ninth-century section of the Book of Cerne, of apparent Mercian origin.[40] Symons lists the liturgical prayers for the Veneration of the Cross set forth in the *Concordia* as an example of a native custom preserved in the *Concordia*,[41] and Julia Bolton Holloway has attempted to demonstrate, with reference to the Ruthwell, Bewcastle, and Brussels crosses and the Old English *Dream of the Rood* that the practice of the *Adoratio* moved from Jerusalem to Britain (by way of the Irish) to the

---

[37] Holloway, "'The Dream of the Rood,'" p. 29.

[38] Talley, *The Origins of the Liturgical Year*, pp. 46ff.

[39] See Kornexl, *Die Regularis concordia*, pp. 87ff; Symons, *Regularis concordia*, pp. 41ff.

[40] Banting, *Two Anglo-Saxon Pontificals*, pp. xxix–xxxii, discusses the interrelationship of these forms in English witnesses, especially in regards to the Egbert Pontifical, which has a form of the prayer *Domine Iesu Christe adoro te in cruce ascendentem* of the 'common' strain represented in Cerne, rather than the 'rare' form represented in the *Concordia* and in the *Portiforium Wulstani*. Gjerløw, *Adoratio Crucis*, prints and discusses fifteen forms in Cerne, the last five of which correspond to the first *Concordia* prayer, concluding that "The Insular character of language and phraseology would seem to indicate an Insular, or Irish-Northumbrian, origin of this text" (16). The prayers are found in a wide range of manuscripts from the ninth to the sixteenth centuries and found their way to France, Italy, Spain, Germany, and Norway (18ff). See also Michelle Brown, *The Book of Cerne* (London, 1996). Brown discusses Bishop's analysis of possible 'Spanish' elements, pointing out that both the Irish and the Carolingian churches were influenced by these Spanish/Gallican forms, and concluding that the *D. I. C. adoro te* prayer "textually embodies the central prayer of the *Mysterium Crucis* from the Good Friday Office of the Mozarabic Missal" (139).

[41] Symons, *Regularis concordia*, p. xlvi. As Gjerløw and Brown have shown, the *D. I. C. adoro te* prayer is found before the *Concordia* in a devotional context, and this seems to have been its primary function in English practice. In the context of the *Adoratio*, however, the only clear antecedents are continental, and Gjerløw points to some examples. See also Robert Deshman, "The Galba Psalter: pictures, texts and context in an early medieval prayerbook," *ASE* 26 (1997), pp. 109–38, esp. pp. 122–4. I am grateful to Professor Sarah Keefer for this point.

continent.[42] Such an idea involves a good deal of supposition, but her argument does illustrate to what degree the themes and images of the Adoration of the Cross, with its corollary theme of the Cross as infused with the power of Christ, were natural to the Anglo-Saxon church from at least the eighth century.

The *Concordia's* instructions for the ritual surrounding the *Adoratio* are extensive. At the hour of None (regularly the time of the *Adoratio* from the Gelasian to the Anglo-Saxon witnesses), the abbot and the brethren proceed to the church. After a pair of lessons with tracts and responds, the Passion according to John is read. This aspect of Good Friday worship is perhaps the most ancient (in the Roman liturgy) and, along with the *orationes sollemnes*, made up the pre-eighth-century Roman liturgy for the day. Particularly exciting is an instruction for the reading of the gospel Passion (taken from *Ordo Romanus I* and included in Ælfric's Eynsham Letter[43]), "et quando legitur in evangelio *Partiti sunt vestimenta mea* et reliqua, statim duo diaconi nudent altare sindone, quae prius fuerat sub evangelio posita, in modum furantis."[44] The stripping of the cloth from under the gospel book, clearly playing out the role of the 'thieves' stripping away Christ's robe, accompanied by the temporal coincidence, represents an attempt to vivify the gospel account with visual representation, a dynamic exercised throughout the Anglo-Saxon liturgy for the high festivals.

Following the reading from John are the *Orationes sollemnes*. These prayers go back to the earliest Western witnesses, and are represented in both the Gregorian and the Gelasian sacramentaries.[45] The prayers serve to

---

[42] Holloway, "'The Dream of the Rood,'" pp. 31ff, goes on to express her opinion that the *Visitatio*, and even the Orléans Playbook, may have derived from England, but her view swims firmly against the critical stream. Much of Holloway's argument stems from an assumption that the *adoro te* prayers constitute an "*Adoratio Crucis* which is earlier and longer than the Winchester version" (30). Several other critics have made this same assumption, often quoting Holloway (see Earl Anderson, "Liturgical Influence in the Dream of the Rood," *Neophilologus* 73 (1989), p. 294). However, the *adoro te on crucem ascendentem* prayers mentioned in the *Concordia* correspond only to the last five of fifteen *adoro te* prayers in Cerne. Taken together, the fifteen prayers (as printed in Gjerløw, *Adoratio Crucis*, pp. 16–17) adore Christ creating light ("*Fiat lux*"), calling Adam, saving Noah, freeing the Israelites from Pharaoh, descending into the Virgin's womb, being baptized, performing miracles (three prayers), raising Lazarus, and then ascending the Cross, being deposited in the sepulchre, descending to hell to free the captives (where the devils sing 'Who is this king of glory?' reflecting the Gospel of Nicodemus), ascending into heaven (*adoro te ascendentem in caelos*, with the same verb as used for the Crucifixion), and coming in Judgement (specifically referring to Christ's Advent). The forms here are too general to be tied to Good Friday, and should be considered (as does Brown) devotional prayers. That they were actually used as part of the *Adoratio* at some stage is certain, but their presentation in Cerne can be considered at most as analogous to or reflective of the liturgy.

[43] See *LME*, p. 133.

[44] Kornexl, *Die Regularis concordia*, p. 88; see also Symons, *Regularis concordia*, p. 42. "And when *Partiti sunt vestimenta mea*, etc. is read in the gospel, straightaway two deacons shall strip from the altar the cloth, which until that point had been resting beneath the gospel book, in the manner of a thief."

[45] See Wilson, *The Gelasian Sacramentary*, pp. 75–7.

bring all of Christendom, and all of humanity in need of Christendom, under the shadow of the Cross, before the Cross is formally addressed and venerated, including specific mention of the Pope, the "imperatore vel rege,"[46] new catechumens, heretics and schismatics, the Jews who sacrificed Christ,[47] and the pagans, to name a few. Most interesting here is Ælfric's explanation in his Eynsham Letter that "the abbot begins the *orationes solemnes* that follow, because on that same day our Saviour also prayed from the Cross for the whole church."[48]

Now follows the *Adoratio* itself, presented with extraordinary detail in the *Concordia*, and clearly the climax of the day.[49] The Cross is set up before the altar and held up by two deacons who sing the first of the *Improperia*, or the Reproaches (*Popule meus*), "addressed from the Saviour to the ungrateful people."[50] As Gjerløw explains, these chants "have pre-Caroline antecedents,"[51] and they can still be found in modern missals. Barbara Raw discusses vernacular elaborations of Christ's reproaches to the people in the eighth Vercelli homily and in *Christ III*.[52] Their relationship with Vercelli VIII is particularly compelling. Francis Clough describes their apparent role in this eschatological homily, in what seems to be a usurpation of the address to the goats by a series of Reproach-like[53] complaints:

> Delivered in the first person, with no homiletic breaks, this address reminds the wicked of Christ's passion and death, accusing them of forgetfulness and ingratitude, and ends with Christ condemning them to hell. It may be that the author, delivering the address in this way, enacted a kind of mini-drama, with himself playing Christ and the audience the damned souls, thus rendering even more effective and immediate an already dramatic motif.[54]

In its liturgical context, this 'mini-drama,' although it has no biblical antecedent, serves both to make Christ present on the liturgical Cross and to develop some of the tension implicit in being a member of the humanity that caused him to be nailed up there, and that needs to be made to appreciate as much as possible the magnitude of his sacrifice. Between each of the *Improperia*, subdeacons and the *schola* respond in Greek and Latin, respectively, *Agios o Theos* and *Sanctus Deus*, again reminding the audience of exactly who is speaking to them. After the first pair of

---

[46] Ibid. p. 76.

[47] In his Eynsham Letter (*LME*, p. 133), Ælfric, adapting Amalarius, instructs that "All the *orationes* should be performed with genuflexions, except for the one wherein we pray for the treacherous Jews" who derided Christ by bending their knees. But see *LME*, p. 197, n. 219.

[48] *LME*, p. 133.

[49] See Kornexl, *Die Regularis concordia*, pp. 89ff; Symons, *Regularis concordia*, pp. 42ff.

[50] Cross and Livingstone, *The Oxford Dictionary of the Christian Church*, p. 690.

[51] Gjerløw, *Adoratio Crucis*, p. 15.

[52] Raw, *Anglo-Saxon Crucifixion Iconography*, pp. 65–6.

[53] This address comes from the *Admonitio de die iudicii*, also found in Caesarius, and, taken from him, in a homily for Rogationtide (*BC*, p. 126). Although their potential relationship to the Reproaches is uncertain, the similarity of their style and format certainly recalls the *Improperia*.

[54] Francis Clough, Introduction to *The Vercelli Book Homilies: Translations*, ed. Nicholson, p. 6.

responses, the Cross is carried to the altar and laid on a cushion. Ælfric specifies that the Cross should be "mid hrægle be-wæfed."[55] After a second Reproach (*Quia eduxi vos per desertum*) and its responses, the Cross is raised up, and a third Reproach is sung. The Cross is unveiled and turned to the clergy, and the deacons sing the widely-attested antiphons *Ecce lignum crucis* and *Crucem tuam adoramus Domine*, among others. The antiphons draw attention jointly to 'the wood of the Cross' and to Christ on the Cross, and this joint address is central to the rest of the *Adoratio* prayers (and from there to more general prayers in veneration of the Cross). The abbot and the brethren prostrate themselves, and the prayers to the Cross are said "with deep and heartfelt sighs." The prayers are given (unusually) in full. The first, the *Domine Ihesu Christe, adoro te . . .* set, praises Christ ascending the Cross, wounded, laid in the grave, descending into hell to free the prisoners, rising from the grave and ascending to heaven, and coming in judgement.[56] After psalms and a collect, the abbot kisses the Cross, followed by the brethren, and then *omnis clerus ac populus*. Ælfric, in his Second Letter for Wulfstan, gives (not unexpectedly) a simplified version of the rite, with most of the same central elements. After the John gospel (and after "þa collecta swa-swa seo mæsse-boc him tæcð" ("the collects just as the mass book teaches him") which may refer to the *orationes sollemnes*),

> Æfter þam beran twegen gebroþru þa rode forð mid hrægle be-wæfed and singan
> þa fers: *Popule meus*. þwegen gebroþru him andwyrdon on grecisc: *Agios o theos*,
> oþ ende. And hi ealle þonne singan on leden: *Sanctus deus, sanctus fortis*. þonne
> þæt oþer fers: *Quia eduxi uos*: þonne eft: *agios, o theos*, and: *sanctus deus*. þonne
> þæt þrydde fers: *Quid ultra debui* and: *Agios* and: *Sanctus*. Unwreon þonne þa
> rode and singan: *Ecce lignum crucis* and þa oþre antifonas. þa hwile þe þa
> gebroþru hi gebiddað æt þære rode and þæt læwede folc eall-swa do.[57]

The key elements of the *Adoratio* are the Reproaches, sung, as it were, by the Cross as Christ to the people, the responses in Greek and Latin, the revelation of the 'wood of the Cross,' and the veneration, made jointly by brethren and layfolk (where applicable). The Cross here is something more than wood in the same way that the Eucharist is something more than bread

---

[55] Fehr, *Die Hirtenbriefe Ælfrics*, p. 163. "Wrapped in a cloth."

[56] These prayers are distinct from those found in Cerne primarily in the addition of the adoration of Christ wounded on the Cross and in the shortening of the Harrowing adoration, where a quick narrative derived from apocryphal sources and including the voice of the devils is replaced in favour of the simpler "adoro te descendentem ad inferos liberantem captivos; deprecor te, ut non ibi me dimittas introire" (Kornexl, *Die Regularis concordia*, p. 92; see also Symons, *Regularis concordia*, p. 43; "I adore you descending to hell to free those held captive; I beseech you that you not allow me to enter there").

[57] Fehr, *Die Hirtenbriefe Ælfrics*, pp. 163–4. "Afterwards, two brothers should bear the cross forth, wrapped in a cloth, and sing the verse: *Popule meus*. Two brothers should answer him in Greek: *Agios o theos*, until the end. And they all should then sing in Latin: *Sanctus deus, sanctus fortis*. Then the second verse: *Quia eduxi vos*: then afterward: *agios, o theos*, and *sanctus deus*. Then the third verse: *Quid ultra debui* and: *Agios* and: *Sanctus*. Unwrap then the cross and sing: *Ecce lignum crucis* and the other antiphons. Meanwhile the brothers pray at the cross, and the layfolk do as well."

and wine, and Ælfric in a homily for the Invention of the Holy Cross, explains its nature:

> Cristene men sceolon soðlice abugan to gehalgodre rode on ðæs hælendes naman, for ðan ðe we nabbað ða ðe he on ðrowade, ac hire anlicnys bið halig swa ðeah, to ðære we abugað on gebedum symle to ðam mihtigan drihtne þe for mannum ðrowade, and seo rod is gemynd his mæran þrowunge, halig ðurh hine, ðeah ðe heo on holte weoxe.[58]

Particularly on Good Friday, each adored cross is to be seen as just as holy as the actual Cross, a connection made easier by the mixed addresses to the Cross and to Christ both in the liturgical forms for the day and elsewhere.

The power of the Cross, specifically as somehow standing in for or reflecting Christ's power, often depicted in terms of light conquering darkness, was certainly a familiar theme in Old English treatments of it. In a Lives of Saints homily on the Exaltation of the Holy Cross, "drihtnes rode" is seen "deorwurð-lice þær scinan" in the heavens.[59] At times, the Cross is granted even more kinetic power. In one of a series of prayers to the Cross found in the Portiforium of Wulstan is one addressed to "sancta et veneranda crux," beseeching the Cross, serving as an agent of Christ, to protect the supplicant, free him from the devil and from sin, confirm him in good works, and rescue him from the darkness, fire, and judgement of the end of the world.[60] The Cross here, through which Christ rips away the darkness of the devil's dominion, is granted his saving power, such that the supplicant is in a sense praying to both at once.[61] Following this prayer is a series of orations in Latin and in English, translations of the prayers to the Cross for the *Adoratio*, as well as many of the accompanying forms. Many address Christ himself; a few address the Cross instead:

> Drihten þine halgan rode we geadmedað 7 we heriað 7 wuldriað þine þa halgan æriste forþam soðlice blis com eallum middanearde þurh þa halgan rode . . . Hala þu gebletsode rod þu ðe ana wyrðe wære to beorenne heofona cyning 7 hlaford.[62]

It is quite rare to find direct English translations of parts of the liturgy. We have translations of baptismal rubrics in the Red Book of Darley[63] and of the *Absolvimus*, the key element of the Reconciliation, in the Pontifical of

---

[58] CH II.xviii, p. 175. "Christians must truly revere the sanctified cross in the Lord's name, because we do not have the one on which he suffered, but its likeness is holy nevertheless, to which we bow in prayers constantly to the great Lord who suffered for mankind, and the cross is the remembrance of his great Passion, holy through him, although it grew up in a forest."

[59] Skeat, *Ælfric's Lives of Saints*, vol. II, p. 150. "The Lord's cross . . . shining there brilliantly."

[60] See Hughes, *The Portiforium of Saint Wulstan*, vol. 2, p. 20.

[61] The Cross as a focal point of the End is developed in a number of places, including the Blickling Easter homily, discussed below, pp. 134–5.

[62] Ibid. p. 21. "Lord, we humble ourselves before your holy Cross and we praise and glorify your holy resurrection because truly bliss has come to all the world through the holy Cross . . . Lo, blessed Cross, you who alone are worthy to bear the Lord and king of the heavens."

[63] Page, "Old English Liturgical Rubrics in Corpus Christi College, Cambridge, MS 422," pp. 149–58.

Egbert.[64] The latter might provide for the lay participants understanding of at least the central part of the ritual, and perhaps the translations here are for much the same purpose (although there is no indication here that they were intended actually to be used in the Good Friday liturgy).[65] It is not at all rare to find translations of private devotional prayers, from which at least the *adoro te* set derive, but the selection of translated passages here, and their layout (with Latin original followed by English translation with the headings "Latine" and "Anglice," and interspersed psalms and readings), reveal at least an awareness of the place of these prayers in the liturgy. In any event, their translation here shows a vernacular interest in the *Adoratio*, reflective of the consequences of elements of the *Adoratio* liturgy such as the *Improperia*, making those before the Cross hear Christ himself speaking from it, or through it, to them.

This relationship between the Cross and Christ is strengthened in the Deposition, a natural extension of the *Adoratio* but not so widely attested. The *Concordia*'s directions are worth quoting in full because of their wonderfully self-conscious sense of reenactment:

> Nam quia ea die depositionem corporis salvatoris nostri celebramus, usum quorundam religiosorum imitabilem ad fidem indocti vulgi ac neofitorum[66] corroborandam equiperando sequi, si ita cui visum fuerit vel sibi taliter placuerit, hoc modo decrevimus: Sit autem in una parte altaris, qua vacuum fuerit, quaedam assimilatio sepulchri velamenque quoddam in gyro tensum, quod, dum sancta crux adorata fuerit, deponatur hoc ordine: Veniant diaconi, qui prius portaverunt eam et involuant eam sindone in loco, ubi adorata est. Tunc reportent eam, canentes antiphonas *In pace in idipsum, Habitabit*; item: *Caro mea requiescet in spe*, donec veniant ad locum monumenti. Depositaque cruce, ac si Domini nostri Ihesu Christi corpore sepulto, dicant antiphonam *Sepulto Domino signatum est monumentum, ponentes milites, qui custodirent eum*. In eodem loco sancta crux cum omni reverentia custodiatur usque dominicam noctem resurrectionis. Nocte vero ordinentur duo fratres aut tres aut plures, si tanta fuerint congregatio, qui ibidem psalmos decantando excubias fideles exerceant.[67]

---

[64] See Banting, *Two Anglo-Saxon Pontificals*, p. 132, n. 30.

[65] They are, rather, part of a set of devotional Cross prayers, possibly reflecting a number of liturgical offices. See Brian Møller Jensen, "An interpretation of the Tropes to the Inventio Sanctae Crucis," *Ecclesia Orans* 3 (1991), pp. 305–23, for a discussion of the interrelationship of the festivals in praise of the Cross, by which "the Inventio as commemorated on the third of May somehow reflects the veneration of the Cross in the Good Friday liturgy" (318). Barbara Raw, *Anglo-Saxon Crucifixion Iconography*, discusses more generally the devotional nature of the prayers in the Portiforium of Wulstan and of the *Adoratio* prayers as they appear elsewhere (56ff).

[66] The Old English gloss for "neofitorum" is "gedwolena." See above, p. 55, n. 16, and Kornexl, *Die Regularis concordia*, pp. 307–8, n. 1111.

[67] Kornexl, *Die Regularis concordia*, pp. 94–6; see also Symons, *Regularis concordia*, pp. 44–5. "Now since in that day we commemorate the burial of the body of our saviour, if it seems fitting or pleasing to anyone to imitate a practice of certain religious men, worthy to be followed for the strengthening of the faith of unlearned common persons and neophytes, this much we have decreed: on one part of the altar, where there is space for it, there shall be as it were a likeness of a sepulchre, with a curtain stretched around it, into which the holy cross, when it has been adored, shall be placed according to the following arrangement: the deacons who previously carried the

As with the *Tenebrae* elaborations, the instructions here have the feel of an importation, and Symons seems to regard it as one, although there is no clear evidence of it in the Lotharingian or Cluniac forms of the time, and the antiphons are taken from those for Nocturns on Holy Saturday.[68] The Deposition of the Cross was quite well known in the later Middle Ages, drawing a good deal of attention, along with a corresponding *Elevatio* on Easter morning. To see it here in such an early form, and with such a clear understanding of its dramatic characteristics, is exciting, but hardly surprising, given the clear sense of dramatic possibility seen elsewhere. The practice is set forth specifically as a visual supplement to the story of the Burial of Christ (recently provided from John's gospel) for "the strengthening of the faith of unlearned common persons and neophytes." In fundamentally the same way as the later liturgical dramas, faith is strengthened by allowing these folk actually to see Christ wrapped in a cloth, borne away to the sepulchre by the two deacons (here perhaps a nice parallel to Joseph and Nicodemus, who wrap and bury Christ's body in John's account, and who are generally present in illumination of the Deposition from the Cross), placed inside, and guarded. That the burial was carried out in a processional fashion, and therefore would bear little resemblance to the actual events of the burial, is a non-issue, for these "unlearned common persons and neophytes" would have reaped their primary understanding of biblical events from the liturgy, and it is anachronistic to think that they would see it as somehow unrealistic. As we have seen throughout the Temporale, most notably at Candlemas and Palm Sunday, liturgical commemoration commonly determines how biblical history is visualized in art and in vernacular narratives, even in translations of the gospel. Illumination of the Crucifixion and Deposition not infrequently present Christ on what looks like a liturgical Cross, more a dramatic portrait of a crucifix than an historically accurate presentation (see plate 3). That it is the Cross itself, rather than Christ, that is literally taken down and buried is likewise not a hindrance to reenactment, for totems like the Cross and the Candle frequently stand liturgically for the

---

Cross shall come forward and wrap it in a cloth in the place where it was venerated. Then they shall carry it, singing the antiphons *In pace in idipsum*, *Habitabit*, and *Caro mea requiescet in spe*, until they come to the place of the sepulchre. When they have laid the cross inside, as if for the burial of the body of our Lord Jesus Christ, they shall sing the antiphon *Sepulto Domino signatum est monumentum, ponentes milites qui custodirent eum*. In that same place the holy cross shall be guarded with all reverence until the night of the resurrection of the Lord. And truly during the night let two brethren be appointed, or three or more, if so many may be found from among the community, who, singing psalms, will keep faithful watch there."

[68] Indeed, there is little good evidence for the Deposition of the Cross, either native or continental, antedating the *Concordia*. For an examination of the evidence, see Solange Corbin, *La déposition liturgique du Christ au Vendredi Saint* (Paris, 1960). It may be that the *Concordia*'s *Depositio* ritual represents tenth-century English innovation. This point was suggested to me by Professor Sarah Keefer, who in her current work on the Veneration of the Cross is examining the possible relationship between the theoretical prescriptions for the *Adoratio* and *Depositio* in the *Concordia* and reflections of their actual use in Corpus 422.

presence of Christ, and come thereby to absorb much of his divinity, and to warrant reverence accordingly. In the *Adoratio* and the *Depositio*, then, the participants watch in awe Christ dead on the Cross, taken down, and buried, yet all the while burning with conquering power, with the promise of Harrowing and Resurrection.

The *Concordia* representation is carried on throughout the weekend, as the brethren hold vigil before the tomb. There seem to be two sets of brethren remaining at the tomb, one possibly representing the historical guards,[69] the other (chanting psalms in groups of two or three) perhaps reflecting the idea expressed by the author of a sermon for Holy Saturday, that the faithful (specifically, for this homilist, Christ's mother and the other women) on the night before the Resurrection kept awake all night, visiting the tomb repeatedly.[70] This continuation of the *Adoratio* and *Depositio* through the night, and until Easter Vigils, again draws attention to the different relationships of the monks and the lay-people to the Good Friday liturgy. The instructions for the *Adoratio* provide another rare instance where the joint participation of monks and lay-people is made explicit. The relationship between monastic and lay participation in these events would differ greatly, of course, from place to place, but at a monastic cathedral like Winchester, given the universal nature of *Adoratio* celebration in the Western church, one might imagine the entire demographic of Anglo-Saxon England, from King to slave, adoring the Cross. Both the *Concordia* and Ælfric specify at least that monks and then lay-people (*Concordia* "popu-lus," Ælfric "þæt læwede folc") would kiss the Cross.[71] A greater role, however, must be played by the deacons and the brethren. The *Concordia* has deacons holding up the Cross before the altar, singing the Reproaches (subdeacons sing the Greek responses), then raising and revealing, wrap-ping, and burying the Cross.[72] The abbot and those brethren 'of the right hand side of the choir,' after all present are reproached and the Cross is unveiled, prostrate themselves before it, singing the penitential psalms and the *Adoratio* prayers (*adoro te*, etc), and are then the first to kiss it. Brethren also then guard the 'tomb,' singing songs in vigil. After the *Depositio*, the

---

[69] Egeria provides a wonderful explanation for the two guards at the Jerusalem *Adoratio*. She was told, she reports, that the Cross was guarded because someone had made off with a piece of the true Cross by taking a bite out of it. See George Gingras, trans. *Egeria: Diary of a Pilgrimage* (New York, 1970), p. 111.

[70] See Ruth Evans, ed. "An anonymous Old English homily for Holy Saturday," *LSE* n.s. 12 (1981), pp. 137–8.

[71] Ælfric does not actually specify that the Cross is kissed, just that the brethren and then the layfolk "gebiddað æt þære rode" (Fehr, *Die Hirtenbriefe Ælfrics*, p. 164). One manuscript (X) has as a gloss to "gebiddað" *adorant*, which could include both the actions of praying and kissing. The *Concordia* does seem to specify that the Cross is kissed (*decosculans*) by the abbot and the brethren, and then the clergy and the people *hoc idem faciat*.

[72] Ælfric assigns all these actions simply to "gebroþru," again revealing the monastic model from which he is trying to extract, on behalf of Wulfstan and thus in the interest of lay observance, an explanation of the fundamental elements of these festivals.

presence of the guards and the vigil-holding faithful demonstrates the degree to which the monastic communities might enjoy a richer sense of reenactment than the common folk, as is the case year-round. Their expanded role in the *Adoratio* and *Depositio* themselves, however, sets up more immediately a separation between the two groups, which might be roughly analogous to an 'actors-audience' dichotomy. The brethren have the job of staging this event for the *indocti vulgi*, and creating the atmosphere whereby they can feel that they are witnessing first-hand what has just been set forth in John's Passion narrative. The purpose of the ritual, as expressed here, is to make the audience assume the role of those witnessing the burial, and all of the ceremonial elements, as 'unrealistic' as many of them may be, like the Reproaches, the kissing of the Cross, and the procession to the sepulchre, are crucial to the reenactment, serving to bring the divine presence of Christ into the ritual, and establish the relationship between the people and the Cross. The deacons and brethren play shifting roles, and any attempt to describe them as 'actors' would become bogged down in the fact that they don't hold down biblical roles in any clear or sustained way (as is often the case in liturgical reenactment). For this reason, descriptions of dramatic ritual as early drama often resort to expressions like 'quasi-dramatic,' concluding that these are awkward attempts at impersonation, constrained by ritual habit from fully realizing their histrionic potential. Such a description, however, would not do justice to the power of these Good Friday ceremonies. It is the ritual *Improperia* that bring the power of the Cross to life. It is through the liturgical expressions of shame and wonder that all present come to terms with the fact that Christ is on the Cross before them, both in agony to pay for their sins and in power to free them from hell.

Although we have no substantive liturgical witnesses to the *Adoratio* before those in the *Concordia*, Anglo-Saxon treatment of the Cross, in particular of Christ on the Cross, reveal from as early as the seventh century a deep familiarity with the central elements of the liturgical reenactment, which to a large extent dominate any exploration of the Crucifixion. Vernacular treatments of the events of Good Friday in many ways seem to reflect this familiarity. The first Vercelli homily resonates quite well with the Good Friday liturgy.[73] The homily is actually a translation (or version) of the Passion according to John, and may itself have been part of the services for the day, in place of a sermon. Ælfric claimed that no sermon should be preached on the three "swigdagas" of Thursday, Friday, and Saturday, and therefore did not provide any, but several manuscripts of the

---

[73] For the two versions of this sermon and its relationship to manuscripts of Ælfric's Catholic Homilies, see Paul E. Szarmach, "The Earlier Homily: 'De Parasceve,'" in *Studies in Earlier Old English Prose*, ed. Szarmach and Huppé, pp. 381–99. See also D. G. Scragg, "The Corpus of Vernacular Homilies and Prose Saints' Lives Before Ælfric," *ASE* 8 (1979), pp. 223–77, and *The Vercelli Homilies*, pp. 1–5. Only the A version provides the Harrowing of Hell.

Catholic Homilies include anonymous sermons for these three days, added later, including Vercelli I for Good Friday.[74] In general, the writer follows John's account quite closely, at times bringing in details from other accounts (often to illuminate the fulfilment of prophecy), or filling in his own. From the account of Christ's scourging by the soldiers, the homilist changes the colour of Christ's robe from purple to red ("mid reade hrægle"[75]), seemingly drawing from the 'scarlet' robe of Matthew. This adaptation fits nicely with the idea of a gold-covered adored Cross, which is itself part of the vision in *The Dream of the Rood*.[76] He also brings in the account of the hours and of the darkness that covered the earth (in the A version only), absent in John:

> Wæs hit middæg þa hie hine on rode hengon. And þa he on rode ahangen wæs, þa geþystrode hit 7 efne fæstlice genihtode ofer eallne middangeard fram middum dæge oð non. And sio sunne 7 ealle þa heofontungulu hira leoht betyndon 7 behyddon, þæt hie þæt morðor geseon ne woldon þæt men her on eorþan wið hira scyppend fremedon.[77]

Matthew mentions the darkness, and Mark adds more specifically the failing of the sun's light, but the Vercelli homilist's elaboration is extra-biblical. The entry for 25 March in the Old English Martyrology (typologically the day of the Crucifixion, as of the completed creation of the world and the Annunciation) similarly draws from Luke, mentioning the darkness and the failing sun, but not the 'heaven-stars,' and certainly not the anthropomorphic motivation of the heavenly bodies.[78] Of course the account of the hours and the emphasis on the darkness covering Christ on the Cross go back to the earliest days of the church, and are expressed in a variety of ways, but their inclusion here certainly must reflect the liturgy potentially surrounding their use on Good Friday. In any event, the homilist apparently felt that the inclusion of the hours and the elaborated account of the darkness were important enough to Good Friday reckoning of the Passion to interrupt John's liturgically prescribed account with them.

The importance of light overcoming darkness and the liturgically established divinity afforded the Cross are developed in more potent ways in the

---

[74] See Hill, "Ælfric's 'Silent Days,'" pp. 118–31. See also *LME*, pp. 184–6, n. 171.

[75] Scragg, *The Vercelli Homilies*, p. 28.

[76] Rosemary Woolf, "Doctrinal Influences on *The Dream of the Rood*," *Medium Ævum* 27 (1958), pp. 137–8, notes the relationship between *The Dream of the Rood* and both jewelled and red crosses used in the liturgy.

[77] Scragg, *The Vercelli Homilies*, p. 36. "It was midday when they hung him on the Cross. And when he had been hung on the Cross, then it became dark and quickly turned into night over all the earth from midday until None. And the sun and all of the heaven-stars shut off and hid their light, because they did not want to see that murder that men here on earth committed against their Creator."

[78] See Günter Kotzor, ed. *Das altenglische Martyrologium*, vol. II (Munich, 1981), pp. 43–5, or George Herzfeld, ed. *An Old English Martyrology* (Oxford, 1900), p. 48. Raw, *Anglo-Saxon Crucifixion Iconography*, pp. 158–9, points out illustrations of the Crucifixion in which figures representing the sun and moon hide their faces.

Blickling homily for Easter. Because of the Cross' ability to transport the faithful to the saving events of Christ's Passion and Resurrection, it frequently appears in accounts of the End. The constant eschatological overlay to discussion of the Crucifixion and Resurrection led, naturally enough, to expect the end either at None on 'Long' Friday or on Easter itself, as does the writer of the Blickling homily, claiming that "seo wyrd on þas ondweardan tid geworþan sceal, þæt se ilca Scyppend gesittan wile on his domsetle."[79] After a brief account of the Resurrection, the audience is given a lengthy and quite dramatic rendition of the Harrowing of Hell. Christ, we are told, sent his spirit to hell, troubling its inhabitants, breaking down its gates, and bringing out the elect, so that "þæra deofla þeostro he oforgeat mid his þæm scinendan leohte,"[80] as he did, symbolically, at the New Fire, and at Easter Vigils. His victory is brought to life first in the long speech of the devils, asking their chief why he brought Christ into hell so that they were defeated. In the course of the speech, the devils note that those who have been taken away by Christ, "þeah hie ær þæs ecan lifes orwene wæron, hie synt nu swiþe bliþe."[81] It is specifically through the Cross that the people are freed, as the devils lament, "þurh Cristes rode is eal þin blis to unrotnesse geworden."[82] After the Harrowing is an account of the Last Days, and the Cross appears again, as a power, presumably shining, among the stars: "seo rod ures Drihtnes bið aræred on þæt gewrixle þara tungla, seo nu on middangearde awergde gastas flemeþ."[83] These sorts of developments of the nature of the Cross both reflect the veneration granted it on Good Friday and help strengthen understanding of its divinity for the sake of the liturgical adoration.

As does the liturgical arrangement for Good Friday, illumination of Christ on the Cross emphasizes more the power implicit in Christ's self-sacrificial mounting than the tragedy of the dying Christ. If the Cross is to be seen as standing in for Christ, to the degree that it is adored and buried in a sepulchre, it might not be surprising that Christ, in turn, comes to resemble the impersonal, enigmatic, and powerful Cross. This portrayal of Christ is often compared to later gothic depictions of him suffering, very personal and very human. These depictions come in conjunction with the gothic usurpation of the Cross in liturgical drama and in art with the figure of the suffering Christ himself.[84] While Anglo-Saxon portrayals of Christ on

---

[79] Morris, *The Blickling Homilies*, p. 83. "That fate shall happen at this present time, that this same Lord will sit on his Judgement seat."

[80] Ibid. p. 85. "He overcame the darkness of the devils with his shining light."

[81] Ibid. "Although they previously were despairing of this eternal life, they are now very happy."

[82] Ibid. "Through Christ's Cross all our joy is turned to sorrow."

[83] Ibid. p. 91. "The Cross of our Lord will be raised up in the concourse of the stars, which now on earth puts cursed spirits to flight."

[84] It is perhaps in relation to this shifting portrayal of Christ that later medieval versions of the *adoro te* prayers "as a rule have the beginning 'Adore te, D. I. C. in cruce pendentem' " (Gjerløw, *Adoratio Crucis*, p. 17), abandoning Christ's 'mounting' the Cross in favour of a much more passively tragic image.

the Cross allow for pity, Christ is also seen ruling from the Cross, as if only after mounting the Cross has he fully come into his power.[85] The account of the Harrowing and the description of Doomsday in the Blickling Easter homily combine this intricate relationship between the Cross and Christ in power with the images and moods of the pre-Easter ceremonies, and with the expectation of the Second Coming nurtured throughout the pre-Paschal season, a combination that has particular resonance with the *Adoratio*.

Other vernacular descriptions of Christ or the Cross as glowing in opposition to darkness are plentiful. Perhaps the most exciting manifestation of the Cross in Old English literature is that in *The Dream of the Rood*, which describes the Cross as a still but dynamic representation of, and window to, the events of Good Friday. A number of critics have attempted to describe parallels between this poem and the *Adoratio*. One of the first to deal with this tantalizing relationship was Howard Patch. Patch discussed the possible relationships between the vision of the jewel-adorned Cross in the poem and evidence for jewelled (and possibly red) crosses in England. He also looked for reflections of Latin hymnody in the poem. While mentioning a few hymns and liturgical forms that reflect many of the same ideas, he was forced to admit that "the results of our search for liturgical influence are surprisingly small."[86] Much more recently, Earl Anderson tried to find sources or analogues for a number of passages in the poem, pointing to, among other things, two hymns of Fortunatus, readings in the Leofric Missal and in the Missal of Robert, the Book of Cerne, and the 'horae passionis' tradition. Like Patch, Anderson had to conclude that he had at most "clarified only three or four phrases in the poem,"[87] and even these represented similarities, not sources. Because of the difficulty of connecting directly liturgical forms with the poem, Rosemary Woolf saw its importance as doctrinal rather than liturgical, expressing Christological debate.[88] Éamon Ó Carragáin, while agreeing with Woolf's shift away from "the rather mechanistic search for verbal parallels for individual passages" in *The Dream of the Rood*, asserted that (focusing on early bits of the poem) "the genesis of the Ruthwell Cross poem should be sought not in Christological controversies but in the liturgical innovations of the Northumbrian Church in the early eighth century" and that "the sort of cleric who, in the tenth century, read the Vercelli *Dream of the Rood* would also have found such liturgical concerns comprehensible and important."[89] Ó Carragáin discussed in great

---

[85] See Raw, *Anglo-Saxon Crucifixion Iconography*, pp. 87ff.

[86] Howard Patch, "Liturgical Influence in The Dream of the Rood," *PMLA* 34 (1919), p. 257.

[87] Earl Anderson, "Liturgical Influence in The Dream of the Rood," *Neophilologus* 73 (1989), p. 301.

[88] See Woolf, "Doctrinal Influences."

[89] Éamon Ó Carragáin, "Crucifixion as Annunciation: The Relation of 'The Dream of the Rood' to the Liturgy Reconsidered," *English Studies* 63 (1983), pp. 487, 488.

detail the relationship between the enduring Cross and the accepting Mary at the Annunciation (illustrating the connection between the time of the Annunciation and the Crucifixion). He also talked about the possible relationship between the poem and the experience of confronting the Ruthwell Cross itself, with its range of devotional and (possibly) liturgical meanings. Peggy Samuels, making reference to Ó Carragáin's article, attempted to describe the poem as "a dramatic re-creation of the communicant's cathartic experience during the ritual drama of the Easter liturgy, especially as highlighted at the most intense moment of the lenten agon, the commemoration of the Crucifixion on Good Friday."[90] Edward B. Irving, discussing the poem in terms of dramatic narrative rather than drama (as did Samuels), gave an account of "the operative elements in The Dream of the Rood's massive emotional power" with reference to Good Friday.[91] The general consensus of those looking to place *The Dream of the Rood* in some sort of liturgical context is that, due to the individual genius of the poet of the Vercelli version (and due to the fact that we know little about the liturgical forms at the stages of the poem's development), we can find only echoes of the liturgy, not direct borrowings, and that we must therefore discuss the poem and the liturgy in terms of analogues, not sources. However, almost all agree that there is some sort of relationship between the poem and the liturgy, which is why there remains an interest in exploring it despite the difficulties experienced decades ago by Patch. However we conceive its origin and its context, the poem encapsulates the dynamic elements of the Cross established in the Good Friday liturgy. Most importantly, the poem says something about the experience of confronting a Cross that one has been trained to see both as a Cross and as the central figure of the reenactment of Christ's Passion.

The poet's initial vision, dropping to him 'from midnight,' presents a shining, gold-sheathed beacon.[92] The poet is humbled before it, "forwunded mid wommum" ("wounded with sins"), while around him are invoked angels, spirits, and men, bringing all creation into its presence. The vision then shifts into a dual one, with the Cross at once bedecked with shining gold and jewels and bleeding in agony from its right side, as if it were pierced along with Christ. The Cross shifts back and forth between blood-red and gold, allowing the poet to see in the gold-wrapped Cross the actual Crucifixion. In the Cross's memory, the Saviour 'mounts' the Cross, active, not passive, the poet using the same root word ("gestigan") as did the

---

[90] Peggy Samuels, "The Audience Written into the Script of *The Dream of the Rood*," *Modern Language Quarterly* 49 (1988), p. 320.

[91] Edward B. Irving, "Crucifixion Witnessed, or Dramatic Interaction in The Dream of the Rood," in *Modes of Interpretation in Old English Literature*, ed. Phyllis Brown, et al. (Toronto, 1986), pp. 101–13.

[92] See George P. Krapp, ed. *The Vercelli Book* (New York, 1932), pp. 61–5.

translator of the *Adoratio* prayers in the Portiforium of Wulstan ("asti-gende," translating "ascendentem"). The Cross shares Christ's wounds, and darkness descends over the shining body:

> Geseah ic weruda God
> þearle þenian. þystro hæfdon
> bewrigen mid wolcnum wealdendes hræw,
> scirne sciman, sceadu forðeode,
> wann under wolcnum. Weop eal gesceaft,
> cwiðdon cyninges fyll. Crist wæs on rode.[93]

The Cross sees Christ's followers actually chisel out a new tomb then and there and place the body inside. That there is more than one person involved in the burial corresponds best with John's account (and with illumination of the *Depositio*), as the synoptic gospels mention only Joseph of Arimathea. They then "ongunnon . . . sorhleoð galan/ earme on þa æfentide, þa hie woldon eft siðian,/ meðe fram þam mæran þeodne. Reste he ðær mæte weorode."[94] The singing of the dirge and procession from the tomb are extra-biblical details that certainly might have invoked a Good Friday liturgy, perhaps a service intended to end at Vespers, which is often referred to as "æfentide" or "æfensang."[95] If, as Symons seems to think, the *Depositio* ceremony is a recent importation, it might be too early to look for parallels in *The Dream of the Rood*. The *Adoratio*, however, certainly seems to have been in practice in some form. If so, it would not be too difficult to imagine a *Depositio* elaboration (whether or not one similar to that in the *Concordia*), for in a culture that has so fully developed the idea of the power of Christ bestowed upon the Cross, the taking down of the Cross after the *Adoratio* might be performed with some dignity, and therefore be naturally parallel to the deposition (and perhaps burial) of Christ's body, perhaps accompanied by prayers, or a 'dirge in the dusk.'

In any event, whether the 'dirge' reflects an *Adoratio* or a Deposition song, the return of the poet's voice brings us back to the adoration of the Cross. The Cross is described as having the power to heal, to lead people to Heaven and open its gates, and to transport the faithful to the Lord. The Cross itself, in commanding that people pray to it, perhaps announces the pre-paschal season (if we can take "sæl" to mean 'season' rather than, more generally, 'time' or 'age of the world'): "Is nu sæl cumen/ þæt me

---

[93] George P. Krapp, ed. *The Vercelli Book*, lines 51–6. "I saw the God of Hosts painfully stretched out. Darkness had wrapped with clouds the Ruler's body, shining brightly, the shadows advanced, darkness under the clouds. All creation wept, bewailing the king's fall. Christ was on the Cross."

[94] Lines 67–9. "Began . . . to sing a lament, wretched in the eventide, they then desired afterwards to depart, crestfallen from the great Prince. He rested there with a small troop."

[95] In his Second Letter for Wulfstan, Ælfric specifies that the Mass for Easter Vigils and the "æfensang" should end with one collect (Fehr, *Die Hirtenbriefe Ælfrics*, p. 170). The *Concordia* also instructs that the Mass and Vespers should end with one prayer on that day (Kornexl, *Die Regularis concordia*, p. 102; Symons, *Regularis concordia*, p. 48).

weorðiað wide ond side/ menn ofer moldan ond eall þeos mære gesceaft,/ gebiddaþ him to þyssum beacne."[96] The verb "gebiddaþ" is the same used by Ælfric in his instructions for the *Adoratio*, and which was understood by one glossator as *adorant*. The poet, at the close of the vision, himself offers 'cheerful prayers to that Cross,' as should the poet's audience on Good Friday. The possible relationship between *The Dream of the Rood* and an early *Adoratio* ceremony has particular resonance if one might consider, as does Holloway, the possible use of crosses bearing part of the poem in the Good Friday liturgy. In any case, the Cross seen by the Dreamer, shining against the descending darkness, speaking to the Dreamer about the events of Christ's death (describing the wounds and tortures suffered by both together), demonstrating both the blood of the Passion and the gold and jewels of Christ crowned, and revealing through itself the story (a story with ritual elements) of the Passion, seems above all else to represent the reaction of a masterful poet to the mixed horror and wonder that is the heart of the Good Friday liturgy. The poet must have been familiar with the liturgical idea that it is through the gold Cross that contemporary appreciation of the Passion is translated, and both the structure and the emotional power of the poem are determined by the mental disjunction between seeing the familiar liturgical Cross, understood as one with the True Cross and thus the celebrant's witness to the events, and seeing through it the bloody Christ mounting the Cross, shining against the darkness, taken down, and processionally buried. Whatever the liturgy for Good Friday before the tenth century, *The Dream of the Rood* demonstrates that the highly dramatic liturgy presented in the *Concordia* was, in its central themes and dynamics, entirely native to Anglo-Saxon understanding of the Cross and of commemoration of the Crucifixion.

THE HARROWING OF HELL AND THE EASTER VIGIL

After Christ's death, according to the apocryphal Gospel of Nicodemus, Christ descended to hell and freed those righteous who died before Christ's Passion opened up the way to Heaven for them, and who were being held in some shallow part of Hell (as opposed to the abyss into which Christ proceeds to throw the devil). There are numerous accounts of this Harrowing, many quite short, as is the entry for 26 March (representing Holy Saturday) in the Old English Martyrology,[97] and it is occasionally represented in illumination (see plate 4). Harrowings can also be found in

---

[96] Lines 80–83. "The time has now come that people all over the earth honour me far and wide, and all this great Creation adores this sign."

[97] See Kotzor, *Das altenglische Martyrologium*, vol. II, pp. 45–7, or Herzfeld, *An Old English Martyrology*, p. 50.

Plate 4. The Harrowing of Hell, Tiberius Psalter
London, BL MS Cotton Tiberius C.VI, fol. 14r (by permission of the British Library)

140

three Easter weekend sermons.[98] The sermon in Corpus 41 begins with a passage indicating its sense of time:

> Men þa leofestan, her sagaõ an þissum bocum ymbe õa miclan gewird þe to õisse nihte wearð, þæt ure Drihten, Hælend Crist, on õas niht gewearð, þe nu to niht wæs, þæt he of deaõe aras to midre nihte, and he astagh niõer to helwarum to þan, þæt he wolde þa helle bereafian, and swa gedyde, and þæt ealdordeoful oferswiõan.[99]

Another version of the same sermon from Corpus 303 begins with the rubric *Sermo in resurrectione domini*, and then follows with more or less the same passage. If we can take the rubric to mean that the homily was proper to Easter Vigils (rather than to Friday night), it would seem that the adapters of this sermon understood Saturday evening as being the time first for the Harrowing and then for the Resurrection. In the third, the homily from Cotton Vespasian D.xiv[100] (based more broadly on the *Acti Pilati*), the introduction mentions that its initial events are proper to Friday, including the begging of the body by Joseph and the council inquiries, and then specifies that Sunday has arrived before Carinus and Leuticius, two of those freed from hell and raised with Christ, come along to tell of the Harrowing. These three homilies reveal some of the complex questions confronting those attempting to come to grips with the Anglo-Saxon sense of just what happened between the time of Christ's death on Friday afternoon and his resurrection sometime in the early hours of Sunday. The differences in the various accounts of the Descent into Hell are far too complicated to be dealt with here in any complete way, and I will discuss only briefly its relationship to the liturgy.[101]

When exactly did Christ harrow hell? The Old English Martyrology assigns it generally to 26 March, which stands for Holy Saturday (25 March is dedicated to the Crucifixion, and 27 March to the Resurrection), but this tells us nothing about whether Christ began harrowing hell on Friday night/early Saturday morning or waited until closer to the time of the Resurrection. Liturgically, the final *Tenebrae* early on Saturday, with its dramatic use of darkness, might certainly remind the participants of the darkness of Hell as well as the darkness that covered the world at the

---

[98] Cameron numbers B8.5.3.1–3. The first and second (from London, BL MS Cotton Vespasian D.xiv and from Cambridge, Corpus Christi College MS 41), were edited by William Hulme, "The Old English Gospel of Nicodemus," *Modern Philology* I (1903–4), pp. 570–614. The third, from Cambridge, Corpus Christi College MS 303 and closely related to the sermon in Corpus 41, is unedited.

[99] Hulme, "The Old English Gospel of Nicodemus," p. 610. "Dear men, it speaks here in these books about the great event that belongs to this night, that it happened to our Lord, Christ the Saviour, on this night which was now, tonight, that he arose from death in the middle of the night, and he descended down to the inhabitants of hell, with the intention that he would rob hell, and he did so, and overpowered the ancient devil."

[100] Ibid. pp. 591–610.

[101] See James Cross, ed. *Two Old English Apocrypha and their Manuscript Source* (Cambridge, 1997) for an introduction to and bibliography for a study of these texts.

time of the Crucifixion. In fact, the version of the ritual in Corpus 190 prescribes for Saturday the antiphon *Vita in ligno moritur, infernus ex morsu expoliatur.*[102] But *Tenebrae* is thematically wrong for a com-memoration of the Harrowing, for the light is being extinguished, and the faithful are left in the terror of darkness, rather than freed from it. Actually, the idea that the faithful are in darkness awaiting the light of Christ resonates wonderfully with the idea that by early Saturday morning those in hell still awaited the light of Christ. Many versions of the Harrowing are so extensive, however, that one might imagine the various addresses of prophets and kings to take a day and a half, with the Harrowing beginning quite early. Even in the accounts of Christ's release of the captives from hell we can get no clear sense of time. In the earliest Greek and Latin versions of the Descent,[103] Christ blesses Adam and the others, takes them out of Hell, and delivers them to the archangel Michael, who leads them to Paradise, where they meet Enoch, Elijah, and the thief. There is no further mention of Christ, and no reason to think that he has accompanied them to Paradise. The thief had already arrived, bearing his Cross as a means of gaining entry, and there is no indication as to how long he had been there. He had arrived by himself, and it would seem from the narrative that his first post-death contact with Christ must have happened at some other time. If we can imagine that they had already met sometime Friday night, after the thief had entered Paradise, then the promise, 'Today you will be with me in Paradise,' would have been fulfilled, and the events of the Harrowing could still have happened later. In any case, the question is avoided. Certain of the freed (such as the witnesses Carinus and Leuticius) are then sent back down to earth, where they seem to be raised along with Christ, to give testimony on Sunday. Whether this happens directly, or many hours later, is not specified. There is certainly no consistency in Anglo-Saxon treatment of these issues. According to the Martyrology, Christ releases the prisoners and sends them forth, "ða he wolde gesigefæsted eft siðian to þæm lichoman,"[104] with no indication whether Christ himself went to Paradise or Heaven, or how long it all took. The homilies in Corpus 303 and Corpus 41 seem to have a different arrangement, as the destination of the prisoners has changed:

---

[102] Fehr, *Die Hirtenbriefe Ælfrics*, p. 238. "Life dies on the cross, hell is robbed of its sting." The use of three antiphons, one for each day, is hinted at in the Verdun ritual (although only the first is given), but not in the *Concordia*. See Symons, "Regularis Concordia: History and Derivation," pp. 57–9, for the Verdun ritual and discussion.

[103] See M. R. James, trans. *The Apocryphal New Testament* (Oxford, 1924), pp. 94–146, for translation and comparison of many of the Gospel of Nicodemus passages and recensions. An Old English version of the Gospel was printed by Hulme, "The Old English Version of the Gospel of Nicodemus," *PMLA* 13 (1898), pp. 471–515.

[104] See Kotzor, *Das altenglische Martyrologium*, vol. II, p. 47, or Herzfeld, *An Old English Martyrology*, p. 50. "When he desired afterwards to travel to his body."

Ure drihten nam þa Adam be his handa 7 teah hine of þære helle 7 ealle þa halgan sawla þe þær on wæron. And on þone dæg þe nu todæg is, mycele here hi þa haligra sawla he lædde mid him up of þære helle 7 brohte to heofonu 7 gefeolde þa setl mid þam sawlum þe lange ær weste stodon.[105]

Christ himself seems to bring Adam and the company to heaven (rather than 'paradise'[106]), here explained as filling the place in Heaven that had lain waste, presumably after the fall of the angels (a motif discussed elsewhere, in a different context, by Ælfric). The homilist then goes on to hint at the relationship between Christ's arising on this First Easter eve and his coming at the End. The rest of the homily is an account of the End, including the Reproach-like address of Christ in judgement also found in Vercelli VIII.[107] Again, the gap between the delivery of the freed and the resurrection of Christ is passed over silently. It would seem, from the opening passage of the homily, that the events take place on Saturday evening, but this is by no means certain, and much hinges on whether we are to take the phrase "he of deaðe aras to midre niht," after which he descends to hell, to mean that his spirit arose and went to hell (which could refer to any time) or that he bodily arose on Saturday night, bodily went to hell, freed the prisoners, and took them to heaven. The latter explanation is particularly intriguing, although for the homilist to be saying that Christ went bodily to hell would be surprising.[108]

The Blickling Easter homily may be following a different tradition. After the thanksgiving prayers of Adam, Eve, and the crowd of holy souls, "þe Drihten þa þa here-hyhþ þe on helle genumen hæfde, raþe he lifgende ut eode of his byrgenne mid his agenre mihte aweht, 7 eft mid his unwemmum lichoman hine gegyrede."[109] If indeed Christ has straightaway taken the

---

[105] See Hulme, "The Old English Gospel of Nicodemus," pp. 611. "Our Lord then took Adam by his hands and drew him from hell, and all the holy souls that were therein. And on the day which is now today, he led a great army of holy souls with him up out of hell and brought them to heaven and with those souls filled the places which long before had stood waste."

[106] Cross's parallel edition and translation of the Latin and Old English version of the Gospel of Nicodemus highlights the confusion evident on the part of some writers of this account. According to the Latin, Christ hands Adam over to Michael, who leads all into Paradise (it does not say whether or not Christ went along, although he does not seem to have). The Old English version says that Christ gives Adam to Michael, then goes up to heaven himself ("on heofenas") while the others are led to paradise ("neorxenawang," Cross, *Two Old English Apocrypha*, pp. 232–3). Perhaps the account in the two Corpus homilies reflects a confusion from these sources of Christ's going to heaven and the saints to Paradise.

[107] Both of these homilies include both the Reproach address and that to the sheep and the goats. The Corpus 41 version also has the apocryphal accounts of Holy Mary, St. Michael, and St. Peter each praying for the forgiveness of a third part of those to be saved.

[108] See Zbigniew Izydorczyk's discussion of this apparent arrangement in the Corpus 41 homily, as well as in the Exeter Book's *Descent into Hell*, as "an early instance of the practice that achieved some currency in later medieval art and literature, in spite of its divergence from the usual patristic and credal chronology" in "The Inversion of Paschal Events in the Old English Descent into Hell," *Neuphilologische Mitteilungen* 91.4 (1990), p. 441.

[109] Morris, *The Blickling Homilies*, p. 89. "The Lord, when he had taken that plunder that was in hell, quickly he went out living from his tomb, awakened by his own might, and afterwards girded himself with his unstained body."

freed, the 'plunder,' with him to his own resurrection (there is no indication of where they go after that), then the Harrowing and the Resurrection are concurrent. The account in the Martyrology is short, but it too gives no indication of the destination of the freed. In fact, they are not led out by Christ, but are sent forth before him ("unrim bliðes folces him beforan onsende") as Christ prepares to return to his body in triumph. The fact that there are so many arrangements of the events leading up to the Resurrection and that none of them provides a clear, unambiguous indication of just when the events occurred probably demonstrates more than anything else that the Anglo-Saxons themselves did not know, and that therefore the entire time between late Friday and late Saturday/early Sunday might be considered as the time of the Harrowing.

Liturgically, references are made to the Harrowing both in the final *Tenebrae* and in the liturgy for Easter Vigils. The first benediction for the Easter Vigil Mass in the Canterbury Benedictional invokes the Harrowing: "Deus sacratissime noctis huius splendor lucifluus, qui virtute divina mortis confractis viribus, leo fortis, claustra disrupit tartarea, benedicat vos."[110] The prayers for the blessing of the Paschal candle (from the Winchcombe Sacramentary), in singing about the wonder of the holy night of the Resurrection, seem to include the Harrowing as one of the events relevant to that night:

> Haec est nox, in qua primum patres nostros filios Israel eduxisti de Aegypto, quos postea rubrum mare sicco vestigio transire fecisti. Haec igitur nox est, quae peccatorum tenebras columnae inluminatione purgavit. Haec nox est, quae hodiae per universum mundum in christum credentes, a vitiis saeculi segregatos, et caligine peccatorum, reddit gratiae, sociatque sanctitati. Haec nox est, in qua destructis vinculis mortis, christus ab inferis victor ascendit. Nihil enim nobis nasci profuit, nisi redimi profuisset . . . O beata nox, quae sola meruit scire tempus et horam, in qua christus ab inferis resurrexit.[111]

The idea that Christ's light purged away the darkness of sin certainly reflects the central image of the Old English Harrowings, the appearance of the light in the darkness. The reference to Christ breaking the chains of death might refer to his own resurrection rather than to the freeing of those in hell, but that he, after breaking the bonds, rose up as victor from hell,

---

[110] Woolley, *The Canterbury Benedictional*, p. 45. "God, lightgiver, brilliance of this most holy night, who, strong lion, by divine strength, with the power of death having been broken, shattered the gates of hell, bless us."

[111] Davril, *The Winchcombe Sacramentary*, p. 82. "This is the night, in which first you led our fathers, sons of Israel, from Egypt, whom afterwards you made to cross the Red Sea with a dry step. This, then, is the night, which purged the darkness of sins with the light of the pillar of fire. This is the night, which at this present time restores to grace and unites in holiness those believing in Christ throughout the whole world, removed from the vices of the world and from the darkness of sin. This is the night, in which, having destroyed the chains of death, the triumphant Christ ascended from hell. Not at all, indeed, would it profit us to be born, if we had not been redeemed . . . O blessed night, which alone merited to know the time and the hour in which Christ rose from hell."

seems to make it a reference to both events, as he both exits hell and rises from the dead on the same night, celebrated in Easter Vigils, specifically at the part of the liturgy for the day where light first appears. The reference to the mystery of exactly what time Christ 'rose up from the netherworld' reflects the inability of medieval Christians to pin down this chronology, and allows the conflation of commemoration both of the Harrowing and of the Resurrection at Vigils.[112] Perhaps the tradition evident in the Blickling homily, in which the destination of the freed saints and the whereabouts of Christ between the Harrowing and the Resurrection are passed over, reflects the force of the liturgically established idea that Christ defeated death and rose from the dead concurrently.

The Harrowing of Hell can have dramatic force not just because it makes an exciting story, but because those reading the story, or hearing the sermon, or partaking in the liturgy are themselves being freed from the darkness of hell, mimicked by the darkness of the church before the lighting of the Paschal candle.[113] This connection is implied in the prayer above for the candle blessing, where the ideas of Christ arising the victor from hell and of each of the faithful needing to be not just born but redeemed are juxtaposed. Anglo-Saxon treatments of the Harrowing reveal an interest in establishing sympathetic identifications with those being freed. From at least the ninth century, the Harrowing of Hell has been made personal to the Anglo-Saxons, devotionally, through narrative technique, and in the liturgy. Although, as was the case with the *Adoratio*, we can say little about the particulars of the Easter liturgy before the tenth century, exploration of the Harrowing in Anglo-Saxon England shows great familiarity with the idea of direct identification with those freed from hell, a familiarity that had dramatic consequences for Easter Vigils.

The central elements of the Harrowing, in its narrative developments, include the appearance of a light in the darkness of hell, the complaints/ questions of the devils in response to the light, the breaking of the gates, the driving of the devils into the abyss, the plaints of the faithful (including the likes of Abraham and David, and often several of the prophets) to be freed, and then of Adam and, especially, Eve, who invokes her daughter Mary. Quite frequently, the Harrowing is followed by an account of the end of the world. Vercelli homily I (in the A version) and *The Dream of the Rood* both end with the Harrowing, a natural conclusion for a Good Friday homily and for a poem that reflects so strongly the liturgical and thematic dynamics

---

[112] Perhaps, as well, it reflects the related desire to expect the End at the time of commemoration of the Resurrection. Matthew 24:36ff makes clear that "about the day and the hour [of the end of the world] no one knows," and the phrasing of this parallel liturgical clause might allow just enough ambiguity to conform with Christ's prophecy and still expect the Second Coming some time during the night.

[113] The church is to be understood as dark before the appearance of the light from the New Fire from which the Paschal candle is lit, even though the Mass would have been celebrated, according to recent Roman custom, in the afternoon (see below, p. 153).

of Good Friday. Most dominant is the importance of light versus darkness. In the Martyrology's account, Adam and Eve "asmorede wæron mid deopum ðeostrum" until they "gesawon his þæt beorhte leoht æfter þære langan worolde."[114] The Cotton Vespasian Harrowing homily (following more closely the Gospel of Nicodemus than do many Anglo-Saxon versions of the Descent) allows Carinus and Leuticius to describe Christ's arrival in Hell:

> Carinus and Leuticius þa ongunnen writen, "Efne we wæron þa mid eallen uren fæderen on þære deopen helle, þær becom mycel brihtnysse ofer us ealle swylce sunne leome. Sathanas and eall hellewerod wæron afyrhte and þuss cwædon, 'Hwæt is þiss liht þæt her swa færlice scinð?' þa wæs sona eall þæt mænnisc cynn blissigende and Adam mid eallen hehfæferen and witegan for þan mycelan lihte, and heo þuss cwæden, 'þiss liht is of Godes lihte . . .'"[115]

This sort of narrative device, putting the explanation of the Harrowing into the mouths of those freed, encourages the audience to sympathize with these two protagonists, and by proxy prepares them to see themselves freed from sin by the light of Christ appearing, fittingly, on Easter eve.

The dramatic potential of the Harrowing story, especially in its core petitions by Adam and Eve to be freed, was realized in more devotional forms as well. In many ways, its earliest extant manifestation is still its most interesting. At the end of the ninth-century section of the Book of Cerne is a Latin version of the Harrowing, from the general prayers of those in hell to the petition of Eve (during which the text breaks off). The Cerne Harrowing was edited and discussed by David Dumville.[116] The text consists of a series of petitions separated by rubrics indicating the shift in speakers. Of particular interest to Dumville are two points. First, red ink seems to have been used "in order to differentiate clearly between narrative and spoken sections,"[117] possibly so as to assist performance by three soloists (a narrator, Adam, and Eve) as well as the full choir. Dumville also postulates that the red sections may be "rubrics or 'stage directions' in our earliest surviving example of Christian dramatic literature, written specifically to be acted."[118] Second, many of the verbs used in the narrative sections are in the

---

[114] See Kotzor, *Das altenglische Martyrologium*, vol. II, p. 46, or Herzfeld, *An Old English Martyrology*, p. 50. "Were smothered with deep darkness . . . saw that bright light after that long time."

[115] See Hulme, "The Old English Gospel of Nicodemus," p. 600. "Carinus and Leuticius then began to write, 'Indeed, we were then with all our fathers in the deep hell, where there came a great brightness over us all just like a sunbeam. Satan and all the hell-dwellers were frightened and thus said, "What is this light that here so beautifully shines?" Then was all that humankind immediately joyful, and Adam with all the patriarchs and prophets because of that great light, and they said thus, "This light is the light of God."'"

[116] David Dumville, "Liturgical Drama and Panegyric Responsory from the Eighth Century? A Re-Examination of the Origin and Contents of the Ninth-Century Book of Cerne," *JTS* 23 (1972), pp. 374–88.

[117] Ibid. p. 380.

[118] Ibid. p. 381.

present tense (although a few remain in the past tense, which Dumville attempts to explain or emend). I will give an outline of the extant piece, providing the rubrics as printed in Dumville[119] and extracting or summarizing the prayers so as to demonstrate the structure of the piece:

> *Hæc est oratio innumerabilis sanctorum populi qui tenebantur in inferni captivitate. Lacrimabili voce et obsecratione Salvatorem deposcunt, dicentes, quando ad infernos discendit . . .*[120]

(A prayer in response to Christ's appearance in Hell beginning "Advenisti Redemptor mundi; advenisti quem desiderantes cotidie sperabamus; advenisti quem nobis futurum lux nuntiaverat et prophetae; advenisti donans in carne vivis indulgentiam peccatoribus mundi. Solve defunctos captivos inferni!" followed by more penitential petitioning. Christ also sets up his cross-sign in Hell.)[121]

> *Postquam autem audita est postulatio et obsecratio innumerabilium captivorum, statim iubente Domini omnes antiqui iusti, sine aliqua mora ad imperium Domini Salvatoris resolutis vinculis, Domini Salvatoris genibus obvoluti, humili supplicatione cum ineffabili gaudio, clamantes . . .*[122]

(A short prayer in the plural regarding the breaking of the chains, beginning "Disrupti, Domine, vincula nostra.")

> *Adam autem et Eva adhuc non sunt desoluti de vinculis. Tunc Adam, lugubri ac miserabili voce, clamabat ad Dominum, dicens . . .*[123]

(A prayer in the singular that the chains be broken, beginning "Miserere mei, Deus," and further praying that the speaker's spirit not be left in the inferno.)

> *Tunc, Domino miserante, Adam, e vinculis resolutus, Iesu Christi genibus provolutus.*[124]

(A prayer of thanksgiving for forgiveness, beginning "Benedic, anima mea, Dominum" and making no specific reference to the Harrowing, instead speaking generally in terms of freedom from 'langour' and destruction.)

> *Adhuc Eva persistit in fletu, dicens . . .*[125]

(Another quite general prayer for mercy, making no reference to the Harrowing itself or to the intervention of Mary, before ending, as Dumville believes, imperfectly.)

---

[119] Ibid. pp. 376–7.

[120] "This is the prayer of the innumerable holy people who were kept in the captivity of hell. With a mournful voice and with supplication, they entreat the Saviour, saying, when he goes down into hell . . ."

[121] "You have come, Redeemer of the world; you have come, he for whom we, longing, have hoped daily; you have come, he whom the prophets announced for us, the coming light; you have come, offering in living flesh pardon for the sins of the world. Save the lost captives of hell!"

[122] "Then after the petition is heard, and the entreaty of the innumerable captives, immediately all, by the decree of the Lord, the ancient just one, without any delay to the authority of the Lord Saviour for the destroyed chains, remaining on knees, in humble supplication with ineffable joy, saying . . ." Dumville discusses problems with this introduction (p. 383), attributing the lack of a main verb, and other difficulties, to problems in authorial editing.

[123] "However, Adam and Eve yet have not been freed from the chains. Now Adam, with a grievous and miserable voice, was crying out to the Lord, saying . . ."

[124] "Now Adam, having been freed from the chains with lamenting to the Lord, [is] bent forwards on his knees to Jesus Christ."

[125] "Yet Eve continues to weep, saying . . ."

147

Perhaps the inconsistency in verb tense in these rubrics is due to an imperfect adaptation from a narrative original to a set of rubrics providing context for a series of vocal prayers. Dumville sees in this Harrowing "very early evidence for the development of the liturgical drama, antedating the earliest extant *Quem quaeritis* text (from Saint-Martial de Limoges) by a century."[126] He goes on to postulate that the version in this ninth-century text (dated c. 800–820 by Dumville, c. 820–840 by Brown[127]) is a copy of an earlier Northumbrian text of the eighth century, such that "The possibility of an original home for the liturgical drama would be shifted from a continental to an Irish-influenced Anglo-Saxon context."[128] To support the idea, he points to "an eighth-century MS (probably from a Northumbrian centre) containing the Gospels of Luke and John" (from Luke 22ff and John 18ff, covering the Passion) which "has a series of liturgical lection-marks entered in the margin by a later Anglo-Saxon hand. These occur in the sections on the Passion, an *l* denoting the words of Christ, a *c* those of the narrator."[129] This presentation certainly bears similarity to later medieval chanting of the Passion narratives according to parts, as part of the development of liturgical drama. With such an early appreciation for the possibilities of sung parts differentiated by character, perhaps Cerne's Harrowing is indeed "the earliest example of liturgical drama which is extant."[130]

Brown, however, is dubious about its role in terms of performance:

> Whatever the original function of this text, its appearance in Cerne lies, I would suggest, in the relevance of its theme to Cerne's overall preoccupation with the *communio sanctorum*. In such an interpretation of Cerne's major theme, the Harrowing therefore would appear as a motif of the Church Expectant, rather than as a functioning piece of liturgical drama.[131]

Taken this way, the Harrowing texts are more parallel to the *Adoratio* prayers earlier in the manuscript, more devotional than performance-based. The Harrowing of Hell, in a narrative context, would have been quite well known to the compilers of this manuscript (Dumville[132] and Brown[133] discuss certain sources) who here have adapted prayers taken largely from the Psalms (the Harrowing is preceded by an Irish-influenced Breviate Psalter) and mixed them with details and rubrics placing the prayers in the context of the Harrowing of Hell. Whether or not the piece had a liturgical function, it is certainly consonant both with the elements of the liturgy that

---

[126] *JTS* 23 (1972), p. 381.
[127] Brown, *The Book of Cerne*, p. 18.
[128] David Dumville, "Liturgical Drama and Panegyric Responsory," p. 381.
[129] Ibid. pp. 381–2, n. 2.
[130] Ibid. p. 374.
[131] Brown, *The Book of Cerne*, p. 146.
[132] David Dumville, "Liturgical Drama and Panegyric Responsory," pp. 386–8.
[133] Brown, *The Book of Cerne*, p. 145.

refer to the Harrowing and with other vernacular and devotional treatments of the idea. Actually, it may be misleading to refer to this piece as a 'Harrowing of Hell,' even though that is clearly its inspiration. There are no laments of the angels, no casting of the Devil into the abyss. We are given simply the voices of those in chains, seeing Christ appearing as a light and begging him to free them. General, psalm-based devotional prayers are given to Adam and Eve, so that the voices of those freed from chains are joined with the voices of those singing these prayers. This is the primary purpose of the rubrics, whatever their functional context, to make the singer feel that he or she is one of those seeing the light of Christ, begging for release, and being granted specific pardon. It is this sense of unity with those in the Harrowing, developed, as we shall see, in the liturgy, in particular in the liturgy for Holy Saturday, that makes the piece dramatic. Although it would be too much, with this, to look for an Irish-influenced Anglo-Saxon tradition of liturgical drama, we can say that the Anglo-Saxon church from an early stage was intimate with the idea of dramatic identification which was the impetus for and heart of the liturgical drama throughout the Middle Ages. We can also say more specifically that from an early stage Anglo-Saxons were developing devotional pieces that allowed them to sing with the voices of Adam and Eve, praying to be forgiven and released from the darkness of sin and praising God for his saving power. By the time of the tenth-century liturgy, developing this identification with those in hell in the prayers for the new light at Vigils might have been merely a dramatic adaptation of a widespread and longstanding native dynamic.

The most complete vernacular account of this strain of the Harrowing is in the Blickling Easter Homily. Many of the elements of the Gospel of Nicodemus, including the witnessing of the twins and the chain of prophets and kings who proclaim at length, are absent, and the story focuses on the light of Christ and the prayers of Adam and Eve, such that it seems more indebted to Cerne (or, as is generally posited, to a common lost Latin original[134]) than to Nicodemus. Christ's victory is specifically described as "overcoming the devil's darkness with his shining light." The kinetic details and the dramatic use of dialogue in the sermon make its audience sympathise with the main protagonists, Adam and Eve. The connection between the congregation and those delivered from hell is strengthened in the account of their forgiveness. The other captives have been sent on ahead, and the devil cast into the abyss. Adam and Eve, however, the first sinners, are specifically left in bonds. Adam begs forgiveness in a few lines, is set free, and responds with a song of thanksgiving (both of his prayers are, with minor differences, the psalm-based prayers given him in Cerne). Eve, through all this, "þa gyt on bendum 7 owope þurhwunode."[135] Her

---

[134] See Dumville, "Liturgical Drama and Panegyric Responsory," p. 375.
[135] Morris, *The Blickling Homilies*, p. 89. "Still remained on knees, weeping."

prayer is longer, and more heartfelt. It follows her prayer in Cerne until Cerne breaks off, at "ne declines in ira ab ancilla tua."[136] She acknowledges her guilt, that "ic wæs mid weorþmende on neorxna wange, 7 ic þæt ne ongeat"[137] and, pointing to her time of weeping and lamentation, admits that she is dust and ashes. She begs him, by Mary, who is 'flesh of her flesh,' to release her, after which she is freed. This plea reminds us of the role of Mary as expressed in the Blickling homily on the Annunciation of St. Mary, where Mary is portrayed as the direct contrast of Eve, succeeding exactly where Eve failed (a common topos). As Adam's failure was absolved by the new Adam, Christ, so Eve's was absolved by the new Eve, Mary. The dramatic forgiveness of Adam and Eve, presented to the audience in direct dialogue, focuses forgiveness for Lenten repentance to this one point. Particularly given the intense associations between the participants and Adam established in Lent, Adam's forgiveness is theirs. It is at this moment, the triumphant return of Christ with the original sinners to which the homilist then points, that the fruits of correct and zealous Lenten and Holy Week observance are realized.

In fact, this dramatic, liturgically consonant understanding of the Harrowing may even have influenced certain versions of the *Acti Pilati* itself. A few aspects of the Harrowing presented in Cerne and developed in Blickling do not seem to have been properly part of the *Acti* until a later date. Regarding Cerne's relationship to the *Acti*, Dumville points out:

> Evidence seems to be lacking in this text for a direct knowledge of the *Acti Pilati*. While there is a certain similarity with the Latin A Recension, Art ii, c. viii, the B recension, cc. ix/x, introduces Eve, Christ's placing His Cross in Hell, and the use of the verb 'provoluere.' The most likely explanation is that our text's source, now represented only by the Blickling version in Old English, was responsible for the introduction of these features.[138]

The Harrowing story developed separately from the rest of the *Acti Pilati*, and was only later attached to it. Other English Harrowings (see the homilies based on the Gospel of Nicodemus) focus on Recension A, with the prayers of Esaias, Simeon, John the Baptist, David, and Isaiah, among others, with elements of Recension B (to which the Blickling version is related) mixed in (M. R. James provides a schema comparing the elements of the two recensions and presenting them in parallel[139]). Recension B is shorter and, while it keeps speeches from Seth, Isaiah, John the Baptist, and David, the story of the actual removal of the faithful from hell focuses on Adam and Eve and the setting up of the Cross in Hell rather than, in Recension A, the greeting of Adam, speeches from several others, and

---

[136] Dumville, "Liturgical Drama and Panegyric Responsory," p. 377.
[137] Morris, *The Blickling Homilies*, p. 89. "I was living in glory in paradise, and I did not perceive it."
[138] Dumville, "Liturgical Drama and Panegyric Responsory," p. 377, n. c.
[139] See James, *The Apocryphal New Testament*, pp. 118ff.

meetings with Enoch, Elias, and the thief. This section of Recension B is altogether more dramatically concise, and more personally applicable, perhaps because of its development in terms of dramatic identification by the Anglo-Saxon adapters.

This dramatic identification informs part of the liturgy for Holy Saturday, specifically the lighting and blessing of the Paschal candle with which Easter Vigils begins. The Mass at the end of Vigils was the original Easter Mass, and probably from apostolic times the commemoration consisted of an all-night vigil. Its early development has been discussed by most historians of the early church liturgy.[140] From at least the third century, it has been associated with baptism, which would be performed at the end of the Vigils (and before the Mass), in the early dawn. Talley discusses the ritual in fourth-century Jerusalem, and its result: "Topologically, as well as sacramentally, the newborn are introduced into the Church having just stepped from the tomb of Christ" at the time of the Resurrection.[141] Also from an early stage, at least in Africa, in the churches of Gaul, and in parts of Italy, the lighting of the Paschal Candle has been a dominant feature.[142] The Vigil was shortened over the centuries, however, possibly due to a decrease in Easter baptisms, and sometime between the eighth and tenth centuries it was anticipated on the previous afternoon (at None in most Anglo-Saxon witnesses). In the Gelasian, the liturgy for Saturday begins with the *Abrenuntio*, given the catechumens, and then goes on to the blessing of the Paschal candle, which includes several references to the Harrowing, especially in terms of light and darkness, and the participants speak as those seeing the light and being freed:

> Deus qui iacentem mundum in tenebris luce perspicua retexisti . . . in quo Dominicae resurrectionis miraculo diem sibi introductum *tenebrae* inveteratae senserunt, et mors, quae olim fuerat aeterna nocte damnata, inserto veri fulgoris lumine, captivam se trahi Dominicis triumphis obstupuit, et quod praevaricante primoplasto tenebrosa praesumptione fuerat in servitute damnatum, huius noctis miraculo splendore libertatis irradiat. . . . Nam ut, praecedente huius luminis gratia, tenebrarum horror excluditur, ita, Domine, lucescente maiestatis tuae imperio, peccatorum sarcinae diluuntur.[143]

---

[140] See Talley, *The Origins of the Liturgical Year*, pp. 5ff. Also, Jungmann, *The Mass of the Roman Rite*, pp. 261ff; Duchesne, *Christian Worship*, pp. 234ff; and Cross and Livingstone, *The Oxford Dictionary of the Christian Church*, pp. 1226–7.

[141] Talley, *The Origins of the Liturgical Year*, p. 51.

[142] See Duchesne, *Christian Worship*, pp. 252ff.

[143] Wilson, *The Gelasian Sacramentary*, p. 80. "God, you who revealed with clear light the world sleeping in darkness . . . in which the ancient darkness itself perceived the intruding daylight by the miracle of the Lord's resurrection, and death, which was formerly eternal with the damned night, was stupefied by the triumph, made captive by the Lord, by the intruding light of true brilliance, and which, colluding with the primordial darkness, was employed in damned servitude, he illuminated with the splendor of freedom by the miracle of this night. . . . So as the dread of darkness is removed by the surpassing grace of this light, so, Lord, let the burdens of sinners be washed away by the shining authority of your majesty."

The Gelasian then gives ten scriptural lessons from the Old Testament,[144] and all proceed to the font for its blessing and for baptism, followed by the first Easter Mass, and the first communion for the newly baptized, at the end of Vigils. The reading for this Mass, which originally would have been coincident with the time of the Resurrection, seems to have been Matthew's account of the women at the tomb. Later on Easter day was a second Mass, which had for its reading the following passage in Matthew, where Christ appears to all the disciples at Galilee. Although we can only speculate as to the liturgy of eighth-century Northumbria, this seems to be the liturgical arrangement with which Bede was familiar, and which his homilies reflect. Bede has a homily for Holy Saturday, apparently for a Main Mass preceding Vigils, discussing Mark 7:31–7, the deaf-mute healed by Christ with the word "Effeta."[145] His exegesis makes clear and repetitive references to baptism, explicitly an upcoming baptism for catechumens in his audience. For Easter Vigils, Bede gives exegesis for Matthew 28:1–10, the story of the women at the tomb.[146] After mentioning the time of the Passion and the 'declining' sun (not obscured totally, but declining naturally in the afternoon), he explains how the women could be approaching both the night before and in the dawning of Easter, claiming that, on this night,

> Our Lord, the author and controller of time, he who rose [from the dead] during the final part of the night, surely caused the whole of it to be festal and bright by the light of his resurrection. . . . we who have come to know that this special night has been illuminated by the grace of our Lord's resurrection must also take particular care lest any part of it become dark in our hearts. All of it should become light as day for us, especially now when we are keeping vigil with the devotion of worthy praise, and are awaiting with a pure and sober conscience the feast of Easter Sunday when we have completed this vigil.[147]

However long Bede's vigil actually went on, it was still understood as lasting all night, and ending with a Mass that represented the main Easter Mass, with the reading of the first proof of his resurrection.

---

[144] The later Gelasian witnesses present the classic twelve lessons (see the Murbach *comes*). Twelve Old Testament lessons were prescribed in the Armenian lectionary, which Talley postulates as reflecting the use in Egeria's Jerusalem. The twelve lessons were taken up in many places in the West, especially in Spain and Gaul, with some variation in makeup of the twelve (a detailed comparison is given by Talley, *The Origins of the Liturgical Year*, pp. 48ff). He considers the spread of the twelve lessons to reflect a "community of tradition" for the Vigil spreading from Jerusalem to Gaul. In the Gregorian form, a longer vigil was reduced to four readings (always beginning, as did the twelve, with Genesis 1:1), possibly from an earlier seven-reading format (Talley, *The Origins of the Liturgical Year*, p. 53). The Gregorian Sacramentary sent to the Carolingians had apparently the four forms (see Deshusses, *Le sacramentaire grégorien* pp. 183–5), but the Supplement, drawing from Gelasian witnesses, provides the Gelasian twelve. Reflecting either this doubling in their primary liturgical sources or a lingering influence from their own earlier Gelasian forms, later Anglo-Saxon witnesses inconsistently provide four or twelve. The Robert Missal, the *Concordia*, and the instructions for Vigils in Corpus 190 (see Fehr, *Die Hirtenbriefe Ælfrics*, pp. 228–31) have only four. Leofric A and the Winchcombe Sacramentary have twelve.
[145] See Martin and Hurst, *Bede the Venerable: Homilies on the Gospels*, vol. 2, pp. 51–7.
[146] See ibid. pp. 58–68.
[147] Ibid. pp. 60–1.

A passage in the Old English Life of St. Machutus seems to reflect this early arrangement:

To þæm mynstre wæs cumende sancte machutes modor on þone halgan easteræfen, 7 þa niht þær to wacianne, 7 heo þa þær on þa niht hire sunu cende sanctum machutem. *De baptismo eius*: þone brendanus [the abbot] gefulgade 7 hine of þon fonte uparærde, 7 syþþan hine for gastlice sunu hæfde, 7 hine getrywlice 7 geleaffullice fedde fram fruman his yldo oþþæt he sprecan mihte 7 andget hæfde.[148]

A future saint can have no more holy a start in life than to be born early on Easter Vigils, baptized at its end (presumably in the morning, if Machutus' mother planned to stay awake all night), with the abbot as his godfather, speaking for him in the baptismal Credo, and given his first Mass on the feast of the Resurrection. One could hardly be born in a manner so directly parallel to Christ's 'rebirth' over the same course of time and not become a saint. Awareness of the early Vigil arrangement allows for the hero's birth story. By the time of the tenth-century church, however, Vigils had been moved to None on Saturday afternoon, ending in the early night (with "æfensang" in Ælfric's Letter and Vespers in the *Concordia*[149]). A few witnesses provide the Old Testament lessons and baptismal forms for Holy Saturday, but their place in Easter is by the Anglo-Saxon period tenuous, and while the font is still blessed, Easter baptisms are not assumed in instructions for the day.[150] Directions are given in the *Concordia*, in Corpus 190, and in Ælfric's Second Letter for Wulfstan, and all agree as to its fundamental elements, although the *Concordia*, typically, has elaborations.[151] According to the *Concordia*, at None, the new fire is brought in and used to light the Paschal candle, which had been placed on the altar. The candle, freshly lit, is blessed, 'as is the custom,' with the prayer *Exultet iam angelica turba coelorum*.[152] This prayer and the following readings come

[148] Yerkes, *The Old English Life of St. Machutus*, p. 5. "The mother of Saint Machutus was approaching the minster on the holy Easter Eve to keep vigil there overnight, and she then on that night gave birth there to her son, Saint Machutus. *De baptismo eius*: Brendanus the abbot baptized him and lifted him up from the font, and afterwards took him as a godson, and truly and faithfully fed him from his infancy until he could speak and had understanding."

[149] A rubric in the Leofric Collectar, following None on Holy Saturday, reflects the combined monastic/secular nature of the Vigil and the intended time of its conclusion: "Vespertinalis sinaxis infra missam et cum missa ipsius diei completur" (Dewick and Frere, *The Leofric Collectar*, p. 133). This combined nature is highlighted by the *Concordia*'s instruction that the Monastic Office be replaced by the Secular Office from Maundy Thursday through Easter Week (See Symons, *Regularis concordia*, p. 49, n. 3).

[150] See below, "Baptism in Anglo-Saxon England."

[151] Kornexl, *Die Regularis concordia*, pp. 99–103; Symons, *Regularis concordia*, pp. 47–9; Fehr, *Die Hirtenbriefe Ælfrics*, pp. 228–31 and pp. 168–71.

[152] Among the relics listed at Exeter (see Max Förster, ed. *Zur Geschichte des Reliquienkultus in Altengland* (Munich, 1943), p. 70), along with a piece of the True Cross and relics from the Sepulchre, Christ's garment, the manger, the spear, the Burning Bush, and the altar that 'Christ himself hallowed' (presumably on Maundy Thursday), is "Of þære candele, ðe Godes engel ontende mid heofenlicum leohte æt ures Drihtenes sepulchre on easteræfen" ("From the candle, which God's angel kindled with heavenly light at our Lord's sepulchre on Easter Eve"). The idea

153

from the Supplement to the Gregorian Sacramentary.[153] As did the Gelasian prayers, they describe those present as freed from the bonds of darkness by this new light of Christ. After a second candle is lit (the second candle is not mentioned in Ælfric's Letter or in Corpus 190), the four Gregorian lessons are given. All then process to the font singing seven litanies, and the font is blessed, along with five more litanies. They return to the altar with three more litanies for the return of the *Gloria in excelsis Deo*, which had been absent from the liturgy since Septuagesima Sunday.

In the vernacular accounts, now follow the *Gloria* and the Vigil Mass, including the *Alleluia*. The Benedictions for this Mass (see above) again make reference to the Harrowing in terms of light. Nothing more is mentioned, and the service has most certainly lost the sense of an all-night vigil. However, it still retains much of the flavour of its original function as the primary Easter Mass, with the reintroduction of the *Gloria* and the *Alleluia*. The *Concordia* adds a bit of drama to the anticipated *Gloria* (as an elaboration of the Vigil Mass). With only the two candles lit,

> antequam cantatur *Gloria in excelsis Deo*, magister scholae dicat alta voce: *Accendite*. Et tunc illuminentur omnia luminaria ecclesiae et, abbate incipiente *Gloria in excelsis Deo*, pulsentur omnia signa,[154]

followed by the Collect of the Mass. This elaboration, with the powerful *Accendite*, the sudden lighting of the whole church, the triumphant *Gloria*, and the pealing of the bells, certainly reflects the idea that the *Gloria* is reintroduced to the liturgy in response to Christ's resurrection. The fact that the Eucharist can be blessed, as it could not on Friday or earlier on Saturday, indicates that Christ has risen, as does the gospel for the Mass, the account of the women at the sepulchre. Also, it would seem that the guards set before the buried Cross after the *Depositio* and told to keep watch "usque dominicam noctem resurrectionis"[155] end their vigil at this time. We are told that no lights are to proceed the gospel book as it is processed to the altar, but only incense, a practice that Amalarius describes as in imitation of the holy women.[156] Alongside this recognition of the Vigil's original import, however, is a sense that, as it is still Saturday evening, Christ has not indeed yet risen. While the dominant mood at the

---

that God's angel kept a candle burning in vigil at the tomb on Easter eve shows how dependent Anglo-Saxon perception of the events at the tomb was on the liturgical expression.

[153] See Deshusses, *Le sacramentaire grégorien*, pp. 360–1.

[154] Kornexl, *Die Regularis concordia*, p. 101; see also Symons, *Regularis concordia*, p. 48. "Before the *Gloria in excelsis Deo* is sung, the master of the schola shall say in a loud voice, *Accendite*. And now all of the candles in the church shall be lit and, with the abbot beginning the *Gloria in excelsis Deo*, all of the bells shall be rung . . ." Ælfric in his Eynsham Letter says that the *Accendite* is to be said three times (*LME*, p. 135).

[155] Kornexl, *Die Regularis concordia*, p. 96; see also Symons, *Regularis concordia*, p. 45. "Until the night of the resurrection of the Lord."

[156] See Fehr, *Die Hirtenbriefe Ælfrics*, p. 231, n. dd. Ælfric repeats Amalarius' interpretation in his Eynsham Letter (*LME*, p. 135).

end of Easter Vigils is one of triumph in the Resurrection, there remains a feeling of expectation. The *Concordia* and the ritual of Fleury are peculiar in prescribing a chapter announcement for Holy Saturday. Throughout the year, the festival for the following day is announced from the Martyrology at Chapter. In the *Concordia*'s instructions for Christmas, the feast of Christmas is announced on the Vigil, in expectation of Christ's coming on the following day. Then follows the instruction:

> Sabbato quoque sancto paschae, dum a puero *Resurrectio Domini nostri Ihesu Christi* legitur, quamquam in martyrlogio id non habetur, propter eius glorio-sissimi victoriam triumphi, quam destructis herebi claustris secum fideles quosque in celos advexit, nobis etiam redivivis spem ascendendi concessit, uniformiter agatur.[157]

The chapter announcement leads the brethren to expect on Sunday to celebrate Christ's rising with those rescued from Hell. What we see here is the same sort of thing that happened to the Christmas liturgy. As both Bede and the anonymous author of a homily titled *In Sabbato sancto* (discussed below, pp. 156ff) tell us, Christ rose from the dead during the night (the Old English writer actually specifies that he rose "on ðysse halgan nihte ufanweardre"[158]), just as he had been born during the night at Christmas, and was revealed to the world sometime in the dawning of the day. When the *In Nocte* Christmas Mass, at which the *Gloria* is reintroduced after Advent (in its original significance, whereby the angels reveal to the shepherds that Christ has been born), was moved earlier and earlier in the night, a previously unrelated Mass for the Byzantine Anastasia was shifted to early dawn on Christmas morning, and the celebration of Christ's birth was split by the two (see chapter 2 above, "Christmas and Epiphany"). So here, when Easter Vigils lost some of its temporal coincidence, a new Mass was introduced on Easter morning, with another reading about the women at the sepulchre, and the revelation of Christ's resurrection was celebrated in both. Early Easter morning is also, for the same reasons, the prescribed time for what was developed as a liturgical highlight to this Easter morning revelation, the *Visitatio Sepulchri*, a ritual based on these same two readings (those from Matthew and Mark).

Easter Vigils is fundamentally a festival of the Resurrection. However, with the relative loss of temporal coincidence with the Resurrection and the proliferation of liturgical forms that make reference to the Harrowing, along with the lingering sense of anticipation, Easter Vigils can be examined

---

[157] Kornexl, *Die Regularis concordia*, pp. 58–9; see also Symons, *Regularis concordia*, p. 28. "It shall be done in the same way as on Holy Saturday, when *Resurrectio Domini nostri Ihesu Christi* is read out by one of the children, although this is not set down in the Martyrology, in honour of his most glorious triumph of the victory by which, having broken the locks of hell, he carried with him into the heavens certain of his faithful ones and gave to us, newly restored to life, the hope of ascending there."

[158] Evans, "An anonymous Old English homily," p. 138. "At the peak of this holy night."

as a reenactment of the events preceding the Resurrection. The congregation, thoroughly familiar with the voices of those in the darkness of hell (many of them might have heard or read about the Harrowing in some version on this day, reinforcing the potential identification), see a new light spring up in the mouth of the serpent (the third New Fire), sing its praises in terms of the Harrowing as the light becomes, in the lighting of the Paschal candle, clearly revealed as the light of Christ here to free them from the darkness of their sins, and expect soon Christ's resurrection, the inevitable outcome of the defeat of sin and death that is the point of the Harrowing. The distance between the lighting of the Paschal candle and the final Mass, when the gospel of the women at the tomb is read, can be understood as the distance between Christ's appearance as a light in Hell and the full revelation of his victory in the early hours of the morning, the second following hard upon the first, and celebrated more fully the following morning.

EASTER MORNING AND THE *VISITATIO*

This brings us to the ritual that, as Peter Dronke laments, has "received an almost inordinate amount of scholarly attention – and controversy – in the last half-century" in the study of the earliest forms of Western drama.[159] It is hard to divorce the *Visitatio Sepulchri* from this general history of drama, of which it has been for so long the cornerstone, although more and more critics urge that we do so. Exploration of the function and significance of the *Visitatio* must begin with an understanding of the liturgical milieu from which it was never made distinct. The same interest in sympathetic identification evident in the rituals discussed so far is what makes the *Visitatio* so dramatic. As with the other instances of dramatic ritual evident throughout the Temporale in late Anglo-Saxon England, the vernacular preaching texts and other treatments of the events of Easter morning help establish and strengthen the identification with the holy women that is the driving force of the Easter reenactment.

The *Visitatio* represents a curious mix of details from various gospel accounts, and is therefore related to the readings both for Vigils and for Easter day. Witnesses for Holy Saturday and Easter seem to reveal a discrepancy in the understanding of which gospel accounts are proper to which Mass. There is one anonymous homily entitled *In Sabbato sancto*, one of the three sermons that, along with Vercelli I, was inserted into several manuscripts of the Catholic Homilies to fill out the days for which sermons were forbidden by Ælfric (see above, pp. 133–4). Based on the reading from Matthew 28:1ff, it takes much of its exegesis from Bede's homily for Easter

---

[159] Peter Dronke, *Nine Medieval Latin Plays* (Cambridge, 1994), p. xvii.

Plate 5. *Visitatio Sepulchri*, Benedictional of Æthelwold
London, BL MS Additional 49598, fol. 51v (by permission of the British Library)

Vigils (although this homilist has expanded and rearranged a good deal), which owned the Matthew 28 pericope. It also draws on Augustine (possibly indirectly) and Smaragdus. If this sermon ever was preached at Vigils, it would have been fundamentally redundant with Ælfric's First Series sermon for Easter, which itself seems to give an exegesis of the Matthew gospel. Bodley 340 and Corpus 198 present the two in conjunction.[160] The anonymous *In Sabbato Sancto* and Ælfric's CH I.xv take remarkably different avenues of exegesis, and seem to have different sources (while coinciding in one stunning regard, discussed below, pp. 166–8), but each deals with the material presented in the Matthew reading. The standard allocation of gospel lections in the West gives Matthew 28:1ff to Vigils and Mark 15:47ff to Easter day. This is the arrangement used by St. Augustine and by Gregory.[161] It is attested in Leofric A, in rubrics to the Old English Gospels,[162] and throughout the later medieval missals. Bede used the Neapolitan arrangement, found in the Gospel Book of St. Cuthbert (c. 700) and representing the use of Naples in the early seventh century, whereby Matthew 28 is split between Vigils and the main Mass for Easter.[163] There are a very few instances where the lections, according to the Roman arrangement, may have been switched. The Lectionary of St. Peter Chrysologus, Bishop of Ravenna (d. 450) assigns Matthew 28 to Easter Day.[164] Amalarius may also have understood the Matthew reading as proper to Easter. Ælfric's focus on Matthew for Easter day may be related to prescriptions for Vigils in the Corpus 190 texts, in a passage derived from Amalarius, related to the procession with incense at Vigils, in which the Mark reading is used in reference to the Vigils, which might leave the Matthew material for Easter Day:

> Ante evangelium non portantur luminaria in ipsa nocte, sed incensum tantum, ad imitationem mulierum, quia hoc tantum modo obtulerunt mulieres, ut dicit evangelium: *Cum transisset sabbatum et reliqua* [Mark 16:1].[165]

In his *Liber Officialis*, Amalarius, quoting Bede on Mark, again discusses the Vigil in terms of Mark's account; "Evangelium narrat secundum Marcum modum conventus feminarum et dicat: *Cum transisset . . .*,"[166] proceeding to explain the possible meanings of the gospel lection and the omission of the lights before the gospel book:

[160] See CH I, pp. 9, 11.
[161] See G. G. Willis, *St. Augustine's Lectionary* (London, 1962), pp. 66, 84.
[162] See R. M. Liuzza, ed. *The Old English Version of the Gospels* (Oxford, 1994), pp. 61, 96.
[163] See Willis, *St. Augustine's Lectionary*, p. 90.
[164] Ibid. pp. 94–5.
[165] Fehr, *Die Hirtenbriefe Ælfrics*, p. 231. "Before the gospel, lights should not be carried on this night, but only incense, in imitation of the women, because this alone the women offered, as the gospel says, *Cum transisset sabbatum et reliqua.*"
[166] "The gospel according to Mark describes the manner of the coming together of the women, and says: *Cum transisset . . .*"

Ut opinor, propter mulierum imitationem dicit romanus Libellus non portari hac nocte ante evangelium aliud nisi timiama, sive quia dubitat utrum iam carnem suam plenam munere lucis revexisset ab inferis Dominus. Hoc tantummodo obtulerunt mulieres.[167]

Hanssens considers this use of Mark at Vigils an error and points to related examples.[168] Both readings, Mark 15:47ff and Matthew 28:1ff, treat the account of the women at the tomb, and many of the elements of Bede's and the anonymous Old English author's exegesis of Matthew, such as the explanation of the purchase of the spices, are taken from Mark's account, perhaps allowing for the confusion. Ælfric recognizes the standard arrangement, and gives for his incipit *Maria magdelene et maria iacobi, et reliqua*, the beginning of the Mark pericope (Mark 15:47), but then goes on to present in his Old English 'translation' the petition of the Jews that the tomb be guarded, from Matthew, and continues using Matthew as his base (with details from other gospels). Perhaps his preference for the Matthew material for the Easter sermon stems partly from the influence of Amalarius, partly from the fact that many of his sources are Vigil homilies (or other exegetical discussions of Matthew 28), and partly from a desire to focus on certain aspects of the story, both exegetical and liturgical, that required him to conflate the gospel accounts in certain ways.

The standard order of Matthew for Vigils and Mark for Easter Day might have had a particular temporal quality when the two would have been only a few hours apart (before the Vigil was anticipated in the afternoon). It is possible to read the two accounts as sequential. In Matthew, Mary Magdalene and another Mary approach as the day is dawning, see the angel come down and roll back the stone (frightening the guards), then hear of the Resurrection and go away. In Mark, the three women (one of them Mary Magdalene) approach after the sun has already risen, see the stone already rolled away, and hear an announcement from what seems to be a different angel, seated inside the tomb rather than on the stone. This order works particularly well when the first is read at Vigils, before the sun has risen, and the other later in the day. There are problems with such a reading, however, including the question in Mark, "Who will roll away the stone?" (if Mary Magdalene had already seen it rolled away, there should have been no worry). In any case, Anglo-Saxon treatments of these two passages seem to follow the efforts of Augustine, Bede, and Smaragdus to explain these difficulties synthetically and harmonize the

---

[167] Hanssens, *Amalarii episcopi opera liturgical omnia*, vol. 2, p. 160. "So, I expect, because of the imitation of the women, the Roman book says that on this night before the gospel nothing should be carried other than the incense, or else because it is uncertain whether the Lord had yet brought back his full body from hell by the tribute of the light. This alone the women offered."

[168] "Evangelium namque Marci (16, 1–7) non in nocte, sed ipsa resurrectionis die canendum erat" (Ibid. "On the other hand, the Gospel of Mark was recited not during the night, but on the actual day of the Resurrection").

gospel accounts.[169] The fact that for Ælfric Vigils was on late Saturday afternoon (and that, therefore, the Matthew reading was somewhat removed from the primary commemoration of the announcement) might have inspired him, who as we have seen had a great interest in making sure that his audience understood the liturgical significance of the high festivals, to himself compose a single, synthetic account of the announcement to the women, one that has particular resonance with the rituals proper to Easter morning, especially the *Visitatio*.

Although Ælfric omits it from his Letter to the Monks at Eynsham, Symons claims (following Karl Young) that the *Visitatio* was "widespread."[170] However, the *Concordia*'s ritual is one of the very earliest, and certainly the earliest to include such a wealth of directions. It is founded on the *Quem quaeritis in sepulchro* dialogue, also found in the Wincester Troper, and has been discussed widely. There is little consensus concerning the origins of the *Quem quaeritis*, and I will discuss only its function in the Anglo-Saxon liturgy.[171] The *Concordia*'s instructions for the 'play' are as follows:

> Dum tertia recitatur lectio, iiii fratres induant se, quorum unus, alba indutus ac si ad aliud agendum, ingrediatur atque latenter sepulchri locum adeat ibique, manu tenens palmam, quietus sedeat. Dumque tertium percelebratur responsorium, residui tres succedant, omnes quidem cappis induti, turribula cum incensu manibus gestantes, ac, pedetemptim ad similitudinem quaerentium quid, veniant ante locum sepulchri. Aguntur enim haec ad imitationem angeli sedentis in monumento atque mulierum cum aromatibus venientium, ut ungerent corpus Ihesu. Cum ergo ille residens tres velut erraneos ac aliquid quaerentes, viderit sibi adproximare, incipiat mediocri voce dulcisone cantare: *Quem quaeritis [in sepulchro O Christicolae]*? Quo decantato finetenus, respondeant hi tres uno ore: *Ihesum Nazarenum.* Quibus ille: *Non est hic. Surrexit sicut praedixerat. Ite, nuntiate, quia surrexit a mortuis.* Cuius iussionis voce vertant se illi tres ad chorum, dicentes: *Alleluia. Resurrexit Dominus.*

---

[169] Augustine, in his Harmony of the Gospels (Book III, Ch. XXIV), while allowing that there might have been two angelic announcements, explains them as immediately sequential, such that the women might have seen the stone rolled away, heard the first announcement, gone inside, seen the second angel sitting on the right hand side, and then gone out. Even from this he shies away, however, explaining alternatively that the 'second angel' may be the same as the first, as his 'sitting on the right side' could still refer to the stone before the tomb (see Findlay and Salmond, trans. *Sermon on the Mount; Harmony of the Evangelists* (Edinburgh, 1873), pp. 441–55). Although these explanations don't appear in Anglo-Saxon exegesis, other attempts to harmonize the gospels (in particular the time of day of the announcement) draw frequently on Augustine's and Smaragdus' efforts to explain a single incident. See also Augustinus Hipponensis, *De consensu Evangelistarum*, Book III, Ch. XXIV, PL 34, 1196ff, and Smaragdus S. Michaelis, *Collectiones in epistolas et evangelia*, PL 102, 222Bff.

[170] Symons, *Regularis concordia*, p. 49.

[171] Hardison, *Christian Rite and Christian Drama*, p. 219, believes that the *Quem quaeritis* first developed as a ceremony associated with the Vigil Mass and was moved to Easter Matins as the Vigil lost its temporal coincidence. That the *Visitatio* in the *Concordia* was set at Matins for the sake of temporal coincidence is well taken, although the shift of the Vigil Mass to Saturday afternoon may have happened well before the direct ancestor of the *Visitatio* took form. The weight of critical opinion holds that the *Quem quaeritis* was developed somewhere on the continent during the ninth or tenth century.

Dicto hoc, rursus ille residens, velut revocans illos dicat antiphonam: *Venite et videte locum.* Haec vero dicens, surgat et erigat velum ostendatque eis locum cruce nudatum sed tantum linteanima posita, quibus crux involuta erat. Quo viso, deponant turribula, quae gestaverant. in eodem sepulcro sumantque linteum et extendant contra clerum[172] ac, veluti ostendentes quod surrexerit Dominus etiam non sit illo involutus, hanc canant antiphonam: *Surrexit Dominus de sepulcro* superponantque linteum altari.[173]

Critics of liturgical drama have lauded the ceremony's designation of roles, its use of costuming and stage directions, and its clear dialogue. This is the first of the representative dramas for which Young, Chambers, and Hardison are looking, with its relative verisimilitude. Its more ritualistic elements, it is claimed, work against the play's effectiveness (as drama), and these critics then look to more 'advanced' versions, versions which have shed many of these ritualistic tendencies in favour of more realistic impersonation. Referring primarily to the ritual action of presenting the gravecloth to the congregation, Hardison concludes that, "judged by representational standards, this sequence is awkward and illogical. It is best understood as a ceremonial survival rather than as an addition to an already representational form."[174] It is interesting to note, however, the resistance of the *Visitatio* scene to this 'shift from ritual to representational mode.' The twelfth-century St. Lambrecht *Visitatio*, despite some innovative scenes surrounding it, retains what to Young and Hardison is an "inept arrangement arising apparently from a reverent unwillingness to disturb the original simple structure of the trope *Q. Q.* – and from a lack of dramatic resourcefulness."[175] The twelfth-century Ripoll Resurrection play, which otherwise "shows a conscious desire

---

[172] The Old English glossator provides for "clerum" the potentially more general "þæne hired" (Kornexl, *Die Regularis concordia*, p. 106).

[173] Kornexl, *Die Regularis concordia*, pp. 104–7; see also Symons, *Regularis concordia*, pp. 49–50. "As the third lesson is being read, four of the brethren shall dress, one of whom, dressed in an alb as if for some other purpose, shall enter and go secretly to the place of the sepulchre and, holding a palm in his hand, shall sit there quietly. Then, as the third respond is being sung, the other three shall enter, all of them dressed in copes and holding thuribles with incense in their hands, and step by step, in the likeness of those seeking something, they should come before the place of the sepulchre. Now truly these things are done in imitation of the angel sitting on the tomb and of the women coming with perfumes so that they might anoint the body of Jesus. When, therefore, the one seated shall see these three draw near, acting just like those wandering and seeking something, he shall begin to sing in a moderate and sweet voice, *Quem quaeritis?* As soon as this has been sung completely, the three shall answer with one mouth: *Ihesum Nazerenum.* Then the seated one shall say: *Non est hic. Surrexit sicut praedixerat. Ite, nuntiate, quia surrexit a mortuis.* At this command the three shall turn to the choir saying: *Alleluia. Resurrexit Dominus.* When this has been said the seated one, as though calling them back, shall say the antiphon: *Venite et videte locum.* Saying this truly, he should rise, lift the veil, and show them the place void of the Cross, with only the linen in which the Cross was wrapped. When this has been seen, the three shall lay down the thuribles, which they were carrying, in that same sepulchre and shall take up the linen and show it to the clergy and, as if showing that the Lord had risen and is not now wrapped in it, they shall sing this antiphon: *Surrexit Dominus de sepulchro* and they shall place the linen on the altar."

[174] Hardison, *Christian Rite and Christian Drama*, p. 233.

[175] Karl Young, *The Drama of the Medieval Church* (Oxford, 1933), pp. 246–7, reprinted in Hardison, *Christian Rite and Christian Drama*, p. 233.

for verisimilitude," leaves "the *Quem quaeritis* in the form established in the tenth century, retaining even the *Te Deum*."[176] To Hardison this resistance to evolution is a flaw, a settling for "something less than pure representation."[177] However, the *Visitatio* and its core *Quem quaeritis* are powerful and successful not because they are almost representational, but because they are ritual. It is misleading to judge the ceremony by representational standards, as it was not intended to be representational. Johann Drumbl describes these dramatic rituals as attempts to recast growing dramatic impulses (developed outside of the liturgy) into something more consonant with liturgical expression.[178] That there was a good deal of cross-fertilization between liturgical and secular forms of reenactment over time is certain (although describing their exact relationship is notoriously tricky), but the idea that a ritual like the *Visitatio* might work the same way, and thus can be discussed in the same terms, as later secular drama is misleading. Surely there is something 'dramatic' here. Both modern drama and medieval dramatic ritual use sympathetic identification to connect all present to the world that is created in the playing space. The liturgy, however, has its own way of uniting the space of the church with the world of biblical history, and the participants with the biblical figures, through the ritual expressions and actions that had for a thousand years unified the bread and wine with the body and blood of Christ himself. The *Visitatio* uses this same liturgically dramatic language to unify the congregation with the holy women, juxtaposing the contemporary church with the sepulchre of Christ and making the congregation play a role, not so much the 'actors.' Its ritual elements, not the details that resemble characteristics of modern drama, are the key to its success. In this context, the *Visitatio* is dramatic in the same way as the rituals for the rest of the high festivals, and its elevation above the rest of the Anglo-Saxon dramatic liturgy is based on a misunderstanding of its ritual power.

Ritual substitutions for historical details are not necessarily 'unrealistic' here. Illustrations of the women at the sepulchre in the Benedictionals of Archbishop Robert and of Æthelwold show the foremost woman holding not a jar of ointment, but a thurible of incense. This detail reflects Amalarius' instruction that incense only be carried before the gospel book in imitation of the holy women approaching the tomb. The tomb itself is understood both liturgically and in illumination as a modern church structure (itself a stylized representation of the Jerusalem site), as Barbara Raw discusses concerning the illustration of the women at the tomb in the mid-eleventh-century Tiberius psalter:

---

[176] However, after the long, melodramatic *planctus* of the three Marys at the place of the ointment merchant, the staid, conservative *Quem quaeritis* dialogue is a striking contrast, providing much the same effect as the conservative worshipping of the infant Christ scene at the end of the Second Shepherds' play. The solemnity of the scene is heightened, not diminished, by its context.

[177] Hardison, *Christian Rite and Christian Drama*, pp. 247, 244, 248.

[178] See Johann Drumbl, *Quem quaeritis* (Rome, 1981).

. . . the drawing of the three Maries at the sepulchre . . . shows the tomb as a circular staged tower with a square base and a crypt beneath, which is closely similar to the western church of the Saviour at Saint-Riquier and which may perhaps have been modelled on the tower built by Bishop Ælfheah at the Old Minster and dedicated in 993–4. . . . the ritual tomb [for the *Concordia*'s *Adoratio* and *Depositio*] must have stood under Ælfheah's tower and it would have been appropriate to represent the historical tomb by a picture of this tower in the Psalter.[179]

The ritual action of presenting the graveclothes to the audience, rather than ruining the emerging representational mode, solidifies the identification between the holy women and the congregation, drawing focus to the purpose of the ceremony, to wonder and exult in the risen Lord, as did the three holy women. This gravecloth is similarly important in illumination, and is featured in the illustrations in the Robert Missal and the Benedictional of Æthelwold (see plate 5). As much as the announcement of the angel, the fact of the shroud is understood as the emotional climax of the story of the women at the tomb, and the redactors of the *Concordia*'s *Visitatio* have accordingly made it the dramatic climax. Hardison and others, in attempting to map the first sprouts of the sort of church drama seen at the time of the Corpus Christi cycles, are looking for 'verisimilitude' as a yardstick for dramatic maturity. The problem is, they are looking for verisimilitude with a much later conception of the events of Easter morning. Whether or not a sense of realism was important to the liturgical participants, there is no reason to believe that the Anglo-Saxon participants of the ritual, as of other rituals year-round, saw anything unrealistic in the *Visitatio*. Certainly they would have known that the monks were men, wearing liturgical garb. Perhaps they might even have enjoyed seeing some of their familiar brethren trying to follow the instruction to walk about as women 'as if seeking something.' There is no reason to divorce aesthetic enjoyment from ritual power, either in describing the *Visitatio* or in describing the development of later drama. However, the ritual 'tomb' was still the sepulchre, the brethren seeking the Lord, and through them all present, were one with the women approaching the proof of Christ's resurrection, and the cloth was still the shroud in which Christ was wrapped, to the degree that these ritual elements are central to every presentation of the events, liturgical, artistic, and textual. This is the same dynamic in which the Anglo-Saxon church has proved itself fluent year-round, both in native practices like the *Adoratio* and in its enthusiastic adaptations of the successful experiments of other churches, readily accepted and integrated into the services that already held the seeds for the liturgical establishment of identification and dramatic objective.

As the identification with the holy women is the dramatic core of the *Visitatio*, so it is what is personalized in other parts of the liturgy, and in

[179] Raw, *Anglo-Saxon Crucifixion Iconography*, pp. 46–7.

vernacular preaching. In the Canterbury Benedictional, the *Benedictio ad Matutinales Laudes* sets forth the example of the women as a means of seeing the proof of the Resurrection:

> Laetificet vos sanctum pascha dominicae resurrectionis, et beatae in christo participemini gloria inmortalitatis . . . Quique, sanctarum mulierum exemplo, orto iam sole christum veneramini in sepulcro, cum angelis cooperti stola candida, crucifixum resurrexisse videamini in gloria.[180]

In Ælfric's First Series sermon for Easter, he relates the believing Christian to the holy women:

> Ac þeos dæd getacnað sum ðing to donne on Godes gelaðunge. We ðe gelyfað Cristes æriste, we cumað gewislice to his byrgene mid deorwurðre sealfe gif we beoð gefyllede mid bræðe haligra mihta, 7 gif we mid hlisan godra weorca urne drihten secað.[181]

Also like the holy women, the faithful stand in awe of the signs of Christ's resurrection evident on Easter and expect soon to see him in person. The *Visitatio*, as part of the Easter liturgical scheme, is not so much interested in having the 'actors' seem like the holy women as it is in making all present feel that they are at one with the women, seeing the cloth along with them.

The force of this connection is more subtly evident in Ælfric's translation of the Matthew account of the women at the tomb, demonstrating how fully biblical narrative and liturgical commemoration have become conflated for the Anglo-Saxon perception of the events of Easter morning. That this account is going to be distinct is immediately clear from its cast of characters. Biblical commentators have always striven to reconcile the inconsistent gospel accounts of exactly which women were involved in the events of Easter weekend. Pope, in a long note to his first supplementary homily of Ælfric, for the Nativity, discusses some of the problems involved in the gospel lists of the women present at the Crucifixion. Following a string of suppositions, Ælfric, seemingly following Haymo, asserts that the mother of James and John, the sons of Zebedee, was Mary Salome (the third woman at the tomb on Easter morning according to Mark), and that she was a sister of the Virgin Mary.[182] Jerome, Augustine, Gregory, and Bede, as Pope shows, followed a different line of supposition in conflating these accounts, one that conflicts with the position apparently taken by Ælfric.[183] The

---

[180] Woolley, *The Canterbury Benedictional*, p. 45. "May the holy Paschal festival of the Resurrection gladden you, and, blessed in Christ, may you participate in the glory of immortality . . . You who, by the example of the holy women, venerate Christ in the sepulchre, by the now risen sun, covered in a bright stole with the angels, may you see the crucified one to be risen again in glory."

[181] CH I.xv, p. 302. "But this deed betokens something to be done in God's church. We who believe in Christ's resurrection, we come truly to his tomb with precious ointment if we are filled with the breath of his holy might, and if we seek our Lord with the glory of good works."

[182] See Pope, *Homilies of Ælfric*, vol. I, pp. 217–20, n. 5b.

[183] Ibid.

question of which women were at the tomb is equally problematic, and Ælfric's Matthew-based solution is particularly curious. The synoptic gospel accounts present women who saw where Jesus' body was laid on Good Friday, those who bought and/or prepared spices, and those who approached the tomb on Easter morning (John is distinct, and tells only of Mary Magdalene finding the empty tomb). Luke's account is general, discussing "mulieres quae cum ipso venerant de Galilaea" (Luke 23:55a), and the same nameless band of women seems to perform all three functions. Matthew and Mark give more detail, and it is from Mark that Ælfric draws many of his innovations to his Matthew base, despite the fact that these two accounts are somewhat hard to reconcile. Mark tells us that "Maria autem Magdalene et Maria Ioseph aspiciebant ubi poneretur" (Mark 15:47), and then gives us a separate set of women for the purchase of the spices (Mary Magdalene, Mary the mother of James, and Salome, also known as Mary Salome), and it seems by syntax to be these three who approach the tomb on Easter morning. Witnessing the burial, Matthew has "Maria Magdalene et altera Maria" (Matthew 27:61) which fits well enough with Mark, but Matthew makes no mention of the purchase of spices, and for Easter morning relates simply, "venit Maria Magdalene et altera Maria videre sepulchrum" (Matthew 28:1b).

Some creative juggling might have brought the accounts together, specifically alternative interpretations of Matthew's 'the other Mary' and the assumption of a silent third Mary at the tomb, but Ælfric takes a surprisingly original tack, and one that has no obvious purpose. On Good Friday, according to Ælfric,

> þa beheold Maria þæs hælendes moder, 7 þa wimmen þe hyre mid wæron, hwær he bebiriged wæs, 7 eodon ða ongean to ðære birig 7 seo Magdalenisce Maria 7 Maria Iacobes moder bohton deorwyrðe sealfe þe bið geworht to smyrigenne deadra manna lic mid, þæt hi scolon late rotian, 7 eodon ða ða wimmen on þisum dæge on ærnemerien 7 woldon his lic behwyrfan, swa hit þær gewunlic wæs on ðære þeode.[184]

There seems to be no authority for including Mary Christ's mother among those witnessing the burial. The general account in Luke might allow for it, and less likely, one might interpret 'the other Mary' to mean the Virgin, but Mark's account, from which Ælfric takes the bulk of his collated additions, and which provides the actual pericope for the day, leaves no room for her. Also curious, Ælfric, in bringing in from Mark the purchase of the 'precious ointment,' reduces the number of purchasers from three to two, Mary Magdalene and Mary Jacobi. This reduction leaves him with

---

[184] CH I.xv, pp. 299–300. "Then Mary the Lord's mother, and the women who were with her, saw where he was buried, and they went towards the city and Mary Magdalene and Mary Jacob's mother bought precious ointment that is made to smear onto the bodies of dead people, so that they rot more slowly, and then the women went on this day in the dawn and desired to prepare his body, as was the custom among that people."

(possibly, by syntax) these two women approaching the tomb on Easter morning, bringing it more or less into accord with the Matthew base, and perhaps this is his reason here. If so, however, this care for consistency with Matthew makes his addition of Mary Christ's mother at the tomb (seeing where the body was buried) and his implicit expansion of the number of women present at the burial beyond two all the more inexplicable. Further, in Ælfric it is not so clear as it seems to be in Mark that the women who bought the spices were the ones to approach the empty tomb. Rather than resorting to the unspecific (implied in the Latin) pronoun 'they,' as does Mark, Ælfric relates that "eodon ða ða wimmen on þisum dæge on ærnemerien." The construction here separates this bit somewhat from the account of the ointment purchase, leaving unclear exactly to which group "ða wimmen" refers, and therefore just how many women were involved. Perhaps this is Ælfric's purpose here, for in leaving his audience with an indefinite number of unspecified women he makes it easier to make the association between the liturgical participants and the women at the empty tomb (as Amalarius seems to have done in his general discussion of the 'mulieres' approaching the tomb with spices/incense).

The idea of the Virgin at the sepulchre does occur in one other place in Anglo-Saxon witnesses, in the anonymous homily *In Sabbato sancto*, and it is presented in terms strikingly similar to those used by Ælfric. Scragg considers the set of homilies of which this is a part to represent "what was available in Canterbury when Ælfric's work first arrived there."[185] Here, it seems to be precisely through the unlikely interpretation of Matthew's 'the other Mary' as the Virgin that she is introduced to the tomb. A more complete study of the sources and structure of this sermon would be valuable, but its core (at least in its exegetical first part) is related to the first part of an exegetical homily for Easter Vigils by Bede on Matthew 28:1–10. After a discussion of the solemnity of the time and of Christ's joint humanity and divinity (focusing on the proof of his bodily resurrection, echoed by those resurrected with him), the Old English homilist begins his translation of the gospel. With no recourse to authority or explanation, he translates "venit maria magdalene et altera maria videre sepulcrum" as "þa com Maria seo Magdalenisca 7 oðer Maria, þæt wæs Cristes lichamlice modor, to ðære byrigenne."[186] In three other places in the translation, he inserts "þa halgan wif" where the gospel account has either an implied pronoun or the more general 'women.' Finally, as he begins his exegesis, he makes the same silent yet startling shift made by Ælfric, claiming:

[185] Scragg, "The Corpus of Vernacular Homilies," p. 266.
[186] Evans, "An anonymous Old English homily," p. 136. "Then came Mary Magdalene and the other Mary, that was Christ's bodily mother, to the tomb."

Hwæt, we gehyrdon þæt se godspellere cwæð, þæt Sancta Maria, Cristes lichamlice modor, 7 þa oðre wifmen þa ðe eac mid hire wæron, þæt heo to ðære byrgenne comon þy æfenne þæs restedæges.[187]

Of course, we have heard no such thing, but the homilist has subtly prepared the reader to accept this. Bede, here, describes Mary Magdalene and the other Mary as representing the Jews and the Gentiles, respectively, come to celebrate the Passion and Resurrection from those who believe the world over.[188] This section comes after Bede's discussion of the time of the approach to the tomb, and he then goes on to talk about the shaking of the earth and the role and characteristics of the angel who rolled away the stone. The anonymous homilist gives no explanation concerning the women, simply presenting us with a group of women headed by Christ's mother. It would seem that he has had the idea in his mind that the story should feature 'Mary Christ's mother and the women who were with her,' and his translation of the Latin followed by his general insertion of 'the holy women' has been his excuse, and his way of making the idea seem authoritative. Again, while explaining the time of day according to Augustine and Smaragdus, he claims (as Augustine and Smaragdus did not)[189] that

. . . ac heora æghwylc þæs soð sæde, forðanðe heo Sancta Maria 7 þa oðre wifmenn, þa ðe eac mid hire wæron, ealle þa niht wacedon 7 gelomlice to ðære byrgenne eodan 7 eft fram, for ðære micclan lufan þe heo to him Drihtne hæfdon.[190]

Finally, after his long discussion of the time of day, with several comparisons of darkness and light, he presents a version of the approach to the tomb that by now bears little resemblance to Matthew, and that we know is based on Matthew only because of the steps he has used to bring us here:

þæt wæs on ðam dæge þe to merigene bið, ðætte Sancta Maria and þa halgan wifmen mid swetum wyrtum 7 mid deorwurðum smyrenyssum to ðære drihtenlican byrgenne coman, þæt heo his þone halgan lichaman mid þam smyrian woldan, þy læs he brosnian mihte. Mid þy wæs getacnod þæt we ealle, þe on ðone ilcan Drihten gelefað 7 his naman andettað, þæt we hine sceolon þurh halige lustas 7 þurh manige halige dæde gelomlice secan.[191]

---

[187] Ibid. p. 137. "Lo, we have heard what the gospeller said, that Holy Mary, Christ's bodily mother, and the other women who also were with her came to the tomb during the evening of the Sabbath."

[188] See Martin and Hurst, *Bede the Venerable: Homilies on the Gospels*, vol. 2, p. 61.

[189] See Augustinus Hipponensis, *De consensu Evangelistarum*, Book III, Ch. XXIV, PL 34, 1196ff, and Smaragdus S. Michaelis, *Collectiones in epistolas et evangelia*, PL 102, 222Bff.

[190] Evans, "An anonymous Old English homily," p. 137. "But each of them said this truth, because Holy Mary and the other women who also were with her kept watch all that night and frequently went to the tomb and back again, because of the great love that they had for the Lord."

[191] Ibid. p. 138. "That was on that day that is tomorrow, that Holy Mary and the holy women with sweet herbs and precious ointments came to the tomb of the Lord, because they desired to smear his holy body with the ointment, lest he decay. With that it was signified that we all, who believe in that same Lord and confess his name, that must seek him frequently through holy desires and through many holy deed."

This passage bears a striking resemblance to Ælfric's, with the expression 'Mary Christ's mother and the holy women,' the mention of the ointment and its purpose, to prevent rotting, and the idea that the women present for us a model. The choice of words and phrasing is quite different, and neither the mention of the spices (also in Bede) nor the idea that the women provide a model are particularly original. But the mention of the Virgin, and in particular the phrase used earlier, 'Holy Mary Christ's mother and the women who were with her,' is too similar to Ælfric's to ignore, particularly as it is the only other extant witness to the idea. It is certainly possible that the anonymous homilist, in response to the popularity of the cult of the Virgin in England, simply combined Matthew's ambiguity with a natural desire to place the Virgin, whom he knew to have been present at Christ's death, at the site of the most important event in Christian history. If the idea were spontaneously his, then Ælfric may have seen it and liked the idea, recasting the anonymous passage into one reflecting his own style and keeping Mary Christ's mother at the burial, where Matthew might allow her, but not clearly at the Resurrection (Ælfric separates the two, as the anonymous homilist does not). And yet, that he would bother to (possibly) separate her from the Resurrection and yet keep her and the women at the burial does not seem like him. Ælfric is notoriously distrustful of anonymous and apocryphal details, and looks for biblical and patristic authority for everything. As such, it seems unlikely that he would make such a drastic departure from scripture and from established exegesis on the authority of one local homilist.[192] The gradual presentation of the idea in the anonymous homily is a bit forced, and seems to reflect a desire to justify some tradition expressed in the later two passages. Perhaps Ælfric's partial allowance of the idea has the same basis.

Illumination gives no direct support for such an idea, as in the Æthelwold and Robert illustrations of the women at the sepulchre none of the women are nimbed, as the Virgin surely would be. There is an exegetical connection between Mary and the tomb taken up by Ælfric in his Second Series Palm Sunday sermon:

Rihtlice wæs seo byrgen swa niwe gefunden, and nænne oðerne næfre ne under-feng, swa swa Maria wæs moder Cristes mæden and modor, and oðerne ne gebær.[193]

This passage is given in the course of an exegetically-expanded gospel narrative at the point at which Christ is laid in Joseph's new tomb, and would correspond narratively with the women watching the burial in

---

[192] However, Ælfric does seem willing at times to creatively manipulate orthodox positions for pastoral reasons (on which see Bedingfield, "Anglo-Saxons on Fire," *JTS* vol. 52, no. 2 (2001), pp. 658–77).

[193] CH II.xiv, p. 149. "Rightly was the tomb so newly made, and never received any other, just as Mary was a maiden and Christ's mother, and bore no other."

Matthew. Still, if this is part of its origin, there is quite a step to be accounted for between describing Mary as a mirror of the tomb and actually placing her there in what is supposedly a translation of the gospel pericope. The Virgin does appear at the tomb in later medieval accounts, as she does in the Second Greek Form of the Gospel of Nicodemus.[194] After Joseph begs the body of Christ, a whole company, including the Virgin and Mary Magdalene, prepare and bury Christ, after which the Virgin and Mary Magdalene lament at the tomb. There is no known copy of this text earlier than the fifteenth century, however. As such, this use of the Virgin probably reflects more an expansion of the *planctus* proper to her in later liturgical drama than any tradition from as early as the tenth century. In any case, while the presence of Christ's mother remains a mystery, the general conflation of the specific women to 'the women' seems to be consonant with the liturgical imperatives.

What certainly carries liturgical resonance in these similar passages, whatever their ultimate sources, is the introduction to the Matthew base of the 'precious ointment' bought after the burial and carried by the women to the empty tomb. Ælfric's most jarring innovation, however, comes right at the end, after the words of the angel to the women:

> þa lagon ða scytan innon þære byrgene þe he mid bewunden wæs, 7 þa wif gecyrdon þa to Cristes leorningcnihtum mid miclum ege 7 mid micelre blisse, 7 woldon him cyþan Cristes ærist.[195]

There is no mention of Christ's burial cloth in Matthew or in Mark. Luke and John each mention the gravecloth, but in each case it is seen and/or handled by Peter or John, and nowhere in the four accounts is there any relationship between the women and the cloth. Here, however, the fact of the gravecloth, the symbol and proof of Christ's Resurrection, is transferred to the women, who then turn to proclaim it to the apostles. This innovation, as of the introduction of the ointment, seems to derive not from biblical or patristic authority but from methods of presenting the women at the tomb that were quite familiar to the Anglo-Saxons, both in illumination and dramatically in the *Visitatio*. The *Concordia*'s instructions for the occasion reenact a story that, compared to scriptural accounts, is partly composite and partly original in its symbolism. The *Concordia* arms the women at the tomb with thuribles of incense meant to represent the ointment bought by the women in Mark with which to anoint Christ's body and gives them the extra-biblical honour of taking up the 'gravecloth' and turning to show it to the 'disciples,' announcing the Resurrection as commanded by the angel.

---

[194] See James' (*The Apocryphal New Testament*) Greek Recension B of the *Acti Pilati*, summarized, pp. 115–17.

[195] CH I.xv, p. 300. "Then lay inside the tomb the sheet with which he was wound, and the women turned then to Christ's disciples with great fear and with great joy, and desired to proclaim to them Christ's Resurrection."

While relating a story dissimilar from any of the individual gospel accounts, the outline of this ritual resonates well with Ælfric's account particularly on those details that differ from Matthew. It is specifically these women, carrying ointment to the sepulchre, that Ælfric admonishes his audience to emulate. The sympathetic association with the holy women established so creatively in the liturgy is both reflected in and strengthened by Ælfric's reinvented version of the gospel story.

The joy granted the women, and through them the entire church, as expressed dramatically in the *Visitatio*, brings them into a state of revelation, and the festival continues until Pentecost. The readings for Easter Week, described as an extension of Easter Sunday, tell of the appearances of Christ to his disciples and of other proofs of his Resurrection, looking forward to his Ascension, in which the faithful, having been freed from the darkness of sins by the power of the Cross and been shown first-hand the proof of Christ's Resurrection, can now participate. They are brought to this unity by a marriage of dramatic elaboration of the liturgy and vernacular explanation and reinforcement, allowing them to understand, and plumb the depths of, the significance of the liturgical reenactments of the Holy Season. As evident in pre-tenth-century explorations of these commemorated events, the mechanism of sympathizing with biblical figures already had currency by the time of the *Concordia*, and was explored and developed liturgically thereafter. An Anglo-Saxon absorbing explanations and narrative presentations of the biblical accounts and then participating in the liturgy that brings the events into the space of the church will have relived directly, carried along by the events of Christ's life from his birth to his Resurrection, God's plan of salvation.

7

Baptism in Anglo-Saxon England

NOTABLY OMITTED from the above description of the Anglo-Saxon Easter liturgy is the ritual of baptism, the very ritual by which Christians are made, and which makes the rest of the liturgy applicable. From the time of St. Paul, Christian theologians have consciously interpreted baptism as a sort of reenactment of, primarily, the death and resurrection of Christ, an association that tied the ceremony to Easter and largely defined the rite. Baptism and communion, according to Wulfstan (and in accordance with canonical decree), are the two ceremonies that are "þurh Godes mihte swa myccle 7 swa mære þæt æfre ænig man ne mæg ðæron ænig ðing awyrdan ne gewanian."[1] As the point at which a heathen becomes a Christian, baptism is the standard denouement in Christian narratives and the defining moment in a Christian's life. Those who describe the dramatic nature of the liturgy have traditionally put forth the baptismal rite as a mimetic or quasi-mimetic ceremony, as it is, at least theoretically, rich in the type of coincidence-based associations that spur mimetic interpretations.[2] However, changes in the application of baptism from the time of the early church to the late Anglo-Saxon period, specifically a confused sense of the role of the baptismal candidate caused by the predominance of infant baptism, the decline of a structured catechumenate, and its related disassociation from Easter, have muted much of the ceremony's dramatic potential. In eleventh-century English explorations of the rite, the relationship between baptism and Christ's resurrection that tends to dominate dramatic discussions of the liturgy gets lost in favour of a description of baptism more appropriately applied to an infant, as a fulfilment of birth, an exorcism of the devil's taint, and an initiation through Mary into the church. In particular, identifications in the liturgy, as explained by Anglo-Saxon homilists, are used in relation to the water rather than the participants of the baptismal rite, making it difficult to speak of baptism in dramatic terms.

The confused sense of role-playing in baptism, having to do predominately with the fact that infants replace adults as the standard protagonists of the 'drama,' is intrinsic to post-Augustinian baptismal practice, as a brief

---

[1] Bethurum, *The Homilies of Wulfstan*, p. 177. "Through God's might so great and so powerful that noone may ruin or diminish anything therein."
[2] See for example Hardison, *Christian Rite and Christian Drama*, pp. 81, 95–6.

historical background to late Anglo-Saxon baptism will illustrate. Whitaker in *The Baptismal Liturgy* gives a general history of the baptismal liturgy, from the time of the early church to the development of the Sarum Missal.[3] Although no actual liturgical evidence exists from the patristic period, Whitaker gleans much from the accounts of Tertullian and Augustine, among others. That infant baptism was performed at this time is evident in the fact that Tertullian, in the third century, opposed it, on the grounds that children could not make promises before they could speak. However, the paradigm was still adult baptism, demonstrating baptismal practice at the time of the persecutions. The Western baptismal liturgy consisted of three main stages, the catechumenate (begun with the christening), when the candidates were prepared spiritually and mentally, baptism itself, at which time they were cleansed, and confirmation, bestowing the Holy Spirit. Baptism was also tied to Easter from at least patristic times, as Whitaker asserts:

> Tertullian evidently regarded Easter as the most suitable season, "for then was accomplished our Lord's Passion, and in it we are baptized." In any case it was not long after this date that baptism came to be normally restricted to the Paschal season, and the development of Lent was related to the preparation of the candidates.[4]

This preparation, at least spanning much of Lent, could last years. Prospective Christians had to prove their fidelity over a period of time, learning the basics of the faith and preparing themselves for cleansing. When deemed ready, they would pass through a series of scrutinies, which were basically exorcisms. Whitaker relays a dramatic account of a scrutiny from this period, during which candidates would sometimes fall away screaming, a sign that the devil had not been fully expunged and that they should wait until the next year as catechumens.[5] After the scrutinies, and before baptism, came the Delivery of the Creed, the words of which could not be known to non-Christians. Before baptism, candidates had to 'Return the Creed,' proving that they had it memorized, and they were exhorted not to let anyone else know the words, and not to commit them to writing. The ceremonies described by Whitaker could only have had adult participants, as they commanded actions and responses that infants could not have made, and the idea of death to the world and resurrection in a new body dominated the preparatory catechuminal period, leading up to Easter.

Augustine's assertion that infants who die unbaptized go to hell, however, had serious repercussions for baptismal practice, and created tensions in the baptismal liturgy that resound even today. In societies that

---

[3] E. C. Whitaker, *The Baptismal Liturgy* (London, 1981). See also his translations of documents pertaining to the liturgy of baptism over this period in *Documents of the Baptismal Liturgy* (London, 1970).

[4] *TBL*, p. 11.

[5] *TBL*, pp. 42–3.

had already been Christianized, infant baptism became the norm. However, the liturgy was still based on the same adult model as that described by Whitaker. The earliest liturgical evidence for baptism comes primarily from two traditions, the first extant in a series of *ordines* collected in the eighth century, printed by Andrieu as the *Ordines Romani*,[6] and the second in the Gelasian Sacramentary (both reflecting, theoretically, sixth-century Roman practice, although extant only in eighth- and ninth-century Frankish texts). Both sources present a baptismal liturgy based firmly around Easter and beginning in mid-Lent. As both demonstrate the same problems mentioned above, I will focus on the Gelasian Sacramentary as represented in Vatican MS Regenensis 316.[7]

The first scrutiny begins on the Third Sunday in Lent, at which time the names of the elect, specified as "infantum," are called, and supplications are made for their preparation as part of the scrutiny Mass. It is specified in the *Ordines*, and understood here, that the infants are not to take part in the eucharist until they have been baptized (in *OR* XI, the primary witness for baptism in the group, the dismissal of the candidates is formalized). Two other Masses of the same type are to follow (*Ordo* XI has seven scrutinies in all, versus the three in the Gelasian), but before them is the Notice of the Scrutiny, announcing the time of the Making of the Catechumen and setting the tone for the following services by stating their purpose, to destroy the devil and open the doors of heaven.[8] From the start, the procedure is defined as an exorcism, in the same militaristic terms later to be used by Anglo-Saxon prose writers.

The names of the infants are written down, and they are called one at a time into the church for the Making of the Catechumen. After a prayer for expulsion of the devil, divine protection, and hope for a second birth, the salt is exorcized, sanctified, and placed in the infants' mouths. The elect are then exorcized, the priest invoking the exodus from Egypt under Moses, beseeching God to send his angel to guard them until baptism, as he did for the Israelites. The devil is told to honour God and not to violate the cross with which the elect are signed. A series of prayers drive out the devil, each one reminding the devil of God's power as evidenced in Christ's miracles.

Following are the Exposition of the Gospels, at which the four gospels are processed to the altar and the beginning of each is read, and the Introduction of the Creed and of the *Pater Noster*, each of which is presented and explained (the Creed after the presentation and the *Pater Noster* interlinearly). The Creed is presented both in Greek and in Latin and is not broken up with commentary as is the *Pater Noster*. It is in these instructional sections that the survival of an adult form is most evident. The elect are addressed at the beginning of the Exposition with an explanation:

[6] Michel Andrieu, ed. *Les ordines romani* (Louvain, 1931).
[7] Wilson, *The Gelasian Sacramentary*, pp. 45ff, and translated by Whitaker in *DBL*, pp. 166ff.
[8] *DBL*, p. 169. Subsequent page references are to this text.

Beloved children, we shall open to you now the gospels, that is, the story of the divine life. But first we must explain what the gospel is, and whence it comes, and whose words are written therein, and why they be four who wrote of this life, and who are the four who, as the prophet foretold, have been marked by the divine Spirit: lest haply without this explanation we should confuse your minds: and because it is for this that ye are come, that your ears should be opened and not that your senses should be blunted. (172–3)

At the Introduction of the Creed, the infants are exhorted not to write the Creed on "any corruptible material" and are afterwards told that "we transform you from the old man to the new" (176). The picture of a group of infants warned not to write down what they hear and joyfully told that they will be transformed from old men is logically awkward, but the tone of the exhortation is most serious, as the salvation of the catechumens depends on the protective power of the Creed, assumed by them in the approaching renunciation of the devil and the confession of belief (the *Abrenuntio* and the *Credo*, performed on Holy Saturday). Following are exhortations to the baptismal candidates urging them to keep themselves protected from the devil by the Creed. The extent to which the catechumens are instructed in the fundamental tenets of the faith before baptism, addressed directly in ways that assume a rather mature level of understanding, demonstrates the tension between the fear of hell for one's children and the logical incongruities inherent in the baptismal forms.

The preceding ceremonies took place before Palm Sunday, followed by a Chrismal Mass on Maundy Thursday. The infants return early on Holy Saturday to, as the rubric specifies, "make their return of the Creed." The devil is again told to flee, the elect are anointed with spittle (for the *Effeta*) and with oil, followed by the *Abrenuntio*, a series of three questions renouncing the devil, his works, and his pomps, after each of which they (or, rather, their sponsors) reply "Abrenuntio." Then, as the infants cannot actually return the Creed (on the adult model, this occasion is designed to ensure that the baptismal candidates have learned it), it is said instead by the priest to the infants, and they are commanded to go outside. They return later in the day for the twelve lessons and process to the font chanting a litany. The font is consecrated, and the reading for the day describes the various levels of significance of the water. The priest is instructed to change his voice, a final prayer of consecration is made, and each is asked three questions, testing belief in the Father, the Son, and the Holy Spirit respectively, to each of which the candidate (or rather, again, the sponsor) replies *Credo*. They are baptized, during which they are dipped three times, once for each part of the Trinity. The infants are signed with chrism, told that God has regenerated them through water and forgiven their sins, and (assuming a bishop is present, as does the Gelasian), confirmed. After confirmation, they receive their first communion.

Almost all passages in the baptismal liturgy extant in Anglo-Saxon manuscripts stem from the Gelasian (possibly by way of the Supplemented Hadrianum or derived from earlier Gelasian sacramentaries that might have been used in England before the tenth century), and they have inherited the same tensions. Sarah Larratt Keefer lists four sources for the baptismal liturgy as practised in Anglo-Saxon England: The Missal of Robert of Jumièges, The Red Book of Darley, The Leofric Missal, and the Corpus 163 copy of the Romano-German Pontifical.[9] All four examples are of the Gregorian/Gelasian type, and I will focus on the first, and to a lesser degree the second. The baptismal services in the Robert Missal do appear in the midst of a series of Masses for Holy Saturday (the services in Darley and the Leofric Missal have been moved out of the main cycle and placed towards the back). Most notable about the service in Robert (as in the others) is its condensed nature. The scrutiny Masses are gone, the services beginning with the *Ordo Ad Caticuminum Faciendum*, which has been moved from mid-Lent to (it seems) the day of baptism. In fact there is no indication, either in the order of sections or in rubrics, that the ceremonies are not to be performed all at once. The infants are exorcized, given the salt, and prayed over in the exact words extant in the Gelasian (indeed, every passage but two, the first and the second to last, is verbatim from the Gelasian). The formal Exposition of the Gospels is replaced with a simple reading from Matthew, and the *Pater Noster* is presented (with only the incipit in the MS). In Darley, the Creed is presented in full following the incipit for the *Pater Noster*, although in Robert the presentation of the Creed has been, remarkably, meshed with the *Credo*, where the three questions are expanded to include the entire Creed (Robert is unique in this respect). Following the *Pater Noster*, in Robert, are the pre-*Abrenuntio* warning to the devil, the *Effeta*, and the *Abrenuntio*, as in the Gelasian (Darley moves the *Effeta* and *Abrenuntio* until just before the *Credo*. Winchcombe moves only the *Abrenuntio*, so that it is removed from the *Effeta*, and instead directly precedes the *Credo* and the actual baptism). Following the *Abrenuntio* in Robert (or following the Creed in Darley) is the procession to the font for its consecration. The Gelasian specifies a litany during the procession. Although Robert makes no mention of it, Darley presents one, spanning five pages in the manuscript (pp. 378–82). After the Benediction of the Font, which is the same in the Gelasian, Robert, and Darley, is the mixing of the chrism and the water, in which the chrism is poured into the water in the form of the cross, followed by the *Credo* and the actual baptism, the vesting of the infants with white garments, and, "si episcopus adest statim," confirmation. The whole ceremony, although in the same basic form, is a good deal shorter than that in the Gelasian. Although it would be dangerous to make too much out

---

[9] See Sarah Larratt Keefer, "Manuals," pp. 101–2. The Winchcombe Sacramentary also contains an *ordo* for baptism, integrated with the Vigil Mass.

of a lack of rubrics specifying that the ceremonies should be performed separately, as different ceremonies are often lumped together without such rubrics, the series of passages from the Making of the Catechumen to the vesting has the feel of a single ceremony, closer to the quick ceremonies for the infirm that follow in each manuscript than to the structured, month-long process presented so carefully in the Gelasian. Such a condensing allowed the ceremony to move away from the kind of firm tie to Easter demonstrated in the Gelasian.

Ælfric's translation and discussion of the *Abrenuntio* and the *Credo* in his Second Series Epiphany sermon supports such a view.[10] Even if we are uneasy taking his account as a direct reflection of the liturgy, he at least seems to imply that the two sets of responses, originally part of the christening and baptism respectively and over half a day apart, are part of the same ceremony. More important is Wulfstan's explanation of baptism in his *Sermo de Baptismate*.[11] He presents the ceremony in accordance with the basic Gelasian order: christening, delivery of the Creed, *Effeta*, Benediction of the Font, baptism, and vestment. He does not mention the *Abrenuntio* in his first quick account (lines 29–99), as he discusses it later in the text, but he does specify that the *Effeta* and the pre-*Abrenuntio* chrism precede the procession to the font, so we might assume that the *Abrenuntio* does as well.[12] In any case, his explanation of *Abrenuntio* and *Credo*, "þe man æt fulluht-þenung on gewunan hæfð" ("that one customarily has at the baptismal service") assumes a single "fulluht-þenung" of which both are a part. Of particular interest is his transition between the *Effeta*/chrism and the benediction of the font:

> And ðonne þis gedon bið eal fullice wel swa to ðære Cristnunge gebyreð, þonne is æfter eallum þisum mid rihtum geleafan to efstanne wið fontbæðes georne.[13]

Whether we can take "georne" to mean 'quickly' or just as a general intensifier (e.g. 'in earnest'), Wulfstan seems to imply a continuity, that christening and baptism can be thought of as a single ceremony, as with the ceremony for the baptism of the infirm, rather than two distinct phases of the baptismal liturgy.[14] If so, then the candidates are catechumens for too short a period of time to mean much, and the ceremony is more readily portable to any time of the year.

---

[10] See CH II.iii, pp. 26–8.

[11] Bethurum, *The Homilies of Wulfstan*, VIIIc, pp. 175–84.

[12] In this respect, and because of the importance Wulfstan places on the delivery of the Creed, which neither Robert nor Leofric has in this position, his account, if it can be taken as chronologically accurate, must follow a version slightly different than that of Darley, Robert, or Leofric (unless, as is possible, the Delivery of the Creed in Leofric is assumed and not stated).

[13] Bethurum, *The Homilies of Wulfstan*, p. 179. "And when this is done fully as well as befits a christening, then it is after all these things to hasten with true faith quickly to the font-bath."

[14] See also Susan Irvine's comments on infant baptisms and on Ælfric's assumption of the union of christening and baptism in her introduction to Ælfric's homily on The Healing of the Blind Man (*Old English Homilies from MS Bodley 343*, Item III (Oxford, 1993), pp. 58–60).

The idea of the catechumenate is not entirely absent from Anglo-Saxon baptismal thought. According to Bede's Ecclesiastical History, King Edwin was catechized for a period of time by Paulinus before being baptized on (in the Old English translation of Bede) "þy halgestan Eastordæge," in the year 627 according to the Anglo-Saxon Chronicle.[15] His daughter Eanfled, the first of the Northumbrians to be baptized, born on Easter Sunday, was 'consecrated to God' and then baptized at Pentecost. The importance of the two Roman baptismal days in the accounts of Edwin and Eanfled and the suggestion of a period of preparatory time before baptism (although we have no indication of what might have been involved liturgically before or during baptism) seem to be in agreement with early Roman practice. At least, Edwin seems to be christened well before his baptism ("Siðþan he gecristnad wæs, swylce eac his lareowe 7 biscope Paulini biscopseðl forgeaf "),[16] building a timber church in the interim, while being instructed.[17] The West-Saxon king Cynegils was catechized before his baptism, and was received from the font by King Oswald of Northumbria. While Bede indicates that this pre-baptismal period was catechetical, the Old English translator more certainly separates his christening from his baptism:

Itaque euangelizante illo in praefata prouincia, cum rex ipse cathecizatus fonte baptismi cum sua gente ablueretur.[18]

[He] lærde þær godcunde lare 7 þone cyning to Cristes geleafan gecerde, 7 hine gecristnade, 7 hine eft æfter fæce mid fulwihtes bæðe aþwoh mid his þeode Westseaxum.[19]

---

[15] Thomas Miller, ed. and trans. *The Old English Version of Bede's Ecclesiastical History of the English People*, vol. I (London, 1890), p. 138. D. P. Kirby, "Bede and Northumbrian Chronology," *EHR* 78 (1963), pp. 514–27, ascribes the conversion of Edwin to 628.

[16] Miller, *The Old English Version of Bede's Ecclesiastical History*, p. 138. "After he was christened, so also he gave a bishopric to his teacher and bishop, Paulinus." The expression "Siðþan he gecristnod wæs" has been grammatically shifted from its position in the Latin, where it has a closer relationship with the preceding sentence, which tells of Edwin building his church: "Baptizatus est autem Eburaci die sancto paschae pridie iduum Aprilium, in ecclesia sancti Petri apostoli, quam ibidem ipse de ligno, cum cathecizaretur atque ad percipiendum baptisma inbueretur, citato opere construxit" (Colgrave and Mynors, eds. *Bede's Ecclesiastical History of the English People* (Oxford, 1969), p. 186). In any case, the Old English translator seems to understand Edwin's period of catechetical instruction as a post-christening catechumenate.

[17] While we get no specific detail regarding the length of Edwin's catechumenical period, the subsequent reference to Paulinus, having baptized many of the royalty and nobility of Northumbria, catechising and baptizing for thirty-six days while staying with the king and queen is perhaps an echo of the Gregorian Lent, which lasted for thirty-six rather than forty days (see chapter 4 above, "Ash Wednesday and Lent").

[18] Colgrave and Mynors, *Bede's Ecclesiastical History*, p. 232. "And so, [he remained] preaching the gospel there in that aforementioned province, when the king himself, a catechumen, was washed in the baptismal font with his people."

[19] Morris, *The Blickling Homilies*, p. 168. "He taught there godly lore and converted the king to Christ's faith, and christened him, and after a time washed him with the bath of baptism along with his people, the West Saxons."

Often in Bede, adult candidates must be catechized before they can undergo baptism, although we have no way of knowing whether this involved a structured liturgical progression from christening to baptism.

The practice of Easter baptism following a preparatory period should not have been unfamiliar to Bede. In a homily for Holy Saturday, Bede may refer to a period of Lenten preparation for baptism:

> As to his saying "Effeta" (that is, "be opened"), he did this in order to heal the ears which a longstanding deafness had closed up, but which his touch now opened that they might hear. Hence I believe a custom has prevailed in the Church that his priests, first among all the elementary stages of consecration [that they perform] for those whom they are preparing to receive the sacrament of baptism, touch their nostrils and ears with saliva from their mouth, while they say, "Effeta" . . . Each one of us, dearly beloved brothers, who has received the baptism of Christ according to the sacred rites, has been consecrated in this way. All who are going to receive this healing and saving bath according to the sacred rites, either at the approaching time of Easter, or at some other time, will be consecrated in this way.[20]

This passage does stress the importance of Easter (while possibly leaving room for baptism outside of Easter or Pentecost), although if it does invoke a catechumenical period, it does so vaguely. Sarah Foot, in her thorough survey of baptism in early Anglo-Saxon England,[21] points out that while Bede's story of the conversion of Edwin does indicate a catechumenical period, other conversions, such as that of Æthelbert of Kent, do not. Regarding these early conversions, she conjectures

> circumstances in which missionaries might have thought it more politic to proceed relatively swiftly with the rituals of initiation, and reserve the more thorough education of the neophytes to a later point, rather than risk the alienation of potentially hostile converts anxious for the outward forms of the ceremony.[22]

By the time of Bede, a more settled system of baptism might have been codified, but eighth-century evidence, as Foot demonstrates, suggests "considerable diversity in liturgical practice between different English minsters."[23] This evidence does seem to indicate a baptism centred primarily on Easter and involving some sort of preparation. Because of the nature of missionary work, the ideal of Easter baptism might certainly have been compromised, and "it is difficult to see how the preparation of candidates could have involved a prolonged period of fasting, exorcism and instruction, unless the clergy had been able to stay amongst their flock for weeks at

---

[20] Martin and Hurst, *Bede the Venerable: Homilies on the Gospels*, vol. 2, pp. 54–5. See also D. Hurst, ed. *Bedae Venerabilis homeliarum evangelii*, p. 222.

[21] Foot explores the available (all non-liturgical) evidence concerning the form, time of year, setting, ministers, and recipients of baptism through the ninth century. On early baptisteries, see Birthe Kjølbye-Biddle, "Anglo-Saxon Baptisteries of the 7th and 8th Centuries: Winchester and Repton," *Acta XIII Congressus Internationalis Archaeologiae Christianae*, vol. II (Vatican City, 1998), pp. 757–78.

[22] Foot, " 'By water in the spirit,' " p. 176.

[23] Ibid. p. 175.

a time."[24] However, the weight of patristic exegetes, for whom baptism and Easter were intertwined, would have (at least theoretically) encouraged the older system, such that in ninth-century France, Amalarius of Metz wrote about baptismal candidates as integral to the festivities of the Easter Vigil.

By the time of the Benedictine Reform, however, baptismal practice had changed a great deal, and appreciation of this earlier ideal of Easter baptism following a catechumenate seems even less clear. The newborn St. Rumwold, in his eleventh-century Anglo-Latin Life, asked to be 'made a catechumen,' although it is not clear whether this was distinct from his baptism, both ceremonies being performed by the priest Widerin.[25] St. Machutus, however, according to the anonymous author of his Life, was born during Easter Vigils and baptized at its end, with no time or need for a catechumenical period.[26] The various versions of the Life of St. Martin (represented in the Blickling and Vercelli collections and in two versions by Ælfric, all based on Sulpicius' Latin Life) demonstrate an ambiguous understanding of the separation of christening and baptism. St. Martin, in Ælfric's account of the bishop's life in his Lives of Saints, was christened ("þa wearð he gecristnod") against his heathen parents' will when he was ten years old.[27] He was not baptized until age eighteen, and Ælfric expresses amazement (as had Sulpicius) that in the three years between his being sent to war and his baptism, he was unspotted, fulfilling "þæs fulluhtes dæda mid fulfremedum weorcum."[28] It is during this time that Martin famously divides his cloak and then dreams of Christ with the cloak, who proclaims that "Martinus þe git nis gefullod me mid þysum reafe gescrydde."[29] Ælfric recognizes what was done to St. Martin at age ten as a pre-baptismal christening, but he is not described as a catechumen, simply as someone who has not yet been baptized. The Blickling homily for the festival of St. Martin shows even more self-consciousness in the separation of Martin's christening from his baptism, explaining that "ðeah he þa gyt nære fullice æfter oþerre endebyrdnesse gefulwad, ah he wæs gecristnod, swa ic ær sægde, hweðre he þæt geryne þære halgan fulwihte mid godum dædu heold 7 fullade."[30] The account of his christening in the Vercelli homily demonstrates more clearly the later Anglo-Saxon need to interpret the Latin "catechumenum fieri postaulauit" in Sulpicius (see Scragg's parallel Latin text to Homily XVIII, *De Sancto Martino Confessore*).[31] The Vercelli

---

[24] Ibid. p. 176.
[25] See Foot, " 'By water in the spirit,' " pp. 171–3.
[26] See Yerkes, *The Old English Life of St. Machutus*, p. 5.
[27] See Skeat, *Ælfric's Lives of Saints*, vol. II, p. 220.
[28] Ibid. p. 222. "The deeds of baptism with perfect works."
[29] Ibid. p. 224. "Martin, who is not yet baptized, has clothed me with this garment."
[30] Morris, *The Blickling Homilies*, p. 213. "Although he was not yet then fully baptized according to another arrangement, but he was christened, just as I said previously, nevertheless he upheld and fulfilled the mystery of holy baptism with good deeds."
[31] Scragg, *The Vercelli Homilies*, pp. 291–309.

homilist translates this expression as "bæd þæt hine man þær gecristnode" and then adds an explanatory appositive, "þæt bið sio onginnes 7 se æresta dæl þære halgan fulwihte."[32] To come to terms with the idea of a catechumenate, the translator must envision a divided baptismal ceremony, of which the 'christening' represented merely the first part. After Martin builds a monastery, "sum gecristnod man" (translating the Latin *catechumenus*) comes to him to be trained, dies unbaptized while Martin is away, and is raised from death and baptized upon Martin's return. The man is called 'a christened man' in the Blickling and Vercelli versions and in Ælfric's Lives of Saints account. In Ælfric's Second Series homily on the Deposition of Saint Martin, however, the man is simply a heathen:

> Æfter ðisum geðeodde sum hæðen wer him to, and se binnon feawum dagum swa færlice swealt þæt he on fulluhte underfangen næs, for ðan ðe Martinus ða on neawiste næs; ac com ða to huse hearde gedrefed, and hine sylfne astrehte sona ofer ðone deadan, drihten biddende þæt he him lif sealde, and he wearð ða geedcucod æfter lytlum fyrste, and sona gefullod.[33]

While there has always been an awareness of the distinction between the state of being of a catechumen and that of the baptized, as evident in Sulpicious' incredulity regarding Martin's purity as a catechumen, this fluidity between the labels 'gecristnod mon' and 'hæðen' perhaps indicates an appreciation of baptism that is much more binary – one is either baptized, or one is a heathen, even if some sort of christening rite has been administered – than the three-part appreciation of early baptism, where many would remain catechumens for a long period of time, and were recognized as in some ways elevated above the state of the heathens. If there is an appreciation in later Anglo-Saxon England of the earlier catechumenical period, it is a vague one, defined almost solely by a separation in time between christening and baptism, and with almost no indication of what happened during that time.

It is a staple of Anglo-Saxon penitential texts (as well as the Irish texts to which they owe a great deal) that adult candidates must learn the Creed and the Pater Noster and be spiritually and mentally ready before being baptized. An Irish canon attributed to St. Patrick prescribes forty days of penance to any brother seeking baptism. The early eighth-century (and heavily influenced by Irish custom) 'Penitential of Theodore' mentions that "Baptized persons may not eat with catechumens."[34] Nowhere in the

---

[32] Scragg, *The Vercelli Homilies*, p. 292. "Asked that the man christen him there . . . that is the beginning and first part of the holy baptism."

[33] CH II.xxxiv, pp. 290–91. "After this a certain heathen man came to him and within a few days he died so quickly that he had not received baptism, because Martin at the time was not in the area, but he came then to the house, sorely troubled, and stretched himself immediately over the dead man, praying to the Lord who gave him life, and he was then re-quickened after a little time, and was immediately baptized."

[34] Gamer and McNeill, trans. *Medieval Handbooks of Penance* (New York, 1979), p. 202.

Anglo-Saxon codes is there any mention of a period of time, or of anything specific that must be done, with the exception of learning the Creed and the Pater Noster, and generally readying oneself. It is this general sense of a need for instruction in the Creed and the Pater Noster that survived of the adult catechumenate, and Ælfric and Wulfstan both stress the same requirement.

Evidence for an infant catechumenate in Irish and Anglo-Saxon penitential texts is less consistent, and has much more bearing on the regularity of formalized Easter baptism. It existed in Irish practice, as attested in a canon attributed to St. Patrick:

> 19. Of the proper age for baptism. On the eighth day they are catechumens; thereafter they are baptized in the solemn feast days of the Lord, that is at Easter, Pentecost, and Epiphany.[35]

This would imply, in some cases, a fairly long period of time between christening and baptism, as would be necessary to keep Easter (or, as a secondary option, Pentecost or Epiphany) baptism a regular part of the liturgy. Theodore's penitential instructs that "one person may, if it is necessary, be [god]father to a catechumen both in baptism and in confirmation," referring to christening and baptism as two separate occasions, with (usually) two different sponsors.[36] By the time of Ælfric and Wulfstan, however, canons referring to baptism are concerned not with the time of year or with the christening of infants, but with the need to baptize quickly. The fifteenth Canon of Edgar, probably by Wulfstan (taken from the version in Junius 121) firmly stresses this need:

> And riht is þæt preosta gehwylc fulluhtes and scriftes tyðige sona swa man gyrne, and æghwær on his scriftscyre beode þæt ælc cild sy gefullod binnan vii nihtum and þæt ænig man to lange unbiscopad ne wyrðe.[37]

The Northumbrian Priests' Law calls for baptism within nine days,[38] and various penitential codes prescribe heavy penances for those whose children die unbaptized.

Both Irish and Anglo-Saxon canons dealing with baptism tend to

---

[35] Ibid. p. 84.

[36] Ibid. p. 202.

[37] Roger Fowler, ed. *Wulfstan's Canons of Edgar* (London, 1972), p. 5. "And it is right that every priest give baptism and confession as soon as someone asks, and everywhere in his shrift-shire bid that every child be baptized within seven nights, and that noone remain unconfirmed too long." Fowler points out that the version in Corpus 201 reads "xxxvii" instead of "vii," which he explains as "a scribal error combining an original xxx with a correction to vii based on Ælfric" (26). If so, we have some evidence of a controversy about the correct age for infant baptism (as Fowler discusses briefly in his note for canon 15), perhaps demonstrating the tension between the fear of allowing a child to die unbaptized and the desire to maintain the tradition of baptism at the high festivals.

[38] See Dorothy Whitelock, et al., eds. and trans. *Councils and Synods*, vol. I (Oxford, 1981), p. 455: "æghwilc cild sy, we lærað, gefullod binnan nigon nihton" ("each child should be, we instruct, baptized within nine nights").

contradict one another, and one often finds contradictions within the same body of text. Most notably, the debate over re-baptism shows some volatile disagreement. On this issue, the Penitential of Theodore says:

12. If through ignorance anyone has been ordained before he is baptized, those who have been baptized by that pagan ought to be rebaptized, and he himself shall not be ordained [again].

This, again, is said to have been differently determined by the Roman Pontiff of the Apostolic See, to the effect that not he who baptizes, even if he is a pagan, but the Spirit of God, ministers the grace of baptism: but also this matter was differently decided in the case of a "pagan" presbyter – he who thinks himself baptized, holding the Catholic faith in his works – these cases are differently decided – that is, that he should be baptized and ordained.[39]

In the Confessional of Egbert, this canon has been compressed into one even more confusing and self-contradictory:

7. If any mass-priest knows that he is unbaptized, he and all those whom he previously baptized shall be baptized. A Roman pope declared that though a priest be sinful or a heathen, nevertheless the ministry of the Holy Ghost, not that of the man, is in the grace of baptism.[40]

Whether one attributes this version to carelessness in transmission or to a genuine lack of consensus on the issue, the debate stands until the time of Ælfric and Wulfstan. Wulfstan, concurring with the more orthodox view, interrupts his account of the christening in his *Sermo De Baptismate* to assert definitively:

Twa ðing syndon þurh Godes mihte swa myccle 7 swa mære þæt æfre ænig man ne mæg ðæron ænig ðing awyrdan ne gewanian, fulluht 7 huslhalgung. Nis se mæssepreost on worulde swa synful ne swa fracod on his dædan, gyf he ðæra þenunga aþere deð swa swa ðærto gebyreð, þeah he sylf ælc unriht dreoge on his life, ne byð seo þenung þæs na þe wyrse. . . . Do swa hwylc swa hit do, Godes sylfes miht byð on þære dæde þurh halig geryne.[41]

Wulfstan's statement represents the final word (for the Anglo-Saxons) in a debate that had spanned the whole of early Christianity. Both he and Ælfric consistently make this assertion, that never should a correctly administered (i.e. according to the Triune formula) baptism be repeated regardless of the state of the person performing the baptism.

It is characteristic of Ælfric and Wulfstan to settle theological debates and present a consistent theology, and Wulfstan does so in regards to

---

[39] Gamer and McNeill, *Medieval Handbooks of Penance*, p. 193.
[40] Ibid. p. 245.
[41] Bethurum, *The Homilies of Wulfstan*, p. 177. "Two things are through God's might so great and so powerful that noone may ruin or diminish anything therein, baptism and the Eucharist. There is not a mass-priest in the world so sinful or so wicked in his deeds, if he should otherwise perform the service as is befitting, although he himself might engage in every wickedness in his life, the service is not at all the worse because of that. . . . Do whatever may be done, God's own might is in the act through the holy mystery."

baptism, concerning the issues discussed above. While Wulfstan too seems, at first glance, to succumb to baptism's confused sense of the age of baptismal candidates (in Bethurum VIIIb, the priest christens "þone cild" and gives the salt to "þam cilde," but he touches with spittle "þæs mannes nose," and "se man" is worthy of the Eucharist), he presents in his *Sermo De Baptismate* a consistent and unified description of baptism that accounts for both adults and children, and makes logical sense for each, avoiding the kind of confusion intrinsic to the liturgy.[42] All references to the candidate have been changed to the unspecific "þone man," rather than switching awkwardly between "cild" and "man." He makes a clear distinction between those who have "þære ylde 7 ðæs andgytes" ("age and understanding") and those who do not. His description, general as it is, could apply to either group, and he makes it clear how each bit should be understood in each case. The former must be "gewisod þæt he cunne hu he of hæþendome mæge to cristendome ðurh rihtne geleafan 7 þurh fulluht cuman."[43] These must learn the *Pater Noster* and the Creed, which signify the true faith. For infants, the Delivery of the Creed is understood to be more applied then learned; rather than pretending that the child can learn and understand it, the candidate plays a passive, not an active role, as the priest, singing the Creed to him, "trymeð he his geleafan 7 mid ðam geleafan gefrætewaþ 7 gewædaþ his hus . . . gegearwað his heortan Gode on to wunianne."[44] When it must be pretended that a child can respond, for the *Abrenuntio* and the *Credo*, Wulfstan makes it clear that, while "his freonda forspæc forstent him eal þæt sylfe swylce hit sylf spæce,"[45] it is then the prime responsibility of those relatives to make sure that the first things that the child does learn, when it can, are the *Pater Noster* and the Creed. The forms are clearly rationalized and explained, and the theology surrounding them is codified. Baptism in late Anglo-Saxon England is discussed generally as a sacrament for infants,[46] but Ælfric and Wulfstan recognize the need for some malleability in the application of the ceremony.

However, in the process of revision and doctrinal clarification, the relationship between this experience and the Holy Season is lost, and we see clearly a single ceremony, performed at any time, not explicitly tied to a

---

[42] See ibid. p. 31 on the relationship between VIII a, b, and c.

[43] Ibid. p. 175. "Instructed so that he might know how he may come from heathendom to christendom through true faith and through baptism."

[44] Ibid. p. 178. "He trims his faith and clothes him with that faith and equips his house . . . prepares his heart as a dwelling for God."

[45] Ibid. p. 182. "The testimony of its relatives stands for it entirely just as if it spoke itself."

[46] Bazire and Cross, eds. *Eleven Old English Rogationtide Homilies* (Toronto, 1982), p. 68, discuss an anonymous Rogationtide sermon which compares rebirth at baptism to confession, when one is "gewintrod." See also the examples put forth by Irvine, *Old English Homilies*, pp. 58–60, concerning statements by Ælfric and Wulfstan reflecting an assumption that baptism is a sacrament for infants.

particular time of the year. A rubric in a sixteenth-century version of the Sarum missal demonstrates a later solution to the same tension between the theoretical appeal of Easter or Pentecost baptisms and the need for quick baptism that we see in Anglo-Saxon exploration of the rite. After describing the benediction of the font, it states:

> At the vigils of Easter and Pentecost this office should not be continued further, unless there were somebody to be baptized . . . Note that at the vigil of Easter and of Pentecost when the fonts have been consecrated neither the oil nor chrism shall be poured into them, unless there be present some who are to be baptized: but let them be covered with a clean cloth, and kept until the end of the Paschal or Pentecostal season, so that, if it happen that during those days someone comes to be baptized, then the fonts may be made fruitful and sanctified by the infusion of oil and chrism, and he may be baptized.[47]

This was the compromise reached by Ælfric in a letter for Wulfsige, discussing Holy Saturday: "Ne do man nænne ele to þam fante, buton mann þær cild on fullige."[48] While recognizing the traditional propriety of baptism in the Paschal season, this seems to suggest that it was not the norm for those that used this text, but that the urgency of quick baptism was deemed more important. In his Letter to the Monks of Eynsham, Ælfric seems to give baptism more weight than one might expect, given its general disassociation from Easter. After the blessing of the Paschal candle and a set of readings and antiphons on Holy Saturday, the baptismal font is blessed. Into the *Concordia*'s account of Holy Saturday, Ælfric inserts some interesting baptismal instructions:

> When infants are baptized they should be anointed on the top of the head by the priest, because the bishop should anoint on the forehead, where the high priest used to wear a plate of gold. The candle that is placed in the hand of the baptized infant is likened to the lamps of the wise virgins.[49]

This passage is derived from Amalarius, except for the likening of the candle to the wise virgins. Jones discusses Ælfric's use of Amalarius here,[50] emphasizing that this material, and especially its placement in the discussion of the Easter Vigil, is close to the version of Amalarius' *Retractatio prima* in a post-Conquest manuscript, Salisbury, Cathedral Library MS 154, which Jones argues "confirms the existence of an augmented version of the *Retractatio prima* from which Ælfric's exemplar, like Salisbury 154, clearly derived."[51] Although the instruction concerning the candle does not appear elsewhere in Anglo-Saxon witnesses, the directions for the applica-

[47] *DBL*, p. 244.
[48] Fehr, *Die Hirtenbriefe Ælfrics*, p. 28. "One should not put any oil in the font, unless one is going to baptize a child there."
[49] *LME*, pp. 134–5. "Infantes, quando baptizantur, in cerebro unguendi sunt a presbitero, quia episcopus debet in fronte unguere ubi laminam auream pontifex ferebat. Cereus qui infanti baptizato datur in, manum coadunatur lapadibus sapientium virginum."
[50] See *LME*, p. 201, n. 230, 231.
[51] *LME*, p. 64.

tion of the chrism[52] are echoed in Ælfric's Second Letter for Wulfstan, where they have no particular relationship to Easter:

> Mid þam haligan ele ge scylan þa hæþenan cild mearcian on þam breoste and betwux þæm gesculdru on middeweardan mid rode tacne, ærþanþe ge hit fullian on þam fantwætere. And þonne hit of þæm wætere cynð, ge scylan wyrcan rode tacen upp on þæm heafde mid þam haligan crisman.[53]

Granted Ælfric's reliance on Amalarius here, the inclusion of baptismal forms for the Easter Vigil in his Eynsham letter should probably be seen in the light of the insinuation in his letter for Wulfsige that Easter baptisms were a possibility rather than an integral part of Easter worship. Consistent throughout these instructions, in any event, is the assumption of infant baptism.

What is lost here, in a society that thinks of baptism as, predominately, an event for infants, without a Lenten catechumenical period, is the idea of a dramatic Easter submission to death and resurrection. What survives from the Gelasian scrutinies is the sense of christening as an exorcism of the devil and an initiation by birth into the church, applied to the child rather than submitted to in a quasi-mimetic correlation with the events at Easter. That there is some sort of 'dramatic' quality to baptism, in some sense of the word, is certain, given the range and power of its associations. The matter of the sacrament, the water, encompasses most of these. In a key passage in the liturgy for the Blessing of the Font from the Robert Missal (also in the Gelasian), directly preceding the actual baptism, the priest addresses the water directly, making it clear that the water in the font is the same water that God first shaped into the four rivers that flowed from Eden and gave life to the world, that sprang forth from the rock in the desert giving life to the Israelites, that Christ turned to wine at Cana, on which he walked, in which he was baptized (*a johanne in jordane*), and which flowed from his side mixed with Christ's blood (*una cum sanguine*) at the Crucifixion.[54] In the same way that the consecrated host calls forth, in a very real, spiritual sense, the body of Christ, so the consecrated water calls forth the life-giving

---

[52] The inclusion of episcopal baptismal instructions does not mean that a bishop would regularly be participating in the liturgy for Holy Saturday at Eynsham. Ælfric also includes in his Eynsham Letter instructions for the episcopal blessing of the oils on Maundy Thursday, perhaps reflecting "a scholarly interest in the rite itself and in the unusual exposition provided by his exemplar of the *Retractio prima*" (*LME*, p. 192, n. 196). Jones further expresses his suspicion that "LME 39 [the blessing of the oils] reflects its immediate written source more than Ælfric's memory of the actual rite performed at Winchester." Perhaps his interest in episcopal baptismal instructions is equally 'scholarly.' These episcopal instructions, along with other general instructions, probably indicate that Ælfric's Letter was constructed with the possibility of a wider audience than just the Eynsham community (see also *LME*, p. 170, n. 98).

[53] Fehr, *Die Hirtenbriefe Ælfrics*, p. 148. "With the holy oil you must mark the heathen child on the breast and between the shoulders in the middle with the cross-sign, before you baptize it in the font-water. And when it is brought forth from the water, you must make a cross-sign upon the head with the holy chrism."

[54] Wilson, *The Missal of Robert of Jumièges*, p. 98.

power of God, such that the participants are dipped into the actual water that baptized Christ, and that flowed from his side. This blessing is something of a hodge-podge, pulling from events throughout Christian history in order to make them present, not for the sake of establishing a biblical setting for dramatic experience, but to make clear the water's power, its ability to drive out the devil.

Anglo-Saxon prose writers picked up these associations as well, particularly the latter two, to the same effect. Ælfric, in a homily for mid-Lent, specifies that the water from Christ's side was "to urum fulluhte."[55] The first Vercelli homily proclaims: "þæt tacnode hælo middangeardes, þæt ðurh his blod fulwihtwæter gewyrþan sceolde."[56] In his Second Series sermon for Epiphany, Ælfric asserts that at Christ's entry into the Jordan at his baptism, "ða wæs þæt wæter and ealle wyll-springas gehalgode þurh Cristes lichaman to urum fulluhte."[57] One of the most interesting explorations of this theme is in the sixteenth Vercelli homily, where the author, using a prophecy of David, turns the river Jordan into a sort of proto-Font:

> Swylce wearð æt þam dryhtenlican fulwihte se cwide 7 se witedom gefylled 7 geworden þe Dauid se witiga in þam sealme sang 7 toweard sægde, ða he þurh haligne gast þa dryhtenlican fulwihte him toweard geseah . . . "Hwæt is þe, sæ, for hwan fluge ðu? Oððe þu, Iordan, for hwan cerdest ðu on bæclincg?" Iordan is haten seo ea þe se hælend on gefulwad wæs, 7 heo is swiðe mycel wæter 7 swiðe strang stream hafað 7 sæflod on yrneð. And þa wæs geworden in þa tid þe se hælend in þæt wæter astag þa ge-cyrde se sæflod 7 se stream eall on bæcling, 7 swa stille gestod þæt flod swylce he flowan ne meahte, ac he wæs swiðe mid þy godcundan egesan geþreatod þæt he hine styrian ne dorste.[58]

This kind of legend strengthens the coincident relationship between the contemporary font and the Jordan at the time of Christ. The Jordan as a font is a popular hagiographical theme. In Ælfric's life of St. Basilius, Basil travels to Jerusalem to be baptized in the Jordan, whereupon, at the point of baptism, a dove descends from a fire in the heavens and stirs the water in imitation of a priest's consecration of the font. The river, after the dove's descent, is referred to as the "fant-baðe."[59] Such associations give the consecrated water the same apotropaeic power held by the host, to the

---

[55] CH II.xii, p. 116. "For our baptism."

[56] Scragg, *The Vercelli Homilies*, p. 261. "That symbolized the healing of the earth, that through his blood baptismal water should be made."

[57] CH II.iii, p. 22. "Then was that water, and all well-springs, hallowed through Christ's body to our baptism."

[58] Scragg, *The Vercelli Homilies*, p. 269. "It so happened at the baptism of our Lord that the saying and the prophecy were fulfilled and brought about which David the wise man sang in the psalm, and spoke of the future . . . 'What is it to you, sea, why do you flee? Or you, Jordan, why do you turn backwards?' Jordan is the name of the river in which the saviour was baptized, and it is a very great river and has a very strong current and runs to the sea-flood. And then it happened in that time when the saviour descended into the water that then the sea-flood and the entire current turned back, and the river stood so still that it could not flow, but it was so greatly held by divine terror that it did not dare to stir."

[59] Skeat, *Ælfric's Lives of Saints*, vol. I, p. 54.

degree that people would take vials of it to bless their homes and fields, to drive out evil spirits, and to heal the sick.[60] These associations also serve as a conduit for drawing Christ's baptism and his crucifixion into the contemporary baptismal ceremony by infusing the water with the power behind these events.

As the water is understood to be one with that involved in the original events, so the participants are described as, in a spiritual sense, participating in those events. As these events are cataclysmic, demonstrations of God's power and violent desire to purge the world of sin, it is not surprising that baptism is most commonly described as a battle with the devil. In his sermon for the second Sunday after Epiphany, Ælfric, discussing the second water vessel changed to wine at Cana, claims:

> On ðære oðre ylde . . . se swymmenda arc getacnode Godes gelaðunge, and þæt se rihtwisa Noe getacnode Crist, and þæt yðigende flod þe ða synfullan adylegode, gebicnode þæt halige wæter ures fulluhtes, þe ure synna adilegað . . .[61]

In his sermon for Mid-Lent Sunday, Ælfric explains that:

> Seo reade sæ hæfde getacnunge ures fulluhtes, on ðære adranc Pharao and his here samod, swa eac on urum gastlicum fulluhte bið se deofol forsmorod fram us, and ealle ure synna beoð adylegode, and we ðonne sigefæste mid geleafan Godes lof singað . . .[62]

The baptismal liturgy describes baptism as an exorcism of the devil and the devil's taint, making the drowning of Pharaoh in the Red Sea a fitting precursor. The poem *Andreas* contains a powerful use of baptism as a conquering force, in that the soldiers who had killed the saint are literally drowned in a flood and requickened by God into a life of faithfulness. Their baptism is literal enough, in the word's original sense of 'drowning,' to make the poet's assertion that "þa wæs mid þy folce fulwiht hæfen . . . riht aræred" a wonderful litotes.[63] Ælfric's First Series sermon for Pentecost develops more fully the theme of baptism conquering enemies, explaining Easter as an old Hebrew festival celebrating the drowning of Pharaoh (followed fifty days later, at Pentecost, with God's bestowal of his law at Mt. Sinai).[64] The destruction of the devil-Pharaoh is relived in the contemporary baptism, as that same power that rescued the Israelites from

---

[60] In a spectacular illustration of superstition surrounding the power of the consecrated water, a mother in Ælfric's Second Series sermon on St. Stephen dips her hair into a baptismal font as part of a curse on her children (CH II.ii, p. 15).

[61] CH II.iv, p. 33. "In the other age . . . the floating ark symbolized God's church, and the righteous Noah symbolized Christ, and the surging flood that destroyed the sinful betokened the holy water of our baptism, which destroys our sins."

[62] CH II.xii, p. 115. "The Red Sea has the signification of our baptism, in which Pharoah drowned and his army with him, so also in our spiritual baptism the devil is smothered away from us, and all our sins are destroyed, and we then sing God's praise victoriously, with faith."

[63] See Krapp, *The Vercelli Book*, pp. 48–9, lines 1643–5. "Then was having baptism among that folk . . . rightly revered."

[64] CH I.xxii, p. 355.

captivity will rescue the baptismal candidate from the devil's influence. What rings through here, whenever baptism is invoked, is the power of the water, drawn from these Old Testament events, his baptism and his crucifixion into the present ceremony by way of invocations like that in the Robert Missal.

What is most surprising, in looking at late Anglo-Saxon treatment of baptism, is the paucity of overt association with the Resurrection. That there is a spiritual connection between baptism and Easter is undeniable. It is the heart of Christianity that Christ's death and resurrection paved the way for our redemption, realized in baptism, and the parallel is obvious in the very word 'baptism,' signifying a death, followed by a rebirth. Ælfric does find an Old Testament relationship between baptism and Easter by way of the Red Sea in the aforementioned sermon for Pentecost. In the same sermon, he makes the New Testament connection, asserting:

> Nu is his þrowung 7 his ærist ure eastertid, for þan ðe he us alysde fram deofles þeowdome, 7 ure ehteras beoð besencte þurh þæt halige fulluht, swa swa wæs Pharao mid his leode on þære readan sæ.[65]

The relationship here is assumed, but the dominant image is, again, that of conquering water. Even baptismal references to the Crucifixion focus on the water from Christ's side, not on the supposed co-occurrence of 'dramatic' roles. If baptism belonged predominately to Easter, and if the death and resurrection of Christ reenacted by the baptismal participants was a major theme, one might expect to see some reflection of that in sermons for Easter. In Ælfric's First Series sermon for Easter, we find the liturgy for the day reflected in the *Visitatio Sepulchri*, the visitation of the three women to the tomb on Sunday morning. Baptism, however, is conspicuously absent. At one point, Ælfric discusses how Christ 'passed over from passion to resurrection, from death to life, from torment to glory,' a discussion that would be a good occasion for referring to Easter Vigil baptisms in which Christ's passing over comes to fruition in men, yet this is not an imperative for him. Ælfric does mention baptism in his *Sermo de Sacrificio in Die Pascae*, explaining how when a child is baptized, "hit ne bret na his hiw wiðutan, ðeah ðe hit beo wiðinnan awend . . . hit bið aðwogen fram eallum synnum wiðinnan, þeah ðe hit wiðutan his hiw ne awende."[66] This discussion, however, focuses on the nature of the consecrated water, and is really an attempt to explain the nature of the consecrated host, which *is* a central part of the liturgy for the day.

There is a more developed identification between the baptismal partici-

---

[65] CH I.xxii, p. 355. "Now is his Passion and his Resurrection our Eastertide, because he freed us from the service of the devil, and our persecutors are drowned through that holy baptism, just as was Pharoah with his people in the Red Sea."

[66] CH II.xv, p. 153. "It does not at all transform its outward appearance, although it is inwardly changed . . . it is washed from all sins inwardly, although outwardly its appearance does not change."

pant and Christ at his birth. The author of a homily for Tuesday in Rogationtide tells us that, "Ðurh clæne mæden Crist wearð geboren, and þurh clæne fulluht we syndon ealle cristene gewordene."[67] In his Second Series Sermon for Christmas, Ælfric describes baptism as a birth:

> Ælc man bið mid synnum gestryned and geboren ðurh Adames forgægednysse, ac he bið eft Criste acenned on ðære halgan gelaðunge, þæt is on Godes cyrcan, þurh fulluht. þæt wæter aðwehð þone lichaman, and se halga gast aðwehð ða sawle fram eallum synnum, and se gefulloda man bið þonne Godes bearn.[68]

This is a more natural association to make for those who, as Ælfric says in his dual interpretation of the parable of the vineyard in a homily for Septuagesima Sunday, "fram cildcradole to Godes geleafan comon."[69] While identification with Christ has shifted focus from his resurrection to his birth and his own baptism, discussion of baptism belongs, for Ælfric, to Epiphany rather than Easter, highlighting the idea of baptism as a ceremony of birth and initiation more than death and resurrection. As the commemoration of Christ's own baptism, Epiphany is a natural forum for discussing the theology of baptism. However, in Ælfric's Second Series sermon for Epiphany, he not only discusses some of its repercussions, but he presents in translation the heart of the baptismal liturgy, the *Abrenuntio* and the *Credo*. As interested as Ælfric is in explaining in his preaching the liturgy for the day, this inclusion is compelling. Baptism at Epiphany, according to Whitaker, is an Eastern phenomenon, as Rome repeatedly asserted that Easter and Pentecost were the appropriate times for baptism, although there is evidence that Epiphanal baptisms were regular in Ireland (Irish Christianity frequently reflecting an Eastern influence). This is certainly not to say that baptism was part of the liturgy for Epiphany for the Anglo-Saxons, for this passage is couched in a theoretical defence of infant baptism, and there is no evidence for such an idea, except possibly the verse Menologium's inconclusive reference to Epiphany as "fulwihttiid."[70] More likely, discussion of baptism would naturally focus on Epiphany in the wake of a practical diminishment in the importance of Easter baptism. This loss is the result of changes in the baptismal liturgy by the time of Ælfric, the most important of which is the shift from adult to infant baptisms and its corollary loss of the structured catechumenate that had originally been defined by, and helped define, the Holy Season.

---

[67] BC, p. 95. "Through a clean maiden Christ was born, and through clean baptism we are all made Christians." This passage is found in a variety of places, including a composite homily (number 30) printed by Napier and discussed in Scragg, "The Corpus of Vernacular Homilies," p. 25. See also M. R. Godden, "Old English Composite Homilies from Winchester," *ASE* 4 (1975), pp. 57–65.

[68] CH II.i, p. 6. "Each man is filled with sins and is born through Adam's transgression, but he is afterwards born to Christ in the holy community, that is in God's church, through baptism. That water washes the body and the Holy Ghost washes the soul from all sins, and the baptized man is then God's son."

[69] CH II.v, p. 44. "Came to God's faith from the cradle."

[70] Dobbie, *The Anglo-Saxon Minor Poems*, p. 49, line 11.

The common assertion that medieval baptismal ceremonies involve a dramatic recapitulation of the death and resurrection of Christ, bolstered by the temporal coincidence of Easter, loses force in such a baptism, particularly in a case where the supposed lead actor is an infant. The images called up by the Anglo-Saxon liturgists and reflected in the prose are quite strong, and they include a number of biblical events, including those of the Passion, that invite dramatic reenactment, but they are not described in terms compatible with dramatic interpretation. Those involved in the ceremonies are interested in the conquering and protecting might of God, the sacrificial potency of Christ's blood, and the quickening power of the Holy Ghost, all present in the water in which are dipped those in desperate need of exorcism. Noah's Flood, the crossing of the Red Sea, and Christ's birth, baptism, and crucifixion are all certainly present at the time of baptism. One might argue that baptism is 'dramatic' because the desire to conquer the devil in the Red Sea, and at Christ's baptism and crucifixion, becomes one with the desire of those baptizing the *infantes* bearing 'ghostly children' into the fellowship of Christ. However, the dramatic character of the Anglo-Saxon rituals examined in previous chapters depends on packaging the liturgy in such a way that it encourages a clear sense of identification with a biblical model, and in particular on an appreciation by those involved that they are to play a certain role in the proceedings. As such, the shift from traditional explorations of baptism (involving a Christ-like death and resurrection) to the newer paradigm (in which baptism is fundamentally an exorcism and identification is utilized to establish connections for characterization of the baptismal water moreso than for the participants) mutes the dramatic potential of baptism in Anglo-Saxon appreciation of the rite.

8

Rogationtide and the Ascension

FOR AN OBSERVANCE that goes back to the very beginning of Anglo-Saxon Christianity and held such an important place in English liturgical devotion, Rogationtide has been surprisingly understudied. John Blair explores some of the social contexts of Rogationtide, speculating about the place of Rogationtide processions in the shifting allegiances between the laity and either minster churches or the growing parish churches, and also about the potential relationships between Christian holy sites used in the processions and sites treated as holy according to folk religions.[1] Neil Ker and Rudolph Willard helped define the corpus of vernacular homilies proper to Rogationtide, twenty-four in all according to the revised count in the introduction of Bazire and Cross' *Eleven Old English Rogationtide Homilies.* The presentation of eleven of the more inaccessible pieces by Bazire and Cross has made easier examination of the corpus of preaching for Rogationtide. The festival, consisting of three days of processions, attracted such a large body of preaching material partly because its prescribed topics were quite broad, and the sorts of sermons that might be written 'for any time of year' tended to migrate towards this dramatic penitential period. Bazire and Cross provide a short list of the sorts of themes that come up again and again in Rogationtide sermons, themes of penance, the care of the soul, basic instruction (with sermons on the Creed and the Lord's Prayer), the importance of listening to teachers, and appropriate behaviour.[2] Such tracts are quite familiar to penitential literature, and some of the relevant passages appear in sermons for both Lent and Rogationtide. The wealth of topics proper to Rogationtide makes generalizations about its dramatic propensities difficult. As is often the case in the liturgy, several things are happening at once in the Rogationtide processions. Crops are blessed, disaster averted, Christian principles learned and strengthened, and heaven approached. I wish here to focus on the last of these, the recurrent theme of Rogationtide as a preparatory approach to union with heaven on the feast of the Ascension, which directly follows Rogationtide. Although Rogationtide and the Ascension have different origins, by the time of the late Anglo-Saxon church, the relationship between the two has been recognized and enhanced to grant the

---

[1] See Blair, *The Church in Anglo-Saxon Society* (forthcoming).
[2] BC, pp. xxiv–xxv.

Plate 6. The Ascension, Benedictional of Æthelwold
London, BL MS Additional 49598, fol. 67v (by permission of the British Library)

Rogations an eschatological focus and to allow liturgical participants to process to the threshold of heaven along with Christ at his Ascension.

The elevation of humanity, through which this approach to heaven is made possible, is the primary theme of the Ascension. This central idea and its importance to the faithful are expressed by Ælfric in his First Series sermon for the day:

> On his acennednysse wæs geþuht swilce seo godcundnyss wære geeadmet, 7 on his upstige wæs seo menniscnys ahafen 7 gemærsod. Mid his upstige is adylegod þæt cyrografum ure genyðerunge, 7 se cwyde ure brosnunge is awend.
>
> Ða ða Adam agylt hæfde, ða cwæð se ælmihtiga wealdend him to þu eart eorðe 7 þu gewentst to eorþan; ðu eart dust 7 þu gewentst to duste. Nu todæig þæt ilce gecynd ferde unbrosniendlic into heofenan rice.[3]

It is not just Christ in power that ascends to heaven on Holy Thursday, but specifically 'humanity,' the same humanity that Adam ruined when he ate the apple. The Ascension is in essence a celebration of the unity of humanity with divinity, and our entrance into heaven is made possible by this elevation of humanity through Christ. This is the point of the liturgy for the day, that through the liturgical expression of the Ascension liturgy the communicants are made one with Christ, and by that granted unity with the divinity of Heaven. The Vigil of the Ascension, which coincides with the third Rogation day, anticipates these themes, and its liturgical forms focus on the need to prepare oneself, by purification, for joining in Christ's ascension the following day. Although the Rogation days originally had something of a different function, one still retained throughout their treatment, their juxtaposition with the Ascension (dating from the time of Rogationtide's inception) makes them to some degree an extended vigil, reflected in Amalarius' description of them as "ieiunium triduanum in vigilia ascensionis Domini."[4] Ælfric reminds us that Christ will return in the same way that he went up on Ascension Day, and this parallel, along with the general idea of entrance into heaven, drew a good deal of eschatological expectation, so that Rogationtide sermons are filled with quite dramatic visions of Heaven and Hell and accounts of Judgement Day. This emphasis makes the penitential processions of Rogationtide a preparation for approaching heaven, and failure to observe the Rogations, or failure to do so appropriately, carries the threat of punishment in hell. As well as being a recapitulation of the penitential pleading of the Ninevites in the time of Jonah, and of the inhabitants of Vienne under Mamertus, Rogationtide

---

[3] CH I.xxi, pp. 347–8. "In his birth it seemed as if the divinity were made humble, and in his Ascension humanity was raised up and exalted. With his Ascension is destroyed that cyrograph of our abasement, and the enactment has changed our corruption. When Adam had guilt, then the Almighty Ruler said to him, 'You are earth, and you will return to earth; you are dust, and you will return to dust.' Now today that same kind travelled incorruptible into the heavenly kingdom."

[4] Hanssens, *Amalarii episcopi opera liturgical omnia*, vol. 2, p. 178. "Three fasting days in vigil of the ascension of the Lord."

is an instructive and a liturgical preparation for the reenactment of the Ascension into heaven, specifically of its elevation of humanity to heaven, in the Rogationtide and Ascension liturgies.

Bazire and Cross give a good, concise account of the early history of Rogationtide.[5] There are several traditions concerning the origins of the festival (each of which I discuss in more detail below), each one emphasizing a certain aspect of the festival. Some say that it is a descendant of the fast of the Ninevites after the warning of Jonah, who attempted to avert the hovering fire of God's retribution, or that it was begun by Gregory the Great in response to a plague, or by St. Peter in answer to three days of pagan processions for the prosperity of fields and cattle. The standard account, and the one most accepted by modern historians, claims that the three processional days were instituted by the bishop Mamertus of Vienne around the year 470 in response to a rash of afflictions to the city and the surrounding countryside. Accounts of this affliction include earthquakes, attacks by wild animals, and fire. According to reports, Mamertus established before the Ascension three days of fasting and processional supplication, after which the affliction ceased. Whatever its origin, because of its success the practice was picked up in other churches and became general throughout the Gallican church in the sixth century. Rogationtide was not accepted in the Roman church until the pontificate of Leo III (795–816). The three days were referred to as the 'minor Rogations' in the Roman calendar, as opposed to the 'Greater litany' on 25 April. The Council of Clofesho in 747 prescribed both festivals, the Roman 'Greater litany' and the three Rogation days "according to the custom of our forefathers, three days before the Ascension of our Lord into the heavens."[6] These designations are also attested in the Old English Martyrology, but by some time in the ninth century the Rogations were instead considered the 'Greater litanies' in England, and they are referred to as *Letania Maiore* in all late Anglo-Saxon witnesses. The general term, used in most of the vernacular witnesses, is "gangdagas," although Ælfric (and apparently Wulfstan, following Ælfric)[7] calls them the "gebeddagas,"[8] reflecting their original purpose, to show evidence of repentance and to pray that God will withhold the destruction that the sinful people rightly deserve. Byrhtferth similarly calls them "Bendagas," although he uses the more general "gangdagum" when explaining their computational relationship to Easter.[9] The two names reflect the two central elements of the Rogationtide liturgy, the procession and the stational penitential prayers.

---

[5] BC, pp. xv–xvii.
[6] See BC, p. xvi.
[7] One of the homilies printed by Bazire and Cross, Homily 8, seems to be based on a lost homily for Rogationtide by Wulfstan, itself based on one of Ælfric's (BC, pp. 104–7).
[8] CH I.xviii, p. 317.
[9] See Lapidge and Baker, eds. *Byrhtferth's Enchiridion* (Oxford, 1995), pp. 156, 152.

Despite the many descriptions of the Rogations, it is difficult to pin down exactly what took place. One of the earliest references to the processions is in the *Epistola Cuthberti de obitu Baedae*, which testifies that "at nine o'clock we went in procession with the relics as the custom of the day required."[10] This starting time is also attested in Homily 6 of Bazire and Cross, a sermon for the first Rogation day, which instructs:

> Forðan ic bidde eow and manige þæt ge don swa eow Godes bec læra∂, þæt ge mid micclum ege gan mid Godes reliquium, na mid idelum wordum and unnyttum spræcum . . . Forðan us is micel þearf þæt we ∂as dagas rihtlice healdan for Cristes upastygennysse. On þysum ∂rym dagum cristene menn sculon forlætan heora þa woruldlican weorc on þa ∂riddan tid dæges, þæt is on undern sylfne, and for∂gan mid þam halgum reliquium oþ þa nigo∂an tid, þæt is o∂ non.[11]

The twelfth Vercelli homily gives more detail concerning what was in the procession, including relics, the gospel books, the Cross of Christ, and the remains of holy men.[12] The faithful were to fast until the ninth hour, and several homilies warn of diabolical consequences for breaking the fast. The procession went both inside and outside of the church, for Ælfric asserts that we should offer up prayers and "fylian urum haligdomum ut 7 in."[13] It would have involved several stations, and must have ranged through the countryside, for the penitents are warned that they must walk barefoot, not ride. Bazire and Cross's Homily 5 may mention the stations:

> Forþon, bro∂or mine, on þas andweardantide beo∂ reliquias haligra manna uppahafene and for∂aborene mid leofsange and mid gastlicum sange on sunderlice stowe gehwilce swa hwær swa hi gesette beo∂.[14]

Homily 8 specifies that, with the Cross, the books, and the holy relics, "we sceal bletsian ure þa eor∂lican speda, þæt synd æceras and wudu and ure ceap and eall þa þing þe us God forgyfen hafa∂ to brucanne."[15] It would seem that, along with the proscription against riding instead of walking, the procession must have covered at least a sampling of the countryside, stopping periodically at certain sites, probably other churches or shrines, for the prayers. Several witnesses mention visits to shrines as part of the observance of the day, although it is not entirely clear that this is necessarily part of the procession itself, as it tends to be mentioned along with other matters of

---

[10] Translated in BC, p. xvi.

[11] BC, p. 83. "Therefore I bid you and exhort that you do as God's books teach you, that you with great fear travel with God's relics, not at all with idle words and useless speaking . . . Therefore it is very necessary for us that we rightly keep these days before Christ's Ascension. On these three days, Christians must forsake their worldly work on the third hour of the day, that is at Terce, and go forth with the holy relics until the ninth hour, that is until None."

[12] See BC, pp. xxii–xxiv, for a number of translated accounts of Rogationtide observance.

[13] CH I.xviii, p. 318. "Follow our holy things out and in."

[14] BC, pp. 72–3. "Therefore, my brothers, at this present time let the relics of holy men be lifted up and borne forth, with praise-singing and with spiritual singing, in various places, each wheresoever they might be set."

[15] BC, p. 12. "We must bless our earthly places, which are the acres and woods and our cattle and all of the things that God has given us to enjoy."

general observance, including vigils, fasting, and almsgiving. The forms for the first day's procession are to be found in the Leofric Missal, which specify the Roman stations, including *Ad sanctum laurentium, Ad sanctum valentinum, Ad pontem molbi, Ad crucem,* and *In atrio.*[16] The mass forms follow, and possibly the *In atrio* form would precede the re-entrance into the church for mass at None. It is uncertain how well this skeletal processional scheme translated into the Anglo-Saxon observance, however. The forms appear in the Robert Missal (which has a definite relationship with Leofric) in the same order, and with the same invocation of "beato laurentio martyre"[17] in the first prayer, but without any of Leofric's rubrics (all simply headed *Alia*). The same forms appear in the Portiforium of Wulstan, but the order of the forms is jumbled, and the stational rubrics are likewise lost. The set of prayers comes under the heading "In Letania Maiori, Statio Ad Sanctum Vincentium."[18] The first prayer is the same as the *Ad sanctum laurentium* in Leofric, and is identical except that the "beato laurentio martyre" in the first prayer has been changed to "beato vincentio martyre." There is no indication, however, with the loss of stational rubrics, that all of the forms do not fall under the heading "Statio Ad Sanctum Vincentium," even though each form is clearly for a different station in Leofric. Apart from this small hint in Wulstan, rubrics indicating possible stations are hard to come by. Perhaps the stations might change from year to year, and certainly the local nature of the processions and the fact that forms in liturgical books rarely give an indication of locality make it difficult to expect to find that sort of detail. In any case, some of the stations surely would have been outside the church complex for there to be the potential of riders, and for there to have been even a semblance of blessing all the surrounding countryside.

Most of the high liturgical festivals in late Anglo-Saxon England seem to involve ceremonies and liturgical elaborations that were developed in monastic settings and extended, to some extent, to include lay participation. Rogationtide is an exception, for from the time of its inception it was a practice for the common people, and would have involved the whole demographic of Anglo-Saxon society. Bazire and Cross demonstrate in a number of cases that many of the sermons for Rogationtide were clearly directed at the unlearned.[19] Instructions for liturgical festivals for monks tend to assume absolute involvement in the spirit and purpose of the ritual elements. Instructions for Rogationtide do not. Throughout the exhortations are injunctions against riding, hunting, bearing a weapon, and gaming, from 'vain deeds and empty words,' and from "idele spellunga and hlacerunga" in God's house.[20] These sorts of proscriptions tend to be

[16] See Warren, *The Leofric Missal*, p. 107.
[17] Wilson, *The Missal of Robert of Jumièges*, p. 111.
[18] Hughes, *The Portiforium of Saint Wulstan*, vol. 1, p. 62.
[19] See, for example, their comments on Homily 3, BC, p. 41.
[20] BC, p. 96.

featured in those sermons most clearly directed at the unlearned, along with highly emotional warnings of eternal retribution and descriptions of hell, constructed more to arouse than to inform. The tendency of the people to misinterpret the fast as a festival is reflected as early as the Council of Clofesho, which beseeches that the three days not be "intermingled with vanities, as is the custom among most people, neither with negligence, nor with ignorant wickedness, that is, with games and horse-races and too great feasts; but rather that the whole people should humbly pray . . . with fear and trembling."[21] The gap between how the wise teachers expected the people to understand these festivals and how they actually did, a gap that is impossible to define, has important consequences for our appreciation of the nature of Anglo-Saxon dramatic ritual. It is precisely this gap that is being addressed in vernacular preaching, for the inspiration behind most of these sermons is clearly to make the people appreciate first that they are under the direct threat of divine retribution for their sins, as were the Ninevites and the people of Vienne, and that they must purify themselves before the upcoming Ascension, where they can either join Christ's elevation of humanity to heaven or fall under this divine punishment.

The liturgical dynamics of Rogationtide and the Ascension include everybody, and in many places there must have been quite a throng of people marching barefoot in procession through the land. Wulfstan assumed that there would be a crowd when he instructed in the Canons of Edgar:

> And riht is þæt preostas folc mynegian þæs þe hi Gode don sculon to gerihtum on teoþungum and on oðrum þingum. And riht is þæt man þisses mynegige to eastrum, oðre siðe to gangdagum, þriddan siðe to middan sumera þonne bið mæst folces gegaderod.[22]

The Vision of Leofric offers a compelling glimpse at contemporary perception of the Rogation crowd. The dreamer, having crossed a bridge and come to a bright field with a sweet smell, sees a throng of people, in a description very similar to that of the place where the faithful wait to enter Heaven in the vision of Drihthelm, presented by Ælfric[23]:

> Ða þa he ofere wæs, þa com him lateow ongean 7 hyne lædde to anum swyðe wlitigan felde 7 swyþe fægeran, mid swetan stence afylled. þa geseah he swyþe mycele weorud swylce on gangdagan, 7 þa wæron ealle mid snawhwitum reafe gescrydde, 7 þæt on þa wisan þe se diacon bið þonne he godspell ret. And wæs an þæra on middan standende on mæssepreostes reafe, swyþe heah 7 swyðe mycel ofer eal þæt oþer folc.[24]

---

[21] BC, p. xxiv.

[22] Fowler, *Wulfstan's Canons of Edgar*, p. 13. "And it is right that priests remind the folk of what they must do for God to fulfill right practice in tithing and in other things. And it is right that one exhort this at Easter, a second time at the Rogation days, a third time at Midsummer when most people are gathered."

[23] For the description in the vision of Drihthelm, see CH II.xxi, p. 201.

[24] See A. S. Napier, ed. "An Old English Vision of Leofric, Earl of Mercia," *Philological Society Transactions* (1908), p. 182. "When he was across, then the guide came towards him and led him

Where the vision of Drihthelm describes the "ungerime meniu hwittra manna" ("countless number of radiant/white people") the dreamer here invokes an image of the Rogation crowd, which at least for him must have been tremendous. Particularly as the Rogation crowd are specifically trying to make themselves worthy to wear white and approach heaven, actualized in the Ascension Mass (in the Vision of Leofric, the highlight is a Mass performed by St. Paul himself), the Vision presents a nice portrait of the spiritual fulfilment of the liturgical aims of the season, realized by all the participating folk.

The Rogations are, first of all, a recapitulation of the penance exercised by the Ninevites and the inhabitants of Vienne, as both the liturgical forms and the vernacular texts make clear. The prayers make frequent reference to current afflictions, describing them as deserved, and beg God to recognize the penance of the supplicants:

> Deus, qui culpas delinqentium districtae feriendo percutis, fletus quoque lugentium non recuses, ut qui pondus tuae animadversione(is) cognovimus, etiam pietatis gratiam sentiamus.[25]

It is not difficult to see the affliction of Vienne underlying prayers like these. Other prayers specifically recall the Ninevites (from the Mass for the second day in Robert, different from that in Leofric):

> Clamantium ad te quaesumus domine praeces dignanter exaudi, ut sicut Ninivitis in afflictione positis pepercisti, ita et nobis in praesenti tribulatione succurras.[26]

Those processing are to realize the danger of their sinful state by seeing themselves as one with the people of Ninevah and of Vienne, under the threat of direct and fiery retribution from God, needing desperately to turn God's anger. The depictions of the tribulations of Ninevah and Vienne in many of the vernacular accounts reinforce this connection by describing them in similar ways, and by extending the threat, often in terms of fire, to the Rogationtide participants. Bazire and Cross' Homily 1 recasts the account of the Ninevites in a way that seems to reflect Mamertus' account, and through that the contemporary arrangement. Following the Old Latin reading (as did Caesarius), this homilist speaks of a three-day fast in Ninevah after Jonah's warning, rather than the forty days of the Vulgate reading. The forty days are mentioned later (in a rather confused way),

---

to a very bright field, and very beautiful, filled with a sweet smell. Then he saw a very great crowd as on a Rogation day, and they were all clothed with snow-white garments, and in that way in which the deacon is when he reads the gospel. And one of them was standing in the midst in a masspriest's robe, very high and very great over all the other folk."

[25] Warren, *The Leofric Missal*, p. 107. "God, you who pierce the sins of the wicked with disruptive striking, may you not reject those weeping and mourning, so that we may recognize the weight of your reproach, and also that we may perceive the grace of your mercy."

[26] Wilson, *The Missal of Robert of Jumièges*, p. 112. "Hear fittingly, we pray Lord, the prayer of those crying out to you, so that just as you spared the Ninevites in the place of suffering, so also you may help us in the present tribulation."

when the homilist reports that, after the Ninevites' fast, God removed the "fyrene clyne"[27] that had been hovering over the city, and was to destroy it within forty days. Bazire and Cross suggest that the extra-biblical presence of the fiery ball might be drawn from the account of the fire that burned the palace in Mamertus' Vienne. Ælfric mentions this fire in his First Series sermon when discussing the institution of the fast by Mamertus. Ælfric claims that Mamertus was inspired by the Ninevites, and Ælfric too considers their fast as lasting three days. Although Ælfric has no fiery ball, the threat of heavenly fire still hangs over the Ninevites for him, as he claims that God did not destroy them "swa swa he ær þa twa buruhwara, Sodomam et Gomorram, for heora leahtrum mid heofenlicum fyre forbærnde."[28] Ælfric goes on to connect the current Rogation-goers with the Ninevites, asserting that 'we also should on these days offer up our prayers, and follow our relics in and out.' Ælfric's specification of the threat as 'heavenly fire' reminds the current Rogationtide participants, who are doing the same fast for the same reasons, of the danger facing them. Fire (usually hellfire) is frequently mentioned as a threat against contemporary participants, either for failing to follow in the rogations or for doing inappropriate things, like wearing shoes or speaking vainly. Ælfric dramatizes the sense that the fire of retribution hangs over the current world in two Second Series pieces, the visions of Furseus and of Drihthelm. Drihthelm sees, as the ultimate threat, a vision of hell that cannot be described visually, as could Purgatory, but only as an overwhelming sense of darkness and flames. For Furseus, the danger is more immediate. As he is being led about by the angels, he sees the world as a low, darkened valley, over which are poised four fires, waiting to devour sinners:

> He geseah ðær feower ormæte fyr atende, and se engel cwæð him to, "þas feower fyr ontendað ealne middaneard, and onælað þæra manna sawla þe heora fulluhtes andetnysse and behat ðurh forgægednysse awægdon."[29]

Each of the fires is intended for sinners of a certain kind, and the implication is that for everyone in the audience there is a fire ready to devour that can only be turned aside by prayer and penance. Even Furseus, whose sin is tremendously small (he accepted a piece of cloth from a sinful man), cannot entirely escape the fire, and he receives a burn that transfers over to his body after he is sent back to it, as a testimony to others. This sort of dramatic portrayal of the threat facing the sinners at Rogationtide solidifies the connection with the Ninevites and the inhabitants of Vienne developed as well in the processional liturgy, and in the Masses with which they end.

---

[27] BC, p. 21. "Fiery ball."

[28] CH I.xviii, p. 318. "Just as he previously burned with heavenly fire the citizens of the two cities, Sodom and Gomorrah, because of their sins."

[29] CH II.xx, p. 193. "He saw there four huge fires burning, and the angel said to him, 'These four fires will burn the whole world, and will consume the souls of all those who have annulled the confession and the vow of their baptism through transgression.'"

There is much more to the processions than just a recapitulation of these appeasing fasts, however. Besides praying that God turn aside his anger, the procession is intended to dedicate fields, woods, cattle, and so forth to God. This dynamic of the Rogations is related to an alternate tradition concerning its origins. The first three Vercelli homilies for Rogationtide (Vercelli XI–XIII) claim that the festival was begun by St. Peter. According to this homilist, "geo hæðene liode hæfdon þry dagas synderlice beforan hira oðrum gewunan þæt hie onguldon hira godum, 7 hiera ceapes wæstma 7 ealle hira æhta hie hira gode bebudon."[30] The three Rogation days, according to this tradition, were set up by St. Peter to counteract this heathen practice. The attribution to St. Peter is a mystery, although he does make a brief appearance in the processional prayers, in the *In atrio*, in which the supplicants pray for help in the form of a heavenly shield "intercedente beato petro apostolo tuo."[31] Although the attribution to Peter is without a known source, pagan Rome did know three days of procession, at about the same time of year (in May), the Amburbale, and the idea that Mamertus' festival is a usurpation of this pagan one would have been compelling, whether or not there is any truth to it. In any case, a central element of the Rogations is to mark off territory as God's. It is more than just a dedication of fruits, trees, and livestock to God. What vernacular descriptions of the procession illustrate is that those walking about with Christ's Cross and the holy relics are spreading about the presence of God, marking God's territory by allowing the divinity that has been accorded the Cross, the gospel books, and the holy relics to drive out the presence of the devil and to unify the earthly places with God's divinity, which is also the central idea of the Ascension. This is what Augustine was doing when he approached Canterbury in 597, holding aloft the Cross and the image of Christ, singing a litany from the Gallican Rogationtide liturgy, claiming the city as God's.[32] The prayer that they sang is similar to those found in the later Anglo-Saxon liturgy, "We beseech thee, O Lord, in thy great mercy, that thy wrath and anger may be turned away from this city and from thy holy house, for we have sinned."[33] The prayers that God's anger be turned were from the beginning married to the idea of claiming territory by infusing it with God's presence.

This latter idea is part of the nature of all liturgical procession, to bring

---

[30] Scragg, *The Vercelli Homilies*, p. 228. "The heathen people had three days specially before their other customs that they offered sacrifices to their gods, and they offered to their god the increase of their cattle, and all their possessions."

[31] Warren, *The Leofric Missal*, p. 107. "By the intercession of your apostle, the blessed Peter."

[32] But see Cubitt, *Anglo-Saxon Church Councils*, p. 130, who cautions that the account of Augustine's Rogation-like approach "is more likely to reflect a later tradition (of Canterbury origin?) engrafted on to tales of Augustine's arrival than the introduction of a Frankish custom by the Gregorian missionaries." Still, there is no reason, given Gregory's mandate, why Augustine might not have introduced elements of the Gallican liturgy, and the festival certainly seems to have had a history by the time of the Council of Clofesho in 747.

[33] See BC, xv.

the benevolent presence of God into the processed space, and by that to drive out the powers of the devil. The rubrics to the procession before the Maundy Thursday *Consecratio Chrismalis* in the Canterbury Benedictional provide a wonderful examination of the general function of processions in the Anglo-Saxon liturgy.[34] After *cena domini*, those present, wearing sacred garb, carry the Cross, "quasi contra diaboli versutas nequitias christi invicto auxilio pugnaturi."[35] At the beginning of the procession, the conflict is set forth, the 'crafty evils of the devil,' and they are to process as if ready to fight them with Christ's power. Two carrying candles follow, "ut christi virtute victores, caelesti lumine flagrare dinoscantur."[36] The candle light is the light of heaven, infusing the space of the church, and making it an extension of heaven. Two more follow carrying thuribles, "ut deifico lumine calentes, christi bono odore fraglare conprobentur."[37] Twin gospel books accompany them, "ut iam christi bono odore referti, dominica dicta scutari conservare corde puro conentur."[38] Only with this infusion of the presence of heaven, in the divine light and the odour of Christ that have filled the room, driving out the dangers of the devil, can the chrism be brought in. This ability of the liturgical procession to define a space as God's is exploited at Rogationtide. In Bazire and Cross' Homily 5, the special 'meeting-place' that surrounds the relics at the processional stages is defined as a 'ghostly place,' a pocket of God's presence, in which those present are before Christ's throne, both for current edification and for final judgement. Explaining how men with a conflict find a "gemotstow" in order to find reconciliation, the homilist defines the space:

> Be þære bysne we magon ongytan þas halgan tide, forþon ðe þas dagas syndon ure gemotdagas gastlicra gemota, þonne bið ure gastlice gemotstow on ymbhwyrfte ure reliquia, swa on cyrican swa butan swa on hwylcre stowe hi on gesette beoð.
> Wite þonne þæt æghwylc mann þæra þe in þysum gemote wunige and þis godspell gehyreð, þæt he eac þam georne mid eadmedum ontyne þære heortan earan to manunge þyses godspelles and to þæs gastlican Deman Cristes sylfes. . . . Gyf we þas gastlican domas gelæstan willað, þe Crist sylf on his godspelle beodað on þisse gemotstowe þonne beoð we beforan Cristes heahsetle . . . and we þonne motan gehyran þone cwyde þe he sylf cwæð to þam þe he sette on þa swyðran healfe, "Cumað, ge gebletsode . . ."[39]

[34] Woolley, *The Canterbury Benedictional*, p. 36.
[35] Ibid. "As if they were to fight against the crafty evils of the devil with the unconquered help of Christ."
[36] Ibid. "So that, triumphant with the strength of Christ, they may be seen to be burning with the light of heaven."
[37] Ibid. "So that, inflamed by the consecrated light, they may be proved to be fragrant with the good odour of Christ."
[38] Ibid. "So that now, filled with the good odor of Christ, they may attempt with a pure heart to preserve with a shield the Lord's words."
[39] BC, p. 73. "By that example we may appreciate this holy time, because these days are our meeting-days of ghostly meetings, when our ghostly meeting place is in the area around our relics, as much in the church as outside as in any place in which they are set. Know then that everyone who remains in this meeting and hears this gospel, that he also that eagerly with humility may open the ears of the heart to the exhortation of this gospel and to the spiritual Judge, Christ

It is not just the church that can be set aside as a 'ghostly' space, but 'in whatever place' the relics are put in the course of the procession. It is the divinity radiating from these objects, driving out the presence of the devil, that allows the space to become otherworldly. Those who lose themselves to this space, and incline the 'ears of their hearts' to the message held therein and emanating from the gospel books, can through that find themselves on the right side at the Judgement (indeed, they are already there). It is unity with this space that allows their approach to heaven. This is the purpose and the result of the dedication of all the space and goods to God, to allow through that the unity of the faithful who inhabit that space with heaven.

This unity with heaven permeates the various Rogationtide themes. In particular, there is an interest in Christ's humanity, in the unity of body and soul, and in the relationship of the body to Heaven that is repeated throughout the week. It is the ultimate aim of the liturgical forms. While the processional forms (of which we have far too few examples) focus on turning away God's wrath, the Mass forms look increasingly forward to the Ascension. The Preface for the second Rogation day (Feria iii in Ascension week) beseeches God to free the supplicants from "noxiis voluptatibus" and from "mundanis cladibus."[40] These sorts of prayers to be separated from the corrupting and damaging influence of the world are, of course, general to any penitential period, but the Mass for the third Rogation day, also the Mass *In vigilia ascensionis*, explains this desire in terms of unity with Christ as a means to reach heaven. The collect for the Mass (I discuss the forms in Leofric, but this Mass is quite general) begins by invoking Christ's entrance into glory. The second form (the *Secreta*) personalizes the event, as "nunc praevenimus ascensione."[41] In particular, the faithful anticipate joining him in this ascension: "et nos per ipsum his commerciis sacrosanctis ad caelestia consurgamus."[42] The Preface mentions Christ's humanity, his defeat of the devil, and his elevation of the substance of humanity. The *Ad complendum* again personalizes the idea, as the faithful think of themselves as part of the same substance that is about to ascend: "Tribue, quaesumus, domine, ut per haec sacramenta quae sumpsimus, illuc tendat nostrae devotionis affectus, quo tecum est nostra substantia, ihesus christus dominus noster."[43] Finally, the *Ad vesperos* reminds God that we are the members of the body of which Christ is the head, with the implication that where the head goes, the body will follow. The Vigil Mass is essentially a preparation, spiritual and mental,

himself. . . . If we desire to survive the spiritual judgements, which Christ himself in his gospel bids in this meeting place when we are before Christ's high throne . . . and we then may hear the proclamation that he himself said to those whom he set on the right side, 'Come, you blessed . . .' "

40 Warren, *The Leofric Missal*, p. 108. "Harmful pleasures . . . worldly calamities."
41 Ibid. "Now we come to the Ascension."
42 Ibid. "And may we rise up to the heavens through these holy exchanges."
43 Ibid. "Grant we pray, Lord, that through these sacraments which we take up, the love of our devotion may extend there, by which our substance is with you, Jesus Christ our Lord."

for the celebration of the Ascension, in which the faithful will take part, on Thursday. As the Rogation days can be thought of as 'three days in vigil of the Ascension,' the interest in humanity approaching heaven abounds as well in the vernacular witnesses. The first Vercelli set of Rogationtide homilies and the set of Rogationtide pieces by Ælfric demonstrate how two authors used this same focus in different ways to help define the purification and separation from the world at Rogationtide as a preparation for ascension into heaven with Christ.

The Vercelli manuscript has two sets of Rogationtide homilies. The first set (Vercelli XI–XIII) is perhaps the more interesting, as all three pieces seem to have been written or pulled together by a single author, who makes references back and forth between them. In the sermon for the first Rogation day, after describing the procession and relating it to St. Peter, and after a paragraph on the need to seek true joy in Heaven, the homilist returns to a theme that throughout the Temporale has stood for the present state of mankind in relation to the salvation history that is reenacted and commemorated in the liturgy. He explains that:

> For þæs ærestan mannes synnum, Adames, we wurdon aworpene of neorxna-wanges eðle 7 on þas wræcworuld sende, 7 we swa syndon on þyssum mid-dangearde swa we her nænig eðel ne habbað.[44]

It is only in the next world that we can find true joy and have a homeland, which we seek by departing this world for the joy of heaven. The homilist then describes the heavenly city, where we will see our kin and our ancestors, and where the angels are our townspeople. The rest of the sermon deals with the idea of the 'spiritual chapman,' trading earthly things for heavenly, with an emphasis on love for the eternal homeland, and finally with a reminder of the approaching End. The homily is primarily an adapted translation of a sermon by Caesarius[45] for another occasion, but its use here, especially with its expanded account of the evil of present days, describes the time not only as one of dedication to God in opposition to pagan practice, but also of appreciation of the benefits of eschewing the worldly for the heavenly. Vercelli XII, after a longer description of the procession, and after specifying that God is present in the Rogationtide company, further develops the idea of the 'spiritual chapman' in terms of approaching heaven personally. Speaking of the fear of God, the homilist tells us:

> Mid þam egesan we us geceapiað heofenlicu þing, englas for mannum, lif for deaðe, god for yfele, swete for bitere, leoht for þiestrum, soðfæstnesse for unsoðfæstnesse, yðnesse for niðe, sawle mægen for licumlicre mettrymnesse. Gif

---

[44] Scragg, *The Vercelli Homilies*, p. 223. "Because of the sins of the first man, Adam, we were cast out from the homeland of paradise and sent into the exile-world, and we are such in this world that we do not have any homeland here."

[45] See ibid. pp. 219ff on the relationship between the homily by Caesarius and the Vercelli homily.

we wilnigan rixian mid Criste, bebigen we ða woruldcundan lustas for undeað-
licnesse, 7 don we symle eal þa þing mid dryhtnes egesan. Se egesa us gelædeð fram
helwarum, 7 he us onfehð to þam uplican rice . . .[46]

The idea of the 'spiritual chapman' taken from Caesarius has here been
expanded and reinterpreted in a way that is specific to a processional, pre-
Ascension time, described in terms of movement from hell to the upward
kingdom. The homily for the third day makes this connection between
Rogationtide and the Ascension explicit, explaining that one of the reasons
for the establishment of the three days is so that any uncleanliness practised
in the forty days between Easter and the Ascension can be purged, allowing
the celebrant to be "þys mergenlican dæge æt þære halgan dryhtnes
upastignestide clæne æt dryhtnes wiofode, 7 þær onfon weddes þæs ecan
rices, þæt is Cristes sylfes lichoma 7 his blod þæt we nu nemnaþ husl."[47] Of
course, the celebrants have been receiving Christ's body and blood all week,
but there is a special need that they be prepared to do so the next day, as
unity with Christ on that day is unity with Christ ascending to heaven.
Much of the rest of this sermon is lost, but the end features the dry bones
speaking to the audience from the grave about the certainty of death, along
with a reminder of Doomsday, when all men will be either 'in the height of
the kingdom of heaven' or 'in hell-pains,' ending with an exhortation to
listen to the holy teaching so that the congregation can be better prepared
for both lives (this and the next), and to live together in eternity with the
three members of the Trinity. Much of the end here is from a general
sermon by Caesarius. The Vercelli homilist has appropriated its material,
and many of the more general themes of Rogationtide, into a strong,
consistent exhortation, using emotionally dramatic devices like the speaking
of the dry bones to the audience and the polarization of Judgement Day to
encourage the folk to make themselves prepared to ascend to Heaven with
Christ on Thursday.

Ælfric's sermons for Rogationtide deal with many of the same themes,
but he also branches into more theological discussions on such topics as
praying, the Pater Noster and the Creed, chastity, and so forth. Many of his
theological discussions have a particular relevance to the Ascension. In his
First Series homily for the second Rogation day, in explaining the Lord's
Prayer, he discusses prayer in terms of what is pertinent to this life and what
to the life to come. His description of heaven includes both a short version
of the quite common topos of the "Joys of Heaven" (at times called the

[46] Scragg, *The Vercelli Homilies*, pp. 229–30. "With that fear we buy ourselves heavenly things,
angels for men, life for death, good for evil, sweet for bitter, light for darkness, truth for
falsehood, kindness for hatred, a powerful soul for bodily weakness. If we desire to rule with
Christ, we shun worldly lusts for immortality, and we do always these things with fear of God.
That fear leads us from the hell-dwellers, and he receives us in the high kingdom."
[47] Ibid. p. 234. "Tomorrow at the holy Lord's Ascensiontide clean at the Lord's altar, and there to
receive the security of the eternal kingdom, that is Christ's own body and his blood that we now
call housel."

"Seven Joys," although the number and nature of them varies) and the doctrine of the unity of humanity with divinity: "þær beoð geþwære sawul 7 lichama þe nu on þysum life him betwynan winnað; ðær ne bið an untrumnyss ne geswinc, ne wana nanre godnysse, ac Crist bið mid us eallum."[48] The idea of Christ being with us is further explained using the description of Christ as the head of the body, and of all Christian men as one man. This interest in the relationship between the body and the afterlife comes up again in his homily on the catholic faith for the following day, when he, after explaining the doctrine of the Trinity, asserts that "ælc lichama þe sawla underfeng sceal arisan on domes dæge mid þam ylcan lichaman þe he nu hæfð, 7 sceal onfon edlean ealra his dæda."[49] The good will have eternal life, while the evil will suffer. The relationship between our re-assumed bodies and Christ's humanity is strengthened in Ælfric's next homily, for the Ascension, in which he explains, while exploring the theme of 'godhead humbled, humanity exalted,' that just as Christ's re-assumed body did not need food (he ate only so as to make manifest his true body), so ours will not: "Soðlice æfter þam gemænelicum æriste ne behofað ure lichaman nanre strangunge eorðlicra metta."[50] As did the Vercelli homilist (for Rogationtide, not for the Ascension), Ælfric explains Christ's new, ascending humanity as the same that Adam ruined.

This emphasis on the elevation of humanity, both in Rogationtide and in the feast of the Ascension, permeates his Second Series pieces as well. Although he explains at the beginning of his tract for Monday that his first imperative is to teach evangelical lore, his account of the End encourages his audience to hope that, through prayer, "we moton forfleon ða toweardan frecednysse, and standan on gesihðe his soðan menniscnysse."[51] The visions of Furseus and of Drihthelm deal intensely with the relationship between the soul and the body. The latter vision presents vivid portrayals of heaven and hell (as of Purgatory and of the place of those waiting to enter into heaven), concluding with a prayer that refers to the audience's potential future in one of these places. His Second Series sermon for Wednesday, being a discussion of the Ascension, deals almost entirely with the nature of Christ's humanity and our unity with it, concluding that "on ðam dæge [tomorrow] abær se ælmihtiga Godes sunu urne lichaman to ðam heofonlican eðle, þær ðær næfre ær ne becom nan ðing ðæs gecyndes."[52]

---

[48] CH I.xix, pp. 332–3. "There body and soul will be united, which now in this life war with each other; there will not be there any sickness or toil, nor lack of goodness, but Christ will be with us all."

[49] CH I.xx, p. 344. "Each body that received a soul shall arise on Judgement Day with the same body that it now has, and shall receive the recompense for all its deeds."

[50] CH I.xxi, p. 346. "Truly after the general resurrection our bodies will not need any nourishing from earthly food."

[51] CH II.xix, p. 188. "We may flee the coming danger, and stand in the sight of his true humanity."

[52] CH II.xxii, p. 211. "On that day the son of the Almighty God bore our body to the heavenly homeland, where nothing of its kind had ever before come."

He then goes on to explain why he has been so concerned that his audience learn these things, summing up his imperatives for Rogationtide preaching:

> Nu behofige ge læwede men micelre lare on ðisne timan, for ðan ðe þeos woruld is micclum geswenct ðurh menigfealdum gedrefednyssum, and swa near ende þyssere worulde swa mare ehtnys þæs deofles, and bið unstrenge mennisc ðurh maran tyddernysse. Nu behofige ge ðæs þe swiðor þæs boclican frofres þæt ge ðurh ða lare eowere mod awendon of ðisum wræcfullum life to ðam ecum þe we ymbe sprecað.[53]

Both the Vercelli homilist and Ælfric are addressing laymen, and each of them encourages the folk to better themselves in relation to the significance of the time, the first through emotional and dramatic exhortation, the second through a combination of reasoned instruction and vivid portrayals of where the laymen might go if they attain unity with Christ's perfected humanity (and where they will go if they don't). This preparation for ascension to heaven with Christ is the thematic centre of Ascension week, and is a key part of the Rogationtide processions as well.

Bazire and Cross have said of their anonymous Homily 10 that "this sermon must have been worth hearing" and that "its unknown composer deserves remembrance."[54] This homilist brings together nicely the polyvalent significance of the Rogationtide processions. He begins with an assertion of the need for penance and the remedy of the soul, reminding the audience of the time's original function. The importance of this remedy is that it will allow the faithful to be placed on the right side at Judgement Day. Specifically, their cleanliness is for presentation to God, in preparation of being returned to him: "he wilnað þæt we clænsien ure sawla and ure lichaman, þæt we magon heo him swa clæne agyfan swa he hi us ær clæne befæste."[55] This is a cleansing of both the soul and the body, both of which are to be returned in their idyllic, pre-Fall state. The homilist includes a dramatic account of the End, including the *Admonitio de die iudicii* that featured so prominently in Easter sermons. He also includes descriptions of the joys of heaven and the pains of hell, reminding all of what is at stake. At the close of the sermon, he explains how the processions relate to the entrance into heaven:

> Men þa leofestan, geþence we geornlice and smealice forhwan eall cristen folc þas andweardan tide þus lufiað and weorþiað and ða halgan reliquias folgiað. Buton tweon swutolice we magon þurh þa halgan gesamnunga ongytan þa ecan reste, and æghwylcum þara bið heofona rices duru ongean untyned þe þa halgan

---

[53] CH II.xxii, p. 212. "Now you layfolk need great learning during this time, because this world is greatly vexed through manifold troubles, and the nearer we are to the end of this world, the greater the attacks of the devil, and humanity is weaker through great frailty. Now you need more urgently this bookly consolation, that you through that learning turn your minds from this miserable life to the eternal one of which we speak."

[54] BC, p. 129.

[55] Ibid. p. 132. "He desires that we cleanse our souls and our bodies, that we may return them as clean as they were when he previously entrusted them to us."

reliquias mid geleafan folgiað. We þonne, men ða leofestan, habbað nedþearfe þæt we mid soðre lufan and mid rihtan geleafan þa gesamnunge secan and ða godcundan lare gehyran. þonne beo we æt urum ytemestan dæge gewlitegode mid Godes þæm gecorenum, be þæm is awriten and ðus cweden, "Ðær þa soðfæsten men scinað . . ."[56]

By following the relics about, as a 'holy assembly' reflective of the white-clad crowd in the visions of Drihthelm and of Leofric (which compared the crowd to a Rogationtide crowd), the doors of heaven are opened to them, and they can approach the threshold with Christ on Holy Thursday. It is through love and true faith, two topics about which Ælfric expounds thoroughly in his Rogationtide sermons, that unity with this assembly is made possible, and through them with the chosen of God, who will enjoy the wonders of heaven.

Rogationtide is a polyvalent festival, and the multiple theories of origins reflect the multiple directions granted the liturgical forms and, especially, the preaching for the period. Binding all of these strands of meaning, however, is the theme of the elevation of humanity as a means of approaching heaven with Christ on Thursday. The processions range across the countryside, but they are increasingly given an upward direction as the Ascension approaches. The abiding image of the Ascension, realized in the liturgy for the week, is that explored poetically by Cynewulf in *Christ II*. Setting up a contrast between Christmas and the Ascension, as the beginning and the end of Christ's time in the world, the poet establishes the 'thanes' as a sympathetic model for his audience:

> Hwæþre in bocum ne cwið
> þæt hy in hwitum þær   hræglum oðywden
> in þa æþelan tid,   swa hie eft dydon
> ða se brega mæra   to Bethania,
> þeoden þrymfæst,   his þegna gedryht
> gelaðade, leof weorud.   Hy þæs lareowes
> on þam wildæge   word ne gehyrwdon,
> hyra sincgiefan.   Sona wæron gearwe,
> hæleð mid hlaford,   to þære halgan byrg,
> þær him tacna fela   tires brytta
> onwrah, wuldres helm,   wordgerynum,
> ærþon up stige   ancenned sunu . . .[57]

---

[56] Ibid. p. 135. "Dear men, let us consider eagerly and thoroughly why all Christian folk at this present time thus love and honour and follow the holy relics. Without doubt we may clearly perceive through the holy assembling the eternal rest, and for each of those who follow the holy relics with faith, the opening of the doors of the heavenly kingdom is approached. We then, dear men, have need that we seek that assembling with true love and with right faith and that we hear that godly lore. Then we will be glorified at our final day with the chosen of God, about whom it is written and said thus, 'There the faithful will shine . . .'"

[57] Bernard Muir, ed. *The Exeter Anthology*, vol. I (Exeter, 1994), p. 66, lines 453–64 (for compatibility with other editions, I give the traditional lineation, which Muir provides alongside his own). "However in books it does not say that they appeared there in white rags in that noble time, as they afterwards did when the great ruler, the mighty prince, the lord summoned his thanes, dear troop, to Bethany. On that joyous day they did not despise the words of the teacher,

His thanes have accompanied him to 'that holy city,' to a liminal place that serves as a gateway to Heaven, akin to the middle-place in the visions of Furseus and Leofric. This place is contemporized by describing it as a temple with an open roof. A loud harmony is heard, the angels approach, and "Cyning ure gewat/ þurh þæs temples hrof þær hy to segun/ þa þe leofes þa gen last weardedum/ on þam þingstede, þegnas gecorene."[58] This is the same temple described so vividly in the Blickling homily for the Ascension,[59] with Christ's final footprints still in evidence, and able to perform miracles, anachronistically extended back to the time of the actual Ascension.

Through the rest of the poem, we are positioned with the accompanying disciples, hearing the words of Christ and of the angel, feeling joy at his return to Heaven and sorrow that we must remain awhile on earth. These thanes cannot yet enter Heaven, although they participate in it vicariously, and Christ does not enter alone. Extra-biblically, the poet brings in the host of those freed from hell on Easter eve. Cynewulf describes the throng – "Wel þæt gedafenað/ þæt to þære blisse, beorhte gewerede,/ in þæs þeodnes burg þegnas cwoman,/ weorud wlitescyne"[60] – and then explains from whence they have come: "þær he of hæfte ahlod huþa mæste/ of feonda byrig, folces unrim,/ þisne ilcan þreat þe ge her on stariað."[61] Then, with the angel giving commentary, we see humanity and divinity entering Heaven together, as one unified body:

> Geatu ontynað.
> Wile in to eow   ealles waldend
> cyning on ceastre,   corðre ne lytle,
> fyrnweorca fruma,   folc gelædan
> in dreama dream,   ðe he on deoflum genom
> þurh his sylfes sygor.   Sib sceal gemæne
> englum ond ældum   a forð heonan
> wesan wideferh.   Wære is ætsomne
> godes ond monna . . .[62]

This is the elevation of humanity, approached in Rogationtide and realized at the Ascension, that is the point of the dramatic liturgy for the week. At

their treasure-giver. Immediately they were ready, warrior with lord, to the holy city, where the famous prince revealed himself with many signs, the lord of glory, with mysterious words, before the only-begotten son ascended . . ."

[58] Ibid. p. 68, lines 494–7. "Our king departed through the roof of the temple where they saw, those who then yet remained watching, the chosen thanes, the footprint of the dear one in that assembly-place."

[59] See Morris, *The Blickling Homilies*, pp. 125–9.

[60] Ibid. p. 70, lines 551–4. "It is truly befitting that to that joy, in a bright company, the thanes came, shining white troop, into the prince's city."

[61] Ibid. p. 71, lines 568–70. "There he from fetters brought forth great plunder from the city of the enemy, a large host of folk, this same troop on which you here gaze."

[62] Ibid. lines 576–84. "The gates open. The king, ruler of all, desires to lead the folk into the city, ancient work of creation, into the joy of joys, the large troop, which he took from the devils through his own triumph. Always henceforth there shall be lasting peace in common between angels and men. The bond is united between God and men . . ."

Christmas, the faithful participating in the liturgy were allowed, as the shepherds, to see heavenly things in the union of humanity with divinity in Christ. At the Ascension, they are allowed to see the consummation of this union in the reconciliation between men and angels and the opening of heaven to humanity.

9

The End and the Beginning

THE BROAD DEMOGRAPHIC of Rogationtide testifies to the wide-spread appeal of dramatic ritual in late Anglo-Saxon England. The efforts of Ælfric, Wulfstan, and others to extend monastic practice to the laity and to ensure understanding of what is happening in the liturgy surely enhanced the experience. This experience extended beyond Rogationtide and the festival of the Ascension into Pentecost and on to the end of the liturgical year, at Advent. That some sense of completion was engendered by the commemoration of the Ascension is reflected in the concluding exhortation of the Blickling homily for Ascension Thursday, "teolian we þonne þeos halige tid eft cume embe twelf monaþ, þe se lifge þæt he betre sy þonne he nu is."[1] After providing a rousing account of the Lord's ascension and a lengthy description of the glowing temple surrounding his last footprints (intended to connect his audience with past events and present miracles), the homilist establishes this festival as a yearly yardstick for measuring personal growth towards unity with God. This is a fitting dynamic for a festival that so thoroughly links liturgical participation with the reunion of humanity and divinity in Christ's reunion with heaven.

PENTECOST

However, while the commemoration of the life of Christ has ended with his Ascension, those left on earth still have a directive to follow, to wait for the empowerment of the Holy Spirit. This happens for the liturgical celebrants, as it did for Christ's disciples, at Pentecost. Liturgically, Pentecost is celebrated as the beginning of the new age, in which mankind is no longer under the law, but under grace. It is a day when, as Ælfric specifies, men are turned to gods by the infusion of the Holy Ghost. In the Whitsunday liturgy, participants call on the presence of the Holy Ghost in the same terms used to describe the original events in Acts, and vernacular treatments of the day and illumination portray Pentecost as a celebration of unity with God, of full confirmation of the participants' place

---

[1] Morris, *The Blickling Homilies*, p. 131. "We expect when this holy time comes after twelve months, that the living one will be better than he now is."

210

Plate 7. Pentecost, Benedictional of Æthelwold
London, BL MS Additional 49598, fol. 64v (by permission of the British Library)

in God's plan and eventual place in Heaven. As such, the festival serves as something of a denouement to the liturgical celebrations from Christmas through Easter and the Ascension, and it continues the practice of establishing biblical figures as models for liturgical commemoration.

The Festival of Pentecost goes back to the earliest days of the Christian church. It developed as an extension of the Hebrew Feast of Weeks, on the fiftieth day after Passover (seven weeks plus one day), when the first fruits of the corn harvest were presented.[2] In the earliest days, there was some evident confusion as to whether 'Pentecost' referred to the fifty-day period or the final day of that period, but its connection to Easter was always clear. The fifty days are treated as an extension of the victory won at Easter, and the canons of the First Nicene Council (325) forbade the faithful from fasting or kneeling in prayer during the season. The final day was from an early stage seen as a recapitulation of sorts of Easter, and the liturgical similarities between Easter and Pentecost are evident in all of the pre-tenth-century continental witnesses that provide for the festivals. The Pentecost liturgy featured an all-night vigil, which was geared towards baptismal candidates, who would receive the sacrament at the end of the vigil, just as at Easter. Because Easter and Pentecost were the two festivals officially sanctioned for the application of baptism in the West, Pentecost quickly grew into one of the most important festivals of the church calendar.

Bede's description of the day highlights that importance. The festival is, of course, fundamentally a celebration of the coming of the Holy Spirit, both to the apostles soon after Christ's ascension, as described in Acts 2:1–42, and to all Christians since at the confirmation that follows baptism. The gospel reading for the day is Christ's promise to send the Holy Spirit as a Comforter (or "Paraclete") after his departure.[3] Bede tells his audience at length that Christ's promise was to both his disciples (fulfilled at Pentecost) and to contemporary Christians. He then describes the meaning of the festival. After instructing that Pentecost was originally dedicated to a commemoration of the giving of the Law by God to Moses, he then summarizes the events described in Acts, ending with the detail that, after the application of the Holy Ghost in the form of 'tongues of fire,' the disciples' words being heard in all languages, and the amazement of the surrounding people, three thousand people were baptized and received the Holy Spirit. This leads him into a discussion of the importance of baptism to the festival:

---

[2] See Talley, *The Origins of the Liturgical Year*, pp. 57ff, and Cross and Livingstone, *The Oxford Dictionary of the Christian Church*, pp. 1253, 1738.

[3] The gospel lection explicated by Bede is John 14:15–21. This is the lection for the Vigil of Pentecost, as in all Old English witnesses. Glosses to the Old English Gospels state for John 14:15ff that "Ðys sceal on pentecostenes mæsse æfen" and for John 14:23ff that "Ðys godspel sceal on pentecostenes mæsse dæg" (Liuzza, *The Old English Version of the Gospels*, pp. 188–9).

Today is the annual celebration of this event; this is the always-welcome festivity of [the bestowal] of heavenly grace. In order to stamp the memory of this more firmly on the hearts of believers, a beautiful custom of holy Church has grown up, so that each year the mysteries of baptism are celebrated on this [day], and as a result a venerable temple is made ready for the coming of the Holy Spirit upon those who believe and are cleansed at the salvation-bearing baptismal font. . . . in veneration of the reception of the law, a new sacrifice was ordered to be offered to the Lord annually on the day of Pentecost, from the time of the reception of this grace; and it never stops being carried out spiritually, also on this our festivity. Indeed the Church offers a new sacrifice on this [day], when on the Saturday that marks the beginning of the holy feast of Pentecost, she consecrates to the Lord through baptism a new people of adoption.[4]

Bede makes much of the appropriateness of the fact that in baptism the Spirit is applied in the same way as it was on the occasion in Acts, and centres his exegesis of the day on that connection.

However, the change in baptism from a seasonal occasion to a variable one affected Anglo-Saxon appreciation of the day. The Vigil of Pentecost is still an important occasion, and is represented in several liturgical books. It includes a series of Old and New Testament lessons, as at the Easter Vigil, and culminates in the blessing of the baptismal font. This arrangement is made clear in the *Concordia*,[5] the Leofric Missal,[6] the Robert Missal,[7] and the Missal of the New Minster.[8] While rubrics in all of these manuscripts mention the procession to the font, however, only one mentions baptism, and it is in this respect an uncertain witness.[9] It seems most likely that, as at Easter, while a historical and theoretical relationship between Pentecost and baptism remained to an extent, a practical one (for the most part) did not.

The liturgy both for the Vigil and for Pentecost itself is quite regular throughout the Anglo-Saxon witnesses, and is essentially that of the Gelasian and Gregorian Sacramentaries. All of the expected themes, based on Christ's promises in John 14 and the events described in Acts 2, find resonance in the liturgical forms: the unity of the faithful, the fire and wind that accompanied the application of the Spirit, the gift of tongues, the preaching of Peter, the conversion and baptism of the three thousand, and the subsequent expansion of the church. Also important in the extant forms is the idea that participation in the Pentecost liturgy is a means of purification from sin and entry into heaven. Several antiphons and prayers

---

[4] Martin and Hurst, *Bede the Venerable: Homilies on the Gospels*, vol. 2, pp. 170–1, 173.

[5] Kornexl, *Die Regularis concordia*, pp. 121–3; Symons, *Regularis concordia*, pp. 57–8.

[6] Warren, *The Leofric Missal*, pp. 110–11.

[7] The *ordo* for the Vigil in the Robert Missal is extremely close to that in the *Concordia*. See Wilson, *The Missal of Robert of Jumièges*, pp. 115ff.

[8] Turner, *The Missal of the New Minster*, pp. 11ff.

[9] While Turner prints the rubric directing the procession to the font as "Deinde descendens ad fontem cum letania *celebrabis baptismum* sicut in pascha," he also admits in a footnote that "The words here are very faded, but *celebrabis baptismum* as in the similarly worded rubric on the vigil of Pentecost in the Sacramentary of St. Amand may be presumed" (Ibid. p. 12).

for the gift of the Spirit are phrased in such a way as either to recall the event in Acts or to mimic it, often mixed together with a concern for contemporary edification. A benediction for the day of Pentecost in the Robert Benedictional is a typical example, and is found widely: "Ille ignis qui super discipulos apparuit, pectorum vestrorum sordes expurget, et sui luminis infusione corda vestra perlustret."[10] An antiphon for Vespers on the eve of Pentecost demonstrates another quite common form, where the Holy Spirit is addressed, and the unity of the faithful is emphasized: "Veni sanctae spiritus, reple tuorum corda fidelium et tui amoris in eis ignem accende, qui per diversitatem linguarum cunctarum gentes in unitatem fidei congregasti . . ."[11] As the description in Acts makes clear, the apostles were in a unified frame of mind at the time of the gift, and this unity was solidified and expanded as the new Christian community established itself. Other liturgical forms echo this unity of the early Christians, in beseeching for a similar state of being (from the Collect for Vespers, the Eve of Pentecost):

> Deus cuius spiritu totum corpus ecclesiae multiplicator [sic] et regitur, conserva in nova familiae tuae progenie sanctificationis gratiam quam dedisti, ut corpore et mente renovati, in unitate fidei ferventes tibi domino servire mereantur.[12]

The attainment of this state of being, by means of the gift of the Holy Spirit, is the ultimate objective of participation in the Pentecost liturgy.

These themes are reflected in sermons for Pentecost by both the Blickling homilist and Ælfric. While the role of baptism is not stressed by Anglo-Saxon homilists, the gift of the Spirit, with its subsequent state of being, is. The Blickling homilist begins by invoking Christ's promise that "ne forlæte ic eow aldorlease, ac eow sende frofre Gast."[13] He stresses the importance of the day, asserting that it consists "næs þara gifena læs þonne Drihtnes ærist,"[14] and then explains the festival as one of new beginnings:

> Forþon us is swiþe mycel nedþearf, broþor mine, þæt we swiþe geornfullice ⁊ eaþmodlice us geþydon on þysne andweardan dæg to urum reliquium ⁊ to urum halgum gebedum; forþon þe we witon þæt se dæg wæs fruma þyses lænan leohtes, ⁊ he biþ fruma þæs ecan æfterfylgendan.[15]

---

[10] Wilson, *The Benedictional of Archbishop Robert*, p. 22. "May this fire which appeared over the disciples cleanse the filth of our sins, and fill your hearts with the infusion of his light."

[11] Dewick and Frere, *The Leofric Collectar*, p. 179. "Come, Holy Spirit, fill the hearts of your faithful ones, kindle the fire of love for you in them, you who brought together people of different languages into one faith."

[12] Ibid. "God, by whose spirit the whole body of the church is multiplied and guided, preserve in the new progeny of your family the grace of the holy mystery which you gave, so that, renewed in body and mind, those burning in the unity of the faith may merit to serve you, Lord."

[13] Morris, *The Blickling homilies*, p. 131. "I will not leave you orphaned, but will send to you a comforting Spirit."

[14] Ibid. p. 133. "Of no less distinction than the Lord's resurrection."

[15] Ibid. "Therefore it is very necessary for us, my brothers, that we very zealously and humbly on this present day come to our relics and to our holy prayers; because we know that this day was the beginning of this transitory light, and it is the beginning of the eternal light to follow."

This eschatological thrust lends the commemoration a more personal sort of urgency, as the new beginning established by the gift of the Holy Spirit is equated with the end of the world, and the new beginning in heaven. The homilist then, after descriptions of the wind-like sound and the tongues of fire, stresses the unity of the apostles, saying that, with their hearts burning perpetually with the love of God, it was meet that "on heora heortan 7 on willan on God gecyrred wæron"[16] as are (ideally) all Christians in the Pentecost liturgy. He briefly discusses (following Gregory) why the Spirit appeared as a dove to Christ, but as fire to the apostles, explaining that while Christ was devoid of the sorts of sins that fire must cleanse, the apostles were not, and the gift of the Spirit is therefore cast in terms of freedom from sin: "þonne wæs se Halga Gast ahafen ofer þa Godes leorneras on anlicnesse fyrenra legea, 7 þurh þæt hie wæron fram eallum synnum alesde, 7 to þæm ecean life gelædde."[17] Reflecting this dual form of appearance by the Holy Spirit, Anglo-Saxon illustrations for Pentecost often feature not just the tongues of fire, but the dove as well, from which the fire extends to the apostles (see plate 7). The rest of the homily is devoted to exploring their 'new state of being' ("þære neowan wyrde"). The audience is told that the Spirit-empowered disciples were able now to bear easily the longing for their Lord, to withstand evil spirits, to be fearless of all earthly kings, and to accomplish whatever they wished. Finally, after establishing the state of being which was reached by the apostles on this occasion as something to be desired, the Blickling homilist makes the connection between the apostles and the contemporary faithful:

> Nis hit þæt an þæt him anum þæm apostolum wære geofu seald, ac eac ðonne eallum manna cynne forgifnes wæs seald ealra synna, 7 eac se freodom þæs unaræfnedlican þeowdomes, þæt is ðæs deofollican onwaldes eallum welwyrcendum. Eac us is alefed edhwyrft to þæm ecean life, 7 heofena rice to gesittenne mid eallum halgum 7 mid Drihtne sylfum . . .[18]

The audience is here encouraged to sympathize with the apostles, being burned clean by the gift of the Holy Spirit, brought to absolute unity with the church and with Heaven, and able to accomplish anything. As this understanding is brought into the liturgy, the antiphons and prayers for cleansing by fire, for the gift of the holy spirit, and for unity with the church and with God bring together the original event with the contemporary petition.

Ælfric's First Series Sermon for Pentecost is more complicated, covering

---

[16] Morris, *The Blickling homilies*, p. 133. "In their hearts and in their will they were turned to God."
[17] Ibid. p. 135. "Then the Holy ghost came over God's disciples in the likeness of flames of fire, and through that they were freed from all sins, and led to eternal life."
[18] Ibid. p. 137. "This gift was not given only to the apostles, but also to all mankind forgiveness of sins was given, and also, to all those who do good, freedom from the intolerable servitude that is the dominion of the devil. Also to us is granted a way of return to the eternal life, and to sit in the heavenly kingdom with all the saints and with the Lord himself."

a broader range of topics.[19] However, as was the Blickling homilist, Ælfric is concerned with this new state of being. He begins with a recounting of the story of Passover, the flight from Egypt, the crossing of the Red Sea, and the destruction of Pharoah's army, all as prelude to his explanation of the Old Testament background to Pentecost as a celebration of the giving of the law to Moses on Mt. Sinai. This is followed by a description of the events in Acts, the New Testament reason for the festival. Ælfric connects the two here both explicitly and more subtly. In describing the giving of the law, he presents the perspective of those watching Mount Sinai from below, waiting for fifty days[20] and seeing up on the mountain "micel leoht, 7 egeslic sweg 7 blawende byman."[21] His description of the gift of the Spirit now parallels the earlier event, featuring a great sound like wind ("micel swegi") and a fire that "gefylde ealle ða upfleringe." He then mentions the baptism of the three thousand, emphasizing their new state:

> þa wæron ealle on annysse mid þam apostolon 7 beceapodon heora æhta 7 þæt feoh betæhton þam apostolon 7 hi dældon ælcum be his neode . . . wearð eall seo geleaffulle meniu swa anmod swilce hi ealle hæfdon ane heortan 7 ane sawle.[22]

This description of the new Christians establishing a communal life, and of the miracles performed by the apostles by means of the Holy Spirit, leads him into an account of the two members of that community who did not live in unity of mind and heart with the rest, Ananias and Sapphira, killed by God for their deceit in holding back part of their property. Ælfric then goes on to discuss the dove and the fire, as well as the gifts of the Spirit, focusing both discussions on the theme of change from sinful to good, and from cold to burning with fervour for God. This change, as he tells his audience, turned a fisherman (Peter) and a tax-collector (Matthew) into apostles, and will similarly change contemporary Christians. He describes the change in such a way that we see this as a fulfilment of a pattern established at Christmas: "On Cristes acennednysse wearþ se ælmihtiga Godes sunu to menniscum men gedoon, 7 on þysum dæge wurdon geleaffulle men godas."[23] Christians 'become gods' because of their union with the Holy Spirit, the change manifesting itself in the seven gifts of the Spirit. Drawing a comparison between those who gave up all they had and

---

[19] As Malcolm Godden explains, in his commentary on CH I.xxii, "In his selection of material and subsequent commentary on it [Ælfric] seems particularly concerned with the models for subsequent Christian practices – episcopal confirmation, the monastic life of poverty and obedience – but also with the ways in which the story of Pentecost relates to the Old Testament . . . and the Gospels . . ." (*Ælfric's Catholic Homilies: Introduction*, p. 175).

[20] Exodus 24:18 says that Moses was on the mountain for forty days and forty nights.

[21] CH I.xxii, p. 356. "Much light, and a terrible sound and blowing trumpets."

[22] Ibid. p. 357. "Then they were all in unity with the apostles and sold their possessions and gave the money to the apostles and they distributed it to each according to his need . . . All the believing company became so single-minded as if they had one heart and one soul."

[23] Ibid. p. 361. "In Christ's birth the son of the almighty God was changed into the form of men, and on this day believing men became gods."

those who did not, desiring gold more, Ælfric makes the connection to his audience.[24] As the apostles laid hands on these faithful ones, at which time the holy ghost came 'through their bishoping,' so

> biscopas synd þæs ylcan hades on Godes gelaðung, 7 healdað þa gesetnysse on heora biscopunge, swa þæt hi settað heora handa ofer gefulludum mannum 7 biddað þæt se ælmihtiga wealdend him sende þa seofonfealdan gife his gastes.[25]

The point of the liturgical commemoration is to effect this change caused by the Holy Spirit, and to celebrate the new state of being. The preaching texts illustrate this by setting up those at the original giving of the Holy Spirit as models for the faithful, who can now expect and receive the fire in the same way, and with similar results, fulfilling God's work with the seven gifts and entering a unity with all those made gods by the Holy Spirit. This unity which was approached during Rogationtide, and made possible by Christ's own raising of humanity to divinity at the Ascension, is now finally realized, as mankind as well is joined with the divine, expecting the eternal continuance of that unity at the Last Judgement.

ADVENT

Although the pace and tenor of the liturgy relax somewhat over the summer, the faithful move in a new direction as the year comes to a close with Advent. Advent serves both as an end and a beginning, and liturgical books giving forms for a year inconsistently begin with Advent rather than Christmas (though Christmas is the usual beginning in Anglo-Saxon witnesses). Its primary function is parallel to that of Lent, to provide a period of reflection and anticipation before the celebration of Christmas. Anticipation of Christ's first coming, however, is echoed by anticipation of his Second Coming, both in the liturgy and in poetic interpretation of the experience of Advent.

As Advent is fundamentally a period of expectation of Christ's birth, it is not surprising to find a proliferation of liturgical forms that emphasize the biblical models for that expectation, the Old Testament prophets and the people 'waiting in darkness.' These prayers and antiphons span the period, and work in the same way as those used in the Christmas Vigil, discussed above.[26] Perhaps the most interesting of these liturgical forms, and certainly

---

[24] This emphasis on giving up possessions as a test of fidelity is, of course, part of the biblical account, but perhaps the fact that Pentecost was a tithing day gave it a certain force. See, for example, the Canons of Edgar, which instructs that Pentecost is the day for "geoguðe teoðunge" (Fowler, *Wulfstan's Canons of Edgar*, p. 13).

[25] p. 364. "Bishops are in this same office in God's church, and they keep the institution in their bishoping, so that they set their hands over baptized men and pray that the almighty Ruler will send to them the sevenfold gifts of his Ghost."

[26] See above, "Christmas and Epiphany."

the most examined by those who study the Anglo-Saxon period, are the 'O' antiphons. Medieval manuscripts show some variety in the number and arrangement of these antiphons, but the core seven, the 'Greater' antiphons, always appear. In Anglo-Saxon studies, these antiphons are best known in the context of the poem known as the Old English *Advent*, or alternately *Christ I*.[27] The liturgical history of the 'O' antiphons has been thoroughly examined by Susan Rankin, who postulates that the poet of *Christ I* probably knew at least fifteen of these antiphons, although extant liturgical manuscripts generally provide no more than twelve, and usually fewer.[28] As Rankin demonstrates, these antiphons were known in England at least from the late eighth century.

Robert Burlin prints and translates the 'Great O's,'[29] which were meant to be sung not all at once, but sequentially, one each night at Lauds or Vespers, leading up to Christmas. A progression of sorts can perhaps be discerned here. All of the antiphons proclaim the need for salvation, but with an increasing sense that Christmas is approaching. The first (*O Sapientia*) is quite general, begging 'Wisdom' to come and provide instruction. The second (*O Adonai*) asks for redemption, invoking the burning bush and the giving of the law to Moses. The third (*O Radix Jesse*) reflects Old Testament prophecy in asking for a deliverer. The fourth (*O Clavis David*) brings in the image of darkness, describing the speaker as captive in prison, sitting in the dark and in death's shadow. The fifth (*O Oriens*) extends this by invoking the light that will pierce that darkness. Finally the sixth (*O Rex gentium*) and seventh (*O Emmanuel*) bring us closer to the expectation of Christ specifically, referred to as the 'cornerstone,' as the prayers to 'come and save us' intensify. Additional antiphons often enhance these images or bring in other themes, such as the praise of Mary, or invocations of Jerusalem or of Joseph. The Leofric Collectar gives ten antiphons, prefaced by a rubric specifying that they are to be chanted at Vespers, after the Gospel, "ab idibus decembris usque Natale domini."[30] Rankin charts the distribution and arrangement of eighteen antiphons in European books.[31]

The poet of the Old English *Advent* has taken fifteen antiphons[32] and rearranged and expanded them, in part to explore the dramatic qualities of

---

[27] See R. B. Burlin, ed. *The Old English Advent: A Typological Commentary* (New Haven, 1968) for an edition and interpretation of the poem.

[28] Susan Rankin, "The liturgical background of the Old English Advent lyrics," in *Learning and Literature*, pp. 317–40.

[29] Burlin, *The Old English Advent*, pp. 40–1.

[30] Dewick and Frere, *The Leofric Collectar*, pp. 15–16. "From the Ides of December until Christmas."

[31] Rankin, "The liturgical background," Appendix I, pp. 338–9.

[32] Although only twelve seem to be reflected in the extant text (several of which are not found in English books), the text begins imperfectly, and it is generally believed that the first three 'Great O's' originally opened the poem.

218

the various invocations. As Edward Irving argues, much of that expansion focuses on the polarities between light and darkness resident in the antiphons and in the surrounding liturgy.[33] The poem is at something of a remove from the liturgy itself, but this dynamic of calling out for salvation, and in particular the identification with those in darkness, is prominent. Irving describes this dynamic:

> Interaction between the two worlds of Light and Dark is expressed in dialogue as well as in image and gesture, as the poem goes on. So dramatic does the dialogue become at one point that some have even called the seventh antiphon, the so-called passus made up of a conversation between Joseph and Mary, an early example of the medieval drama, but the entire series is profoundly dramatized.[34]

This seventh antiphon has received a great deal of attention, in large part because of its shift in first-person voice between Mary and Joseph, making it more a dialogue than an invocation.[35] However, as Irving argues, this antiphon is simply a more obvious example of the dramatic invocation explored generally by the poet, and is integrated with the surrounding material by, among other things, the theme of darkness and light, represented here in terms of ignorance and revelation.[36] Rankin sees a more progressive structure in the arrangement and development of the antiphons by the poet, arguing that they

> have a rhythm corresponding to that part of the liturgical year which they follow: a long period of waiting (lyrics 1–10), a short time of intense emotional reaction at Christmas (lyric 11), and afterwards, a time for comprehension of the Christmas events, before the feast of the Epiphany (lyric 12). . . . By choosing antiphons characteristic of different liturgical periods, and by amplifying their points of contact with the Christmas story, he gave a flow and integrity to the whole cycle.[37]

In anticipating the birth, the poet goes further, imagining some of the repercussions of these events and dramatizing them in his narrative, including the reactions of Mary and Joseph to her pregnancy, the vocal exultation of the angels in the presence of Christ, and post-Christmas recollections on the significance of the birth. These vignettes are presented in such a way as to enhance the relationship between the audience of the poem and the voices invoked in the Advent liturgy. While the exact relationship between the antiphons and the poem is difficult to determine, the poem does represent an aesthetic reaction to them, and an indication that at least one poet appreciated their dramatic possibilites and expanded upon them in his own medium.

---

[33] Edward B. Irving, Jr, "The advent of poetry: *Christ I*," *ASE* 25 (1996), pp. 123–34.

[34] Irving, "The advent of poetry," p. 126.

[35] Of particular interest to critics is the ambiguity concerning how many changes in speaker are represented, and therefore who is speaking which section. See C. G. Harlow, "The Old English Advent VII and the 'Doubting of Mary' Tradition," *LSE* 16 (1985), pp. 101–17.

[36] See Irving, "The advent of poetry," pp. 130–3.

[37] Rankin, "The liturgical background," pp. 336–7.

Particularly interesting in the poem is the fluid nature of time. Recollection is mixed with expectation, in a way that unifies past events with present concerns. As Irving argues, "any dramatic dialogue always has the full immediacy of a voice heard, speaking in the present . . . or in the future."[38] This is an essential aspect of the liturgical forms as well, which pray simultaneously for Christ to arrive as a light for those in darkness, in the voices of the Old Testament beseechers, and for Christ to drive away current ignorance and sin, ensuring a place in the light of heaven. This contemporary dynamic is often presented in eschatological terms. A common preface for the third Sunday in Advent (here from the Leofric Missal) specifies this juxtaposition:

Cuius incarnatione salus facta est mundi, et passione redemptio procurata est hominis procreati, ipse nos quaesumus ad aeternum perducat praemium, qui redemit de tenebris infernorum, iustificetque in adventu secundo qui nos redemit in primo. Quatinus illius nos a malis imnibus defendat sublimitas, cuius nos ad vitam erexit humilitas.[39]

A lot of things are being invoked in the Advent liturgy, in terms of expectation: the coming of light to the people in darkness, the fulfilment of prophecy concerning the Messiah, the union of divine with human in Mary's womb, and the hope of freedom from sin. Irving discusses the various Advents in the Old English poem: "Jesus comes to Jerusalem; God comes to Mary; Jesus is born in Bethlehem; Hope, or grace, comes to man; Christ comes to Harrow Hell; Christ comes to be born in each person."[40] All of these find voice in the Advent liturgy as well. But the expectation of the Second Coming gives this sense of anticipation a certain edge, personalizing the voices of the Old Testament models for those who are, in a sense, in the same position, lost in the darkness of the world and awaiting Christ's judgement, where humanity and divinity will be unified in a more permanent way for those participating in the liturgy.

Although the 'O' antiphons are not themselves explicitly eschatological, the prominence of this sort of appreciation of the voices crying for Christ's coming in the surrounding liturgy surely coloured interpretation of these antiphons, many of which present expectation in somewhat general or ambiguous terms. This mix of past commemoration and contemporary position in the Christian universe is picked up and enhanced by the poet of *Christ I*. In his elaboration of the *O Clavis David*,[41] the poet describes the

---

[38] Irving, "The advent of poetry," p. 127.
[39] Warren, *The Leofric Missal*, p. 127. "May he by whose incarnation the salvation of the world was brought about, and by whose passion redemption was administered for the creation of mankind, may this same one, we pray, who redeemed us from the darkness of hell, lead us to the eternal reward, and forgive us in the second advent who redeemed us in the first. To the same degree may his sublimity defend us from the evils of the enemies, whose humility raised us to life."
[40] Irving, "The advent of poetry," p. 128.
[41] "O Clavis David, et sceptrum domus Israel, qui aperis et nemo claudit, claudis et nemo aperit,

pregnancy of Mary in the past tense, from the perspective of someone ruminating on the mystery from the present age, as a way of appreciating how God delivered humanity. His preceding description of that state of needing deliverance, however, is in the present tense, and encourages the poet's audience to consider themselves in that position now:

> Huru we for þearfe þas word sprecað,
> and myndgiað þone þe mon gescop
> þæt he ne læte to lose weorðan
> cearfulra þing, þe we in carcerne
> sittað sorgende, sunnan wenað,
> hwonne us liffrea leoht ontyne,
> weorðe ussum mode to mundboran,
> ond þæt tydre gewitt tire bewinde,
> gedo usic þæs wyrðe, þe he to wuldre forlet,
> þa þe heanlice hweorfan sceoldan
> to þis enge lond, eðle bescyrede.[42]

The faithful have, over the course of the year, assumed the voices and positions of those cast out of paradise and forced to live in exile, during Lent, and of those in hell awaiting the light of Christ, at *Tenebrae* and on Holy Saturday. In expanding and interpreting the sentiment expressed in the *O Clavis David*, the poet revitalizes these associations and recontextualizes them to highlight the dynamics of the present season, reflecting how the liturgical participants are to relate to this pre-Christmas expectation, as something both commemorative and current. This contemporary need is addressed at the end of the poem. After praising, again, the mystery by which the Lord of heaven was born in the womb of a woman, the poet interprets this in terms of present devotion and the hope of eternal life. For those who honour God,

> He him þære lisse lean forgildeð,
> se gehalgoda hælend sylfa,
> efne in þam eðle þær he ær ne cwom,
> in lifgendra londes wynne,
> þær he gesælig siþþan eardað,
> ealne widan feorh wunað butan ende.[43]

---

veni et educ vinctum de domo carceris, sedentem in tenebris, et umbra mortis." Burlin, *The Old English Advent*, p. 71. "O key of David, and scepter of the house of Israel, you who opens and noone closes, who closes and noone opens, come and lead the captives from prison, sitting in darkness, and in the shadow of death."

[42] Burlin, *The Old English Advent*, p. 68, lines 22–32. "Indeed, because of need we speak these words and are mindful of the one who created man, so that he might not allow the cause of those full of care to be lost, for which we in prison sit sorrowing, and expect the sun, when the lord of life might open the light to us, and become to our spirit a protector, and that frail understanding clothe with glory, and make us worthy of this, which he gloriously forsook, we who miserably had to turn to this narrow land, cut off from the homeland."

[43] Ibid. p. 168, lines 434–9. "The hallowed Saviour himself will grant him the reward of that favour, even in that homeland where he never came before, in the joy of the land of the living, where he afterwards will dwell, happy, live forever without end."

The importance of this eschatological perspective is perhaps reflected in the fact that the illustration in the Benedictional of Æthelwold for the Third Sunday in Advent shows Christ approaching in Judgement (see plate 8). Those participating in the Advent liturgy, then, not only adopt the voices of the people of Jerusalem waiting for light; they also personalize the need expressed by these biblical figures, as they expect the advent of Christ, this time in Judgement, with the promise of entry into the homeland that was lost through sin (as expressed dramatically at Lent), and then re-assured for those participating in the commemorations of Christ's death, resurrection, ascension, and giving of the Holy Spirit.

THE ANGLO-SAXON DRAMATIC AESTHETIC

The dynamic of setting up biblical models in the liturgy, which makes this sort of participation 'dramatic,' is intrinsic to Christian worship, and was certainly not invented by the Anglo-Saxons. It is fundamentally the same strategy employed in fourth-century Jerusalem and in the ninth-century Carolingian church, indeed wherever and whenever the faithful celebrated the life of Christ by means of the action of the liturgy. This brings us back, then, to the initial question: What is happening in tenth-century Anglo-Saxon England? What is so new there that the same critics who scoff at the idea of an Anglo-Saxon drama want to see in this milieu 'the birth of liturgical drama?' It is not the spontaneous introduction of a new, representational form in the *Visitatio*, a virus that over the centuries infected Europe with dramatic fervour. It is, rather, a relatively widespread appreciation of the power and edifying possibilities of liturgical reenactment, of which the *Visitatio* is only one product. Because it is celebrated at Easter, and because it happens to look more like later conceptions of drama than do the rituals for Candlemas, *Tenebrae*, and Rogationtide, it has been mistakenly elevated above these equally dramatic reenactments. Tenth-century England is certainly doing something new, and that something is often expressed as visual representation, with 'actors' playing the roles of those wailing at the Crucifixion, or of the guards at the tomb, or of the women approaching the sepulchre. But this sort of visual representation is not the heart of the drama. It is a supplementary trapping, one of many techniques brought to bear in order to appeal to the aesthetic sensibilities of the people, encouraging them to invest themselves fully in the liturgy and facilitating the establishment of the dramatic identification in the 'audience.' Certainly, in the later Middle Ages, liturgical dramas came to emphasize representation, and look much more like 'plays' than does even the *Visitatio*. This is because many of them were plays, developed not out of a burgeoning tradition of representation in the liturgy but in response to the aesthetics of their own participants. Peter Dronke and

Johann Drumbl have both suggested that dramatic developments in the early medieval liturgy might be due more to attempts to accommodate outside impulses than to a spontaneous generation of drama within the liturgy.[44] Lizette Larson-Miller describes the cultural relationship between a congregation and its liturgy:

> The continuing development of liturgy since its normative formation in the early church was often a cultural action and reaction, allowing the contemporary study of historical liturgy to provide a mirror into what a particular society and its leaders saw as most important and most central to the meaning of life. Nowhere is this marriage of culture and liturgy more evident than in the church of the medieval West.[45]

Rosamund McKitterick, in describing liturgical innovation (specifically the development of the *schola cantorum*) under Pippin, has emphasized the role of aesthetics. Reminding us that "the Frankish clergy did believe they should make the effort to ensure that the laity were comprehending and even delighted participants in the offices of the church,"[46] she asserts that Pippin's contribution

> . . . could also have helped to make the participation of the laity in the services a more active one, for it permitted them to join in the singing of portions of the Mass. The effort to increase the beauty of the liturgical Offices in this manner would also have appealed to the aesthetic sensibilities of the people, and been an incentive to them to go to church.[47]

This marriage of instructional fervour with aesthetically compelling liturgical innovation rules Ælfric's relationship with the liturgy. While, as McKitterick has demonstrated, the Franks showed some interest in this sort of dramatic development, the controversy inspired by Amalarius' dramatic interpretation of the liturgy perhaps reveals a conflicted appreciation of the dramatic propensities of the liturgy. The Anglo-Saxon reformers, however, show less reticence, and Ælfric grants Amalarius nearly the authority of a Church Father. What is new in the late Anglo-Saxon church is the degree to which the appreciation and the enhancement of the dramatic qualities of the liturgy were given free reign.

But if we are going to describe the growth of dramatic ritual in tenth-century England as developing out of an attempt to accommodate a preexisting aesthetic, where did this aesthetic come from? This is a difficult question, and one on which I can only speculate, in part because of the lack of source material, and in part because of the various layers of influence between England and other countries. Many of those involved in the Benedictine Reform had spent a good deal of time experiencing the Frankish liturgy, and travel to other places, with varying practices, is not

---

[44] See Dronke, *Nine Medieval Latin Plays*, p. xviii; Drumbl, *Quem quaeritis.*
[45] Lizette Larson-Miller, ed. *Medieval Liturgy* (New York, 1997), p. ix.
[46] McKitterick, *The Frankish Church*, p. 146.
[47] Ibid. p. 123.

unlikely. While it is hard to trace particular rituals as they move from France to England, the English were without doubt interested in learning what the Frankish churches were doing and, in some respects, emulating that. However, many of the dramatic ceremonies in the post-Reform liturgy that seem to owe something to Frankish influence already had some purchase in England. The Adoration of the Cross is explored in terms of sympathetic identification in the ninth-century Book of Cerne and in *The Dream of the Rood*. The liturgy for the Harrowing is also developed in Cerne, and is taken up by the composer of the Blickling Easter homily. The *Tenebrae* extension, probably an importation, is a development of a ritual that had been part of the English liturgy for some time. The processions at Candlemas and Rogationtide had been in practice, in some form, from at least the time of Bede, and their dramatic propensities recognized at least by the time of the Blickling and Vercelli homilists. When the tenth-century Reformers regularized and expanded the liturgy, they drew on both foreign and native elements in a way that was consistent with, rather than replacing, English aesthetics.

While many of these pre-Reform witnesses are devotional, narrative, or homiletic, rather than liturgical, they do show that the strategy of recognizing and enhancing sympathetic possibilities was a longstanding English dynamic. Many Anglo-Saxon poems are particularly rich in terms of this aesthetic. Poems like *The Wife's Lament, The Wanderer, The Seafarer,* and *The Dream of the Rood* are strategically designed to emphasize empathetic connections with the narrators, rather than reactions to plot. Anglo-Saxon vernacular writers often tend to emphasize direct discourse over summary narration to involve the listener or reader more viscerally in the story, as the author of the Blickling Easter homily does with the petitions of Adam and Eve to be freed from their chains, highlighting those aspects of the story that most directly invite the reader to assume a relationship with the protagonist. This is an option in narrative, one that can be emphasized more or less, and many Anglo-Saxon writers are particularly adept at enhancing these sympathetic possibilities. The story of the Harrowing, with its emphasis on the petitions of Adam and Eve to be freed from their chains, is developed in this way from a very early stage in England, as evident in the version in the Book of Cerne, which emphasizes and develops these first-person prayers at the expense of other traditional elements of the Harrowing.

Perhaps a similarly inclusive aesthetic is nurtured or developed in other aspects of Anglo-Saxon society. Although we have little or no evidence for it, secular dramatic activities, such as mumming, or participatory folk rites, or histrionic performances by scops, any or all might have lent themselves to this dynamic.[48] While the witnesses that we have are compiled by those at

---

[48] Particularly interesting are C. R. Dodwell's speculations regarding a potential knowledge of Terrance by reform-era artists, which raises the possibility of a more comprehensive appreciation

the top of the ecclesiastical order (many of whom may have developed different sets of aesthetics than those developed by the common folk, which may or may not have overlapped in various ways), Karen Jolly's discussion of the way in which Christian and popular religious elements were freely intertwined in the liturgy at a somewhat lower level than the Old Minster in Winchester or Christ Church, Canterbury, gives us some sense of the sorts of practices and tendencies that are not established or recorded by liturgical theorists,[49] and more work on participatory folk practices in England might offer a glimpse at such popular aesthetics. On another level, invoking Hardison's now famous comment at a seminar in 1981 that "medieval drama is a multi-headed beast," Jody Enders explores the dramatic propensities of rhetoric, in particular legal disputation, in Europe between the fall of the Roman Empire and the advent of liturgical drama, and argues for appreciation of aesthetic continuities between various forms of social interaction, from public executions to court proceedings to the Mass itself.[50] Perhaps the author of the Rogationtide homily printed as Bazire and Cross Homily 5, who compares the stational sites of the Rogations with legal "gemotstow," hints at such an appreciation of legal proceedings. One might certainly make connections between liturgy and law in regards to the practice of ritual ordeals. Blair describes "the co-existence – occasionally tense, perhaps more often tranquil – of official and vernacular modes of religious practice" and the usage of both Christian and 'pagan' holy sites on a day-to-day basis.[51] As Enders asserts, "Instead of maintaining, with Young, the imperviousness of liturgical drama to the 'contamination of alien forms,' we might wish to reconsider the unquestionable influence of a tradition that was not, in fact, alien – the rhetorical tradition,"[52] and we might extend this to a range of influences, as those developing the late Anglo-Saxon liturgy were surely involved in various other aspects of the culture, and were directing the liturgy at layfolk who were involved in even more. The sources and permutations of this aesthetic, this propensity for enhancing sympathetic aspects of poetry, or narrative, or public proceedings, evident in Anglo-Saxon England from an early stage, may have contributed to the aesthetics involved in the dramatic rituals recorded in post-Reform Anglo-Saxon sources.

Of course, this sort of generalization must be tempered according to regional, and even individual, variation in taste, and in resources. As Christopher A. Jones reminds us, "in its actuality the liturgy must have

---

of Roman dramatic tradition in England, although we have no direct evidence of such appreciation, apart from the similarities between gestures depicted in some Anglo-Saxon books and those described by Terrance (see C. R. Dodwell, *Anglo-Saxon Gestures and the Roman Stage* (Cambridge, 2000), esp. pp. 101ff).

[49] Karen Jolly, *Popular Religion in Late Saxon England: Elf Charms in Context* (Chapel Hill, 1996).

[50] Jody Enders, *Rhetoric and the Origins of Medieval Drama* (Ithaca, 1992), pp. 15, 103, 110.

[51] Blair, *The Church in Anglo-Saxon Society* (forthcoming).

[52] Enders, *Rhetoric and the Origins of Medieval Drama*, p. 27.

resisted a totalizing view, if only by the sheer diversity and variability of its parts, both written . . . and unwritten."[53] Some places in England are more equipped to explore these dramatic rituals than are others, and some people or communities will be more or less inclined to read the liturgy this way, as the *Concordia*'s description of the *Tenebrae* elaboration as 'optional' may indicate. Liturgical witnesses for various locations reveal a good deal of conscious variety in form and objective. While the identifications with biblical models are resident in the liturgy regardless, enhancement of sympathetic interaction is merely an option in the liturgy, just as it is in narrative. It is intrinsic to the liturgy, everywhere and at all times, to create some kind of connection between the participants and the 'remembered' events. This can be left vague, or it can be enhanced by having the congregation do certain things, say certain things, and move through certain settings that, if done consciously, with benefit of instruction, personalize the commemoration, and set the congregation up as the protagonists. While this sort of approach to the liturgy may not have been ubiquitous in late Anglo-Saxon England, it certainly seems to have been an active one.

In discussing the *Concordia*'s instructions regarding the optional extension of *Tenebrae*, which explain that the ritual is intended to 'set forth the terror of that darkness,' Jones notes that the "Amalarian flavor comes not only from its edifying, symbolic interpretation but also from its historicizing view of the liturgy as an institution subject to embellishment, through time, by human authorities."[54] Describing the practice of blending spiritual commentaries, like that of Amalarius, with liturgical and prayer texts, he considers this "a remarkably consistent feature among what appear to be original Anglo-Saxon attempts at liturgical exposition."[55] The concern for instructing the unlearned in such a way that they perceive and undertake a dramatic relationship with the liturgy is evident in the *Concordia*, and in particular in the sermons of Ælfric, who frequently makes use of Amalarius in this regard. And other things are happening in the tenth century as well. Developments in art and music are evident, the relationship between church architecture and liturgical requirements is being explored, monks are experimenting with sign language that might have been in many respects rather histrionic,[56] and so on. So perhaps all of these forces – a tendency for enhancing sympathy in poetry and narrative; inclusive, participatory public and folk practices; creative manipulation of artistic, musical, and architectural forms; an interest in liturgical exposition; a care for extending monastic dynamics to the laity, with benefit of instruction as to what it all means – are coming together to create the dramatic liturgy of the late

---

[53] Jones, "The Book of the Liturgy," p. 659.
[54] Ibid. p. 685.
[55] Ibid. p. 684.
[56] See Dodwell, *Anglo-Saxon Gestures*, pp. 145–7.

Plate 8. The Second Coming, Benedictional of Æthelwold
London, BL MS Additional 49598, fol. 9v (by permission of the British Library)

Anglo-Saxon period. Whatever the causes, and however far the aesthetic may have extended, many Anglo-Saxon interactions with the liturgy indicate a recognition of its sympathetic possibilities and an attempt to enhance this sort of participatory appreciation of what the liturgy is doing in the year-round celebration of salvation history. Whatever the origins of the Anglo-Saxon dramatic aesthetic, its by-products are widely evident in the richly dramatic late Anglo-Saxon liturgy.

In the interest of examining the *Visitatio* within its own context, I have looked predominately at witnesses contained within a period of just over a century. However, how does this synchronic study of dramatic liturgy in late Anglo-Saxon England relate to the larger history of the development of drama in England, and in Western Europe generally? Although more recent critics of liturgical drama, following Hardison's lead, have rejected the Darwinian model of steady 'dramatic' growth in the complexity of, in particular, Easter and Christmas festivals, replacing it has been an assumption of a progressive growth in the use of representation from the birth pangs of the *Quem quaeritis* to the Passion plays of the later Middle Ages. Certainly, somewhere along the line, some shift to what we recognize as being mimetic (what Hardison calls the 'shift from ritual to representational modes') must take place. However, this is a shift in aesthetics, and nothing can be more difficult to trace. These rituals often work by matching the expectations and aesthetic predispositions of their participants to the liturgical reenactment, and as these qualities change over time so does the nature of liturgical expression. Also, there may be certain communities that react negatively to dramatic liturgical expressions, and influence others with their more understated, contemplative interaction with liturgical forms. As enhancing sympathetic identifications is an option, it will surely find a variety of permutations from decade to decade, as well as from place to place. As such, any attempt to map the influence of the practices of one period on another must move very slowly. In particular, the tumultuous ecclesiastical environment of the Anglo-Norman period makes it extremely difficult to postulate about the effects of Anglo-Saxon interpretations of the liturgy on later practice. Anglo-Saxon dynamics will have thrived in some places (Worcester, with its Anglo-Saxon bishop Wulfstan II remaining in place until 1095, is perhaps a good candidate) and not in others, and one might perhaps trace the movement of some Anglo-Saxon liturgical practices through the Anglo-Norman period, or by way of Anglo-Saxon influence on continental practices, to later observance. However, until the Anglo-Norman liturgy is examined in a more comprehensive way, and is supported by evidence demonstrating attempts to draw out sympathetic aspects of the liturgy in a way similar to that employed by the late Anglo-Saxon church, the place of this Anglo-Saxon interest in dramatic expression within the liturgy in the long-term development of liturgical and secular drama will remain clouded.

Bibliography

PRIMARY SOURCES

Liturgical witnesses

Andrieu, Michel, ed. *Les ordines romani du haut moyen âge*. Spicilegium Sacrum Lovaniense. Etudes et documents; fasc. 11,23–4,28. Louvain: Spicilegium Sacrum Lovaniense, 1931–61.

Bannister, Henry Marriott, ed. *Missale Gothicum*. HBS 52, 54. 2 vols. London: Henry Bradshaw Society, 1917.

Banting, H. M. J., ed. *Two Anglo-Saxon Pontificals: (the Egbert and Sidney Sussex Pontificals)*. HBS 104. London: Henry Bradshaw Society, 1989.

Conn, Marie A., ed. *The Dunstan and Brodie (Anderson) Pontificals: An Edition and Study*. unpub. dissertation. University of Notre Dame, 1993.

Corrêa, Alicia, ed. *The Durham Collectar*. HBS 107. London: Henry Bradshaw Society, 1992.

Davril, Anselme, ed. *The Winchcombe Sacramentary*. HBS 109. London: Henry Bradshaw Society, 1995.

Deshusses, Jean, ed. *Le sacramentaire grégorien: ses principales formes d'après les plus anciens manuscrits*. Spicilegium Friburgense 16, 24, 28. Fribourg: Editions-universitaires, 1971.

Dewick, E. S. and W. H. Frere, eds. *The Leofric Collectar*. HBS 45, 56. 2 vols. London: Henry Bradshaw Society, 1914–21.

Doble, G. H., ed. *Pontificale lanaletense*. HBS 74. London: Harrison & Sons Ltd, 1937.

Frere, Walter Howard, ed. *The Winchester Troper*. HBS 8. London: Harrison & Sons, 1894.

Gingras, George, trans. *Egeria: Diary of a Pilgrimage*. Ancient Christian Writers 38. New York: Newman Press, 1970.

Grant, Raymond J. S., ed. *Cambridge, Corpus Christi College 41: the Loricas and the Missal*. Costerus n.s. 17. Amsterdam: Rodopi, 1978.

Hanssens, Jean Michel, ed. *Amalarii episcopi opera liturgica omnia*. Studi e Testi 138–40. 3 vols. Città del Vaticano: Biblioteca Apostolica Vaticana, 1948–50.

Hughes, Anselm, ed. *The Portiforium of Saint Wulstan*. HBS 89, 90. 2 vols. London: Henry Bradshaw Society, 1958.

Jones, Christopher A., ed. and trans. *Ælfric's Letter to the Monks of Eynsham*. CSASE 24. Cambridge: Cambridge University Press, 1998.

Kornexl, Lucia, ed. *Die Regularis concordia und ihre altenglische Interlinearversion*. Münchener Universitätsschriften. Philosophische Fakultät. Texte und Untersuchungen zur englischen Philologie; bd. 17. München: Fink, 1993.

229

Lowe, E. A., et al., eds. *The Bobbio Missal.* HBS 53, 58, 61. 3 vols. London: Harrison & Sons, 1917.

Prescott, A., ed. "The Text of the Benedictional of St. Æthelwold." *Bishop Æthelwold.* Ed. Barbara Yorke. Woodbridge: Boydell, 1988. 119–47.

Symons, T., ed. and trans. *Regularis concordia Anglicae nationis monachorum sanctimonialiumque: the Monastic Agreement of the Monks and Nuns of the English Nation.* London: Nelson, 1953.

Turner, D. H., ed. *The Claudius Pontificals.* HBS 97. London: Henry Bradshaw Society, 1971.

——, ed. *The Missal of the New Minster, Winchester.* HBS 93. London: Henry Bradshaw Society, 1962.

Vogel, Cyrille, and Reinhard Elze, eds. *Le Pontifical romano-germanique du dixième siècle.* Studi e Testi 226–227. 3 vols. Città del Vaticano: Biblioteca Apostolica Vaticana, 1963–72.

Warner, George F., ed. *The Stowe Missal.* HBS 31–2. 2 vols. London: Henry Bradshaw Society, 1906.

Warren, F. E., ed. *The Leofric Missal.* Oxford: Clarendon Press, 1883.

Whitaker, E. C., trans. *Documents of the Baptismal Liturgy.* Alcuin Club Collections 42. 2nd ed. London: SPCK, 1970.

Wilson, H. A., ed. *The Benedictional of Archbishop Robert.* HBS 24. London: Harrison & Sons, 1903.

——, ed. *The Gelasian Sacramentary.* Oxford: Clarendon Press, 1894.

——, ed. *The Missal of Robert of Jumièges.* HBS 11. London: Harrison & Sons, 1896.

——, ed. *The Pontifical of Magdalen College.* HBS 39. London: Henry Bradshaw Society, 1910.

Woolley, R. M., ed. *The Canterbury Benedictional.* HBS 51. London: Harrison & Sons, 1917.

Unpublished manuscripts consulted (liturgical)

Cambridge, Corpus Christi College MS 44 (Corpus-Canterbury Benedictional)
Cambridge, Corpus Christi College MS 146 (Samson Pontifical)
Cambridge, Corpus Christi College MS 163 (Roman-German Pontifical)
Cambridge, Corpus Christi College MS 422 (Red Book of Darley)
London, British Library MS Additional 28188
London, British Library MS Cotton Vitellius A.vii

Other

Bazire, Joyce, and James E. Cross, eds. *Eleven Old English Rogationtide Homilies.* Toronto Old English Series 7. Toronto: University of Toronto Press, 1982.

Belfour, Algernon Okey, ed. and trans. *Twelfth Century Homilies in MS Bodley 343.* EETS o.s. 137. London: Kegan Paul, 1909.

Bethurum, Dorothy, ed. *The Homilies of Wulfstan.* Oxford: Clarendon Press, 1957.

Bieler, Ludwig, ed. *The Irish Penitentials.* Scriptores Latini Hiberniae 5. Dublin: Dublin Institute for Advanced Studies, 1975.

Burlin, R. B., ed. *The Old English Advent: A Typological Commentary.* Yale Studies in English 168. New Haven: Yale University Press, 1968.

Clemoes, Peter, ed. *Ælfric's Catholic Homilies: The First Series: Text.* EETS s.s. 17. Oxford: Oxford University Press, 1997.

——, ed. *Ælfric's First Series of Catholic Homilies: British Museum, Royal 7 C. XII, folios 4–218.* Early English Manuscripts in Facsimile 13. Copenhagen: Rosenkilde and Bagger, 1966.

Colgrave, Bertram and R. A. B. Mynors, eds. *Bede's Ecclesiastical History of the English People.* Oxford medieval texts. Oxford: Clarendon Press, 1969.

Cook, Albert S., ed. *Biblical Quotations in Old English Prose Writers.* London: Macmillan, 1898.

——, ed. *Biblical Quotations in Old English Prose Writers: 2nd Series.* Yale Bicentennial Publications. New York: C. Scribner's Sons, 1903.

Cross, J. E., ed. and trans. *Two Old English Apocrypha and their Manuscript Source: 'The Gospel of Nicodemus' and 'The Avenging of the Saviour.'* CSASE 19. Cambridge: Cambridge University Press, 1997.

Doane, A. N., ed. *The Saxon Genesis: an Edition of the West Saxon Genesis B and the Old Saxon Vatican Genesis.* Madison: University of Wisconsin Press, 1991.

Dobbie, Elliott Van Kirk, ed. *The Anglo-Saxon Minor Poems.* ASPR 6. New York: Columbia University Press, 1942.

Earle, John, ed. *A Hand-book to the Land-charters, and Other Saxonic Documents.* Oxford: Clarendon Press, 1888.

Evans, Ruth, ed. "An Anonymous Old English Homily for Holy Saturday." *LSE* n.s. 12 (1981): 129–53.

Fehr, Bernhard, ed. *Die Hirtenbriefe Ælfrics in altenglischer und lateinischer Fassung.* Bibliothek der angelsächsischen prosa; ix. bd. Hamburg: H. Grand, 1914.

Findlay, William and S. D. F. Salmond, trans. *Sermon on the Mount; Harmony of the Evangelists.* The Works of Aurelius Augustine, Bishop of Hippo 8. Edinburgh: T. & T. Clark, 1873.

Förster, Max, ed. *Zur Geschichte des Reliquienkultus in Altengland.* Munich: Verlag der Bayerischen Akademie der Wissenschaften, 1943.

Fowler, Roger, ed. "A Late Old English Handbook for the Use of a Confessor." *Anglia* 83 (1965): 1–34.

——, ed. *Old English Prose and Verse.* London: Kegan Paul, 1966.

——, ed. *Wulfstan's Canons of Edgar.* EETS o.s. 266. London: Oxford University Press, 1972.

Gamer, Helena M. and J. T. McNeill, trans. *Medieval Handbooks of Penance.* Records of Civilization: Sources and Studies 29. 2nd Octagon printing. New York: Octagon Books, 1979.

Godden, Malcolm, ed. *Ælfric's Catholic Homilies: The Second Series: Text.* EETS s.s. 5. London: Oxford University Press, 1979.

Haddan, Arthur West and William Stubbs, eds. *Councils and Ecclesiastical Documents Relating to Great Britain and Ireland.* Vol. III. Oxford: Clarendon Press, 1878.

Herzfeld, George, ed. and trans. *The Old English Martyrology.* EETS o.s. 116. Oxford: Oxford University Press, 1900.

Hill, Edmund, trans. *The Works of Saint Augustine.* Vol. III. Brooklyn, N.Y.: New City Press, 1990.

Hulme, William H., ed. "The Old English Gospel of Nicodemus." *Modern Philology* I (1903–4): 570–614.

——, ed. "The Old English Version of the Gospel of Nicodemus." *PMLA* 13 (1898): 457–542.

Hurst, D., ed. *Bedae Venerabilis homeliarum evangelii.* CCSL 122. Turnhout: Brepols, 1955.

Irvine, Susan, ed. *Old English Homilies from MS Bodley 343.* EETS o.s. 302. Oxford: Oxford University Press, 1993.

James, M. R., trans. *The Apocryphal New Testament.* Oxford: Clarendon, 1924.

Jones, C. W., ed. *Bedae Venerabilis opera didascalica: De temporum ratione liber.* CCSL 123B. Turnhout: Brepols, 1997.

Kotzor, Günter, ed. *Das altenglische Martyrologium,* 2 vols. Philosophisch-Historische Abhandlungen N.F. 88. Munich: Verlag der Bayerischen Akadamie der Wissenschaften, 1981.

Krapp, George Philip and Elliott Van Kirk Dobbie, eds. *The Exeter Book.* ASPR 3. New York: Columbia University Press, 1936.

——, ed. *The Vercelli Book.* ASPR 2. New York: Columbia University Press, 1932.

Lapidge, Michael, and Peter S. Baker, eds. *Byrhtferth's Enchiridion.* EETS s.s. 15. Oxford: Oxford University Press, 1995.

Lawler, T. C., trans. *St. Augustine: Sermons for Christmas and Epiphany.* Ancient Christian Writers 15. Westminster, Maryland: The Newman Press, 1952.

Liuzza, R. M., ed. *The Old English Version of the Gospels.* EETS o.s. 304. Oxford: Oxford University Press, 1994.

Lowe, R. C., ed. and trans. *Three Eleventh-Century Anglo-Latin Saints' Lives. Vita S. Birini, Vita et Miracula S. Kenelm et Vita S. Rumwoldi.* Oxford: Oxford University Press, 1996.

Mansi, Giovan Domenico, ed. *Sacrorum conciliorum: nova et amplissima collectio.* Graz: Akademische Druck- u. Verlagsanstalt, 1960.

Martin, Lawrence T., and David Hurst, trans. *Bede the Venerable: Homilies on the Gospels.* Cistercian studies series 110, 111. 2 vols. Kalamazoo: Cistercian Publications, 1991.

Miller, Thomas, ed. and trans. *The Old English Version of Bede's Ecclesiastical History of the English People.* EETS o.s. 95–6, 110. 2 vols. London: N. Trübner & Co., 1890.

Morris, Richard, ed. and trans. *The Blickling Homilies of the Tenth Century.* EETS o.s. 58, 63, 73. London: N. Trübner & Co., 1874–80; reprinted 1967 as one volume.

Muir, Bernard J., ed. *The Exeter Anthology of Old English Poetry.* 2 vols. Exeter: University of Exeter Press, 1994.

Napier, Arthur Sampson, ed. *The Old English Version of the Enlarged Rule of Chrodegang.* EETS o.s. 150. London: K. Paul Trench Trübner & Co. Ltd., 1916.

——, ed. "An Old English Vision of Leofric, Earl of Mercia." *Philological Society Transactions* (1908): 180–8.

——, ed. *Wulfstan: Sammlung der ihm zugeschriebenen homilien nebst Unter-suchungen über ihre Echtheit.* Sammlung englischer Denkmäler in kritischen Ausgaben; 4. bd. Berlin: Weidmann, 1883.

Nicholson, Lewis E., trans. *The Vercelli Book Homilies: translations from the Anglo-Saxon.* Lanham, Maryland: University Press of America, 1991.

Pope, John Collins, ed. *Homilies of Ælfric: a supplementary collection.* EETS o.s. 259–60. 2 vols. London: Oxford University Press, 1967–8.

Raith, Josef, ed. *Die altenglische version des Halitgar'schen bussbuches (sog. Poenitentiale pseudo-Ecgberti).* Bibliothek der angelsächsischen prosa; 13. bd. Hamburg: H. Grand, 1933.

Sauer, H. ed. *Theodulfi Capitula in England.* Texte und Untersuchungen zur englischen Philologie 8. Munich: W. Fink, 1978.

Schaefer, Kenneth, ed. "An Edition of Five Old English Homilies for Palm Sunday, Holy Saturday and Easter Sunday." unpub. dissertation. Columbia University, 1972.

Scragg, D. G., ed. *The Vercelli Homilies and Related Texts.* EETS o.s. 300. Oxford: Oxford University Press, 1992.

Skeat, Walter W., ed. and trans. *Ælfric's Lives of Saints.* EETS o.s. 76, 82, 94, 114. 4 vols. London: N. Trübner & Co, 1881–1900; reprinted 1966 as 2 vols.

Thorpe, B., ed. and trans. *The Homilies of the Anglo-Saxon Church.* 2 vols. London: The Ælfric Society, 1844–6.

Whitelock, Dorothy, et al., eds. and trans. *Councils & Synods with Other Documents Relating to the English Church.* 2 vols. Oxford: Clarendon Press, 1981.

Yerkes, David, ed. *The Old English Life of Machutus.* Toronto Old English series 9. Toronto: University of Toronto Press, 1984.

SECONDARY SOURCES

Alexander, J. J. C. "The Benedictional of St. Æthelwold and Anglo-Saxon Illumination of the Reform Period." *Tenth-Century Studies: Essays in Commemoration of the Millennium of the Council of Winchester and Regularis Concordia.* Ed. David Parsons. London: Phillimore, 1975. 169–83.

Anderson, Earl R. "Liturgical Influence in The Dream of the Rood." *Neophilologus* 73.2 (1989): 293–304.

Anderson, George K. *The Literature of the Anglo-Saxons.* Princeton: Princeton University Press, 1949; reprinted 1997.

Axton, Richard. *European Drama of the Early Middle Ages.* London: Hutchinson, 1974.

Barlow, Frank. *The English Church, 1000–1066.* Hamden: Archon, 1963.

Baumstark, Anton; Bernard Botte, rev.; F.L. Cross, trans. *Comparative Liturgy.* 1st English ed. London: Mowbray, 1958.

Bedingfield, M. Bradford. "Anglo-Saxons on Fire." *Journal of Theological Studies* 52, no. 2 (2001): 658–77.

——. "Public Penance in Anglo-Saxon England." *ASE* (forthcoming).

——. "Reinventing the Gospel: Ælfric and the Liturgy." *Medium Ævum* 68, no. 1 (1999): 13–31.

Bethurum, Dorothy. "Archbishop Wulfstan's Commonplace Book." *PMLA* 57 (1942): 916–29.

Bishop, Edmund. *Liturgica historica: Papers on the Liturgy and Religious Life of the Western Church.* Oxford: Clarendon Press, 1918.

Bjork, David A. "On the Dissemination of *Quem Quaeritis* and the *Visitatio*

Sepulchri and the Chronology of Their Early Sources." *The Drama in the Middle Ages: Comparative and Critical Essays*. Eds. Clifford Davidson, et al. AMS Studies in the Middle Ages 4. New York: AMS Press, 1982. 1–24.

Blair, John. *The Church in Anglo-Saxon Society* (forthcoming).

Blair, John, and Richard Sharpe, eds. *Pastoral Care Before the Parish*. Studies in the Early History of Britain. Leicester: Leicester University Press, 1992.

Bloomfield, Morton W. *The Seven Deadly Sins*. Michigan: Michigan State College Press, 1952.

Brown, Michelle. *The Book of Cerne: Prayer, Patronage and Power in Ninth-century England*. British Library Studies in Medieval Culture 1. London: British Library, 1996.

Brückmann, J. "Latin Manuscript Pontificals and Benedictionals in England and Wales." *Traditio* 29 (1973): 391–9.

Chambers, E. K. *The Mediaeval Stage*. 2 vols. Oxford: Clarendon Press, 1903.

Clayton, Mary. *The Cult of the Virgin Mary in Anglo-Saxon England*. CSASE 2. Cambridge: Cambridge University Press, 1990.

Conner, P. W. *Anglo-Saxon Exeter: A Tenth-century Cultural History*. Studies in Anglo-Saxon History 4. Woodbridge: Boydell, 1993.

Corbin, Solange. *La déposition liturgique du Christ au Vendredi Saint; sa place dans l'histoire des rites et du théatre religieux*. Paris: Société d'éditions Les Belles Lettres, 1960.

Corrêa, Alicia. "Daily Office Books," *The Liturgical Books of Anglo-Saxon England*. Ed. Richard Pfaff. Kalamazoo: Medieval Institute Publications Western Michigan University, 1995. 45–60.

Craig, Hardin. *English Religious Drama of the Middle Ages*. Oxford: Clarendon Press, 1955.

Cross, F. L. and Elizabeth A. Livingstone, eds. *The Oxford Dictionary of the Christian Church*. 3rd ed. Oxford: Oxford University Press, 1997.

Cross, J. E. "Portents and Events at Christ's Birth: Comments on Vercelli V and VI and the Old English Martyrology." *ASE* 2 (1973): 209–20.

Cubitt, Catherine. *Anglo-Saxon Church Councils c. 650–c. 850*. Studies in the Early History of Britain. London: Leicester University Press, 1995.

Dalbey, Marcia A. "Themes & Techniques in the Blickling Lenten Homilies." *The Old English Homily and Its Backgrounds*. Eds. Paul E. Szarmach and Bernard F. Huppé. Albany: State U of New York Press, 1978. 221–39.

Davidson, Clifford. "Space and Time in Medieval Drama: Meditations on Orientation in Early Theater." *Word, Picture, and Spectacle*. Ed. Clifford Davidson. Early Drama, Art, and Music Monograph Series 5. Kalamazoo: Medieval Institute Publications, 1984. 39–93.

De Jong, Mayke. "Pollution, Penance and Sanctity: Ekkehard's Life of Iso of St. Gall." *The Community, the Family, and the Saint: Patterns of Power in Early Medieval Europe*. Eds. J. Hill and M. Swan. International Medieval Research 4. Turnhout: Brepols, 1998. 145–58.

——. "What was public about public penance? *Paenitentia publica* and Justice in the Carolingian World." *La Guistizia nell'alto mediovo II (secoli IX–XI)* Spoleto 44 (1997): 863–902.

Denis-Boulet, Noële M. *The Christian Calendar*. Faith and Fact Books 112. London: Burns & Oates, 1960.

Deshman, Robert. *The Benedictional of Æthelwold.* Studies in Manuscript Illumination 9. Princeton: Princeton University Press, 1995.

——. "The Galba Psalter: pictures, texts and context in an early medieval prayer-book." *ASE* 26 (1997): 109–38.

Dix, Gregory. *The Shape of the Liturgy.* 1st ed. Westminster: Dacre press, 1945.

Dodwell, C. R. *Anglo-Saxon Gestures and the Roman Stage.* CSASE 28. Cambridge: Cambridge University Press, 2000.

Driscoll, Michael. "Penance in Transition: Popular Piety and Practice." *Medieval Liturgy: a book of essays.* Ed. Lizette Larson-Miller, 1997. 121–63.

Dronke, Peter, ed. *Nine Medieval Latin Plays.* Cambridge Medieval Classics 1. Cambridge: Cambridge University Press, 1994.

Drumbl, Johann. *Quem quaeritis: teatro sacro dell'alto Medioevo.* Rome: Bulzoni, 1981.

Duchesne, L. *Christian Worship: its Origin and Evolution.* 5th ed. London: SPCK, 1949.

Dumville, David N. *English Caroline Script and Monastic History: Studies in Benedictinism A.D. 950–1030.* Studies in Anglo-Saxon History 6. Woodbridge: Boydell, 1993.

——. "Liturgical Drama and Panegyric Responsory from the Eighth Century? A Re-examination of the Origin and Contents of the Ninth-Century Section of the Book of Cerne." *JTS* 23 (1972): 375–406.

——. *Liturgy and the Ecclesiastical History of Late Anglo-Saxon England.* Studies in Anglo-Saxon History 5. Woodbridge: The Boydell Press, 1992.

——. "On the Dating of Some Late Anglo-Saxon Liturgical Manuscripts." *Transactions of the Cambridge Bibliographical Society* 10.1 (1991): 40–57.

Enders, Jody. *Rhetoric and the Origins of Medieval Drama.* Ithaca: Cornell University Press, 1992.

Fisher, John Douglas Close. *Christian Initiation: Baptism in the Medieval West: a study in the disintegration of the primitive rite of initiation.* Alcuin Club Collections 47. London: SPCK, 1965.

Flanigan, C. Clifford. "The Fleury Playbook, the Traditions of Medieval Latin Drama, and Modern Scholarship." *The Fleury Playbook: Essays and Studies.* Eds. Thomas P. Campbell and Clifford Davidson. Early Drama, Art, and Music Monograph Series 7. Kalamazoo: Medieval Institute Publications, 1985. 1–25.

——. "The Roman Rite and the Origins of the Liturgical Drama." *University of Toronto Quarterly* 43 (1973–4): 263–84.

Foot, Sarah. " 'By water in the spirit': the administration of baptism in early Anglo-Saxon England." *Pastoral Care Before the Parish.* Eds. J. Blair and R. Sharpe. Leicester: Leicester University Press, 1992. 171–92.

Förster, Max. "Zur Liturgik der angelsachsischen Kirche." *Anglia* 66 (1942): 1–51.

Frantzen, Allen J. *The Literature of Penance in Anglo-Saxon England.* New Brunswick, N.J: Rutgers University Press, 1983.

Gatch, M. McC. "Miracles in Architectural Settings: Christ Church, Canterbury and St. Clements, Sandwich in the Old English Vision of Leofric." *ASE* 22 (1993): 227–52.

——. "The Office in Late Anglo-Saxon Monasticism." *Learning and Literature in Anglo-Saxon England.* Eds. Lapidge and Gneuss. Cambridge: Cambridge University Press, 1985. 341–62.

Gatch, M. McC. "Old English Literature and the Liturgy: Problems and Potential." *ASE* 6 (1977): 237–47.

——. *Preaching and Theology in Anglo-Saxon England: Ælfric and Wulfstan.* Toronto: University of Toronto Press, 1977.

Gem, Richard. "Tenth-Century Architecture in England." *Settimane di Studio del Centro Italiano* 38 (1991), pp. 803–36.

Gjerløw, Lilli. *Adoratio crucis.* Oslo: Norwegian Universities Press, 1961.

Gneuss, H. "Liturgical Books in Anglo-Saxon England and their Old English Terminology." *Learning and Literature in Anglo-Saxon England.* Eds. Lapidge and Gneuss. Cambridge: Cambridge University Press, 1985. 91–141.

Godden, Malcolm. *Ælfric's Catholic Homilies: Introduction, Commentary, and Glossary.* EETS s.s. 18. London: Oxford University Press, 2000.

Godden, Malcolm and Michael Lapidge, eds. *The Cambridge Companion to Old English Literature.* Cambridge: Cambridge University Press, 1991.

Godden, Malcolm. "An Old English Penitential Motif." *ASE* 2 (1973): 221–39.

Gunstone, John. *Christmas and Epiphany.* Studies in Christian Worship 9. London: Faith Press, 1967.

——. *The Liturgy of Penance.* Studies in Christian Worship 7. London: Faith Press, 1965.

Hardison, O. B. *Christian Rite and Christian Drama in the Middle Ages.* Baltimore: Johns Hopkins University Press, 1965.

Harlow, C. G. "The Old English Advent VII and the 'Doubting of Mary' Tradition." *LSE* 16 (1985): 101–17.

Hartzell, K. D. "Graduals." *The Liturgical Books of Anglo-Saxon England.* Ed. R. Pfaff, 1995. 35–7.

Hen, Yitzhak. "The liturgy of St Willibrord." *ASE* 26 (1997): 41–62.

——. "Rome, Anglo-Saxon England and the formation of the Frankish Liturgy." *Early Medieval Europe* 10 (forthcoming 2001).

Hill, Joyce. "Ælfric's 'Silent Days.'" *LSE* 16 (1985): 118–31.

——. "Monastic Reform and the Secular Church: Ælfric's Pastoral Letters in Context." *England in the Eleventh-Century: Proceedings of the 1990 Harlaxton Symposium.* Ed. Carole Hicks. Harlaxton medieval studies, v. 2. Stamford: Paul Watkins, 1992. 103–18.

——. "The 'Regularis Concordia' and its Latin and Old English Reflexes." *Revue Bénédictine* 101 (1991): 299–315.

Hohler, C. E. "Some Service-Books of the Later Saxon Church." *Tenth-Century Studies.* Ed. David Parsons. London: Phillimore, 1975. 60–83.

Holloway, Julia Bolton. "'The Dream of the Rood' and Liturgical Drama." *Drama in the Middle Ages: Comparative and Critical Essays: Second Series.* Eds. Clifford Davidson and John H. Stroupe. AMS Studies in the Middle Ages 18. New York: AMS, 1990. 24–42.

Irving, Edward B., Jr. "The advent of poetry: *Christ I.*" *ASE* 25 (1996): 123–34.

——. "Crucifixion Witnessed; Or, Dramatic Interaction in The Dream of the Rood." *Modes of Interpretation in Old English Literature.* Eds. P. R. Brown, et al. Toronto: U of Toronto Press, 1986. 101–13.

Izydorczyk, Zbigniew. "The Inversion of Paschal Events in the Old English Descent into Hell." *Neuphilologische Mitteilungen* 91.4 (1990): 439–47.

Jensen, Brian Møller. "An Interpretation of the Tropes to the Inventio Sanctae Crucis." *Ecclesia Orans* 3 (1991): 305–23.

Jolly, Karen Louise. *Popular Religion in Late Saxon England: Elf Charms in Context.* Chapel Hill: University of North Carolina Press, 1996.

Jones, Christopher. "The Book of the Liturgy." *Speculum* 73.3 (1998): 659–702.

——. "The Chrism Mass in Later Anglo-Saxon England." *Ritual and Belief: The Rites of the Anglo-Saxon Church.* Eds. M. Bradford Bedingfield and Helen Gittos. HBS (forthcoming).

Jungmann, J. A., and Francis A. Brunner, trans. *The Mass of the Roman Rite.* 2 vols. New York: Benziger, 1950.

Keefer, Sarah Larratt. "Manuals." *The Liturgical Books of Anglo-Saxon England.* Ed. Richard Pfaff, 1995. 99–110.

Ker, N. R. *Catalogue of Manuscripts Containing Anglo-Saxon.* Oxford: Clarendon Press, 1957.

Kirby, D. P. "Bede and Northumbrian Chronology." *English Historical Review* 78 (1963): 514–27.

Kjølbye-Biddle, Birthe. "Anglo-Saxon Baptisteries of the 7th and 8th Centuries: Winchester and Repton." *Acta XIII Congressus Internationalis Archaeologiae Christianae*, v. II. Studi di Antichita Cristiano Pubblicati a Cura del Pontificio Instituto di Archeologia Cristiana. Citta del Vaticano, Split, 1998. 757–78.

Klauser, Theodor, and John Halliburton, trans. *A Short History of Western Liturgy.* Oxford University Press: London, 1969.

Kornexl, L. "The *Regularis Concordia* and its Old English Gloss." *ASE* 24 (1995): 95–130.

Lapidge, Michael. "Abbot Germanus, Winchcombe, Ramsey, and the Cambridge Psalter." *Words, Texts and Manuscripts: Studies in Anglo-Saxon Culture presented to Helmut Gneuss.* Ed. M. Korhammer. Cambridge: Boydell, 1992. 99–129.

——, ed. *Anglo-Saxon Litanies of the Saints.* HBS 106. London: Henry Bradshaw Society, 1991.

——, ed. *The Blackwell Encyclopaedia of Anglo-Saxon England.* Oxford: Blackwell, 1999.

—— and Helmut Gneuss, eds. *Learning and Literature in Anglo-Saxon England: studies presented to Peter Clemoes on the occasion of his sixty-fifth birthday.* Cambridge: Cambridge University Press, 1985.

Larson-Miller, Lizette, ed. *Medieval Liturgy: a book of essays.* Garland Medieval Casebooks 18. New York: Garland, 1997.

Latham, R. E. *Revised Medieval Latin Word-list from British and Irish Sources.* London: Oxford University Press, 1989.

Lees, Clare A. "Theme and Echo in an Anonymous Old English Homily for Easter." *Traditio* 42 (1986): 115–42.

Loyn, H. R. *The English Church, 940–1154.* New York: Longman, 2000.

MacGregor, A. J. *Fire and Light in the Western Triduum: their Use at Tenebrae and at the Paschal Vigil.* Alcuin Club Collections 71. Collegeville, Minnesota: Liturgical Press, 1992.

McKitterick, Rosamond. *The Frankish Church and the Carolingian Reforms, 789–895.* Royal Historical Society Studies in History. London: Royal Historical Society, 1977.

Meens, Rob. "The Frequency and Nature of Early Medieval Penance." *Handling*

Sin: Confession in the Middle Ages. Eds. Peter Biller and A. J. Minnis. York Studies in Medieval Theology 2. York: York Medieval Press, 1998. 35–63.

Metzger, Marcel. *History of the Liturgy.* Collegeville, Minnesota: Liturgical Press, 1997.

Mortimer, Robert Cecil. *The Origins of Private Penance in the Western Church.* Oxford: Clarendon Press, 1939.

Nelson, Janet L., and Richard Pfaff. "Pontificals and Benedictionals." *The Liturgical Books of Anglo-Saxon England.* Ed. Richard Pfaff. Kalamazoo: Medieval Institute Publications Western Michigan University, 1995. 87–98.

O'Briain, Helen Conrad, "The Harrowing of Hell in the Canterbury Glosses and its Context in Augustinian and Insular Exegesis." *Text and Gloss: Studies in Insular Learning and Literature Presented to Joseph Donovan Pheifer,* eds. H. Conrad O'Briain, A. M. D'Arcy, and J. Scattergood. Dublin: Four Courts Press, 1999. 73–88.

Ó Carragáin, Éamon. "Crucifixion as Annunciation: The Relation of The Dream of the Rood to the Liturgy Reconsidered." *English Studies* 63.6 (1982): 487–505.

Oakley, Thomas Pollock. *English Penitential Discipline and Anglo-Saxon Law in their Joint Influence.* Studies in history, economics and public law, vol. CVII, no. 2. New York: Columbia University Press, 1923.

Ortenberg, Veronica. *The English Church and the Continent in the Tenth and Eleventh Centuries: Cultural, Spiritual, and Artistic Exchanges.* Oxford: Clarendon Press, 1992.

Page, R. I. "Old English Liturgical Rubrics in Corpus Christi College, Cambridge, MS 422." *Anglia* 96 (1978): 149–58.

Palazzo, Eric, translated by Madeleine Beaumont. *A History of Liturgical Books from the Beginning to the Thirteenth Century.* Collegeville, Minnesota: The Liturgical Press, 1998.

Parsons, David, ed. *Tenth-Century Studies: Essays in Commemoration of the Millennium of the Council of Winchester and Regularis Concordia.* London: Phillimore, 1975.

Patch, Howard. "Liturgical Influence in The Dream of the Rood." *PMLA* 34 (1919): 233–57.

Pfaff, Richard. "Massbooks: Sacramentaries and Missals." *The Liturgical Books of Anglo-Saxon England.* Ed. Richard Pfaff. Kalamazoo: Medieval Institute Publications, Western Michigan University, 1995. 7–34.

——, ed. *The Liturgical Books of Anglo-Saxon England.* Old English Newsletter. Subsidia 23. Kalamazoo: Medieval Institute Publications Western Michigan University, 1995.

——. *Medieval Latin Liturgy: a select bibliography.* Toronto medieval bibliographies 9. Toronto: University of Toronto Press, 1982.

Prescott, Andrew. "The Structure of English Pre-Conquest Benedictionals." *British Library Journal* 13 (1987): 118–58.

Ramsey, Nigel, Margaret Sparks, and Tim Tatton-Brown, eds. *St. Dunstan: His Life, Times and Cult.* Woodbridge: The Boydell Press, 1992.

Susan Rankin, "The liturgical background of the Old English Advent lyrics: a reappraisal." *Learning and Literature in Anglo-Saxon England.* Eds. Lapidge and Gneuss. Cambridge: Cambridge University Press, 1985. 317–40.

Raw, Barbara. *Anglo-Saxon Crucifixion Iconography and the Art of the Monastic Revival.* CSASE 1. Cambridge: Cambridge University Press, 1990.

——. "Biblical literature: the New Testament." *The Cambridge Companion to Old English Literature.* Eds. Godden and Lapidge. Cambridge: Cambridge University Press, 1991. 227–42.

Rice, D. Talbot. *English Art: 871–1100.* The Oxford History of Art, v. II, ser. ed. T. S. R. Boase. Oxford: The Clarendon Press, 1975.

Samuels, Peggy. "The Audience Written into the Script of The Dream of the Rood." *Modern Language Quarterly* 49.4 (1988): 311–20.

Schnusenberg, Christine Catharina. *The Relationship Between the Church and the Theatre: exemplified by selected writings of the Church Fathers and by liturgical texts until Amalarius of Metz – 775–852 A.D.* Lanham, Maryland: University Press of America, 1988.

Scragg, D. G. "Cambridge, Corpus Christi College 162." *Anglo-Saxon Manuscripts and Their Heritage.* Eds. Phillip Pulsiano and Elaine M. Treharne. Aldershot: Ashgate, 1998. 71–84.

——. "The Corpus of Vernacular Homilies and Prose Saints' Lives before Ælfric." *ASE* 8 (1979): 223–77.

Sellers, Gordon Bailey. "The Old English Rogationtide Corpus: A Literary History." unpub. dissertation. Loyola University, 1996.

Smolden, W. L. "The Melodies of the Medieval Church-Dramas and their Significance." *Comparative Drama* 2 (1968): 185–209.

Spurrell, Mark. "The Architectural Interest of the *Regularis Concordia.*" *ASE* 21 (1992): 161–76.

Stevenson, K. W. *Worship: Wonderful and Sacred Mystery.* Washington, D.C.: Pastoral Press, 1992.

Symons, Thomas. "*Regularis Concordia*: History and Derivation." *Tenth-Century Studies.* Ed. David Parsons, 1975. 37–59.

Szarmach, Paul E. "The Earlier Homily: De Parasceve." *Studies in Earlier Old English Prose.* Ed. Paul E. Szarmach. Albany: State U of New York Press, 1986. 381–99.

Talley, Thomas J. *The Origins of the Liturgical Year.* New York: Pueblo Pub. Co., 1986.

Teviotdale, E. C. "Tropers." *The Liturgical Books of Anglo-Saxon England,* ed. Richard Pfaff. Kalamazoo: Medieval Institute Publications Western Michigan University, 1995. 39–44.

Vogel, Cyrille, translated by William G. Storey and Niels Krogh Rasmussen. *Medieval Liturgy: an Introduction to the Sources.* NPM Studies in Church Music and Liturgy. Washington, D.C.: Pastoral Press, 1986.

Warren, F. E., and Jane Stevenson. *The Liturgy and Ritual of the Celtic Church.* 2nd ed. Studies in Celtic History 9. Woodbridge: Boydell, 1987.

Waterhouse, Ruth. "Ælfric's Use of Discourse in Some Saints' Lives." *ASE* 5 (1976): 83–103.

Watkins, Oscar Daniel. *A History of Penance.* 2 vols. London: Longmans Green, 1920.

Whitaker, E. C. *The Baptismal Liturgy.* 2nd ed. London: SPCK, 1981.

Wilcox, Jonathon, ed. *Ælfric's Prefaces.* Durham Medieval Texts 9. Durham: Durham University Press, 1994.

Willis, G. G. *St. Augustine's Lectionary*. Alcuin Club Collections 44. London: SPCK, 1962.

Woolf, Rosemary. "Doctrinal Influences on The Dream of the Rood." *Medium Ævum* 27 (1958): 137–53.

Wormald, Francis. "The 'Winchester School' before St. Æthelwold." *England Before the Conquest: Studies in Primary Sources presented to Dorothy Whitelock*. Eds. Peter Clemoes and Kathleen Hughes. Cambridge: Cambridge UP, 1971. 305–13.

Wormald, Patrick. *The Making of English Law: King Alfred to the Twelfth Century*, v. I. Oxford: Blackwell, 1999.

Young, Karl. *The Drama of the Medieval Church*. 2 vols. Oxford: Clarendon Press, 1933.

Index

241